From Wake Island To Berlin

WW II Ex-POWs

Turner Publishing Company

TURNER PUBLISHING COMPANY
412 Broadway
P.O. Box 3101
Paducah, KY 42002-3101
(502) 443-0121

Turner Publishing Company Staff:
Editor: Katherine Sredl

Library of Congress
Catalog Card Number: 96-61775
ISBN: 978-1-56311-331-4
ISBN: 978-1-68162-131-9
Limited edition: Additional copies may be ordered directly from the publisher.

Front Endsheet: POWs during the Bataan Death March.

Back Endsheet: Death Railway

Cover Photo: POWs Lee Rogers and John Todd. (MedSearch photo)

Table of Contents

DEDICATION 4
ACKNOWLEDGEMENT 5
INTRODUCTION 6
CHAPTER ONE: Gysgt. Edward Sturgeon-Wake Island 8
Camp Woosung, China
Camp Osaka, Japan
CHAPTER TWO: Pvt. Benjamin Dunn-Java 30
Burma Death Railway
CHAPTER THREE: Sgt. Charles Branum-Bataan 58
Bataan Death March, Camp O'Donald, Philippines, Camp Bilibid, Philippines
Camp, Mukaishina, Japan
CHAPTER FOUR: Cpl. Ralph Lape-Mindanao 75
Camp Mindana, Philippines,Camp Kawasaki, Japan
Camp Niigata, Japan
CHAPTER FIVE: Lt. Thomas Hart-Burma 95
Camp Hosi
Escaped
CHAPTER SIX: P.F.C. John McLaughten-Glider Infantry 108
Stalag IIB, VIIA, Luft III
CHAPTER SEVEN: SSgt. Russell Hulsey-93rd Bomb Group 115
Stalag 17B
CHAPTER EIGHT: TSgt. Gordon Butts-451 Bomb Group 132
Stalag Luft III, Stalag VIIA, XIIID
CHAPTER NINE: Sgt. William Bradley-351 Infantry 143
Stalag IIIA, IIIB
CHAPTER TEN: Sgt. William Carr-398th Bomb Group 160
Stalag Luft IV
CHAPTER ELEVEN: SSgt. Edwin Douglass-134th Infantry 173
Stalag XIIA, IIIC, IIIA
CHAPTER TWELVE: TSgt. Harold Boardman-96th Bomb Group 182
Stalag Luft IV
CHAPTER THIRTEEN: Lt.. Carl Remy-95th Bomb Group 188
Stalag Luft I
CHAPTER FOURTEEN: Cpl. Kenneth Smith-106th Infantry 208
Stalag IXB
CHAPTER FIFTEEN: Sgt. Alvel Stricklin-301 Infantry 221
Stalag XIIA, XC
ABOUT THE AUTHOR 226
APPENDIX A-Japanese Prison Camps 227
APPENDIX B-German Prison Camps 235
APPENDIX C-German Prison Camp Regulations 237
PUBLISHER'S MESSAGE 256
INDEX 257

Dedication

This book is dedicated to all the ex-prisoners of war in World War II and their Families.

Acknowledgement

I would like to thank Steven Arthur for his translation of documents, Terri Rentfro for her computer knowledge, and for their art work Bill Erwin, Robin Greenlee, and Michael Dann.

Introduction

In World War II 130,201 American servicemen were captured and held as Prisoners of War. About twenty-five percent of those were held by the Japanese Imperial Army and the remaining seventy-five percent of them were held by Hitler's Third Reich. Although all of the men were POWs in World War II there were marked differences in the captives' experiences.

The day after the attack on Pearl Harbor, the Japanese begin a massive invasion of the West Pacific Area. This included Wake Island, the Philippine Islands, Singapore, Southeast Asia, Java, New Guinea, Borneo and Malaya. By May 1942, after many bloody battles with Allied forces, the Japanese had successfully seized most of the West Pacific. It was during this early part of the war that the Japanese captured the majority of American POWs. These American captives would be POWs under the Imperial Japanese Army for the entire war.

The Japanese, who believed in fighting to the death, were surprised by the surrender of Allied Forces in the West Pacific. The surrender posed unsuspected problems for the Japanese. What to do with thousands of Allied prisoners? It also posed a problem for Allied POWs, because as the Japanese considered surrender as unacceptable under any circumstance they considered POWs as inferior beings. This resulted in a cold blooded plan on the part of the Japanese of brutality and extermination.

American prisoners were held in camps scattered through the West Pacific Asia area. Many of the camps were military installations that had been seized by the Japanese during the war. However, in some areas barracks were constructed. Often the barracks had dirt floors. Men slept on the floor, in wooden bunks, or bamboo slabs located in the barracks. A latrine was provided, the common open pit with no drainage that was filled with maggots and flies.

The Japanese did not adhere to the Geneva Convention at all. Their treatment of American prisoners was barbaric to say the least. Men were beaten, bayoneted, tortured, and murdered. On the Bataan Death March alone 650 American prisoners of war were murdered.

Those lucky enough to survive the inhumane treatment of the Imperial Army were rewarded with hard labor, starvation and disease. Men were forced to work 12 hour days in all weather conditions with only small portions of buggy rice to eat. The food was not enough for the prisoners to maintain their health and many developed disease from the diet as well as the unsanitary conditions. Due to lack of medical treatment, many died. No other example could explain it better than the construction of the Railway built in Burma and Thailand. The Japanese needed a supply line to their troops in India and put approximately 300,000 POWs and coolies to work in the most diseased jungle and mountains in Asia. The result of 15 months of unspeakable working conditions and treatment? Over half of those men died. The railroad was to become known to the world as the Railway of Death.

During the course of the war many POWs were moved to various parts of Asia and towards the end of the war large numbers were moved to Japan. The transportation method was the Hell Ship, so named because the men in large numbers were stuffed in holes below decks for days and even weeks. There was no ventilation and many suffocated. The dead were thrown over board leaving a trail of dead bodies in the Pacific.

When the war was finally over of those held by the Japanese, no fewer than 37 percent - 12,526 - never came out of the camps alive.

On the other side of the globe Nazi Germany held the other seventy-five percent of American prisoners. The Nazis called then Kriegsgefangen-a term that the prisoners of war shortened to Kriegie. The nickname belied the reality of daily life as a POW.

The first American prisoner of war captured by the Nazis was Navy Lieutenant John Dunn who was captured on April 14, 1942. On September 25, 1942, the first American Army Land Troops were reported as prisoners of war by the Nazis to an agency created by the Geneva Convention - the Central Agency for Prisoners of War. From that point until the end of the war Hitler's Third Reich captured a total of 98, 312 American prisoners of war.

There were three principal types of Nazi Prisoner of War camps: the offizer Lager (officer's camp), a Stalag Stamm Lager (main camp), and Durchgangs Lager (entrance camp). There were seventy five of these camps scattered mostly throughout Germany with a few located in Poland, Czechoslovakia, Austria, and East Prussia. In addition, a number of the prisoners were in Kommandos (work camps) and hospitals.

Most camps had barracks constructed with ten rooms leading from a central hallway that ran lengthwise through the building. The rooms were supplied with triple-deck bunk beds with paper sacks filled with straw or wood shavings as mattresses for the prisoners. The washrooms and a pit latrine were located near the rear of the barracks. As the war progressed, many men had to sleep on the floor in the rooms and it became necessary to use the wash rooms to house prisoners. There was a small stove, a table, and a few stools for furnishings.

The Nazis' adherence to the Geneva Convention was generally correct, but the treatment of American prisoners of war by the Third Reich depended largely on the prisoner's location, the time period of which the prisoner was captured, and what German units were in charge of the prisoners - regular German Army or SS Troops.

For example, Stalag Luft III proved to be a well organized camp of captured Air Force officers with some of the best treatment as compared to other prison camps, while Stalag VII was a camp of captured enlisted ground forces with average treatment as compared to other prison camps, and Stalag IXB, established for enlisted men captured during the Von Rundstedt Offensive of December 1944, gave poor treatment of prisoners.

As for the time period of the war, the deterioration of the German transportation system caused uncontrollable conditions of proper segregation of prisoners according to nationalities and removal of prisoners from danger zones from the air raids. Food, clothing, and medical supplies for the Germans were severely rationed causing shortages of these supplies for the prisoners of war. However, when one takes into account the provisions of the convention, there was no doubt that the Nazis made numerous willful violations ranging from technical circumstances to full-scale atrocities.

The third area affecting the treatment of prisoners was the attitude of the German soldiers themselves. There was a sharp division between the attitudes of the German regular army and Hitler's SS Troops toward the POWs. The regular army willfully violated many rules such as holding back Red Cross packages, clothing, claiming that there was a shortage of food and water as a result of bombing raids, threats of beatings and death, and ignoring medical needs of prisoners, etc. There were atrocities by the regular army - beatings, prisoners killed, terrorizing by police dogs, and placement in solitary confinement to name a few, but atrocities by the regular army were more of an exception than the rule.

The SS troops were a different story. Their main attitude toward POWs and human life was so grossly twisted that even many of the German regular army troops feared them. American prisoners were beaten, tortured, and murdered by the SS troops. Some were beaten and murdered upon capture, others while they were in prison camps, and some after attempting escape. Records from the Nuremberg trials show that among the victims of the death camps - Flossenburg Concentration Camp and Mauthasen Concentration camp - American Prisoners were put to death by the SS troops. Fifteen members of an American mission in Slovakia were executed. Some of the fliers were Negroes. In addition, over six hundred American prisoners of war were found in Gestapo concentration camps - Buchenwald, Dachau - at the end of the war.

The Germans surrendered three months before the Japanese. When the war ended all of 1.1 percent (a little over 1000 POWs) died while in Nazi prison camps.

I could go on and on about conditions and treatment of POWs, but to get a true picture of what life was like as a prisoner of war - to be beaten, threatened with death, to ache with hunger, to watch helplessly as your friends die from common diseases among prisoners such as tuberculosis, ulcers, gastritis, nephritis, dysentery, and diarrhea problems, to face the unknown of what each day might bring - one needs to walk in the footsteps of men who lived as prisoners of war.

This book contains 15 personal accounts of men who fought the Japanese and Nazis only to face the grim reality of daily life as POWs. The stories run the gamut from Wake Island, the Death Railway, The Bataan Death March, and survival in the Jungles of Burma after escaping the Japanese to the D-Day invasion, B-17 crew members shot down over Germany, and the Battle of the Bulge.

I was born in 1945 just before the end of the war and grew up hearing stories and watching movies about World War II. This era had continued to fascinate me and is the inspiration for writing this book. The information for this book came from personal interviews with ex-prisoners of war, personal documents of ex-prisoners of war, military records from the National Archives in Washington D.C., the U.S. Navy Department in Washington D.C., the National Headquarters of American Ex-Prisoners of War, the Provost Marshal's Office of the U.S. Army, American Red Cross Documents, and the War Department in Washington D.C.

The stories in this book are real, they are compelling, and they give a true picture of POW life from soldiers who walked in those shoes as American prisoners of war in World War II.

CHAPTER ONE

GUNNERY SERGEANT EDWARD STURGEON
U.S. MARINE CORPS

1ST DEFENSE BATTALION, 5TH ARTILLERY WAKE ISLAND
CAPTURED WHILE IN DEFENSE OF WAKE ISLAND

PRISONER OF WAR
DECEMBER 23, 1941-SEPTEMBER 6, 1945
WOOSUNG, CHINA AND OSAKA, JAPAN

THE BEGINNING
June 11, 1941-November 2, 1941

On June 11, 1941, 19-year-old Edward Sturgeon joined the Marine Corps and was sent to the Marine Corps Recruit Depot in San Diego, California for boot camp. The Japanese aggression in the Pacific was getting so bad at that time boot camp had been shortened by a month. After eight weeks of rigorous training Ed graduated from boot camp and was assigned to the 8th Marines in San Diego.

One day at roll call the platoon sergeant asked for volunteers for the First Defense Battalion in Hawaii. Those who volunteered would get out of all the day to day training. Ed volunteered. For the next two weeks, the volunteers spent fifteen minutes doing close order drill in the morning and the rest of the day at the Slop Shute drinking beer.

In September 1941, Ed and the other volunteers loaded aboard a ship and headed toward Pearl Harbor. A week later they arrived in Hawaii and were transported to the 1st Defense Barracks located at Pearl Harbor. For the next couple of weeks Ed and the other men stayed busy with infantry training and close order drill.

The first week of October the 1st Defense unit received orders that they were restricted to the base. Ed knew they were going to be shipped out, but information was so secret at the time they didn't know when or where they were going to be sent.

A week later, the 1st Defense Battalion boarded ship and headed west. They traveled in a complete blackout with two Destroyer Escorts. Ed and the rest of the crew all took turns day and night standing submarine watch in case of an attack by the Japs. A few days later they arrived at Johnson Island without incident. After dropping off some supplies they headed out again.

This time it wasn't the Japs they were concerned about. It was the weather. They had headed straight into a typhoon. As Ed recalls, "you could look over the side of the ship and the waves were so high that you couldn't see the destroyers. We had to eat sandwiches and drink coffee for about three days. When you were at a table you didn't know who's coffee you were drinking, you just had to grab a cup as it comes by. I decided I wasn't going to get sick, but I saw all of these other guys vomiting and it made me seasick. Finally, the weather cleared up and we could go above deck. To my surprise we were circling an island. The ship had to anchor out about a quarter of a mile because there were no channels to bring the ships in to dock. We had arrived at Wake Island."

WAKE ISLAND A BRIEF HISTORY

Wake Island is one of the most isolated islands in the world inhabited by people. It sets in the center of the Pacific with the coordinates on the map of 19 16' N., 166 37' E. The islands are 2,000 miles west of Hawaii, 1,200 miles east of Guam, and 1,000 miles southwest of Midway Islands.

Collectively there are three islands that make up the V shaped Island. The largest of the three is named Wake and is located at the point of the V. At each end of the arms of Wake

Boot Camp graduation photo. Ed Sturgeon third from the left on the bottom row.

Island's V are two small islands that are less than a mile long. Peale Island is the northern island and Wilkes Island is on the south side. An ancient volcano and lagoon are centered in the three islands. A coral reef almost encompasses the nine-mile outer perimeter of the islands

The first known sighting of Wake Island occurred in 1586 by a Spanish explorer Alvaro de Mendana. His stay was brief when looking for supplies of food and water he discovered the only inhabitants to be birds and rats that could stand on their hind legs.

In 1796 a British merchant by the name of Samuel Wake visited the island. Again 44 years later in 1840 Commodore Charles Wilkes a U.S. Naval officer and a naturalist Titian Peale surveyed the island. From these three men Wake, Wilkes, and Peale collectively the islands became known as Wake Island.

The island remained uninhabited until Pan-American Airways established a station there for refueling its trans-Pacific Clippers in the mid-1930's. By the time Edward Sturgeon arrived at Wake Island on November 2, 1941 Wake had become a military base. He and his fellow volunteers brought the force on the island to 15 officers, 373 enlisted men, a Navy doctor and one hospital corpsman.

THE FIRST DAYS ON WAKE
November 2, 1941-December 7, 1941

Upon arrival at Wake Island on November 2, 1941, Edward Sturgeon and the other Marines were assigned to living quarters and given duty assignments. Ed's personal account,

"The first thing that I noticed about the island was how white the coral was. It actually hurt my eyes for a while until I got use to it.

We were assigned to four man tents. We had hard cots to sleep on and had to take salt water showers. After the shower I was walking back to the tent and I noticed there were rats all over the place. They went about their business as if none of us were around. I did the same. I put my gear away and hit the bunk. About 2:00 A.M. the next morning they came down the line and wanted a volunteer mess cook. I volunteered for the job.

I went to the kitchen which was just another tent with screen sides built onto it. All we had to cook with was wood. The civilian contractors would dump wood and I would get up each morning about 4:00 A.M. cut up wood and get the stoves fired up. The one day that I

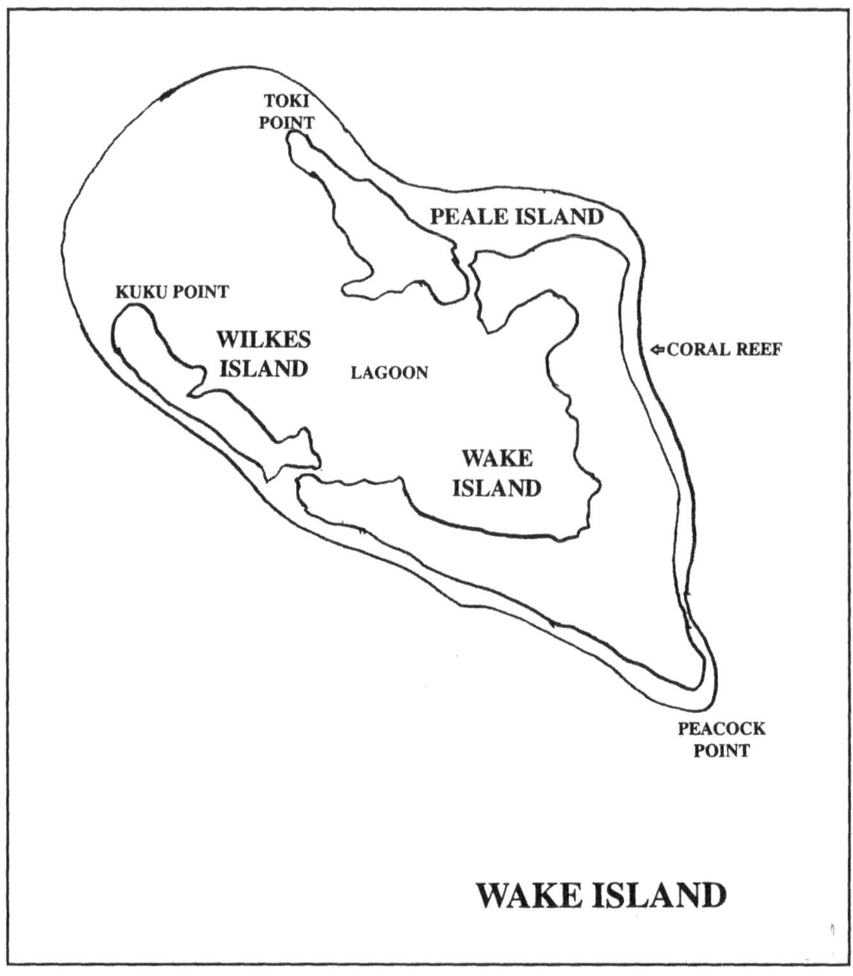

remember most is Thanksgiving Day. We were supposed to have turkey, but when we got the supply of turkey they were all spoiled. Instead we had ox tongue and rice.

I kept busy for about thirty days firing up the stoves, but on December 7, that ended. I lost my job when new diesel burning stoves arrived for the kitchen."

THE BATTLE OF WAKE ISLAND
December 8, 1941-December 23, 1941

The next morning on December 8 Ed, having been temporarily replaced by diesel burning stoves, was milling around his tent. A fellow bunk mate darted through the door, "the Japs attack Pearl Harbor," he yelled out. The two Marines locked eyes and stood silently glaring at each other in awe.

In a short time the entire 1st Defense Battalion had received the news. The United States was at war with the Japs. Four planes were put in the air immediately. They flew at 12,000 feet watching for any signs of an attack by the Japanese. In the mean time Ed had gone to the mess hall for noon chow as he recounts, "we were in the mess hall and the air raid alarms went off. We ran out and got in trucks and headed for our gun position. I was on a 5-inch gun at Toki Point and was there in minutes. We only had 12 planes on Wake Island that had arrived about a week before the war started. The bomb racks didn't fit and had to be reworked. We still put four in the air to look for Japs. A little after 1200 noon 36 Jap bombers came in on us. Our planes couldn't spot them because they came in real low in a

Point of Interest

WAKE ISLAND FIRSTS

During the defense of Wake Island the 1st Defense Battalion became the first military unit to acomplish the following:

1. The first enemy surface warship sunk by American forces in World War II.
2. The first enemy ship sunk by American aircraft in World War II.
3. The first Japanese fleet submarine sunk by American forces in World War II.
4. The first and only abortive amphibious landing operation of World War II.
5. The first Medal of Honor awarded in World War II posthumously to Marine Aviator Captain Hank Elrod.
6. The first Presidential Unit Citation in World War II and the only one awarded by personal direction and signed personally by President Franklin D. Roosevelt.

Ed Sturgeon in 1945. He weights 150 lbs. here. Sept. 6, 1945 after release from the Japs, he weighed 82 lbs.

V formation and cut their engines just before coming over the island. We didn't know they were there until they were right on top of us and then all hell broke loose. They did a lot of damage. All of our planes except the four in the air were destroyed. Some of the men in the air squadron were killed as well as several civilians. They did a lot of damage to Camp one and two and destroyed a lot of our storage tanks. Some of our anti-air craft guns fired back, but we didn't hit a plane.

The next morning, on December 9 before daylight the general quarter's alarm sounded again. Ed and the rest of the gun crew watched in the early morning darkness for signs of the Japs. It wasn't until about 1200 noon when they hit with a bombing raid again. The Marines stayed in position and this time, they were ready for the Japs. The anti-aircraft guns shot into the Japanese tight V-formations with deadly accuracy. By the time the planes left six were trailing smoke and one of those disintegrated in the air.

The Japs were not without some success however. They had rained 500 pound bombs on the island and a number of buildings were destroyed. As Ed explained, "we were lucky because one of the apparent targets was the 3-inch guns at Battery E and the 5-inch guns at Battery A located at Peacock Point. These positions guarded the southern approach to the Island and the positions received some damage. We weren't hit."

On the third day, December 10, the defenders were weary from the lack of sleep and the daily bombing. They were also well dug in. An American F4F-3 Wildcat fighter plane intercepted the Japs before they arrived at the island on this third attack and shot two planes down. The Japanese arrived early with their attack arriving at Wake with 25 planes at about 10:45 A.M. Obviously, they were concentrating on the gun positions with this attack. This

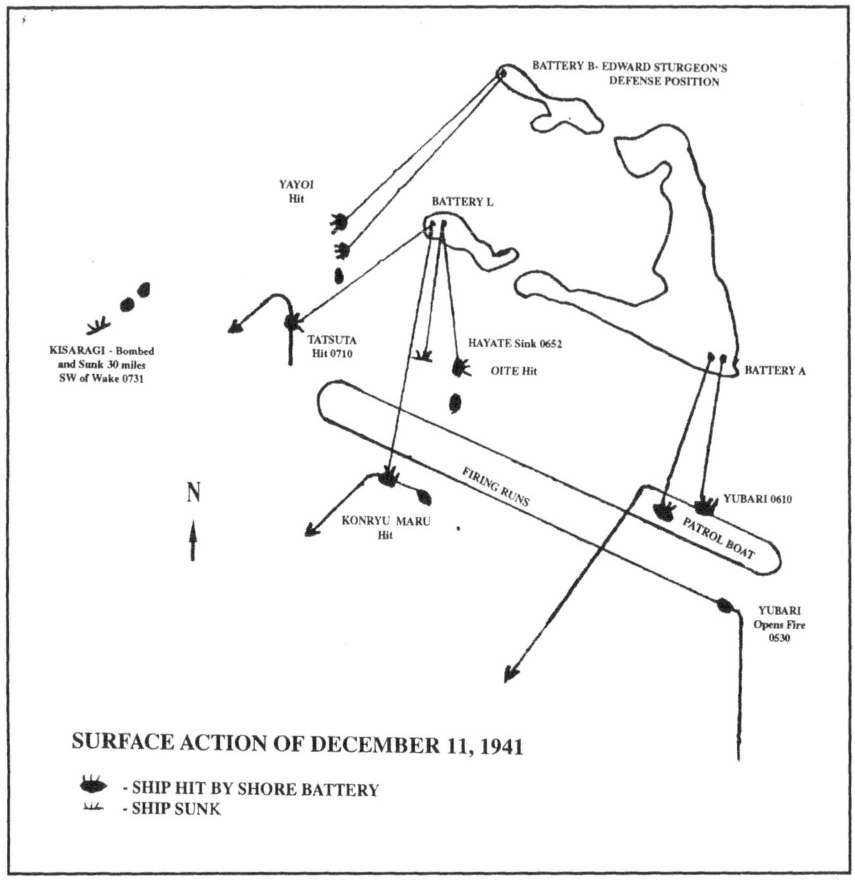

time Edward recalls his crew wasn't so lucky, "One of the first targets was our guns. They did some damage this time knocking out the aiming scope on one gun and they destroyed some of our ammo. One thing paid off though. The night before we moved some of our 3-inch guns and we had constructed some wooden dummy guns. They destroyed the dummies, but didn't touch any of the three inch guns."

On December 11 at about three in the morning the defenders spotted the Jap invasion force. Edward explains, "that night we knew they were going to try an invasion. They wanted to sneak in on us, but the sea was too rough for a landing. We found out later that there were several of their men that were killed as they tried to load aboard landing craft. At daylight, they came in with 13 ships. They started shelling us and artillery rounds were hitting all around us. We held our fire. They came in a little closer and continued firing while we waited. As the ships got closer we could see that they had three cruisers, six destroyers, and four transport ships. Finally they came within 500 yards and we got orders to open fire. The first shot we fired all we could see were feathers. The recoil blew our bedding all to hell. I'll never forget that. We had them in a trap. We hit eight ships and sank two destroyers before they could pull out. We stopped their land invasion and it was the first time in the war that an invasion by the Japs had been stopped."

Ed and the other defender's spirits were high with their victory over the overwhelming odds of the Japanese attack. They spent most of the night moving guns and by morning they were ready to rest. The Japanese, however, planned to continue the pressure on the defenders. They attack at 5:00 A.M. strafing the gun positions and the airfield.

On this fifth day another first came for the defenders when one of the Wildcat pilots spotted a submarine off the shores of Wake. The pilot attacked and made a direct hit on the Japanese submarine which in minutes left only an oil slick on the surface of the ocean.

For the next ten days the defenders fell into a routine. The daily bombings were like clock work. The days came indistinguishable as the men dealt with licking their wounds, burying the dead, and preparing for the next raid.

Life in the foxholes was anything, but pleasant. Rats were running everywhere. Often when the men tried to get a few minutes of sleep they would be awaken by the rats running across their bodies. Dead birds were everywhere. In between bombings efforts were made to get food to the defenders, but often food consisted of cranberries and orange marmalade out of the can for some while many went several days without any food at all.

Then on December 23, after ten days of constant bombing, the Japanese made the final assault. More than 1,000 soldiers with the essential equipment boarded landing craft and landed at approximately 1:00 A.M. The battle for Wake was on. The outnumbered defenders fought savagely against overwhelming odds. Finally, after seven hours of battle the decision was made to surrender. At 8:00 A.M. the command began to alert all units by telephone to cease fire. The battle for Wake Island was over.

PRISONERS ON WAKE

December 23, 1941-January 12, 1942

The Japanese were in complete control of the island and begin to collect the American prisoners. Ed recalls the events of capture and the days to follow on Wake Island, "after we surrendered we waited at the gun sight for them to come after us. We slept as much as we could because we hadn't had any sleep for days. It was about noon when they got us. They

Today's Pictures Today

A Nation's Tribute to the gallant defenders of Wake island has been paid by President Roosevelt. An official citation for the members of the U. S. marine corps who battled to the last in the face of overwhelming odds and sank several Jap warships, was issued at the White house. Here is the citation.

Associated Press Wirephoto

1942

Citation by

THE PRESIDENT OF THE UNITED STATES

of

The Wake detachment of the 1st Defense Battalion, U. S. Marine Corps, under command of Major James P. S. Devereux, U. S. Marines

and

Marine Fighting Squadron 211 of Marine Aircraft Group 21, under command of Major Paul A. Putnam, U. S. Marines

"The courageous conduct of the officers and men of these units, who defended Wake Island against an overwhelming superiority of enemy air, sea, and land attacks from December 8 to 22, 1941, has been noted with admiration by their fellow countrymen and the civilized world, and will not be forgotten so long as gallantry and heroism are respected and honored. These units are commended for their devotion to duty and splendid conduct at their battle stations under most adverse conditions. With limited defensive means against attacks in great force, they manned their shore installations and flew their aircraft so well that five enemy warships were either sunk or severely damaged, many hostile planes shot down, and an unknown number of land troops destroyed."

Franklin D Roosevelt

The first Presidential Unit citation. It is the only PUC ever signed by the President.

A Point of Interest

LIST OF CAPTURED AND KILLED FROM WAKE ISLAND

Killed in action(includes 3 Navy)	44	Civilians on Wake	1,200
Total to be captured	442	Killed in action	82
Died in POW camps(Marines)	18	Died in POW camps	115
Died in POW camps(Navy)	9	Died escaping	2
Number repatriated(includes Navy)	415	Executed by Japs(Oct 7, 1943)	98
		Died after the battle	2
		Number repatriated	901

were jabbering all the time. All they wanted was money. They were running around "money, money, money." Ever once in a while they would find a 10 or 20 dollar bill and they would just throw it in the air. They didn't want that, they wanted silver. "Watch, Watch," they jabbered.

They made us strip so they could search us good then they let us put our clothes back on. We were lucky though because we were the last of the prisoners picked up. The first prisoners they captured they stripped them and tied their hands behind them with telephone wire then ran it up around their necks. Then they started beating them.

They took us to the airfield and made us set there in the open field. The sun was hot and they wouldn't give us any water. The people that were injured had gotten no treatment and they were starting to smell from the infection in their wounds. That first night it rained and the wind began to blow. Some of the guys didn't have any shirts and even for those of us who did it got really cold.

The second day, we were crowded together. The Japs came out with machine guns and set them up all around us. They were just getting ready to put the trigger and it started raining again so they covered their machine guns up. It rained for an hour or so. When it quit raining the Japs came back out and uncovered their guns. They were going to shoot us and just as they were going to start a Japanese Admiral came up waving his hands and yelling at them to stop. They moved their machine guns and left us there for the rest of the day.

Late in the afternoon, they brought us the first food, dried bread. None of us had any water in two days. They used empty gas barrels to carry water to us. The water tasted like gasoline.

On Christmas day, they took us into a barrack that had not been bombed out. They strung barbed wire around the barracks so we couldn't get out. They had guards all around the fence. It was better to be out of the weather and they gave us some stew that day to eat, but I was still getting really hungry. The day that the war started we had scattered food all over the island and hid it. I knew where I had hidden a case of sardines so I went under the fence that night and went out there and got me a few cans of sardines.

Things were really pleasant in the camp at that time. There was no beatings or anything. They pretty much left us alone. We had destroyed most of the weapons before we were captured, but we hadn't got to destroy all of them so a couple of days later some Jap guards came to the barrack and took six of us to a building to clean the 50 caliber machine guns that they had captured. They stood outside while we worked. We took a part out of every gun.

Across the road from us they filled one of the barracks full of food. I went over and all the windows were broken out of the barracks so I climbed in and got some of the Jap crackers. They were like our C-ration crackers and we called them Japanese heart attacks. I liked them better than our crackers because they were sweeter.

Then in January 1942, they came around and told us to pack we were leaving. We had no idea where we were going.

A Point of Interest

OFFICIAL JAPANESE LOSSES IN THE BATTLE OF WAKE ISLAND

Hayate	Destroyer	Sunk
Kisaragi	Destroyer	Sunk
PC-32	Destroyer-Transport	Beached
PC-33	Destroyer-Transport	Beached
RO-62	Submarine	Sunk
Tatsuta	Cruiser	Damaged
Tenru	Cruiser	Damaged
Yubari	Cruise	Damaged
Oite	Destroyer	Damaged
Mutsuki	Destroyer	Damaged
Yako	Destroyer	Damaged
Kongo Maru	Transport	Damaged
Bombers	————	21 shot down
Bombers	————	51 damaged
Japanese Soldiers	————	800-900 killed

This aerial photo of Wake Island was taken just one month after Ed and the other prisoners were moved to Japan.

WAR DEPARTMENT

OFFICE OF THE CHIEF OF THE ARMY AIR FORCES

WASHINGTON

January 7, 1942

Major General T. Holcomb
Commandant Marine Corps
Arlington Annex
Navy Department
Washington, D. C.

Dear Holcomb:

Admiral Towers has sent me a most interesting and inspiring report on the activities of the small group of Marine Officers and ratings in the gallant defense of Wake Island.

This report is the first official or semi-official account I have received of just what happened on Wake Island and I am most impressed with the magnificent work done.

The bravery and ingenuity described in this report are in keeping with the splendid records of the Marine Corps and I feel warrant inscription on a very bright page of those records for all members of the Armed Forces of the United States to strive to emulate.

The memory of those who fell will always occupy a prominent spot in the history of our country and add to the past records of the Marine Corps.

Very sincerely yours,

H. H. Arnold

H. H. ARNOLD,
Lieutenant General, U. S. Army,
Chief of the Army Air Forces.

A Point of Interest

CIVILIAN POWs ON WAKE ISLAND

After the capture of Wake Island, the Japanese retained some civilian contractors to finish construction projects. On October 7, 1943, the Japanese marched the 98 prisoners to a location on the beach and executed them with machine guns.

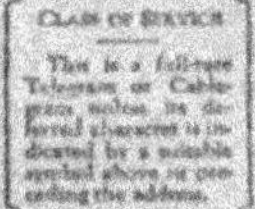

WESTERN UNION

NO 4 CK NL GOVT PD U WASHINGTON DC 31

MR IRA STURGEON
ROUTE ONE
HARVARD ILL

FOLLOWING ENEMY PROPAGANDA BROADCAST FROM JAP HAS BEEN INTERCEPTED QUOTE HELLO FATHER AND ALL COLON THIS IS A BROADCAST MESSAGE FROM YOUR SON I GIVE THANKS TO THE JAP ANESE FOR BROADCASTING THIS MESSAGE I AM WELL HOPE YOU ARE ALSO TELL "MOTHER" , THAT I SAID HELLO WELL I WISH YOU ALL A MERRY CHRISTMAS AND A HAPPY NEW YEAR DO NOT WORRY EVERYTHINGS ALRIGHT YOUR LOVING SON EDWARD STURGEON US MC UN QUOTE THIS BROADCAST SUPPLEMENTS ALL PREVIOUS REPORTS STOP

LERCH PROVOST MARSHALL GENERAL

WESTERN UNION

67 NL 2 EX MF Chicago Ill 12

Ira Sturgeon,
Route 2
Girard Ill..

In the list of missing released by War Department is the name of Private E V Sturgeon, We plan to publish the list with pictures of the missing men in a gallery of heroes in the CHICAGO SUN June 18, Will you kindly send us by special delivery at once a photograph of Private Sturgeon which we will return. May we extend to you our sympathy..

War Heroes Editor,
The Chicago Sun..
Chicago Illinois..925am..

THE VOYAGE ON THE NITTA MARU

January 12, 1942-January 24, 1942

On January 12, 1942, most of the prisoners were able to travel. All but 20 of the Wake Island prisoners were taken to a ship waiting offshore, the Nitta Maru. (The Nitta Maru and other Japanese ships used to transport POWs were named *Hell Ships* by the prisoners because of the inhumane treatment and conditions the prisoners had to endure.) Each was given a set of regulations for prisoners as they came aboard. The regulations read as follows:

JAPANESE NAVAL REGULATIONS FOR PRISONERS OF WAR

Commander of the Prisoner Escort
Navy of the Great Japanese Empire

REGULATIONS FOR PRISONERS

1. The prisoners disobeying the following orders will be punished with immediate death:

   a. Those disobeying orders and instructions.
   b. Those showing a motion of antagonism and raising a sign of opposition.
   c. Those disordering the regulations by individualism, egoism, thinking only about yourself, rushing for your own goods.
   d. Those talking without permission and raising loud voices.
   e. Those walking and moving without order.
   f. Those carrying unnecessary baggage in embarking.
   g. Those resisting mutually.
   h. Those touching the boat's materials, wires, electric lights, tools, switches, etc.
   i. Those climbing ladder without order.
   j. Those showing action of running away from the room or boat.
   k. Those trying to take more meal than given to them.
   l. Those using more than two blankets.

2. Since the boat is not well equipped and inside being narrow, food being scarce and poor you'll feel uncomfortable during the short time on the boat. Those losing patients and disobeying the regulation will be heavily punished for the reason of not being . . . ?

3. Be sure to finish your "Nature Call", evacuate the bowels and urine before embarking.

4. Meals will be given twice a day. One plate only to one prisoner. The prisoners called by the guard will give out the meal quick as possible and honestly. The remaining prisoners will stay in their places quietly and wait for your plate. Those moving from their places reaching for your place without order will be heavily punished. Same orders will be applied in handling plates after meal.

5. Toilet will be fixed at the four corners of the room. The buckets and cans will be placed. When filled up a guard will appoint a prisoner. The prisoner called will take the buckets to the center of the room. The buckets will be pulled up by the derrick and be thrown away. Toilet papers will be given. Everyone must cooperate to make sanitary. Those being careless will be punished.

6. Navy of the Great Japanese Empire will not try to punish you all with death. Those obeying all the rules and regulations, and believing the action and purpose of the Japanese Navy, cooperating with Japan in constructing the "New order of the Great Asia" which lead to the world's peace will be well treated.

The End

During the twelve-day voyage the men endured beatings, starvation, and five of the prisoners were brutally executed. The victims of the horrible atrocity were Seaman First Class John W. Lambert, Seaman Second Class Theodore D. Franklin, Seaman Second

A Point of Interest

NITTA MARU

The Nitta Maru, which transported the Wake Island defenders to Japan, served as a transport until November 25, 1942 when she was sent to the Mitsubishi Nagasaki Shipyard for conversion to an aircraft carrier. After conversation the Nitta Maru was renamed Chuyo.

On November 19, 1943 the U.S. submarine Sculpin was sunk near Truk. The forty-two survivors were taken to Truk, and transferred to the escort carriers Chuyo and Unyo. En route to Japan the Chuyo was torpedoed by the U.S. submarine Sailfish, and only one of the prisoners survived. He and 20 prisoners in Unyo were taken on to Japan.

The first and last duties of the Nitta Maru in World War II were as a prison ship.

Class Roy J. Gonzales, Master Sergeant Earl R. Hannum, and Technical Sergeant William Bailey. All were beheaded and no one knows why or how these five men were chosen for execution. The ship stopped first in Japan then continued to prison camps in Woosung and Kiangwan, China.

Ed recalls his experience of the twelve-day voyage on the hell ship, "The first part of January they came in and told us to pack some of our clothing that we were leaving. We didn't know where we were going so we packed the warmest clothing we had. We got our clothes together and they loaded us on small boats to go out to the ship which was anchored about a quarter of a mile out. The sea was really rough that day. They had a ladder lowered on the side of the ship and we were trying to climb aboard. Guys were getting knocked off the ladder. Some of them were getting injured. The Japs decided that wouldn't work so they took us around on the other side of the boat and lowered a rope. It looked like it was about twenty feet up. The boat we were in would be next to the ship one minute then rock as far as fifteen feet away from it the next minute. Each one of us had to grab the rope, swing against the side of the ship with our feet, and walk and pull ourselves up the side. There were sharks in the water so we had to be careful not to slip. All of us remembered the Jap ships we sank and not a single Jap made it to shore because of the sharks. I grabbed the rope and swung over. I was weak from the lack of food, but I thought about the sharks and I was able to muster enough strength to make it to the deck.

When we got to the top, the whole Jap crew was lined up in two lines. All of the them were carrying clubs. The first thing they did was to take all of our clothes that we had brought with us. Then they made us run through the line while they beat us with their clubs. I did better than some, but I was hit in the head several times. It caused a brain abscess which required me to have a brain operation later. That was the first brutal treatment we got.

Then they put us below deck. We were down there for 12 days. They would come in ever so often yelling and screaming at us, then they would beat us with clubs. We got a bucket to use for human waste. They gave us a little bow of GUI water they called soup. We called it slop. Several days out to sea it started to get cold. We didn't have any clothes other than those on our backs and we thought we were going to freeze to death. One day their general quarters sounded off. We heard later from some of the men that they heard two torpedoes go by.

After approximately one week we pulled up at Tokyo and they took a few prisoners off and then we took off again. When we stopped again, we were at the docks at Shanghai, China. The 12-day voyage ended on January 24, 1942. It was spitting snow and sleet and most of the guys had on shorts and summer shirts. None of us had hats or coats. They made us walk about six miles to Woosung. Many of the guys just about froze to death on the march to the prison camp.

WOOSUNG PRISON CAMP

Woosung prison camp is located 15 miles north of Shanghai and 5 miles northeast of Woosung Forts. It was originally a Chinese Army training camp. The camp was captured by the Japanese in 1937 and used as a Japanese army barracks. The camp consisted of eight one-story barracks, each approximately 200 feet long by 35 feet wide. The barracks were sectioned on the inside and provided living space for 24 men.

The sleeping decks rose approximately a foot from the floor and was used to sit on by the prisoners when they ate. Each prisoner was issued one cotton mattress sack with straw filling, a small straw filled pillow, and two cotton filled blankets to fight off the bitter winter. At night the rats scurried through the barrack freely.

The latrine was located at the end of the barracks. The latrine was constructed as such that waste discharged into large earthen jars located underneath the floor. Chinese coolies, would empty these jars and carry the waste to their fields for fertilizer.

The S.S. Nitta Maru *on her arrival at Yokohama.*

There were two electric fences used to control the 1,500 prisoners in the camp. One was located around the eight barrack and the other bordered the entire camp.

WELCOME TO WOOSUNG
January 24, 1942-September 1942

"They put us in the barracks with no heat," Ed explained. "About midnight they came by and gave us some soup. It had Curie powder in it. You talk about warming someone up.

For the next couple of months they didn't make us do any work. It was a good thing too because we were on a starvation diet of about 500 calories a day. We got a small bowl of rice, a bowl of stew, and tea. After a couple of months the increased the diet to about 650 grams of rice a day plus some meat. It wasn't long before the meat was cut out of the diet. The only supply of water was from a 30 foot well and we were warned not to drink it. All we had was tea. We fed our hogs better, but we had to eat the food because that is all they gave us. Every once in a while we would catch a rat in the barracks and eat it. They didn't taste all that bad.

After a couple of months they started working us ten hour days. We worked at leveling a field which was used for a Japanese parade ground. Some of the men worked on farms and others on roads. I worked on a farm and road repair. It didn't matter what the weather was we had to work out in it. Also, the work was hard considering the lack of food. I was suffering from dysentery, malnutrition, and rapid weight loses.

To add to the misery the guards treatment got worse as time passed. Face slapping became a common occurrence. Mass punishment occurred on several occasions. If just one prisoner messed up all us had to pay. They made us stand in the rain for long hours. Sometimes they stopped food for days. All of us were suffering from the conditions and treatment. Then, I got the word that I was being moved.

OSAKA SHIP YARDS
September 1942 -September 1945

The Osaka Prison Camps housed approximately 10,000 POWs. It was run by Colonial Akami. It was rumored that Colonial Akami had served in China, but had gone mad during the battle and was returned home to his homeland to do a less stressful job. He was brutal to the prisoners and was executed after the war for his atrocities.

The barracks at the prison were wooden houses' approximately 18' wide and 33' long and housed approximately 75 men. Water was provided by outside spigots at wooden wash tables.

The bunks were made of rough cut lumber and were stacked in threes. They were covered by a thin straw mat. The mat was of little comfort against the rough lumber. The personal belongings of the prisoners were placed on a narrow wooden ledge on the wall just behind the sleeping shelves.

Ed was loaded aboard another hell ship, in September 1942, and headed for Japan. The ship held close to the coastal lines going back in case of a torpedo attack. They were more decent to the prisoners this trip. They let the prisoners come up on deck about fifteen minutes a day and gave them some food. The prisoners received no beatings during the trip. A few days later they arrived in Coby, Japan. They transferred the prisoners to a variety of jobs as slave laborers in lumber yards, junk yards, steel mills, cement factories, warehouses, barges, sampans, and coal mines.

Daily life for the prisoners was grueling. The Japs controlled their every move. They told them when to get up, what they would eat, where, when, and how long they would work. In return, the Japs did little more than to provide some of the bare necessities.

Ed was assigned to the ship yards at Osaka. "Several of the men refused to work and they were killed, he explained, " We knew they meant business so when they said to work you worked. We worked at hard labor 12 hours a day. There were no safety precautions for us, but I guess we were better off than some because they had to work in the coal mines without any safety precautions. They made us carry big slabs of steel on our backs from one location to another. The slabs we carried averaged 300 pounds. In the summer it was hot, in the winter freezing cold. The Japs issued us one jacket in the winter and we had to work out in the weather regardless of whether it was snowing, sleeting, or raining. We would get soaked in the rain then go back to the barracks with no heat. I was getting weak from the lack of food and I was afraid I wouldn't be able to work. My weight lose had brought me down to less than one hundred pounds. I had dysentery, and beri beri. We had no medical care so if a prisoner couldn't work any more they were placed in barracks to die. To make it worse their food rations were cut in half.

The Japs decided that they were going to train some riveters. I thought this would be a good way to get away from carrying the steel and get out of the weather.

I volunteered for the training and in a short time I was working on the ships. I watched the Japs and noticed that they weren't checking my work so I started putting loose rivets in the overhead of the ship. Then one day they lined us up and I thought they may have found out what we were doing. In stead, they told us how we were great ship builders. They said they never had any ships return for repairs. We joked about it later because we knew why they weren't coming back. It was because they were being sunk by our Navy as fast as they went out.

This job was easier that packing 300 pound slabs on by back, but I was getting weaker. At that time the rice we got was the sweepings off the floors. The rice was full of rat droppings, and rocks. It just wasn't fit to eat. The Japs got a shipment of tangerines in and we were so hungry we would follow them around and pick up their peelings and eat them.

At the yards they had an old skinny horse. We use to make fun of it all the time. One day it was killed during a bombing raid. It had been hit by incendiary bombs. It was burnt and laying in the mud. The Japs told us we could have the horse to eat. We dragged it out of the mud, cleaned it up, and butchered it. The Japs took the meat and gave us the bones. We actually had every bone in the horse. We ate what we could from the bone and sucked the juice out of the bones.

We knew if we were caught stealing food they would kill us, but we were starving. Some of the guys were stealing rice and I was stealing rock salt. Some guys had stolen electrical parts and had made homemade hot plates with the parts. They hid them in the walls of the barracks. We used the hot plates and traded what food we stole to stay alive.

The Japs were getting short on food and we probably would have forgiven them if they had just starved us, but we had to take the beatings too. They beat us all the time. They made up excuses for the least little thing. Every time we would take back an island or something they would beat the hell out of us with a two-inch bamboo club. They would hit us in the head and around our face. Some of the guys got their ears split from the beatings. I never got my ears split, but I did get hit in the head really hard. Then things got worse when we took back Okinawa. They beat us daily. We laughed at them all the time. They would beat us and we would laugh about it later. It used to make them mad because they couldn't break our spirit.

In 1943, in Osaka, Japan we had an Army Air Corps sergeant that was a radioman. He worked out around the Jap ships and he stole the parts to make a radio. He got the news from the radio. The Japs found out we had the radio, but they couldn't find it. They started beating on everyone to find it. In the mean time he took it apart and threw it in the toilet. After a while he saw that the Japs were beating on everybody else so he told them where it was at. They made him go down in the toilet up to his neck in waste and get the parts out. When he came out, he smelled terrible. Then they took him to this cell and put him in it. All you could do was stand in it. You couldn't set or lay because there wasn't any room. There were sticks sharpened and pointing toward him on all sides so that if he fell or tried to bend they would stick in him. The second day we noticed that the Japs would take him out of the cell and to the toilet at the same time. So we gathered up food and one of us would be in the toilet because the Japs would wait outside. When he came in, we would feed him. We did that day after day. He was getting more food than we were at the time. The Japs never did caught onto what we were doing. They left him there for 12 days just standing there except for the once a day toilet trip. After the 12 days the Japs let him out and went to gibbering and carrying on. They got food and fed him really well. We were surprised until we learned that the Japs thought he was a hero. They couldn't believe that a man could stand for 12 days without food or water.

1945 BOMBING RAIDS OVER JAPAN

Since the Americans had taken Guam and Saipan American bombers were able to operate within the Japanese homeland. Wave after wave of B-29 bombers dropped tons of bombs on the enemy.

Ed recalls, "The first part of 1945, the B-29s started coming over and we figured the war was getting short. Then in March 1945, 300 B-29s burnt the whole city of Osaka out with incendiary bombs. Some of the bombs landed right in our barracks. Some of the guys got their faces burnt and some got teeth knocked out, but none were killed. We were really happy to see that even if the bombs were dropped on us. One of the funniest things was the Japs had a fire department right beside our barracks and it burnt down before they could get the fire trucks out of it.

A few days later they loaded us aboard a train and we headed north through Tokyo and all the way across the island to Aioshi, Japan to the steel mills. The first thing they did was to cut our food rations. We worked day after day and they just kept cutting our food rations lower and lower because of the shortage of the food supply. We would get up each day and work 12 hour days around those hot furnaces. We were told that during the winter it got as low as 30 below zero so we were lucky from that stand point.

Every fifth day we would have to work a 24-hour shift because we would change from day shift to night shift. I was really getting weak. Then the fleas were really getting bad. They were all over me biting. It was terrible. We had to jump up and bow to the Jap soldiers when they came by and I had got my temper up over the fleas and the whole mess we were in, so I decided that I wasn't going to bow to them any more. One of these little Japs came by and I didn't get up. He went to gibbering and grabbed me and took me outside. He started beating me with his club. I decided that I wasn't going to let the little son-of-a-bitch knock me down, but after he beat me for a while he did knock me down. After that he made me stand out there all night long. Every time they changed guards they would beat the hell out of me.

We knew that the Japs had orders to kill all of us in case the Americans landed in Japan. As a matter of fact if they hadn't dropped the atom bomb we would have been. They already had some of the graves dug. We would be working in the factories and we made knives and carried them back to the camp. They would search us. I don't care what you had as long as you showed it to them they didn't care. I don't know why, but the only thing that they had a concern about is what you had hid on the body.

THE FINAL DAYS

The commander of the camp had several ducks and a big pig that were running around the camp. I guess he was trying to torment us because we were so hungry. We wouldn't bother trying to get any of them though because if one person got caught trying to steal food then everyone got punished. They may make us do without food for two or three days or they may make someone go out and stand in the hot sun with their hands in the air until they passed out. One day, about a week after I was beaten, I went out and lined up for work. I was on the night shift. The Japs came out and they were gibbering and carrying on. Then they said "Nice Noto" "Nice Noto." (No work in Japanese.) We got to talking and figured that something was happening. About and an hour later the day shift came walking into the camp. The Japs never told us the war was over, but we thought it might be. That night we got enough nerve up to sleep outside so that we could get away from the fleas. The next morning when we woke up the Jap guards were gone except for a couple of the good guards. They never said a word to us all day.

The second day I got up enough nerve and decided that I was going to get a duck. I waited all day and when it got dark. I went out to get one. There weren't any ducks left. The other prisoners had already got them. Well, I went back in and several of us got to talking about that big hog. We didn't know the war was over, but we knew there was a good chance it was so we went over, got the pig and killed it. The Japs didn't say a word. One of the guys looked down at the gate where the Jap guard was at. He said he had enough and went down to the gate and took the rifle away from the Jap. We headed for town. Women would be outside with their chickens and ducks. We would just walk up in a yard and grab chickens and ducks. Then we found a five-gallon can of peanut oil and that night we had the biggest chicken fry you ever saw.

The next day some of the guys went to town and found a short wave radio set and found out the war was over. That was the first that we officially knew it was over. That same day and American plane came over and dropped a parachute with magazines and cigarettes to us.

The day following another plane came over and dropped some more. They circled and told us that B-29s would be over the next day to drop food to us. So we were excited and the next morning we got up early. Eighteen B-29s came in and they were low. They opened their bomb bay doors and came in right over the top of us. They release several containers, two 55 gallon drums which were welded together, and the parachutes busted on them. We were out in the yard dodging barrels. Some of the guys got hit by them and were injured. They had done this all over Japan and we heard that there were a few of the POWs that were killed. The barrels were full of fruit and all the things we needed. That night one of the guys got on the short wave and made contact with the Americans. They told them that we had gotten the food, but if they were going to try and kill us that we might as well just stay there. They got the point.

The next day the planes came in again. They dropped food again. I had dropped from 165 pounds on Wake Island to 89 pounds at the end of the war. It was estimated that we were gaining three pounds a day on the food we were getting. I could certainly stand to gain; we all could. They also dropped clothing. The thing that always sticks in my mind is the shoes. I guess they wanted to make sure that we got the right size because when we left the camp there was a pile of shoes as high as a mountain.

The morning of September 6, 1945, some of the guys decided that we needed to catch a train and go to Tokyo. We asked one of the Japs to take us and he wasn't going to do it so one of the Marines pulled a gun on him. Then the Jap took us. We shoveled coal and the Jap engineer drove the train. All the men that died in China were buried, but the men who died in Japan had to be cremated. When we left the prison camp, we brought all of them back with us.

We went across the island to the American forces in Yokohama. The first thing that I saw was the American uniforms of the 1st Cavalry Army division. It was a wonderful sight. The Red Cross was there and they gave us a candy bar. Then they took us in and deloused us. Then they gave us new clothes and more food.

HEADING HOME
September 1945-May 1946

The next morning, September 7, 1945, they took us by boat out in the harbor to the USS *Ozark*. It was late when we got aboard the ship and they were going to feed us. We lined up at the chow line. The Navy thought we hadn't eaten and they didn't want to over feed us. They didn't know we had been getting food dropped to us so the first thing they did was drop a vitamin pill and then a sloppy soup. It was just soup, but it was good. It was like they were putting us on a diet. That night we broke into the food lockers and got some good food. The next day they fed us a good meal.

We pulled out and got into Guam a few days later. I got paid and went to the PX and bought some candy bars. I ate 32 chocolate bars that day. It is a wonder it didn't kill me. They put us in a hospital for a few days. It was funny because you would wake up in the

— *A Point of Interest* —

LEGAL CLAIM AGAINST JAPAN

The Center For Civilian Internee Rights (CFCIR) filed a claim against the Japanese government seeking an apology and compensation for American POWs and civilian internees who were brutalized and mistreated by Japanese Forces during World War II. As of yet, they have been unsuccessful in their efforts.

morning and most of the guys would be laying on the floor. We couldn't sleep on the soft mattresses.

A few days later we sailed and arrived in Hawaii. They would let us off at Pearl Harbor and after two days we headed for the States. When we arrived in San Francisco there were newspaper people waiting on us, but we were told that we were not to tell how we were treated in the camps because if we did we would be court marshaled. They took us to the Naval Hospital in Oakland. I stayed there for three or four days.

Then one morning they loaded us aboard a train headed for Chicago. We had about twenty cars to the train. I don't know how many men we had on the train, but they were all POWs from Corregidor, the Philippines, and Wake. Guys started writing on the side of the train. We took off and after a while the train stopped in a town. All the prisoners got off the train and headed across the street to the local taverns. The first stop the train was two hours getting started again. As the guys were getting back on the train, you would see one with a case of beer another with a case of whiskey. We had enough liquor on the train to last six months.

The train started off and just as it did there was a colored woman walking by the train carrying a bucket. One of the guys grabbed the bucket from her and filled it full of whiskey. Then he passed it around. The next stop they had SPs at the station and had us cut off so we couldn't get off the train. We just laughed at it because we had enough liquor to get us to Chicago.

When we pulled in Chicago they pulled in the Navy yard. They took us to the hospital and checked us in. They gave us orders not to leave the hospital. I went to sleep that night and when I woke up the next morning the hospital was empty. All the guys had took off for home without any papers. I got a call from the Red Cross that my folks were unable to locate me. They gave me a number and I called them.

The next day my brother came up and got me and we went home. I didn't have papers, but I didn't care. I stayed home for a month or so and then went back. We were in the hospital one morning and the doctor came in. The waste cans were full of whiskey bottles. He shook his head and said, "I don't know if you guys are tough or just crazy."

I was discharged and sent home a few days later."

PELEIU ISLAND
1946 and 1947

I went to work for the railroad and that lasted for a short time. I didn't like it so I went back and joined the Marines again. In May, 1946, I was sent to U.S. Naval Air Station at Opa-Locka, Florida, but I didn't like the duty station. They wanted 20 volunteers to go overseas and I went in and found out that they already had 20 names so I just wrote my name at the top. The major called me in and said, "You don't want to go back overseas." I said, "Yes sir, I do, I have already made my mind up."

In May 1946, I got orders for Peleiu Island in the Pacific. I arrived there on October 7, 1946. I was assigned as Non-Commissioned Officer in Charge of Security. The island still

Lt. Ei Yamaguchi turns over his battle flag and sword to Capt. Leonard O. Fox on April 21, 1947 on Peleiu Island. Thirty-three other soldiers surrendered with the Lt. In the upper middle of the photo in the background is Gunnery Sergeant Ed Sturgeon Staff Non-Commissioned Officer in charge watches.

Wake Island Defenders at 1994 reunion.

had Jap stragglers on it so I was there for a few months tangling with the Japs again. They would sneak into the base and try to cut our throats. The Japanese government finally sent a Japanese officer over to the islands and we would go out into the jungle areas with him. He would talk over a loud speaker, but the Japs still wouldn't surrender. Then in 1947 one of the Japanese came forward with the names of all the Jap soldiers hidden in the caves. The families of the soldiers were contacted and they all wrote letters which were forwarded to the islands. The one Jap got the letters to the remaining soldiers hidden in the caves. In April 1947, Lieutenant Yamaguchi surrendered his flag and command of 33 men."

Six months later Ed was shipped to Pearl Harbor, Hawaii where he was the Non-Commissioned Officer in charge of the main gate. In May 1948, Ed was transferred to the U.S. Naval Base, Norfolk, Virginia. In May 1949 he was discharged."

EPILOGUE

After Ed was discharged, he landed a job with Rockwell International working as a Maintenance Engineer. Ed worked at the company until 1975 when he took sick leave for a brain operation from complications of the injuries he had received from the Japanese beatings he had received in prison camp. After the surgery he returned to work and took full retirement in 1980.

He and his wife Theresa had three children David 46 who served in the Marine Corps and is a Viet Nam veteran, Linda 39, and Joyce 36. All are now married. Ed has remained active in veteran's organizations. He is a member of the Wake Island Wig-Wag Organization based in Missouri. He receives monthly newsletters with updates on veteran's business and information about Wake Island Defenders and their relatives. In 1994, he went to the fifty-three reunion of the Wake Island Defenders held in Oklahoma City. He also has visited many World War II museums.

He now lives in Richview, Illinois and enjoys living and fishing at the many resorts in the area.

FIFTY YEARS LATER
May 1996

In May 1996, Ed returned to Peleiu Island and spent a week on the Island. He was amazed to find that most of the remains of battle were still just as they had been left. Many of the guns, tanks, and ammunition were still in the same location, untouched except for mother nature. The trip was to bring another surprise. Another man was on the battlefield, Lieutenant Yamaguchi. The two men once enemies walked the battlefields together in memory of a time when they spent their youth in war.

Peleiu Rock Islands in 1996.

Ed Sturgeon with the Marine security guards on Peleiu Island in 1996.

Lt. Yamaguchi climbing into the cave he hid in some 50 years before. Taken in 1996.

Lt. Yamaguchi looking over the old battlefield with a NBC camera crew.

Lt. Yamaguchi with a radio operator in his command.

CHAPTER TWO

PRIVATE BENJAMIN DUNN
U.S. ARMY

131ST FIELD ARTILLERY BATTALION
CAPTURED ON JAVA ISLAND DURING THE JAPANESE INVASION

PRISONER OF WAR
MARCH 8, 1942-SEPTEMBER 2, 1945
JAKARTA, SINGAPORE, BURMA, AND THAILAND

THE DRAFT AND TEACHING SCHOOL
June 1941

In 1941 Ben was teaching school. The draft was going heavy and Ben was afraid that he would be drafted in the middle of the school year, so in the summer of '41 he went down to the draft board to see when they thought he would be inducted. "I had a fairly low draft number, Ben explained, " and they told me that they thought I would be drafted during the middle of the next school year because they were drafting teachers. I asked them if I could go in now and get my time in. They said I could so I went in on a June draft in 1941. I went to Camp Roberts, California and after basic training I was assigned to a regular army unit at the base."

THE MOLDING OF THE LOST BATTALION
November 1941-June 1942

In November 1941 Ben left the States and stopped at Pearl Harbor. On December 1, 1941, six days before the attack on Pearl Harbor Ben headed west with a convoy of nine ships. The convoy was headed for the Philippine Islands. On December 7th, they heard that Pearl Harbor had been attacked and within a day Wake Island, the Philippine Islands, and all the other islands in the Western Pacific. Ben's ship headed for Australia and they were the first American troops to land there in World War II. Ben's ship stayed for about a week and the troops had a great time. "Out of all of the nine ships I don't know what happened to them. We were the only one of the nine that had stopped at Australia," Ben said.

"There was one battalion, the 2nd Battalion from the 131st field artillery out of Texas detached from the 36th Division. My battery was the Brigade Headquarters battery the 16th Field Artillery Brigade. They took the 2nd Battalion and 120 men from my outfit, put us on a Dutch ship and sent us to Java. We were told that there were submarines in the area, but the trip was a pleasant one. I never saw anything that was a threat. We arrived at Soerabaja, Java the second largest city in the Netherlands East Indies. Then they moved us about 30 miles from the city to a Dutch air base. There were no planes at the base, but a few days later what planes were left of the 19th bomb group which had been bombed out at Clark Air Base in the Philippines, landed at the base. There were a number of us that were assigned to the Air Force to help with the planes. I learned to fuel planes and load bombs.

The officer in charge was Colonel Eubanks. He told us the first day we were there that we were going to be bombed by the Japs because there was nothing to stop them. He said, 'remember to take cover and lay down. Don't stand up at any time we are being attacked.'

Within a week about 27 Jap bombers attacked the air field and destroyed four of our bombers. The rest of the bombers were out on a mission so they didn't get them. They only

A Point of Interest

BATTLE OF SUNDA STRAIT

In the Battle of Sunda Strait the USS *Houston* and HMAS Perth each got their share of Japanese ships. Official Japanese records report the following:

SAKURA MARU	Passenger - 7170 tons	Sunk
TOKUSIMA MARU	Passenger - 5975 tons	Sunk
HORAI MARU	Passenger - 9192 tons	Sunk
W-2 (AM TYPE)	Mine Sweeper	Sunk
TSURUMI	Tanker	Damaged
SHIRAKUMO	Destroyer	Damaged
HARUKAZE	Destroyer	Damaged
AS AGUMO	Destroyer	Damaged
KINU	Light Cruiser	Damaged

killed one native during the raid. He was running for cover and we yelled at him to get in a hole, but he couldn't understand English. None of the military personal got a scratch.

This went on day after day. We didn't know what was going on with the war and then one day I got orders to be transferred to the Texas Battalion. There were 17 of the 26 of us from the field artillery that got orders to the 2nd Battalion. The rest of the men went back to Australia.

In the meantime, the Japanese were headed for Java. The allied fleet wasn't organized. The command was under a Dutch commander and there were some Dutch ships, Australian ships, and an American cruiser. They all met the Japanese fleet as the Japs headed for Java. It was the biggest Naval battle since World War I. Most of the allied ships were sunk, but a few got away."

THE USS *HOUSTON*

The USS *Houston* and HMAS *Perth an Australian* cruiser was ordered back to Australia. The two ships already damaged from previous battle with the Japanese limped into Tanjong Priok Harbor, the port of Batavia, to take on oil and make emergency repairs. Then the night of February 28, 1942 they left the harbor, made their way through a mine field, and ran head on into a Japanese invasion fleet in the Sunda Strait northeast of Java. The invasion fleet was supported by an aircraft carrier, two heavy cruisers, several light cruisers, two squadrons of destroyers, and dozens of other support ships. They put up a hell of a fight against the Japs before they were sunk.

Three hundred and sixty-eight crewmen from the *Houston* made it to shore and were captured by the Japanese. One hundred and fifty died in the water trying to make it to shore and over half of the crew went down with the ship. Little did the captured crew know that a short time later they would join with Ben's unit and become known as the Lost Battalion.

THE SURRENDER. . . JAVA
March 8, 1942

On March 1, 1942, the Japanese landed troops on both ends of the island. The defense against the Japanese was next to none. The native troops were abandoning the invasion area in large numbers. The Australians were putting up a good fight against overwhelming odds, but were being all but annihilated. The American forces were constantly being delayed by Japanese superior air attacks. The Dutch's Air Force and Navy were destroyed and most of their ground troops were natives who were sympathetic toward the Japanese and had deserted. The Japs couldn't be stopped.

WESTERN UNION

MRS FRANCES DUNN=

AN OFFICIAL REPORT RECEIVED IN THE WAR DEPARTMENT STATES THAT YOUR SON PRIVATE ERNEST B DUNN IS A PRISONER OF WAR OF THE JAPANESE GOVERNMENT IN BURMA ANY FURTHER INFORMATION RECEIVED WILL BE FURNISHED BY THE PROVOST MARSHALL GENERAL=

ULIO THE ADJUTANT GENERAL.

On March 8, 1942, Ben and a group of soldiers were camping in a Bamboo grove. They were preparing to continue to the Tjilatatjap port on the southern part of the island to board a ship. One of the officers came by the grove and told the soldiers that it would be impossible to reach the port. Ben and his fellow soldiers were told to lay down their arms and surrender. The Dutch had surrendered the island to the Japanese.

It was a real jolt for the soldiers, but with tear filled eyes they followed orders. "We didn't know what to expect from the Japanese, but if we had known what was in store for us we would have probably gone into the jungle and resisted," Ben said. "After the Japs arrived we did find out really quick that they put out rewards to the natives if they found someone who escaped.

With them being sympathetic toward the Japs we would have been unsuccessful. My morale was really low. We had been captured and had put up no fight at all. I really felt bad about that.

The Japanese didn't know what to do with all of us prisoners of war. They didn't believe in surrendering. The stories that I heard from the men that fought against them in the islands said they would run directly into a machine gun knowing they were going to be killed because they believed they would be killed for the emperor and go straight to heaven. Since they hadn't expected so many prisoners they hadn't considered the food supply. We would soon learn that we were going to be on a rice diet.

Here we were prisoners in Java. We were moved several places at first, but none of the locations were actually prison camps. Once we were at a race track for about a week. They took us up to the mountains to an old plantation. There were about five hundred of us that were in the battalion and they captured us pretty much intack. They moved us around and then finally in May 1942 we ended up in a prison camp on the docks of Tanjong Priok.

We worked on the docks doing all kinds of work. We were eating small portions of rice with very little meat mixed in with the rice. It just wasn't enough to eat and especially with the forced hard labor.

One of the worse things at first was trying to get use to their regulations and their language. We couldn't understand Japanese. We got orders in Japanese and according to their standards if we disobeyed they could beat us, slap us or hit us with a butt of a rifle if we didn't follow orders. It wasn't long before we learned to count in Japanese and to sound off in Japanese. We learned Japanese orders. If a Japanese soldier came by regardless of rank we were required to salute or bow. In their eyes we were the lowest thing on the earth. In the morning if a Japanese Lieutenant got up and didn't feel good he might slap a Sergeant around, then the Sergeant would beat up on a private and the private would beat up on the prisoners.

We worked at hard labor on the docks for about six weeks being slapped, beaten, yelled at and starved. Then they moved us again.

THE BICYCLE CAMP

June 1942

This camp was completely encircled by a high barbed wire fence with a single asphalt street running down the middle of it from one end to the other. Four parallel barracks were located on both sides of the street. The first three barracks on the right from the entrance of the camp were for the American prisoners of war. The other barracks on the same side of the street was for Dutch officers and civilians. The barracks on the other side of the street were occupied by the Australians except for the last barracks which was used as a hospital. The mess hall was behind the Australian barracks.

All the buildings were permanent with running water taps near each building. There were no bunks in the barracks so each prisoner found their own spot to sleep.

This photo of Ben Dunn was drawn by Noel Mason soon after their capture in Java.

A Point of Interest

THE LOST BATTALION

Number of the 2nd Battalion 131st Field Artillery taken POW	529
Number of USS Houston CA-30 who survived the sinking and taken POW	368
Number of 131st FA personnel who worked on the Burma Railway of Death	381
Number of the USS Houston survivors who worked on the Railway of Death	269
Number of 131st people who died in Burma and Thailand	65
Number of Houston men who died in Burma and Thailand	66
Number of 131st men who died enroute to Japan on ships that were sunk	16
Number of Houston survivors who died enroute to Japan on ships that were sunk	2
Number of 131st men who died in Japan	2
Number of Houston survivors who died in Japan	2
Number of 131st men who died in Java	5
Number of Houston survivors who died in Java	4
Number of 131st men who died in Singapore	1
Number of Houston survivors who died in Borneo N.E.I.	1
Number of Houston men who died in Saigon F.I.C.	1
Number of Houston men who died on a Japanese ship	1
Total Deaths	166

BEN'S EXPERIENCE

In June Ben's unit was moved to downtown in Batavia-now given the Indonesian name of Jakarta. They were marched from the train station to an old military Dutch camp called the Bicycle camp. The Japanese guard house was located just inside the entrance to the camp on the left side of the street. The porch was always crowded with Japanese guards armed with rifles at fixed bayonet. No one knows the reason why the camp was named Bicycle camp, but the name of the camp was of little concern to the prisoners. The camp would prove to be the best that Ben was to live in during his duration as a prisoner of a war. "It was a better camp then any we had been in. We had electric lights and a couple of outlets. When we got there, there were Americans already in the camp. They were in bad shape. They were half naked and had sores all over them. They were the survivors of the *Houston*. There were 368 out of the 1,100 man crew and they were all in this camp. They were starved. We had some supplies and we started sharing our clothes and blankets with them. We became one unit and some of us would spent the rest of the war together. We were the Lost Battalion.

In a couple of months they started moving prisoners to Japan. All the Navy officers had been sent earlier and then they sent our Colonel and some more officers to Japan. Myself and the other prisoners worked on the docks, built an airport, worked in a rubber plant, and worked in a Japanese headquarters where they were sorting auto parts from cars they had taken from their capturers.

At this time the food wasn't too bad. The rice was cleaner, but the rice we got when we were first captured was dirty. I think it had been swept up off the floor. It had bugs in it and worms. For a while some of the guys wouldn't eat it because it made them sick. When you get hungry, you start eating and after a while everybody picked what bugs and worms they could out of rice. As time passed we just ate the rice worms, bugs, and all. Once in a while we got a vegetable and a piece of meat. We ate everything that we could get our hands on.

We had a radio and since we had electricity we could listen to it. The Japs didn't know it but some of the guys took it apart and rigged it and we were able to get some news once in a while from San Francisco. If we had been caught, they would have shot us.

The Japs started moving some of us. They brought us a piece of paper to sign stating that we would not try to escape. We wouldn't sign it so they took what officers we had left and started beating them. The officers told us to sign whatever they wanted us to because it

A Point of Interest

CATCHING FLIES

The Death Rail prison camps became so infested with flies that the Japanese ordered the prisoners to catch 100 flies each night. The Japanese guards would come around with a bucket. If the guard thought that you had enough flies to make 100 he would let the prisoner put them in the bucket. If he did not think the prisoner had not caught 100 flies the Japanese guards would beat them with bamboo clubs.

didn't mean anything because we were signing it under duress. If we wanted to try to escape, we could. We signed the papers and they quit beating up on the officers.

They wanted to find out how many technicians they had so they give us some papers to fill out. Some of the guys put down the truth and some didn't. Some of the Australian prisoners put down that they were beer tasters. Some of the Americans put down that they were peach fuss removers. The Japs took about 60 of the men that they thought were technicians and they shipped them to Japan. We never saw them again until the war was over.

In another month they took 200 more prisoners and two officers and they shipped them out. We didn't know where they were going. Later we found out that they were shipped to Singapore and then to Burma to work on the rails."

THE DAI NICHI MARU
October 1942

In October 1942, the Japs loaded the remaining Americans and Australians aboard the Hell ship Dai Nichi Maru. "We were down in a hole packed in like rats," Ben explained. "It was hot and lucky for us it was a short trip. We didn't have enough water to drink. They gave us a little cup of rice twice a day. Most of us weren't hungry. It stunk so bad that we couldn't eat. Men were sick and throwing up. The Japs wouldn't let us clean it up. Everyone had dysentery and if you had to use the bathroom you had to go up on the deck and set on a wooden stool that hung out over the edge of the ship. You were setting out over the ocean and the stool wobbled and shook. We were afraid that it would collapse and if we fell in we were dead because the Japs wouldn't try to help us. As a result, most prisoners relieved themselves where they set."

Twelve days later the ship pulled into Singapore. It was a welcome sight for Ben and the rest of the prisoners.

SINGAPORE
October 1942 -January 1943

CAMP CHANGI

This camp was a large sprawling cantonment in the low hills on the east end of the island. The barracks were permanent stone barracks that had been used in peace time by the British army. The prisoners slept on the concrete floor and again picked their own spot.

The camp was surrounded by barbed wire fence and the Japanese guards were posted on the outside of the fence. The camp consisted of English, Scots, Gurkhas, Indians, Australians, and now American prisoners of war. The Japanese had captured about 100,000 British troops in Singapore, Malia, and the islands up and down the area and there were still about 60 thousand troops in the camp when Ben got there. The Japanese turned over the interior operation in the camp over to the British. The Japanese guards were on the outer perimeters and on occasion they would come in and check things out.

A Point of Interest

CONSTRUCTION OF THE RAILWAY

For 15 months prisoners of war and local natives constructed 260 miles of railway from Rangoon, Burma to Bangkok, Thailand. The path of construction took them over some of the most rugged mountains and through some of the most diseased jungles in the world. This Railway of Death was completed without the use of a single machine.

"The food was terrible", Ben told me. "We got dirty rice and rotten vegetables to eat. One day I walked over to a basketball court where some British officers were at trying to play ball. In 1942 the British didn't know anything about basketball. They asked if I knew anything about basketball. I told them I played a little and they asked if we I could get some friends and play them a game. The next day we met and played. We beat them 50 to nothing. After the game was over, the British took us in their barracks and gave us some tea. I looked around and there were cans of food from the Red Cross setting on their shelves. They had taken the Red Cross packages and kept them for themselves while we were eating rotten food. We told the other prisoners what we saw and needless to say the American and British prisoners didn't get along from then on. We would be walking along and see a British officer coming along and we would act like we were going to salute them. They would snap to attention and salute as we were raising our arm, then we would scratch our head. They would report us to our officers, but they wouldn't do anything."

THE JOURNEY TO BURMA
January 1943

After about three months, on January 6, 1943, Ben and about 350 Americans packed their gear, were marched to Singapore, and put us on a train for Georgetown. To their horror they were loaded on another hell ship the Dai Moji Maru. "The conditions were worse than the first ship partly because we were on it longer," Ben said. "We were headed north for Burma. There were two ships. We were within a day of arriving at Burma when we were attacked by American planes. I was setting down in that hole and I looked up through the hatch and I saw the planes. The bomb bay doors opened and here come the bombs. Two bombs hit really close to the ship and it started to list. We thought it was going to sink but we couldn't get up out of the hole because the Japs had machine guns on us. The planes left without making a second run, but they had sunk the other ship. A bomb hit right in the hole where the Jap soldiers were at. The soldiers on top went overboard. There were some Dutch prisoners on that ship and they went overboard. The Japs had life jackets, but prisoners weren't given life jackets. When we picked up the survivors some of the Dutch prisoners had on life jackets. They told us that the soldiers went into the water with their rifle, helmets, and packs. They could hardly move. The prisoners would swim up to them and hold them under until they drown then take their life jackets."

THE DEATH RAILWAY
January 1943 -January 1944

The Death Railway was not yet in the vocabulary of any of the prisoners. It was a project that even the Japanese engineers had said was impossible. Yet, by the command of the Emperor the project began. The railroad was to run from Ban Pong, Thailand to Thanbyuzayat, Burma. The Japanese had chosen to build the railway in order to get much needed supplies to their troops on the India front. It had been in operation only three months when Ben arrived and it would not be until one year later when the railway was finished and the toll was taken on the lives of more than 300,000 men in 260 miles of mountains and the

A Point of Interest

LIVES CLAIMED

The Burma Railway of Death claimed the lives of over 120,000. Although the actual account is difficult to determine: some historians have estimated that as many as 393 men died for every mile of track laid. Approximately 26,000 of those were allied POWs. The remainder were native prisoners.

most diseased jungles of Thailand and Burma that the title The Railway of Death would be burned into the memory of the POWs.

Thanbyuzayat was the jumping-off place for most of the POWs and Ben was no exception. He would listen to the speech by Lieutenant Colonel Y. Nagatoma that had been repeated over and over to the new groups of POWs brought to work on the rails.

Lieutenant Colonel Nagatoma's speech:

> It is a great pleasure to see you at this place as I am appointed Chief of War Prisoners' Camps in obedience to the Imperial Command issued by His Imperial Majesty, the Emperor. The Great East War has broken out due to the rising of the East Asiatic nations whose hearts were burnt with the desire to live and preserve their nations on account of the intrusion of the British and Americans for the past many years. There is therefore, no other reason for Japan to drive out the Anti-Axis powers of the arrogant and insolent British and Americans from East Asia in cooperation with our neighbors of China and other East Asiatic nations and to establish the Greater East Asia Co-Prosperity Sphere for the benefit of all human beings and to establish everlasting peace in the world.
>
> During the past few centuries, Nippon has made extreme endeavors and sacrifices to become the leader of the East Asiatic nations who were mercilessly and pitifully treated by the outside forces of the Americans and British, and Nippon without disgracing anybody, has been doing her best up till now for fostering Nippon's real power. Therefore, you are now only a few remaining skeletons after the invasion of East Asia for the past few centuries and our pitiful victims. It is not your fault, but until your government wakes up from their dreams and discontinue their resistance, none of you will be released. However, I will not treat you badly for the sake of humanity, as you have no fighting power at all.
>
> His majesty, the Emperor, has been deeply anxious about all the POW camps in almost all the places in the southward countries. The Imperial thoughts are inestimable and the Imperial forces are infinite, as such you should wee with gratitude of them and should correct or amend the misleading and improper anti-Japanese ideas. I shall meet with you hereafter, and at the beginning of various times. Although there may be lack of material, it is difficult to meet all the requirements.
>
> (1) I heard that you complain about the insufficiency of various items. Although there may be a lack of materials, it is difficult to meet all your requirements. Just turn your eyes to the present conditions of the world. It is entirely different from prewar times. In all countries and lands, materials are considerably short and it is not easy to obtain a small piece of cigarette or a small match stick and the present position is such that is not possible even for the needy women and children to get sufficient food. Needless to say, therefore, that at such inconvenient places, even our respectable Nippon Army is not able to get mosquito nets, foodstuffs, cigarettes, and medicines, freely and frequently. As conditions are such, how can you expect me to treat you better than the Imperial Japanese Army? I do not persecute according to my own wishes and it is not due to the expense, but do to the shortage of materials at such distant places. In spite of my wish to meet your requirements, I can't do so with money. I shall, however, supply you if I can do so

with my best efforts and I hope you will rely on me and all of you render your lives before me.

(2) I shall strictly manage all of your going out, coming back, meeting your friends, communications, possessions of money, and other things shall be limited. Living manners, deportment, salutations and attitude shall be strict and in accordance with the rules of the Nipponese Army, because it is only possible to manage you all who are merely remnants of a rabble army by the order of military regulations. By this I shall issue separate pamphlets of house rules of war of POW's and you are required to act strictly in accordance wit the rules.

(3) My biggest requirement from you is escape. The rules for escape shall naturally be very severe. This rule may be quite useless and only binding to some of the POWs, but is more important for all of you in the management of the camp. You shall therefore, be contented accordingly. If there is a man who makes a one per cent chance at escape, we shall make him face the extreme penalty. If a man is foolish enough to try to escape, he shall see big jungles toward the east which are absolutely impossible for communications. Towards the west, he shall be faced with boundless ocean, and in all points and most important, our Japanese Army is staying and guarding. You will easily see the difficulty of complete escape. A few such cases of ill-omened matters which happened in Singapore shall prove the above and you shall not attempt such foolish things, although it is a last chance after your complete embarrassment.

(4) Hereafter, I shall require all of you to work, as no one is permitted to do nothing and eat as a prisoner. In addition, the Imperial Army had great works to promote at the places newly occupied by them and this is an essential and important matter. At the time of such shortness of material, your lives have been spared by the military and all of you must reward them by your work. By the hand of the Nipponese Army, railway work to connect Thailand and Burma have started to the great interest of the world. These are deep jungles, where no man comes to clear them by cutting the trees. There are almost countless difficulties, but you should do your best efforts. I shall check carefully and investigate about your non-attendance, so all of you should, except those who are really unable to work, be taken out for labor. At the same time, I shall expect all of you to work earnestly and confidently every day. In conclusion, I shall say to you, "Work Cheerfully" and from thenceforth you shall be guided by this motto.

Lt. Col. Y. Nagatoma
Chief No. III Branch
Thai War Prisoners' Camp

Ben couldn't believe it. How could they possible do it? It was impossible. For the next year he would work daily with one thing in mind. Survival! And against all odds he would survive.

BEN'S STORY

"We made it into Moulmein, Burma on January 16, 1943. That was the beginning of our experience on the railway of death. They took us to a place called Thanbyuzayat which was the jump-off place for building a railroad that was to connect Bangkok, Thailand with Rangoon, Burma. It would be 260 miles long and run through the jungles and mountains. The reason they were building it was because the Americans were sinking the Jap supply ships that were trying to get into Burma. The Japs had an army ready to attack India, but had to hold them up because of a lack of supplies. This railroad was being built to get them those supplies."

18 KILO CAMP

"This camp consisted of several huts. They were made from bamboo and leaves from the jungle. In these huts we chose our spot on the floor and that is where we slept.

They put us to work on this railroad nonstop. We were divided up into groups of fifty.

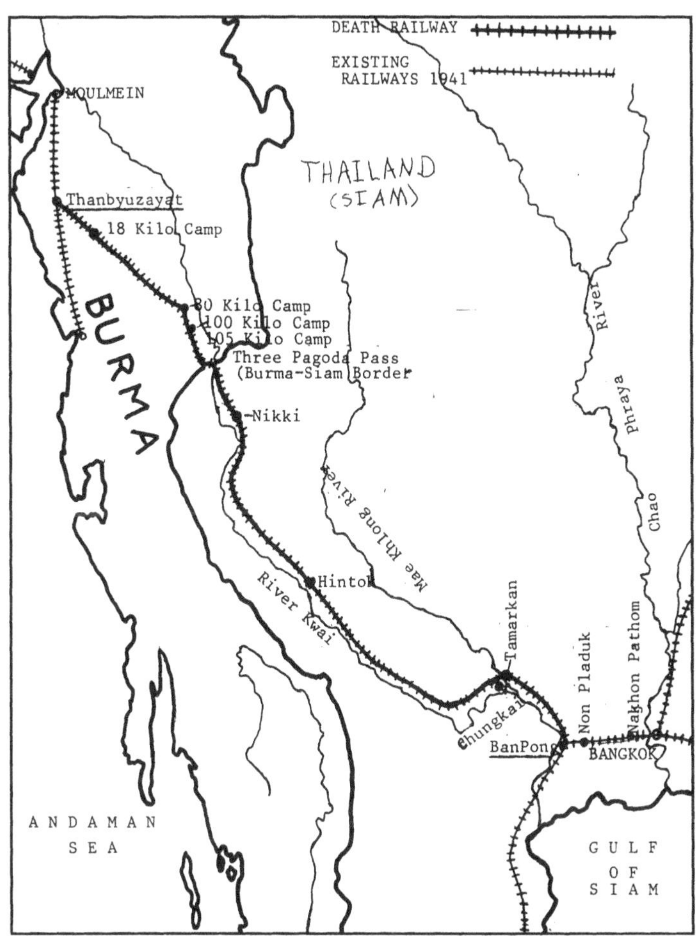

Death Railway–From Ban Pong, Siam to Thanbyuzayat, Burma.

There was usually a second Lieutenant in charge and we also had the Jap guards. We built this railroad without any machines. I never saw a machine until after the railroad was complete. It was picks and shovels and wheel barrels. The first group of American prisoners that had arrived before us had cleared the jungle and we were the dirt moving group. We had picks and shovels, but no wheel barrels. We carried dirt in a basket. When they told us what we were building I couldn't believe that they thought we could build it with no equipment. Each day we marked off the area we were to cover. At first we started out with 1.2 cubic meters. It was in January 1943 and the dry season. We went out there and knocked out our work and went back to camp. After three days they increased the area to 1.5 cubic meters. We knocked that out and would go back to camp and eat rice. We didn't have enough water and we had to boil it. It was hot so we would go back to the camp and boil water and drink all we could. I drank the water hot. I never had a good cold drink of water for three and a half years. This work was what we did day after day.

Then they moved up the area to two cubic meters a day. That was beginning to be really hard work. The Dutch prisoners told us not to finish the work as fast as we could so we could get back to camp for rest, but to string out the work because the Japs would just keep adding more area to work on a daily basis. They were right and we slowed down the work.

It was really hot out there picking and digging. Some of the ground had really gotten hard. This was in the beginning and some of the prisoners started getting sick. They came down with malaria. I knew what the symptoms of malaria was because I had it as a kid when I lived on the Mississippi River. It is hard to describe what malaria is like but you get really hot and almost feel like you are crawling. It goes in stages first there is the high

A Point of Interest

A FAILED RAILROAD

The Japanese over-estimated the ability of the railway. The railway was able to ship 600 tons of supplies daily to the India front. This was only one fifth of the estimated amount. Then information supplied to Americans by recovered POWs resulted in intensified bombing on the railway in November 1944. The railway became inoperable within months of its completion.

temperature and then heavy sweats. Another thing about it is that it will go for four or five days and you think you are over it and then it comes back. I had it come back on me approximately 30 times while I was a prisoner. I was working one day down in the pit and I started feeling it come on me. I stopped working and went over to the side of the pit and set in the shade. I knew that quinine would knock the malaria and we had that in camp. That night I took some quinine and the next day I could go to work. Different ones came down with it and it really hit some of them hard.

Every day we would walk to the point where we were working, work all day, and then walk back to camp. The next camp from us was 12 miles so the more we worked the longer the walk each day. We would go back to camp and boil water and drink all we could hold so that our bodies were saturated for the next days work. We had been told that the food at Burma was going to be better that in Singapore and we were looking forward to it. When we got there, it was better. We got rice with as much as an ounce of meat in it and more of it for about the first two weeks but the work was so much harder."

85 KILO CAMP

"In the Middle of May 1943, they took us by truck to 85 Kilo camp. That was 50 miles from the main base camp and it was deeper into the jungle. It would be the last time we would be moved by truck. At this camp was that there was a stream running down the middle of the camp and we could use it to bath and to get fresh water for boiling. It didn't last long though because we did the same kind of work for about two weeks then they moved us again."

80 KILO CAMP

"We started to work at this camp and we were there until the end of June. It was terrible. By now we had to walk 12 miles to get to the working area. The food was getting worse and there was less of it. Many of the guys were sick with malaria, dysentery, and just weak from the hard work and the lack of food. The healthy ones helped carry the sick to work. We never lost anyone. Then we moved again."

100 KILO CAMP

"It was at this camp that the rainy season really started. The first day in the camp we had one of our prisoners to die on the railroad. The work was really hard here. We had to work in the mud and rain. They cut our food rations in half with no meat and the men started dying fast. One food item we had was a melon. It looked like a watermelon, but it was white. They gave those to us and we cut the melons up, boiled them, and ate them with our rice. They had no vitamins or food value at all. The Australians called the melons "white death" because when we were put on a diet like that prisoners started getting beri beri. That is a disease caused by vitamin deficiency. It usually started with swelling in the ankles. Then it would get in the stomach. Then the face. Sometimes in their scrotum and it would swell many sizes. Then finally it would get in the lungs. A persons lungs would fill with fluid. You would hear your friends gasping for air because of their lungs filling with fluid and you knew that they weren't going to live, within a few hours they would die in their own fluid.

All of us had a little bit of joint disease from vitamin deficiency. Most had malaria.

Then if you worked out and you got a cut on your legs it would get infected and cause a tropical ulcer. It was a sore and that would start eating on the flesh until it would get to the bone and then it would spread out. If you had them long enough, it would even affect the bone. We had two doctors one from the *Houston* and the other from the 131st battalion, but they didn't know how to deal with it because they had never seen a disease like that. The guys would take rags soak them in water, put them on the sores, and try to soak that rotten

Sketch of working in prison camp by Wisecup who was a POW from the USS Houston.

flesh out. They would do that every day, but it didn't heal them. When they really got bad, the men would be taken back to the base camp and the Australian doctor would amputate. They lost more than they saved. The American doctors with us operated on a few and didn't save any.

The group of Americans that had arrived in Burma before us were luckier than we had been. Every one of the 200 Americans in that group had a tropical ulcer of some kind. They

Sketch of grave site in POW camp by Wisecup.

had a Dutch doctor with that group who had lived in the jungles all his life. He had a sharpened spoon that he used to dig out the rotten flesh in the ulcers. He didn't loose a single prisoner.

I had malaria and amebic dysentery. You don't get rid of it without proper drugs and we didn't have any drugs. Our doctor died but right before he did he told me that I couldn't go out and work on the railroad any longer. He told me to stay in or it was going to kill me. I stayed back and when the men that could work left the camp the Japanese would send one of our officers down to the barracks and make everybody that could walk go outside. This major came through one day and asked me what was wrong, "can't you walk." I told him hell yes but I'm not going to the doc told me to stay in here and I'm going to. He told me it was up to me. But there would be a Jap soldier that would be coming through with a club soon. Pretty soon this Jap came by and asked me what was wrong. I told him malaria, beri beri, and dysentery. He felt of my forehead and I must have had a temperature because he went on and never said a word. They would ask some what was wrong and they would say they couldn't walk. The Japs would take them outside and beat them. They had nine prisoners out once and beat them with bamboo poles. They would hit them in their ulcers which made them grow faster. I don't know if they did it to make them die faster or not, but they did die fast.

On the job you would always look to see who was going to be the guard, because some was worse than others. We had one we called liver lips. He was dark and big and when he got mad and started beating on a prisoner it seemed the more he beat the madder he got.

We had another guard called Mocon. Mocon was a word for food and he was always around the kitchen looking for food. He didn't like me for some reason. I found out later that they did not like blue eyes. They called them fish eyes. I had fish eyes."

Sketch of POW cemetary for Death Railway.

OPERATION SPEEDO

"They started operation speedo. The work day got longer and the work got harder. If you were sick, they cut your rations in half. It didn't matter for the Americans because they shared anyway and soon everyone got less food. Then they decided to send the sickliest men back to 80 kilo camp where we had been before. By this time that camp was run down. This was at the end of the rainy season in the fall of 1943. Every day they would take a truck load of sick prisoners to this camp. They were taking them there to die. My name was on the list but I told them that I didn't want to go, I could walk. A friend of mine who had been through all of this with me saw me getting on the truck and came up and said, Dunn I just came from 80 kilo and it is worse than this camp. You don't have to work there but you don't get as much to eat. It's bad there. I explained that I had no choice the Japs were sending 25 today and 20 the next day. They told me I had to go. The Japs paid us ten cents a day and he gave me a dime and told me that maybe I could buy and egg or something with it. I told him he needed it as badly as I did, but he insisted. I got on the truck and when we arrived I couldn't believe it. There were only four or five men that could walk in the whole camp. The rations were half of what we had gotten at Kilo 100. Men were dying like flies.

There were two other Americans that could walk. They were orderlies. I could walk and we did the best we could to take care of each other. I found out that over the past three months that 61 of the Americans that had been sent down to this camp had died. It was a combination of things that killed them. They all had malaria, beri beri, dysentery, tropical ulcers and they just gave out.

I found two of my friends in this camp. We had been in Camp Roberts in the States together. They both had tropical ulcers, malaria, and dysentery. Every day I would go down and visit them. One of them had the worse tropical ulcer I ever saw. It went from the ankle up the leg with the whole shin bone showing white. They both lived through that and I think it was because they were so close. They supported each other and I went down every day to help them too. They were in a ward at one end where the prisoners with dysentery were at. Each day when I would go down I would ask where some prisoner was at. "Oh, he died. We buried him yesterday." It was really demoralizing.

One of the native Dutchmen showed me a plant in the jungle that was good to eat.

The Japs only had two guards and they rarely checked on us. They knew we weren't going any place and they didn't like the smell in the barracks so they didn't come in there either. I could walk about 30 yards before resting so I would slip into the jungle and pick some of these plants. I boiled them and ate them with my rice. It helped some. I also checked the Jap's garbage and picked out what we called Harry Carries. They were a little tube that was about as big as my thumb. I threw them in the fire and roasted them and then ate them. One day I was roasting some Harry Carries and I asked one of the Americans who slept by me if he wanted a couple of them. He said he did. I took them out of the fire and he said, 'they are kinda burnt aren't they.' I said, yeah if you don't want them give them back. He said, 'Oh they are just the way I like them.' He died later.

The two other Americans that could walk were busy, every day burying the dead. They had just returned one day from burying some prisoners and the Japs told us we were moving out. The railroad was finished."

Sketch of the Great White Hunter by Wisecup.

A Point of Interest

HIDDEN CAMERA

A 19-year-old Australian POW kept a hidden camera and took photos in the Death Rail Camps. When the railroad was finished he was put on a train back to Singapore. When the train was stopped to be searched by Japanese guards he quickly smashed the camera into small pieces and hid the film on a dying POW's stretcher. Had he been caught he would have been immediately executed. The film was later used as evidence to prosecute Japanese officers for war crimes. 32 officers were executed and 79 received life in prison.

Sketch of POWs loading on a train by Wisecup.

KILO 105

"They put us on boxcars and took us to Kilo 105. While I was there, I had the worse attack of malaria that I had ever had. Every time my heart would beat a really sharp pain would go right down my spine. I thought to myself, here I have made it through all of this and we are about to get out of here. Am I going to die now that I have gone through all of this? All night long that sharp pain was there. The next morning the pain was gone. Even though it was hot, I stood by the fire all day. We found out that the prisoners that had stayed in the camp while the railroad was being built had a Cholera epidemic and most of them died. Why they brought us back into that camp is beyond me. Maybe they thought we would all die. We stayed there for a few weeks and then they moved us again."

THE RIDE ON THE BURMA RAILWAY OF DEATH

"They put us on a train and made a trip from there into Thailand. It was really exciting. That railroad was crooked and shook. All the prisoners tried to sabotage the railroad as it was being built. They would put stumps in the footing so it would eventually rot out. If they put a bolt in the track and the Japs weren't looking they would take the nut loose. Anything to make the thing fall apart and in places it did."

Photos above and below are the Death Railway.

CAMP TAMARKAN

We made it into Thailand on January 4, 1944, stopped at the Kwai Bridge, and camped there. Most of us couldn't work, but things begin to get better because of the Thai people. The Thai people are good. Anytime they had prisoners of war in Thailand the Thai people would always try to get food to them. I got a lot of duck eggs in this camp. The food was better and many of us started to get better. None of us got well until we got out of the camps, but we started to get better.

There were several thousand of us in the camp and I was there when the Americans bombed the Kwai Bridge the first time. I was in the malaria ward which was the

Photos above and below are the Death Railway.

first hut by the bridge. One morning they came in and moved me to a hut at the other end of the camp because I had malaria. The Americans came in that day and bombed the bridge. They missed the bridge and the bombs hit that hut that I had just been moved out of and killed 17 Australian and Dutch prisoners. It was right where I had been sleeping. They bombed the bridge several more times, but every time they missed it.

We were there for several months. They gave us a glass rod test to check for amebic dysentery. If you didn't have dysentery or malaria at the time, they put us on a list to go to Japan. By this time it was 1944 and it wasn't safe in Japan. I had amebic dysentery. With amebic dysentery you think you have to go to the bathroom all the time. All you will pass is a handfull of blood and puss. Since I had the dysentery, I wasn't going to Japan."

SERVICE DES PRISONNIERS DE GUERRE,

俘虜郵便

FROM P. O. W. No. 10365

NAME Ernest B. Dunn

NATIONALITY American

RANK Private

Camp : No. 3 Branch Thai War Prisoners Camp. NIKE, THAILAND.

泰俘虜收容所 第三分所檢閲濟 昭和19年2月1日

To Mr. Thomas Dunn
Gorham Illinois
U.S.A.

Front of postcard from Ernest B. Dunn while in Nike, Thailand POW camp, to Mr. Thomas Dunn.

IMPERIAL JAPANESE ARMY.

Our present place, quarters, and work is unchanged since last card sent to you. The rains have finished, it is now beautiful weather. I am working healthily (~~sick~~). We receive newspapers printed in English which reveal world events.

We have joyfully received a present of some milk, tea, margarine, sugar and cigarettes from the Japanese Authorities.

We are very anxious to hear from home, but some prisoners have received letters or cables.

Everyone is hopeful of a speedy end to the war and with faith in the future we look forward to a happy reunion soon.

With best wishes for a cheerful Christmas.

Tell mom and dad to write and also my friends.

From Ernest B. Dunn

Back of postcard from Ernest B. Dunn while in Nike, Thailand POW camp, to Mr. Thomas Dunn.

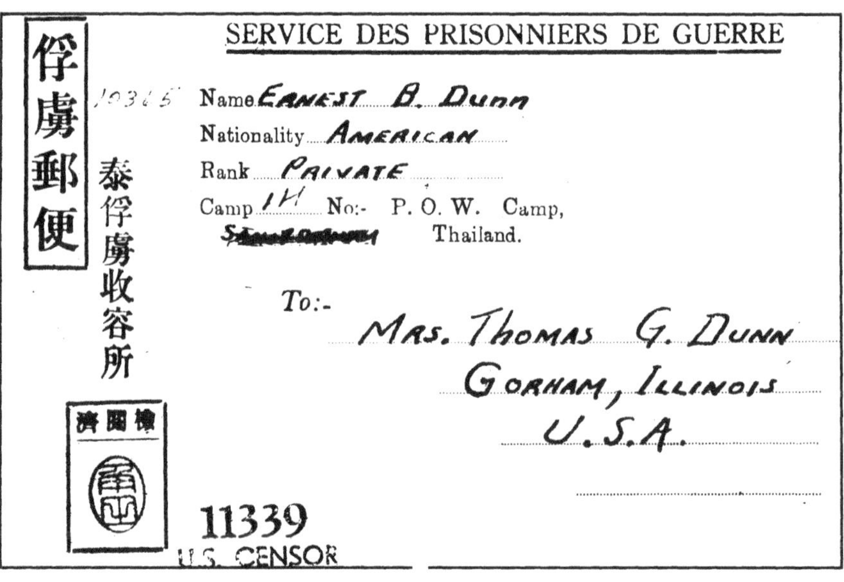

SERVICE DES PRISONNIERS DE GUERRE

俘虜郵便

10365

Name Ernest B. Dunn

Nationality American

Rank Private

Camp 14 No:- P. O. W. Camp, Thailand.

泰俘虜收容所

To:- Mrs. Thomas G. Dunn
Gorham, Illinois
U.S.A.

11339

U.S. CENSOR

Front of postcard from Ernest B. Dunn while in Thailand POW camp, to Mr. Thomas Dunn on June 4, 1944.

IMPERIAL JAPANESE ARMY

Date June 4, 1944

~~Your mails (and) are received with thanks.~~
~~My health is (good, usual, poor).~~
~~I am ill in hospital.~~
I am ~~working for pay (I am paid monthly salary)~~.
~~I am not working~~.
My best regards to ALL THE FAMILY.

Yours ever,

Ken Dunn

Back of postcard from Ernest B. Dunn while in Thailand POW camp, to Mr. Thomas Dunn on June 4, 1944.

GENEVE 228 1??/124 28 1650 COPY
DLT JAPANESE REDCROSS TOKYO

10365 NAK

T00131 KINDLY TRANSMIT MESSAGE TO FOLLOWING POW MOULMEINCAMP PRIVATE ERNEST B DUNN RECEIVED CARD FAMILY WELL KEEP YOUR COURAGE LOVE MOTHER DUNN

INTERCROIXROUGE A1936

Letter to Ernest B. Dunn from his mother. The letters were short because the Japs would only allow letters to be 25 words in length.

Dear Benny: Jan. 18, 1944

Just notified you are prisoner. We are all well. Tommy has two year old boy named Benny.

Dad and Mom

Letter sent to Ernest B. "Benny" Dunn from his mom and dad on Jan. 18, 1944.

SERVICE DES PRISONIERS DE GUERRE

10365

FROM.

NAME ERNEST B. DUNN

NATIONALITY AMERICAN

RANK PRIVATE

CAMP War Prisoners Camp (5)
Moulmein, BURMA.

TO T. A. DUNN
GORHAM,
ILLINOIS
U.S.A.

Front of postcard from Ernest B. Dunn while in Moulmein, Burma POW camp, to Mr. Thomas Dunn.

IMPERIAL JAPANESE ARMY.

I am interned at The War Prisoners Camp at
Moulmein in Burma.

My health ~~is~~ (good, ~~usual, poor~~)

I have not had any illness.

~~I (am) (have been) in hospital~~.

I am (not) working (for pay at ______ per day).

My salary is ______ per month.

I am with friends ______

LET Me know about the family.

From Ernest B. Dunn

Back of postcard from Ernest B. Dunn while in Moulmein, Burma POW camp, to Mr. Thomas Dunn.

CAMP NAKHON PATHOM
February 1944 -March 1945

Ben had survived the Death Railway and was slowly recovering from the terrible conditions at those camps. Then things even got better. He was sent to another camp. "It was the best camp that I had been in Thailand," Ben explained. "It had huts with wooden floors in it that we slept on instead of the bamboo slats. The barrack was built better and was supposed to have been a hospital. There were a lot of doctors, but no medicine. The Japs had received medicine in the Red Cross packages, but they would not give it to the doctors. At one time there were 7,000 sick prisoners in this camp. I was there five or six months and I started getting better. The food was better. The Thai people would get as much food as they could to us. The only work I did there was haul wood a couple of times. Also, they built a brick wall around the camp and I worked on that some. They had a workshop where they were making artificial legs. Some of the prisoners worked in them and they were helping each other. Making limbs for each other and it helped rehabilitate them.

Slim Chambers was in this camp with me. He was funny. I don't care how bad things got in the camps he always had sometime funny to say. He would make up jokes about

May 8, 1944

Dear Benny:

Good baseball news - the Browns are leading the league. Bad river news - flood on the Mississippi again.

Love,

Mom.

Letter sent to Ernest B. "Benny" Dunn from his mom on May 8, 1944.

Bridge over the River Kwai in Kanchanaburi, Thailand.

A Point of Interest

BRIDGE ON THE RIVER KWAI

The movie BRIDGE ON THE RIVER KWAI, released in 1957, won seven Academy Awards. The movie tells the story of World War II British POWs captured by the Japanese and forced to build a bridge over the river Kwai. Colonel Nicholson became obsessed with building the bridge. In the end he saw the bridge finished only to have allied commandos blow the bridge up just as the first Japanese train was crossing over. The truth is that there was no Colonel Nicholson, there were no allied commandos, and the Kwai bridge still stands today.

something I did or sometime someone else did. It was really good that we had someone like that.

A guy by the name of Dempsey Key was in my battery and we became good friends. He could steal more things from the Japs than anybody I ever saw. When we were in Singapore one time, the English officers had a bunch of chickens in a pen. They weren't giving anybody the eggs or chickens, but the other officers. Key sneaked down to the pen and stole nine of those chickens, pulled their heads off, and laid them at the back door of the officer's barracks. The officers blamed it on the Japanese.

Many of the prisoners joints were stiff because of weight lose. When you weigh say 170 pounds and you go down to 80 pounds or so your muscles and joints get stiff. In this camp one of the doctors got a group of healthy prisoners that went around and did rub downs on other prisoners and tried to help them learn to walk again."

THE KWAI CAMP
March 1945 -May 1945

"By now it was the Spring of 1945," Ben told me. "They started shipping us out if we were well. I was in pretty good shape except for a little dysentery problem so I was shipped back to the camp on Kwai. I was only there for a couple of weeks and went through a couple of bombing raids and they finally hit the bridge. A couple of weeks later they put us on a train and took us to Bangkok. There we were put on a barge and started down river. I thought for sure they were taking us to the ocean. We are going to Japan. I thought about trying to escape because I saw the B-29s going over. I knew it would be dangerous. Well, we stopped along the river and they took us to a warehouse where we worked for a few days."

CAMP WHITE PAGODA
May 1945 -July 1945

"They put us on another train and sent us to Ratburi where they were building an air field," Ben said. "I worked there and then at a rock quarry. I hauled wood and kept the fire going. There was a school near us. One day we went by this school and looked in it. We saw a picture drawn on the blackboard with planes dropping paratroopers. We thought it meant something, but we didn't know what. It did mean something because the Thai people were always trying to tell us something, but we didn't understand their language.

Every night there were planes flying over real low and dropping supplies and weapons to the Thais to help fight the Japs. The planes were from the Office of Strategic Services. They were supplying them to help for the big invasion. They were to take over all the prison camps and release the prisoners. The Americans knew that the Japs had issued orders that in the event of invasion that they were to destroy all records and kill all POWs. The Thai people were trying to tell us, but we didn't understand them. The Korean guards

A Point of Interest

SELLING THE BRIDGE

After the war was over the Allies sold the Bridge on the river Kwai back to Thailand. The proceeds were divided among the Prisoners of War. Each prisoner received about $280.00.

saw the end of the war coming and they wanted to take care of themselves. They told us that they had orders to kill all of us if there was an invasion. They told us that almost every day and I could hardly believe it. They told us that if we wanted they would take us to the Americans, but we didn't believe them.

If was only a couple of months before the end of the war. Finally a couple of guys took off. They took them to the OSS and American officers were there and got them back to American hands.

They moved us next to some mountains and we started digging holes in the side of the mountains for the Japs to hide in. We were carrying ammunitions and food to the positions on poles. One day they sent us out to feed some Jap soldiers. They had a basket on a pole and we started out. It was about two miles across the rice patty and I could smell the food. I looked in the basket and it was boiled duck. I started eating on it and I told the other guy that he better get some. By the time that we got there we had eaten almost all that duck. We dropped the basket and ran back across the rice paddy in the dark. I always wondered what happened to those Japs when they opened up that basket and found nothing but bones.

The next day we were outside the tent waiting on the Japs to tell us what they wanted us to do. One of them came out and told me to pick up this 200 lb. bag of rice and take it across the rice paddy. I couldn't pick up a 200-pound rice sack. Even in my best days I couldn't have done it. When I was younger if someone put it on my back I might have been able to carry it. We had never heard this group of Japs say a word in English, not a word. I knew that he knew I couldn't carry it. We were all getting pretty cocky and I said carry it yourself you son of a bitch. He said, 'don't call me a son of a bitch.' Then he hit me up side the head with a bamboo pole. One prisoner that was with me took the pole away from that Jap. I told him that we were in for it now they are probably going to shoot all of us, but the Jap went back into the tent and didn't say a word."

NAKHON NAYOT- THE LAST CAMP
July 1945 -September 1945

"We were sent to our last camp," Ben said. " We worked a couple of days and then about the third day in camp we went out to work. We got about a quarter of a mile for the camp and the guards stopped us. We sat on the side of the road, they jabbered a bit, and then took us back to camp. They told us we were going to have a rest day. We wondered what was going to happen and we wondered if the war was over. That night the Japanese guard house had a bunch of Sake and Key and some other prisoners stole the Sake and a bunch of prisoners started drinking. The next morning at roll call half the prisoners were drunk. The Jap officer took the soldiers out and beat them with his sword for letting the prisoner's steal the Saki. That day we didn't do anything and we still didn't know for sure what was going on, but we soon found out."

LIBERATION
September 2, 1945

"The next morning when we got up the Japanese were gone. We had a formation and this British officer stood before us and said, "this is the happiest day of my life. The war is over." We all started yelling and slapping each other on the back. Some cried, but Chambers was standing beside me. He was about as big around as a sick peach tree. He looked at me and said, "G-- D--- Dunn, I'm going to get home in just enough time to pick cotton."

We all sang our national songs. Then the next thing you know the English, Australians, and Dutch had up their flags. I don't know where they got them, but we didn't have one. We got the liner of some of the English tents, the red from Dutch liners out of their hats, and a white lining I had and made a flag. It took us two days to sew the flag, but when we raised it, it was the most beautiful thing I had ever seen.

It was August 17th when they told us it was over and it had been a couple of days. Then the Japs started coming by in trucks. They were drunk and had lost their discipline. We heard shots fired and thought they were probably killing themselves, but we were told not to fly our flags for a few days.

A week later the Americans came in and got the American POWs. The English, Australian, and Dutch couldn't believe we were leaving that quick, but they took us to a big hospital in India.

We had white sheets, pretty nurses, good food, and a lot of care. It was really hard to believe that we had made it through the imprisonment and that we were really free."

AMERIC[illegible] CROSS
Washington, D. C.

Form 1 DSD
Rev. Sept. 1944

International Red Cross Committee
Geneva, Switzerland

CIVILIAN MESSAGE FORM

Sender

Name Mrs. Frances Dunn.
Street R.F.D. 1, Box 179
City Jeffersonville. State Indiana
Citizen of United States
Relationship to person sought Mother
Chapter Clark County Date Aug. 17, 1945.

Message
(News of personal or family character; not more than 25 words)

Dear Benny:

The family is well and anxiously awaiting your return. Dad and I live at same address as when you left.

Tommy is still teaching at Gorham. He has two little boys.

Catherine is well again, John is still with newspaper. Isabel has two little boys also.

Frances is at Gorham. Wade is in the Navy.

Send us a cablegram the first chance you get. We will gladly pay for it.

Love,

Mom

Addressee

Name Pvt. Ernest B. Dunn
Address J 16816 U.S. Prisoner of War #10365 War Prisoner Camp, Branch 8
Country Nike, Thailand

Identifying Data

Birthplace and date of birth: Gorham, Ill. Feb. 17, 1917
Citizen of: United States

AMERICAN RED CROSS
Washington, D. C.
International Red Cross Committee
Geneva, Switzerland
CIVILIAN MESSAGE FORM

Form 1616
Rev. Sept. 19

Sender

Name Thomas G. Dunn
Street
City State
Citizen of
Relationship to person sought Father
Chapter Date August 18, 1945

Message
(News of personal or family character; not more than 25 words)

Dear Son:

Can hardly wait to see you. All well here.

Please write soon as you can.

Dad, Mom, and Francis

Addressee

Name Pvt. Ernest Benj Dunn
Address U.S. POW #10565
Camp 3 Thai War Prisoners
Camp Nike, Thailand
Country

Identifying Data
Birthplace and date of birth

HOME
October 1945

Ben was in the hospital for several weeks before returning to the Walter Reed hospital in the States. After being assigned to ward 35 he called his parents. It was the first time that Ben really felt free.

After a couple of days one of the officers came into the ward and told the men that the President would like to have a group of the men from the 131st unit to come to Washington to the White House. The officer looked at Ben, "how about you Dunn," he asked? Ben had heard too many rumors and said, "No, I'll take a rain check. Just tell Harry I'll drop in some other time."

The next day Ben picked up the newspaper and there were pictures in the paper of his buddies at the White House with the President and his family. They were having a great time. Although Ben had wished he had gone he was happy for his friends who had been entertained by the President.

On October 13, 1945, Ben arrived home. His parents were at the train station and although they had aged and had developed noticeable lines from worry they looked great to Ben.

Ben's parents saved all the newspaper clippings and magazines during the war. Ben had a chance to catch up on the war. All the major battles and events were news to him. To this day Ben still reads of events in World War II that he had not known about.

Ben was married to Johanna Mifflin in 1949. They have two sons Tom and Joe. A few years later he wrote a book titled *THE BAMBOO EXPRESS* about his experiences as a POW. Ben went back to teaching until his retirement.

FIFTY YEARS LATER
1991

In 1991, John Wisecup a Marine who was captured after the sinking of the USS *Houston* returned to Thailand. A close friend of Ben's he sent photos of the remains of the Death Rail. The POWs had spent 15 months building two hundred and sixty miles of track. Today there is only sixty miles of the original track remaining.

Ben and Robert Coffey in 1992. Coffey was also a POW on the Death Railway.

John Wisecup at the Death Railway in early 1990's.

CHAPTER THREE

SERGEANT CHARLES BRANUM
U.S. ARMY

71ST INFANTRY 5TH INTERCEPTER COMBAT UNIT
CAPTURED DURING THE FALL OF BATAAN

PRISONER OF WAR
APRIL 9, 1942-SEPTEMBER 15, 1945
BATAAN DEATH MARCH, CAMP O'DONALD, BILIBID, & MUKAISHIMA

A VOLUNTEER TO THE PHILIPPINES
1939

After quitting college in 1939 Charles volunteered for the Army. He completed his basic training and then received orders to the Philippine Islands. There Charles was assigned to the 2nd Observation Battalion Squadron in Manila. His unit was moved a short time later to Clark Air Force Base. Charles had regretted quitting college and wanted to better himself. He excelled at his duties as an enlisted soldier and strived to become a good leader. That drive and determination landed Charles a spot in a class of candidates with the West Point Preparatory school. He once again excelled, and looked forward to becoming an officer, but it was not to be, before he could finish the war broke out.

THE JAPANESE ATTACK
December 8, 1941

The Japanese attacked Pearl Harbor on December 7, 1941, and destroyed the U.S. Pacific Fleet. Their strategy was to isolate the Southeast Asia area from any help from the United States. On December 8, 1941, the Japanese began a series of bombing raids throughout the Southeast Asia area which included the Philippine Islands. After 14 air raids the Philippine and American Air Force was all, but totally destroyed.

Two days later, the Japanese made a land invasion at Aparri, Virgan, and at Lingayen. The Allies had no choice, but to retreat to Corregidor and the Bataan peninsula for the protection of rough terrain. There they would make their last stands.

The battle for Bataan begin on January 9, 1942. The Allies were subject to endless bombardment by Japanese artillery and air power. They attacked in full force. In spite of the overwhelming superiority in numbers, arms, equipment, and undisputed air power the defenders held their positions, often in hand-to-hand combat with the enemy.

The attack by the Japs had become so costly that General Homma had seriously thought about abandoning the attack on the Philippine Islands and bypassing the islands in order to meet the schedule of conquest of Southeast Asia.

One more attack however, was in favor of the Japs. They made an attack with 50,000 soldiers supported by 150 artillery guns on the line of defense that had been weakened by starving conditions and disease. The assault lasted for four days ending with the surrender on April 9, 1942 of 76,000 Filipino and American troops.

Following the surrender of Bataan the Japanese immediately began bombardment of Corregidor. Bombardments continued every day until May 5, 1942. The last day of bombardment finished everything on Corregidor-communications, guns, supplies, and even the morale of the defenders. The following day Corregidor had fallen into the hands of the enemy.

From the first day of bombing Charles was involved as a defender. First on Corregidor, then on Bataan. He performed bravely and would later receive six Purple Hearts, two

A Point of Interest

CORREGIDOR

From April 9, 1942 until May 6, 1942, Corregidor ("The Rock") was subjected to the most intensive artillery bombardment ever witnessed. It is estimated that in the 27 day period the Japanese hit "The Rock" with 1,800,000 pounds of shells. This was in addition to the bombs dropped by Japanese aircraft.

Silver Stars, and one Bronze Star for his performance. But, not before he would go through the pure hell of the Bataan Death March and 1,232 days as a prisoner of war under the Imperial Japanese Army.

CHARLES' STORY
December 8, 1942 - April 17, 1942

"The first place they bombed was our school in Baguio. Seventeen bombers came over and we thought they were ours. We went to the windows to look at them and after we looked for a minute we realized they weren't our planes-bombs fell everywhere. They kept making passes all day and tore up the town of Baguio and our base Camp Hay.

After days of continuous bombing, we had to evacuate on Christmas day 1941. We went across headhunter territory. As we traveled, we got acquainted with these headhunters and they agreed to get a Japanese head every chance they got. We got across the mountains and two of us were assigned to a lookout post. The rest of the group headed for this little town, took a bus, and headed for Manila.

The two of us were on the outpost and we could see that the Japs were bombing this little town. The group that went ahead of us had sent a bus for us and when we boarded the bus we told the driver we wanted to go through this town. He didn't want to take us, but we made him. What we didn't know was the Japs had taken the town. He knew it, but we wouldn't listen. When we got to the edge of town, we saw Japs everywhere. It was dust and they were camping around the area cooking their meals. We told the driver to take his time and go on through the town as if nothing was wrong. We leaned back and he drove right through the whole group of Japs. We were so close we could have touched them. They never saw us because we leaned back so they couldn't tell who we were. We made it through and finally reached our troops."

CORREGIDOR

"I couldn't find my unit and I had some training with machine guns so this Lieutenant assigned me to one of the guns. We continued on and came to where the defenders were camping out. The Lieutenant in charge of us came from Corregidor and needed to return. Since I couldn't find my outfit, he wanted me to go with him. We were able to get to a water barge and made it to Corregidor and I stayed there for about three or four weeks. The Japs were bombing the place continuously.

Some of the troops had made a bomb shelter by digging a big hole and placing jungle leaves over it. There were steps going down into the shelter. It looked unsafe to me. One day I was eating breakfast and the Japs came over. We headed for the shelter. I told the cooks as we started in that I wasn't going down in the hole. I didn't trust it. I stayed on the steps and it is was a good thing. A bomb hit near by the shelter and it caved in and killed forty men. I didn't find that out for a while because I was hit on the back of the head and I was out for hours. I was lucky though because I stayed on the stairway and avoided the cave-in."

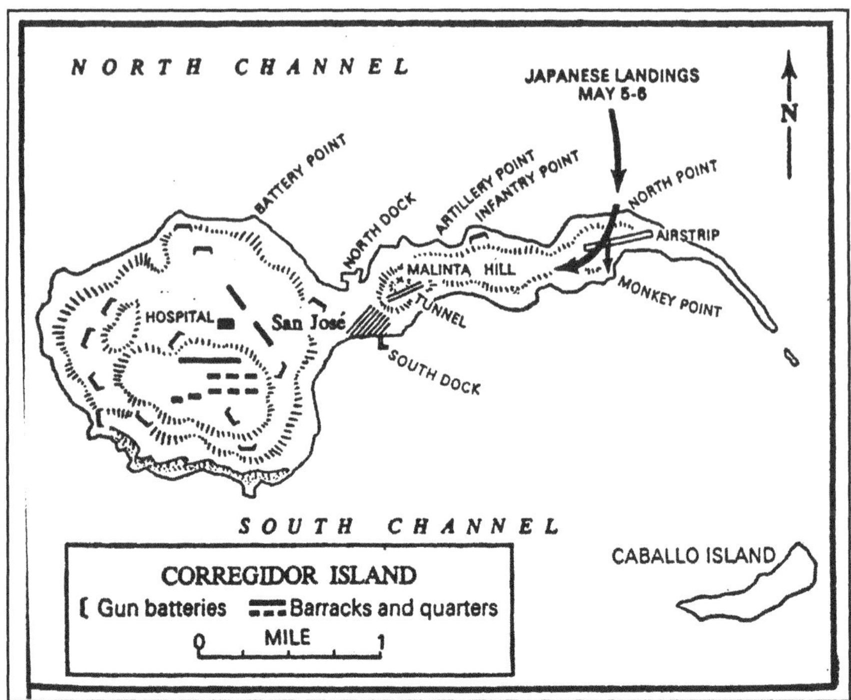

BATTLE OF THE POINTS . . . *BATAAN*

"When I woke up, I found some wounded men and helped them down to the hospital. Some were kept in the hospital, but I was released. I decided that I should go back to my unit on Bataan. So I returned to Bataan, but I never could find my outfit. I was put in the provisional infantry, the 71st Infantry 5th Intercepter Combat Unit. They were good men and they taught me a lot. There were points that the Japs would land on and we would form a line to hold them back. They were trying to get to this road that went around the peninsula. We fought on a point called Aglaloma. I was wounded several times but not too seriously.

Then we moved to a second point and I was wounded in the chest area. We finally had a main line across Bataan, but we were assigned to the battle of the Points. One night the Japs made a night landing. I was looking through a scope and spotted them coming in. I called in artillery and we were hitting them with 155 rounds. Then I moved back up to my machine gun and myself and the other machine gunners emptied 250 belts of ammo into the landing boats. Finally, our P-40s came in and started bombing them. We were doing really well until some of the P-40s mistaken us for Japs and started firing on us. The biggest problem we had wasn't the Japs, but the disease. More than half of us had malaria, beri beri, or dysentery if not all of them. It was a day to day dog fight, but we were able to move them back off the points at least temporarily."

SURRENDER
April 9, 1942

"After we ran all the Japs off of this point, we were assigned to another point. Then we moved to a point near Corregidor. All of the points had been taken back from the Japs when they made their final assault. They had thousands of troops and by now we had the weakest line of defense that we had since the battle started. The battle lasted for four days and then was followed by three days of bombing. Then we got the word on the telephone to surrender. We had wire strung all over the jungle to contact each other and sometimes a Jap would be on there. Some could speak good English and they would try to trick us. When I picked up the phone and they told us, I told them to go to hell because I thought it was a Jap. We found out later we really were supposed to surrender. It was a horrible night.

We were told that if we saved our trucks they would move us in them. We lined our trucks up on the air base. It was a horrible feeling because we didn't know what they would do to us. We had heard that they didn't take prisoners. When they came in, they didn't seem to bother us at first, but they didn't use the trucks. We had to walk. The walk later became known as the Bataan Death march."

BATAAN DEATH MARCH
April 9, 1942 - April 17, 1942

"I was walking by myself and there were no guards around. I could have escaped into the jungle, but there was no place to go. We continued to walk and they begin to group us in groups. Then we had to stay together. I was on the march for nine days. I had to walk about 90 miles. I helped two men that were in my unit. I was healthy and they weren't in good shape because of the wounds they had received while we were fighting the Japs. The march itself is hard to describe. I don't know the words to use, but it was horrible. They were killing men every few minutes. You would hear a gun go off and a short time later we would walk by a dead soldier.

We had stopped for a short time and then the Japs told us to move out. The guy beside me staggered as we stood up and a Jap shot him in the arm. He spun and fell down. This Jap went over and put his foot on the other arm pinning him down and bayoneted him in the chest. He hadn't done anything just staggered. We had to leave him right there.

They inspected us every mile. They would make us lay everything down on the ground in front of us. I didn't have anything because I had lost it all, but they found one guy with razor blades which he had with his shaving equipment. They told us that they were going to kill ten men plus the man that had the razor blades. They started picking the men and the guy next to me is where they stopped. They took the men in front of us and made us line up and they shot them men right in front of us. They just left them on the trail.

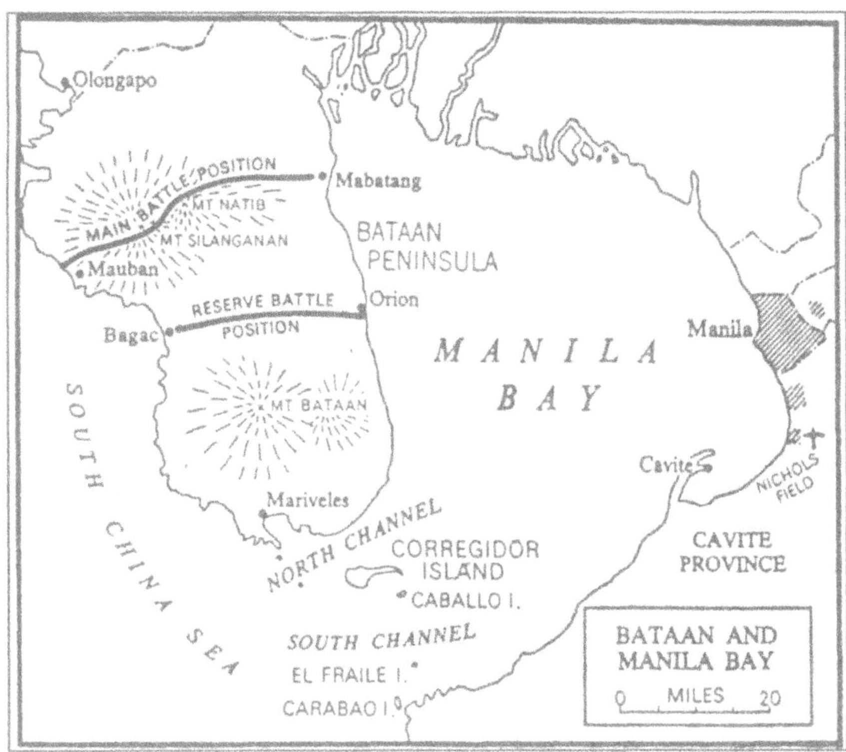

Charles Branum Third Sikeston Youth on Islands Missing

Mrs. P. V. Branum announced Saturday that she had received official notification from the War Department that her son, Charles C. Branum, (pictured) non-commissioned Army officer, was on the missing list.

The letter was similar to others received by parents, whose sons were in the Philippines at the time of the final surrender of the Islands to the Japanese. It stated that young Branum's actual status would be obscure until the Japanese supply through Geneva a list of prisoners taken in the Philippines or until last minute casualties are made available. The department promised to relay promptly any further information.

Last word received direct from Charles came in a letter, written Feb. 10 from Bataan, which arrived in Sikeston April 1. It was the only letter received by the family from him since the outbreak of World War II. Young Branum had been reported mistakenly by radio the day after the war began to have been killed in action. A cablegram, which he sent his family Dec. 14, confirmed that he was alive and well.

Charles Branum earlier had written his parents telling of a meeting in Manila last summer with Capt. W. E. Derris Jr., son of Mr. and Mrs. W. E. Derris Sr. who also has been officially reported missing following action in the Phillipines. Fred Boyer is the third Sikeston young man officially placed in the ranks of the missing at the time of the Phillipines final surrender. They were the only young men from this city known to have been serving in the Phillipines at the time.

POWs during the Bataan Death March.

This captured photo from the Japs shows the limprovised litters to carry comrades who were to weak to walk.

A Point of Interest

BATAAN DEATH MARCH

Americans and Filipinos were herded together, and regardless of their condition, marched to San Fernando, a road distance of about 140 miles. The march lasted for more than a week. Many of the men were forced to march without shoes or covering for their heads.

They were fed only twice during the march and were never given water. No one was permitted to lag behind. Anyone who fell behind or was caught trying to get food or water was either beaten, bayonetted, or shot.

The death march claimed the lives of 16,950 American and Filipinos.

At O'Donald the healthiest POWs were seated at the noon meal. After the photos were taken by the Japs, the rice was thrown out.

All along the trail as we walked, you could see dead Americans and Filipinos lying beside the roadside. After we got out of the mountains into the lowlands there were all kinds of artesian wells but the Japs still wouldn't let us have any water. Some of the men were so thirsty they broke and ran for the wells to get a drank and the Japs shot them all. There were about 20 men and they killed every one of them just because they wanted to get a drink of water.

The next day the Jap guard let us go to a well and fill our canteens and then drink all the water we wanted. It was on the last day of the march. It was nine days of hell."

CAMP O'DONALD

At the end of the march the prisoners were jammed into boxcars and taken to Camp O'Donald, located at Capas, in North Central Luzon. They were housed in Nips (shacks)

A Point of Interest

CAMP O'DONALD

From April 10, 1942 to May 5, 1942 (six weeks) nearly 1,600 American prisoners and 26,768 Filipinos died from lack of quinine and food, although the Japanese Army had plenty of food and medicine on hand.

One month after Camp O'Donald opened the Japs took this photo of the men who were the healthiest to show that their treatment was good. Little did the world know that men were dying rapidly from starvation.

that had been formerly used by the Filipino Army. There were about 1,500 American prisoners who died in this camp.

"After we got to Camp O'Donald the men were dying so fast from dysentery, starvation, and malaria that we had a hard time keeping up with burial," Charles explained. "We had a place called Boot Hill where we buried the men in mass graves. A few days after we buried them, it came a hard rain and washed away much of the dirt. You could see arms and legs sticking up out of the ground."

I volunteered to go on work details because I thought I might get something to eat. On occasion I did and I would bring part of the food back to these two wounded men I had been helping. I was on a work detail building a road. The Japs were trying to build a road from our location to the Philippine sea. There were 300 of us that went on the detail and in two weeks there were only about 50 of us left. I was covered with tropical ulcers and would have died if I had used this medicine that a buddy of mind had stolen from the Japs. The ointment, which had I used it on my body, would have been absorbed so much it would have killed me.

I was lucky in a way that I got sick and was transferred out of the prison camp because the Japs were so brutal there. When prisoners were brought in if the Japs found any Japanese money or tokens the prisoners were immediately beheaded. Prisoners were marched without food or water, made to sit out in the sun without any protective cover, continually beaten, and couldn't lie down at night.

Prisoners too weak to work or march were killed. On one occasion I saw three Americans buried alive. One officer was trying to help another soldier and he was beaten until he passed out. These people were inhuman."

BILIBID PRISON CAMP

This prisoner of war camp was located in the heart of Manila. The camp was designed by the Americans during their occupation of the Islands as a place of detention for Filipino criminals, before World War II.

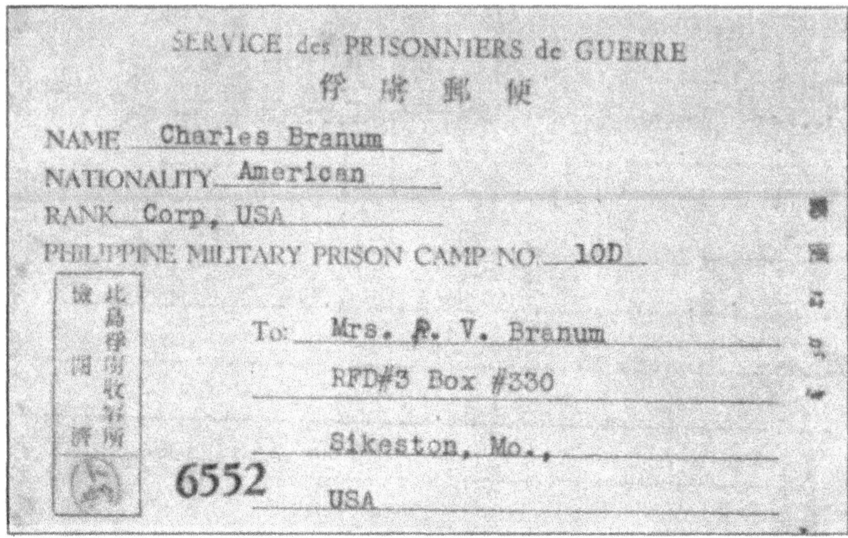

SERVICE des PRISONNIERS de GUERRE

俘虜郵便

NAME Charles Branum

NATIONALITY American

RANK Corp, USA

PHILIPPINE MILITARY PRISON CAMP NO. 10D

To: Mrs. P. V. Branum

RFD#3 Box #330

Sikeston, Mo.,

USA

6552

Front of postcard from Charles Branum to Mrs. P.V. Branum while he was at a Philippine military prison camp.

IMPERIAL JAPANESE ARMY

1. I am interned at—Philippine Military Prison Camp No. 10D
2. My health is—excellent; ~~good fair poor~~
3. Message (50 words limit)

I am well anduninjured. Please see that all my friends are notified I'm still ok. Hope you are all well and that we will be together soon. Regards to Madeline and the others.

Signature

Back of postcard from Charles Branum to Mrs. P.V. Branum while he was at a Philippine military prison camp.

The camp consisted of approximately 11 long, one-story buildings, one large main building formerly used as a hospital, and one and at one end of the grounds, a two-story administration building constructed partly of wood and partly of concrete.

The prison grounds were laid out in the form of a wheel with a stone wall surrounding the grounds forming the rim of the wheel. The long low buildings were the spokes. The wall had three entrances and guard towers were located at several places along the wall.

The Japanese used the camp as a prisoner of war camp. Prisoners were strip searched as they arrived at the camp and were allowed to keep one uniform, a shelter half, and a blanket.

The food was a problem for the prisoners. A poor quality rice diet with an occasional rotten vegetable was all the prisoners were allowed. Outbreaks of dysentery, beri beri, and malaria were common.

The Japs beat prisoners for the smallest infraction or for no infraction at all.

Charles was transported to Bilibid Prison along with 50 other prisoners by truck.

Nine of the prisoners died on the way. Charles arrived at the prison covered with tropical sores. The Japs had captured a medical naval unit and they worked on Charles. The medical team finally got the sores under control. The Red Cross had sent food parcels to the camp and Charles was allowed to split one with another prisoner. Charles stayed in this prison camp until he got well enough to work. From that point on Charles was assigned to a series of work details that would last until late 1943.

CHARLE'S PERSONAL ACCOUNT

"We were sent out to work on Neilson Field making a concrete runway for the Japs. I spent Christmas day 1942 working on the field. We were on a straight rice diet. The rice was full of worms. They were white with black heads. They laid eggs in the rice and it often had webs in it. You would have to eat the worms and pick the webs off like cotton candy. We begin to go blind because of a vitamin deficiency. Everything was a blur. The American doctors didn't know if we would ever get our eyesight back, but as we got used to the food we began to get better. We only got water to drink.

After we completed the air strip at Neilson we were moved to a Filipino army air base. It was really hard work on this field. We hauled rock for another air strip. They would dynamite the rock and it would come down in big rocks. Then we would have to break the rock up with picks. The whole time we worked the Japs would beat us. They would beat us for not working fast enough or really for no reason at all. Several men were beat to death with pick handles. If you had any gold in your teeth, they would knock your teeth out to get the gold.

One day I was carrying rock. This Jap guard came and got me. He took me to the guard house where there were eight other Jap guards. They grabbed my shorts and pulled them off. Then each one of them would take turns putting cigarettes out on my back and testicles. Each time one would do it they would all bust out laughing. When they finished there little game, they beat me with a bamboo club and sent me back out to the rock pile. My testicles begin to swell and I was sick for several days from the incident. I had to keep working though.

One day they were going to set some more dynamite and the Americans were putting the dynamite in the holes the Japs had drilled. I was working near by on a rock edge and I didn't notice this guard go over and he put wires on the generator and set the dynamite. Two Americans who had been setting the dynamite were killed and the rock that I was on slid down and I slid with it. There was a heavy rock landed on my left foot. There were no broken bones, but my foot was smashed really bad.

After I got hurt, they put me to work in the kitchen. The Japs would go into town to get the food and would get some tobacco for the prisoners to smoke if they wanted. I didn't smoke. They were allowed to get a bushel basket of fish to feed six hundred men. All we could do is to make a soup like out of it and pour it over the rice. There were days when all they did was to provide us with shell corn to eat. We had to cook that and the skin wouldn't come off and it was hard to eat. All you could do was swallow it and we didn't have anything to go with it."

*Jap prison camp–**Bottom row** left to right: J. Kuslak, J. Cooper, G.W. Mihalopoulos, W. Lawrence, J. Blackman, P.S. Jakubowski, L. Bowman, E.W. Coxey, G.C. Himes, J.F. Potris, M. Ryan, W.J. Gunnip, T.W. McGee, J.H. Hutson, N.W. Roberts, W.W. McHenry, L.J. Gillespie. **Second row** left to right: E.S. Zielinski, H.E. Lowe, B.R. Rayborn, R.L. Horn, T.T. Harrill, F.E. Cummins, J. Hryn, R.M. Bussell, T.H. Bogie, R.T. Artman, J.D. Gregory, W. Daun, J.D. Copeland, V.A. Wheatley, W.V. Baits, L.V. Pickett, O.L. Simpson, A.J. Reveglia, I.B. Piercy. **Third row** left to right: J.H. Davis, R.S. Barton, A.B. Moore, C.P. Chavez, C.C. Branum (circled), A.P. Ciborek, A.R. Camacho, H.F. Johnson, L.L. Long, C.M. Omtvedt, L.E. Howell, H.F. Johnson, H.O. Shannon, L. Vistula, J.P. Baskin, W.E. Twigg, W.J. Black. **Fourth row** left to right: G.B. Scott, C.A. Coats, D.P. Earing, J. Seamancheck, F. Horton, O.R. Kafer, R. Howard, E.E. Chovan, W. Hopkins, C.A. Plymale, A.R. DeBauche, J.H. Shuford, G. Martinez, C.E. Calvin, H.E. Hicks, A.R. Escalente, S.E. Fort. **Fifth row** left to right: G. Holman, A.A. Angert, N. Whitecotton, D. Gerola, R. W. Rote, E.W. Tyrrell, R. McGuiness, R.E. Baker, I.R. Leavins, G.W. Paden, H.B. Hobbs, L.M. Wagner, F.W. Malikowski, R.A. Lloyd, G.L. Williams, E.L. Milsap. **Sixth row** left to right: M.J. Stambaugh, L.I. Martin, J.E. Edwards, A.J. Stanley, R. Corona, R.E. Joplin, D. Carabine, J. Aragon, H.W. Baker, S.A. Nadolny, E.L. Pope, A.L. Chism, W.D. Arwood, F.J. Meyer.*

HELL SHIP TO JAPAN

In the latter part of 1943 Charles was selected along with a hundred other prisoners to go to Japan. They walked to the docks and boarded a hell ship for Japan. Charles never did know the name of the ship because it was an old rusty freighter and there was no name on it. He simple called it a Hell Ship and rightfully so, "they put 1,000 of us on this old rusty freighter. We didn't have any place at all to lie down. It was so hot in there you couldn't get your breath. Several guys suffocated on the trip. They wrapped them in canvas and they were dumped overboard. I got lucky again because they needed 20 cooks. I never dreamed that my name would be called, but mine was the 19th name called. I stepped out of that hole and got some fresh air. It was wonderful.

Twenty of us getting out of the hole helped for more room for those in the hole, but 20 plus the men that had died about 10 or 15 at the time wasn't much out of 1,000.

I was on top because of being a cook and I watched as we moved across the ocean. We were in a convoy with other freighters. We didn't know if the other ships had prisoners on them or not. On the way to Japan one of the submarines hit and sunk one of the ships in our convoy. We were lucky we weren't hit."

COBY, JAPAN
September 1944

"We made it to Coby, Japan several days later on my birthday, September 4, 1944," Charles said. " I was 24-years-old. It was a good birthday present to get off that hell ship. We were put on a train. They made us pull the shades down on the windows. We went north for about three hours. Then they took us off the train and put us on a ferry and took us to the island of Honshu."

CAMP MUKAISHIMA
September 1944 - September 15, 1945

This camp was located on the Island of Honshu a small island in the Inland sea about 30 miles due east of Hiroshima. It was one of eight camps in the Hiroshima group.

The camp had barracks divided into three rooms for the prisoners and was approximately 30 feet by 130 feet. The barracks contained double deck sleeping platforms.

The buildings were constructed with rough wood, unpainted inside and out. The roof

was made of fireproof paper. The floors were rough wood. There was no heat in the buildings.

The latrines were wooden boxes with six holes covering a concrete pit which had to be emptied every week. The urinal was on the partition that separated the last sleeping room from the latrine.

There were six spigots to wash from, but the water was not drinkable.

This prison camp was by far the best that Charles had been in. The food consisted of rice and steamed barley and although there was never enough it was much better than he had, had in the past. Luckily so because Charles had dropped from a muscle build of 165 pounds down to frail 85 pounds. "There was a dock yard there that repaired ships that had been damaged. I was made an electric welder and I welded plates to patch the holes in the ships. We stayed in this camp for the rest of the war. There was a British camp across the road from us and they had built barracks for us on the opposite side. We worked with the British and they taught us a lot about welding. It was really easy work. All we did was weld, nothing else.

It was a lot better camp than we had been in. It was cold and we had to put up with that and many of the British prisoners had died from the weather years previous to our arriving, but we made it. We got to take a bath once a week. We had a big wooded tub over on the British side. We would heat the water and would have to use small buckets to wash with. We got soap and it was the first I had since being a prisoner. The last ones to use the tub got to get in the tub and it was a pleasure being in the water.

B-29s started bombing Japan daily. They would take us to a mountain side and make us get in sandy caves. They were dangerous to be in especially if the bombs hit near by, but we never had to worry about it because they never came close.

What did worry us were the Japs because we knew the war was getting close to the end. The Japs thought we were going to make an invasion on land. They had signs up all over the place with orders to kill every POW when the first American set foot on Japan. Kill them by any means. No one is to escape. We were all afraid we were going to be killed because there was no place to escape."

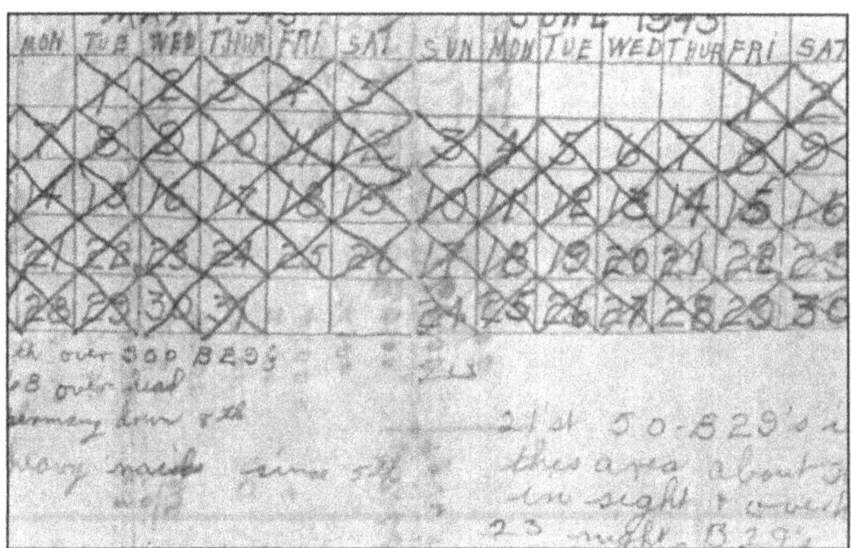

A calendar that Branum kept while a POW.

THE A-BOMB
August 6, 1945

"We went to work at the dock yard as usual on the morning of August 6th. I was on the mast of a ship that was in dry dock. I saw the plane go over. It had been doing this for several days. This day it flew over us and all of a sudden there was big flash. At first I thought I had struck an arc with the welder. Then there was a huge mushroom cloud forming in the sky. There was a mountain range between us and Hiroshima. We watched the cloud until we could feel some of the shock waves. It blew some windows out in a few buildings. We didn't know what it was, we thought a bomb had hit an oil well. The mushroom cloud got higher. It was scary. An uneasy feeling, but we still didn't know what it was.

Around noon that day I got caught with some food I had stolen. The Japs beat me and slapped me around all afternoon. Then they took us back to the camp. They told us that there would be no more beatings or kneeling on the concrete. We weren't sure what had happened yet, but we knew it was something big.

The A-bomb dropped about nine miles from us and we did get radiation. We just didn't know it. None of us in the camp had any problems, but there were twenty men in Hiroshima when the bomb hit. They brought two of them in our camp and one of them had mucous running out of his eyes, nose, and ears.

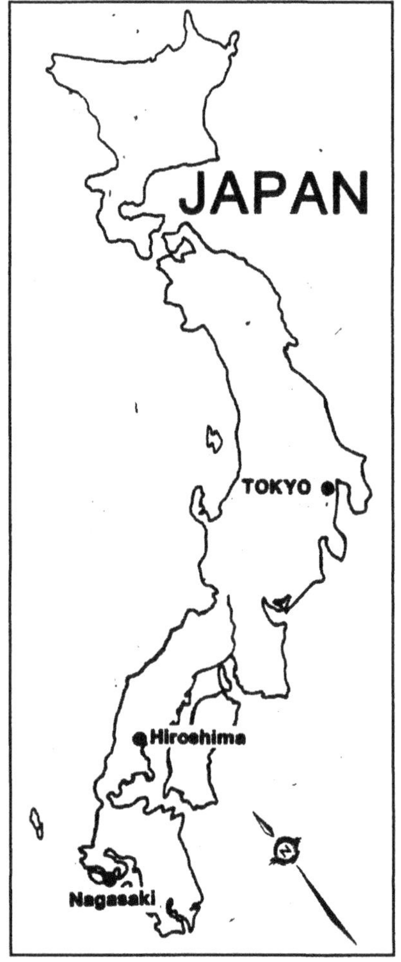

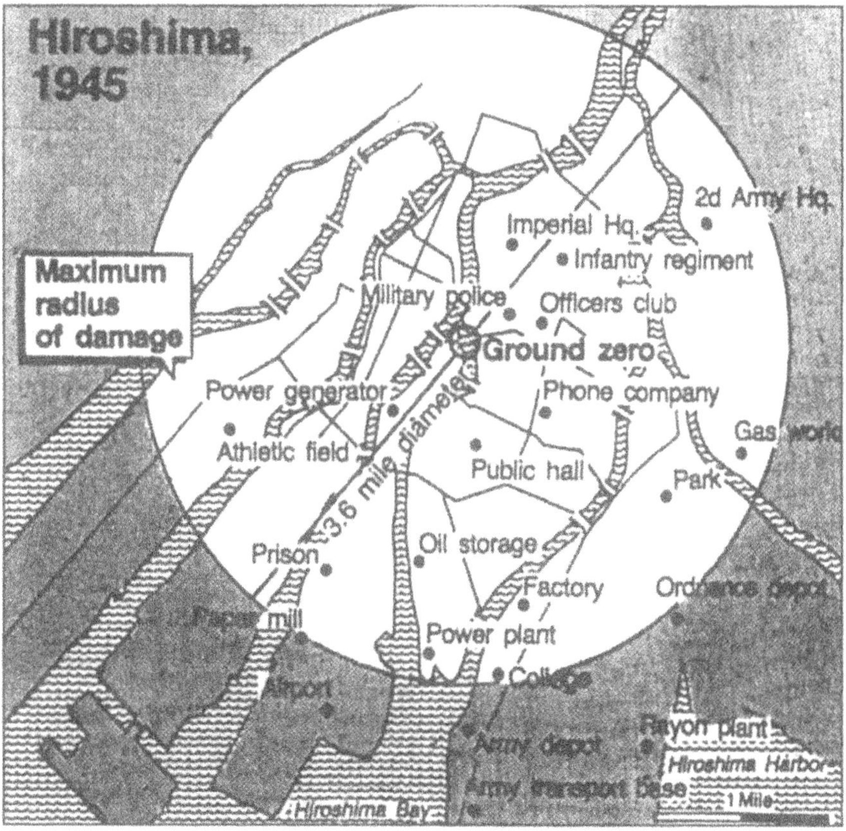

Hiroshima, 1945

Maximum radius of damage

2d Army Hq.
Imperial Hq.
Infantry regiment
Military police
Officers club
Ground zero
Power generator
Phone company
Athletic field
3.6 mile diameter
Gas
Public hall
Park
Prison
Oil storage
Factory
Paper mill
Power plant
College
Airport
Rayon plant
Army depot
Hiroshima Harbor
Army transport base
Hiroshima Bay
1 Mile

Map of Hiroshima showing damage of A-Bomb.

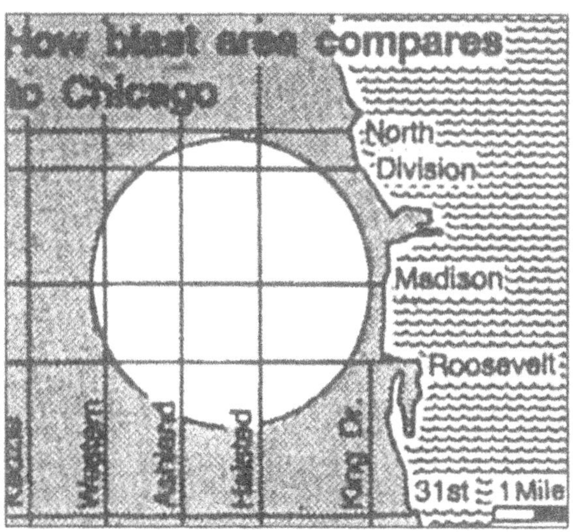

Map of Chicago showing comparison.

Shortly after that the Japanese removed some of the more odious guards from the prison camp.

Then when the bomb was dropped three days later on Nagasaki we saw a big change in the Japanese. They were always bragging about what they had done to us, but this day they wouldn't even look at us. They just walked around with their heads bowed. We knew the war was over, but the Japs wouldn't tell us anything. Finally we were told to go over to the British side. They had stolen a radio and we heard that we were suppose to listen for a message from MacArthur. He told us that the Japanese had surrendered on August 14, 1945. He told us to stay in the compounds, but he might as well have said to get out of them go where you want to because that's what we did.

THE FIRST AMERICAN FLAG OVER JAPAN
August 18,1945

The POWs had a month before they were liberated. While they were waiting the Americans dropped food. The prisoners had lowered the Japanese flag of the rising sun and realized that they didn't have a flag to raise. The planes were dropping food by parachute. The parachutes were red, white, and blue. The prisoners took the material to a local Japanese tailor shop to sew the flag. The Japanese worked constantly to finish the flag as soon as possible. On the morning of August 18, 1945 at 11:00 A.M. 99 of the surviving prisoners fell out for a formal flag-raising ceremony. "I was selected to raise the flag, Charles recalls. "One of the men took a bugle off of an abandoned Jap cruiser and played *To the Colors* while I raised the flag with tear filled eyes."

LIBERATION
September 15, 1945

For the next month the prisoners raised the flag with a formal ceremony each morning. Then spent their time eating and enjoying the freedom of movement for the first time in three and one half years. There were millions and millions of yen left everywhere. Charles picked some up and put it in his billfold as souvenirs because he didn't think it was any good. To his surprise when they were liberated he found out that we could turn it in for money. He had left a barrack full.

On September 15, 1945, the men lined up and marched to the port of Onomichi where they were officially liberated. On this march to freedom the homemade flag was carried and displayed before the liberated prisoners.

Charles and his fellow prisoners caught a plane and landed in Okinawa. "We were getting ready to leave there and we had to go to sick call." Charles recalls. "I didn't want to because I knew that I was sick. Well sure enough I had a fever and they put me in the hospital. This major that made me go to sick call walked nine miles to this hospital just to tell me that he and the other men that I had been with had to leave. While I was there everybody wanted to come to the hospital and look at me because I was the first POW in there. I was moved up into the mountains to another location with fewer men. We had a movie one night and was hit by a Jap that had held up in the mountains. He sprayed the area with an automatic weapon. No one was hurt, but I thought that all this was over with."

HOME
October 1945 - November 1945

"I took a ship back home," Charles explained. "It was rainy night when we left. I got my bunk and didn't notice at the time who was staying by me, but after settling down I took over at the next bunk. Bob Elderge from St. Louis, Missouri was in the next bunk. I had enlisted with him and we had gone over seas together bunked side by side. I couldn't believe that we were returning the same way. It was a long ride back home, but not really because I was going home and it was still hard to believe that I was going home. I knew it, but it didn't seem real.

One day the Captain of the ship called all of us up on deck. When we got up, he said,

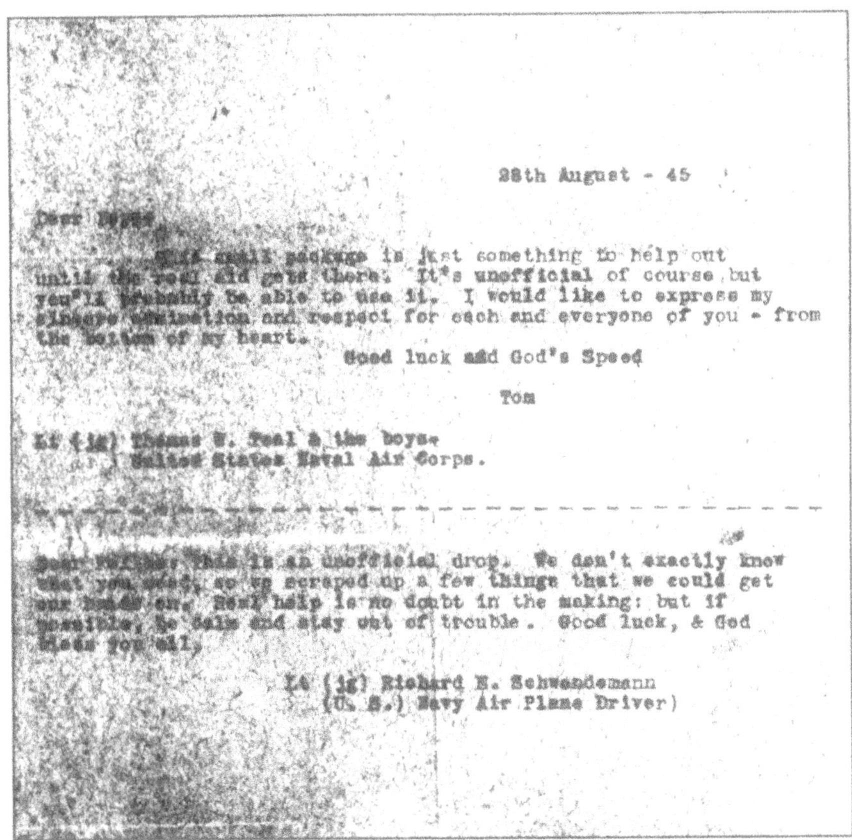

28th August - 45

Dear [illegible],

[illegible] small package is just something to help out until the real aid gets there. It's unofficial of course but you'll probably be able to use it. I would like to express my sincere admiration and respect for each and everyone of you - from the bottom of my heart.

Good luck and God's Speed

Tom

Lt (jg) Thomas W. Teal & the boys.
United States Naval Air Corps.

Dear Fellows, This is an unofficial drop. We don't exactly know what you need, so we scraped up a few things that we could get our hands on. Real help is no doubt in the making: but if possible, be calm and stay out of trouble. Good luck, & God bless you all,

Lt (jg) Richard H. Schwandemann
(U. S.) Navy Air Plane Driver)

Message dropped to the POWs in Japan after the surrender.

"land ho. There it is men, America." It was sure great to see the Golden Gate, but it was hard to see it with tear filled eyes.

We had to stay at the hospital in San Francisco for a few days. One night they put on a big party. We all thought it was for us, but we got a real surprise. It was for POWs all right, German POWs. We couldn't believe it. The staff was giving them a going away party. We left in disbelief.

I was in the hospital for a while. I weighted 185 when captured and 80 pounds when I was released. I couldn't eat. Finally I got enough vitamin B1 shots and got straighten out.

I was discharged and boarded a train for home. One of the women was looking at me and finally spoke up. She said she noticed my ribbons but couldn't figure out where I had been. I told her I was a POW in Japan. She said she was on her way home to see her brother he had been a POW. I asked who he was and she told me. We had been together. I told her he was perfectly all right. She hugged and kissed on me all the way home.

I got home to Sikeston, Missouri in November 1945. My parents met me and hugging started all over again. We drove home. We went down the country road and turned into the road and up toward the house. I remembered every inch of that dirt road and how I played on it when I was a boy as we drove closer to the house. When we got there, I couldn't believe I was home. After all those years I was home again."

EPILOGUE

Charles graduated in 1950 with a degree in Natural Gas and Petroleum Engineering. He worked in Texas for nine years and then moved to Cape Girardeau, Missouri and worked for Missouri Utilities until his retirement in 1984. He married Mary Etta and they have one son David.

THE FIRST FLAG OVER JAPAN

From the time of the freedom march to Onomichi on September 15, 1945 until February 1952, the flag and bugle were in the possession of Clifford M. Omtvedt and were eventually taken to his home in Eau Claire, Wisconsin. In 1952 they were given to Colonel Ralph T. Artman, the former officer in charge of the prisoners, and presently to the chief of military history in Washington.

The flag was donated to the Fort Lee Quartermaster Museum in June 1963, for the museum's opening. Charles had lost tract of the flag until he contacted his congressman who was able to locate the flag. On Independence Day of 1967 Charles took his family to the museum to see the flag that he raised, "the first American Flag to fly over Japan after their surrender in World War II."

Charles at the Ft. Lee Quartermaster museum in Virginia where the first flag raised over Japan after their surrender is located. Branum raised the flag in a ceremony at the POW camp.

Charles and Mary Branum in 1995.

David, their son.

CHAPTER FOUR

CORPORAL RALPH L. LAPE SR.
U.S. ARMY AIR FORCE

HEADQUARTERS AND HEADQUARTERS
5TH AIR BASE GROUP
CAPTURED DURING THE JAPANESE
INVASION OF THE PHILIPPINES

PRISONER OF WAR
MAY 10, 1942-SEPTEMBER 5, 1945
MINDANAO, KAWASAKI, AND NIIGATA

A MATTER OF AGE
1939

Ralph had such an interest in planes that he wanted to enlist in the Army air Corp. The only thing stopping him was his age. Ralph discussed the problem with his mother and the two paired up and lied about his age so he could enlist. It worked and Ralph went into the Army through Jefferson Barrack on December 2, 1939. He was shipped to 19th bomb group Hamilton Air Base in San Francisco, California. After eight weeks of basic training, he was sent to aviation school to work on aircraft engines. He became an aircraft engine mechanic.

The unit received orders to Tacoma, Washington. Ralph didn't want to go because he liked California. He transferred to the Headquarters Squadron 5th Air Base Group at Hamilton Air Base. In a short time, the unit moved to Utah and took over a portion of Salt Lake City's Airport and started a wing there. They trained for months in the Salt Lake Flats. Then the unit moved again this time to Fort Douglas, Utah and started a wing at that location and trained for almost a year. Finally in the fall of 1941 the unit received orders for the Philippines.

THE PHILIPPINE ISLANDS
November 1941-December 7, 1941

Security was tight because of the concern of the Japanese and it wasn't until Ralph's unit left the Hawaiian Islands in the middle of November 1941 that they learned their destination. It was "Plum." Plum was a code name for the Philippine Islands. They traveled in blackout until they reached the destination on Thanksgiving Day. "We stayed at Fort McKinley for about two weeks and found out that we were going to take over Clark Air Force Base," Ralph explained. "By the time the two weeks were up that had been changed. We were going to the island of Mindanao and set up there. They moved us by boat to the island and we set up on the Plato of Del Monte.

Mindanao is the largest of the southern islands of the Philippines. This island is about 500 miles south of Luzon. Most of the air bases were in that area and american commanders realized they needed bases other than those at Luzon, so it was decided to build a base on Mindanao.

There was a big field there and we worked on it to make a runway for B-17s. I was a 747, which meant that I was an aircraft mechanic on the ground and an aerial gunner in the air. About a week after I got there, I saw General MacArthur board a submarine and as he was going aboard he turned and told us, "I shall return." The only problem was he didn't tell us when. We knew something was up because he was leaving. We learned later that he had went to Australia to set up a base defense there."

THE ATTACK
December 8, 1941-May 9, 1942

"We started running missions out over the Pacific and we had completed three missions," Ralph said. " We were sent out on our fourth mission to check on some unidentified boats that were approaching the islands. They ended up being the intersteamers (local boats). We were coming in off of our fourth mission in a Douglas BAT. It was a twin engine bomber built by Douglas Aircraft, we called it a Bucket of Bolts. We had an aerial engineer aboard, a Master Sergeant by the name of Pappy Nettles. I was riding as upper tail gun. We had about a ninety-five percent overcast, through a quick break in the cloud's Nettles saw four air planes flying. They were fighter planes, but that was all that he could tell. We landed and taxed up to the end of the runway and the pilot cut the engines. As they died down, I heard engines. I yelled and asked the rest of the crew if they heard the engines. They did and I said, 'Thems not ours.' They weren't. They came down out of the sun right at us. They were the four planes that Nettles had spotted, four Japanese Zeros. They cut loose with the guns. We jumped out of the plane and ran for a trench nearby. They were spaced so that when one would fire and circle the next plane was firing so we couldn't get out of the trench. On the third pass they hit the plane and set it on fire and it burnt up. The Japs pretty much destroyed the entire Air Force all over the Philippines with the attack mainly because we didn't have many planes there to start with.

Catholic Church–Men of 5th AB Group was quartered and messed around this church till March 1942, then moved to Maramag Forest till surrender on May 10, 1942.

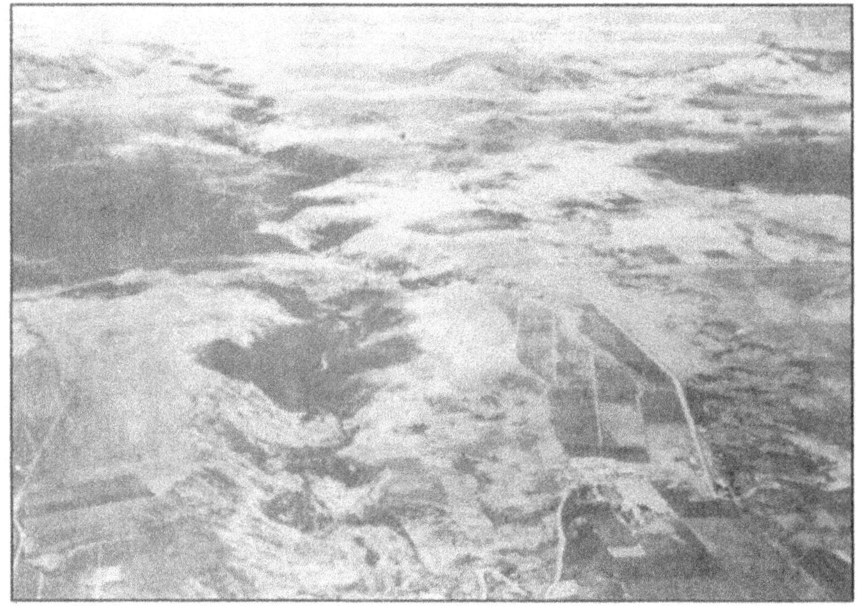

Del Monte Air Field

After the attack we didn't have a plane to fly so they assigned me to twin .50 caliber guns on the air strip. We had built a hangar back into solid rock where we put our P-40's. The Japanese were trying to lob bombs into the hangar, but they never did get the job done.

I was there for four days and Pappy Nettles came over and got me. He told me that I had been assigned with him to a P-40. We were moved into the Maramag Forest for protection. The forest was so dense that planes could not be detected from the air. We made several missions and fought day after day. Supplies were low. We were running out of food and ammunition, but we kept resisting until May 1942."

THE SURRENDER
May 10, 1942

"General Wainwright who had taken over the command of the Philippine Islands got on the radio," Ralph explained. "In the northern part of the Philippines the American troops had already surrendered. General Wainwright gave a message ordering us to surrender because if we didn't the Japs were going to kill all the other prisoners. On the second day he gave the message again, but this time he also sent an officer escorted by Japanese down to meet with us. Our commander decided we should surrender and we did on May 10, 1942. They gathered all of us up and we had to go to a village north of the Maramag Forest called Malaybalay."

This is the P-40 Lape was assigned to. On the wing is Pappy Nettles.

Headquarters of the 5th AB Group, Jan. 1942.

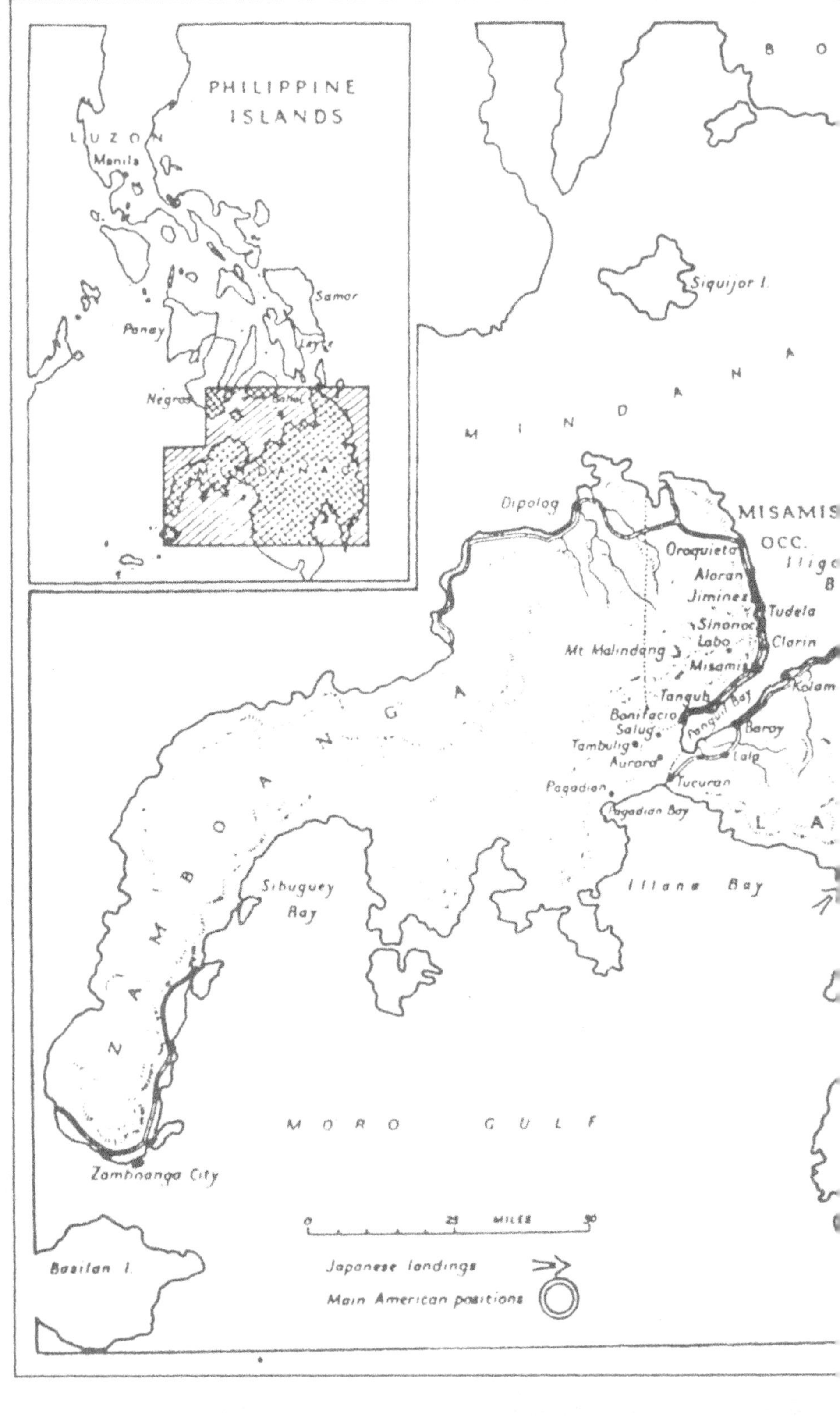

PHILIPPINE ISLANDS
LUZON
Manila
Samar
Panay
Leyte
Negros
MINDANAO
Siquijor I.
Dipolog
MISAMIS OCC.
Oroquieta
Aloran
Jiminez
Tudela
Sinonoc
Labo
Clarin
Mt Malindang
Misamis
Tangub
Kolambugan
Bonifacio
Salug
Tangub Bay
Baroy
Tambulig
Aurora
Lala
Pagadian
Tucuran
Pagadian Bay
ZAMBOANGA
Sibuguey Bay
Illana Bay
MORO GULF
Zamboanga City
Basilan I.
0 25 MILES 50
Japanese landings
Main American positions

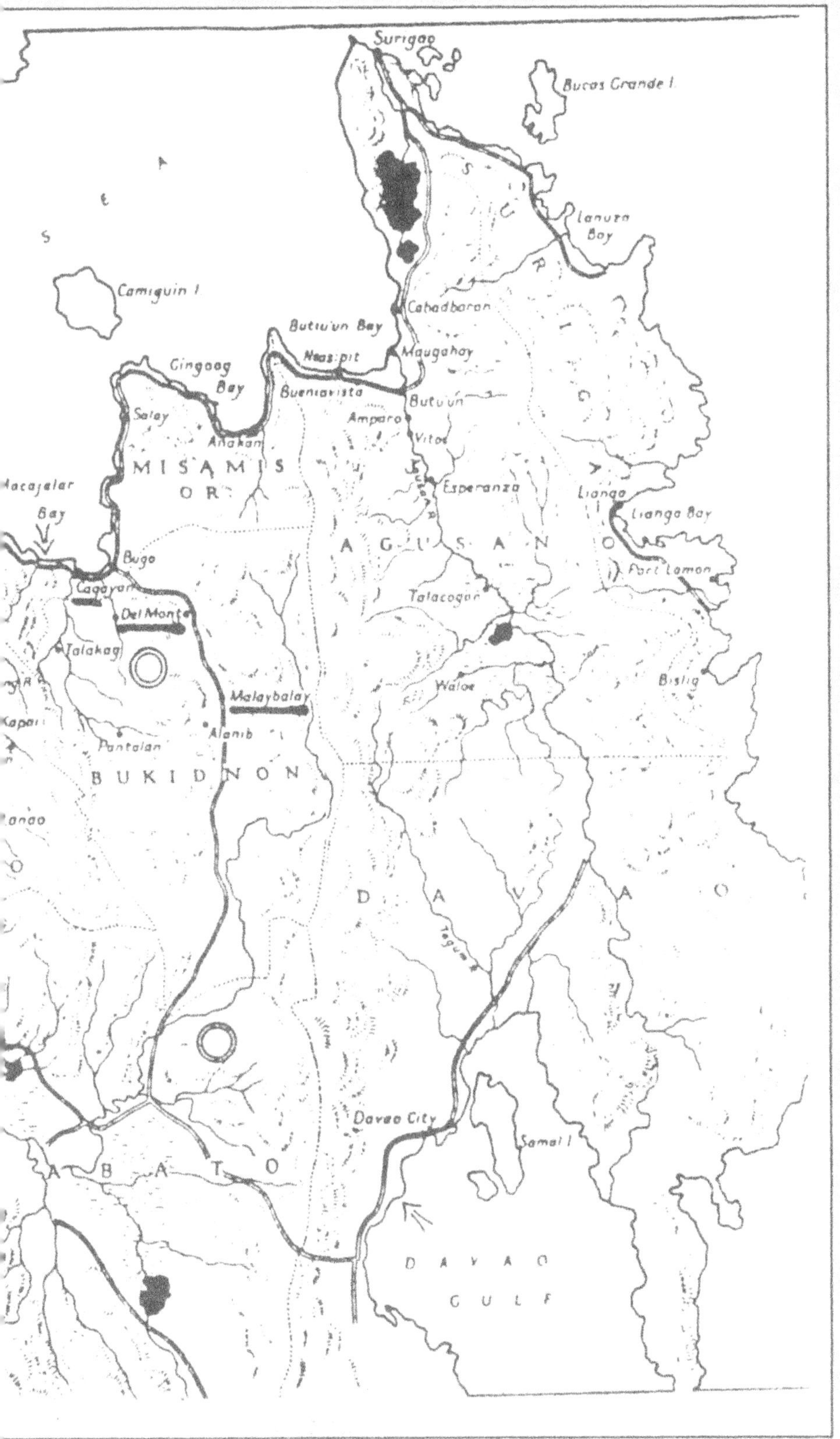
Surigao
Bucas Grande I
S U R I G A O
Lanuza Bay
Camiguin I
Cabadbaran
Butuan Bay
Nasipit
Maugahay
Gingoog Bay
Buenavista
Butuan
Amparo
Vitos
Salay
Anakan
MISAMIS OR
Esperanza
Lianga
Lianga Bay
A G U S A N
Port Lamon
Bugo
Cagayan
Del Monte
Talacogan
Talakag
Waloe
Bislig
Malaybalay
Alanib
Pantalan
B U K I D N O N
D A V A O
Davao City
Samal I
D A V A O
G U L F

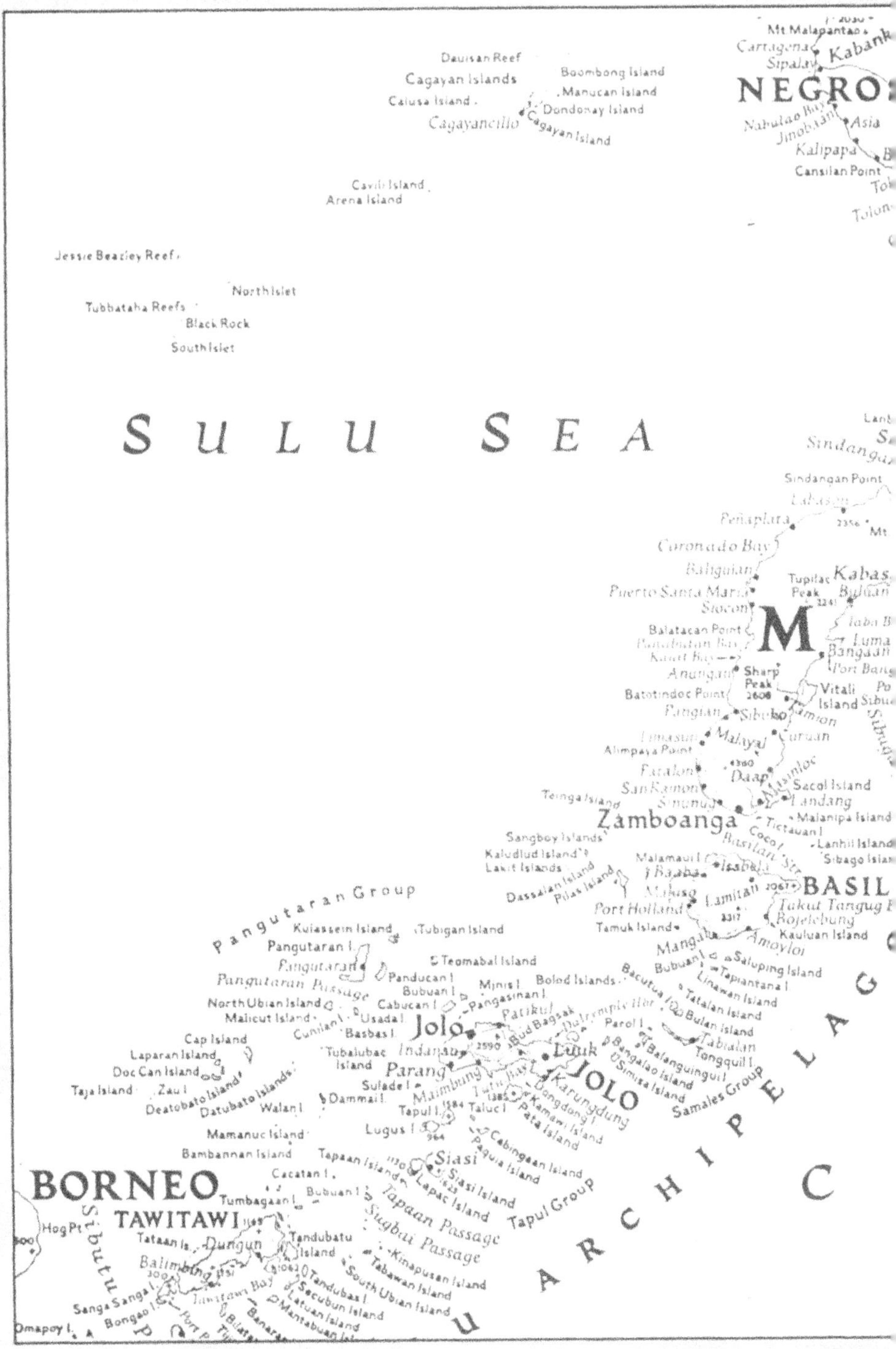

Point of capture is circled.

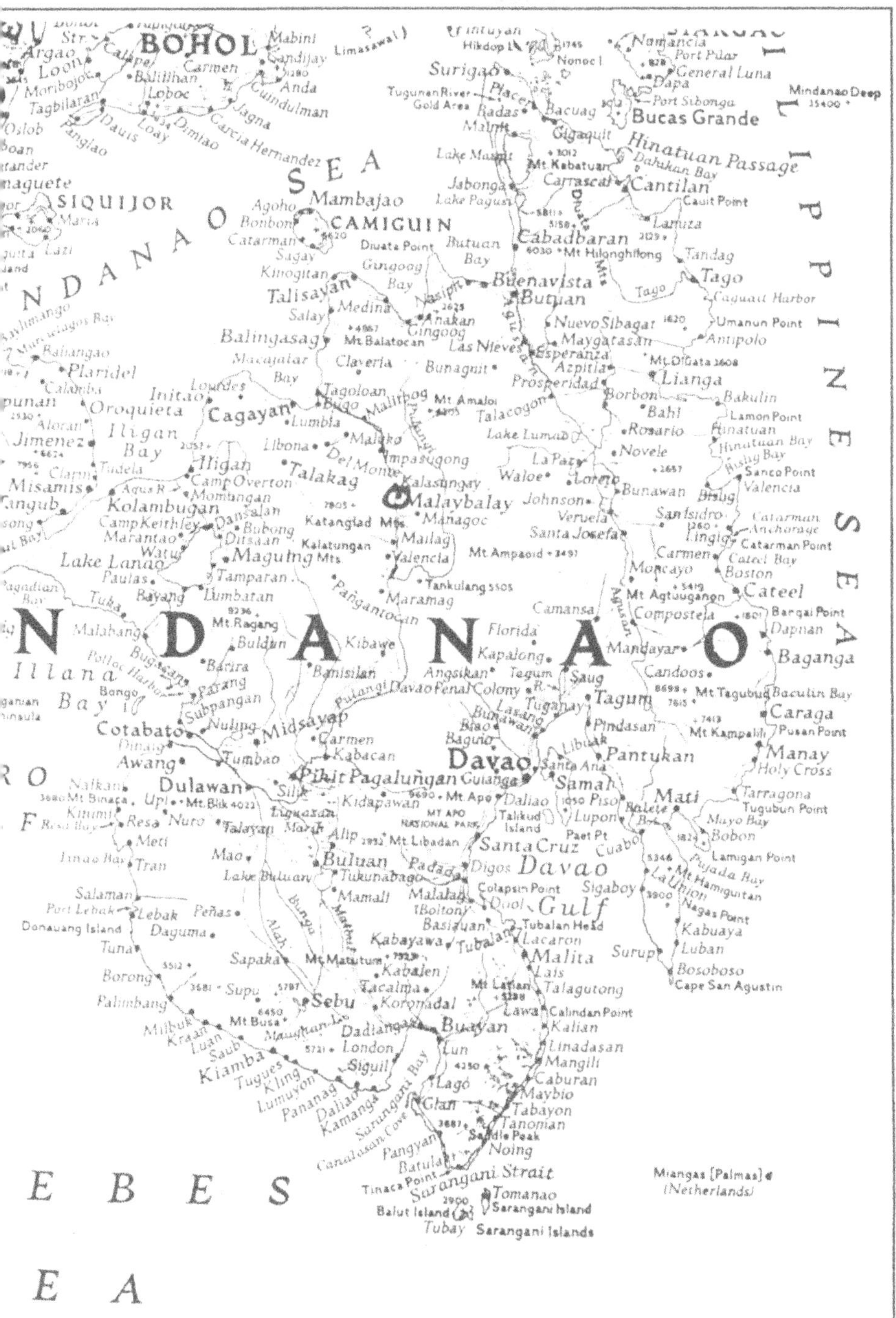
BOHOL
Carmen
Loboc
Tagbilaran
Loon
Argao
Anda
Jagna
Guindulman
SIQUIJOR
SEA
CAMIGUIN
Mambajao
Surigao
Placer
Bacuag
Mindanao Deep
Bucas Grande
Hinatuan Passage
Cantilan
Cabadbaran
Buenavista
Butuan
Butuan Bay
Gingoog Bay
Talisayan
Balingasag
Cagayan
Iligan Bay
Iligan
Misamis
Oroquieta
Jimenez
Kolambugan
Lake Lanao
Marawi
Malaybalay
Talakag
Katanglad Mts
Mt Ampaoid
Tankulang
Maramag
Kibawe
Lianga
Bislig
Tago
Tandag
Lingig
Cateel
Baganga
Caraga
Manay
Mati
Tagum
Davao
Samal
Davao Gulf
Digos
Santa Cruz
Mt Apo
Midsayap
Cotabato
Illana Bay
Dulawan
Pikit
Kidapawan
Buluan
Lake Buluan
Koronadal
Sebu
Buayan
Kiamba
Malita
Sarangani Bay
Sarangani Strait
Sarangani Islands
Balut Island
Cape San Agustin
Miangas (Palmas)
(Netherlands)
CELEBES SEA
PHILIPPINE SEA
MINDANAO SEA
MINDANAO

THE FIRST SIX MONTHS
May 1942 -October 1942

"We were there for six months." Ralph told me. He said, "The village had a barracks that the Filipinos had used and that's where they put us. The barracks was surrounded by barbed wire. We slept on the barracks floor. They fed us a rice stew in camp and it had rice and some kind of sticky soup with it. There were a lot of worms in it and at first we started to try to pick them out, but after a while we just ate it worms and all. Once in a while we would get a small piece of fish. Rice cakes on occasion.

They marked us off in sections of ten and told us that if any one man escapes out of the ten the other nine are going to be shot. They kept their word, too. Several men tried to escape and they would march us out and make us watch them beat men to death or just shoot them. On one occasion I can remember two men that escaped. They made them dig their own graves. Then they staked them up in front of the grave and shot them in the head. Their bodies plopped into the graves. Then a Jap officer went up to them and shot them in the head after they were already dead. Filipinos covered them with dirt, but the Japs acted like the dead men should cover themselves, too.

I saw every horrible inhuman thing that the Japs did, but behead a prisoner. I had two friends that were brothers from West Plains, Missouri that was in the Bataan Death march. They told me that when they were on the march that the Japs wouldn't let them stop and get a drink of water. They forced them to march for several days and they said that these Jap trucks would come by and Jap soldiers would swing their rifles and hit men in the head as they passed. A lot of men died from head injuries. They bayoneted several of them. One man was in a line and the Japs didn't think the line was straight so they took the man on the end of the line and put him in front of the rest of the soldiers and shot him.

After we had been in the camp for a while, they begin to break us up in groups. At first I didn't know what was going on, but then I figured it out. The Japs were putting those of us that were airmen or men that had a technical job into one group. They didn't want anybody there that might be able to escape and help our own side out. They were going to ship us to Japan."

BILIBID PRISON
October 1, 1942

On October 1, 1942, two hundred and seventy-five prisoners of war which included Ralph, boarded the freighter Ama Maru and sailed for Manila. They arrived on October 4, 1942. They were paraded through the streets of Manila to Bilibid Prison. " We were there for a few days," Ralph said. "I never knew that I would see a skeleton walk, but they can

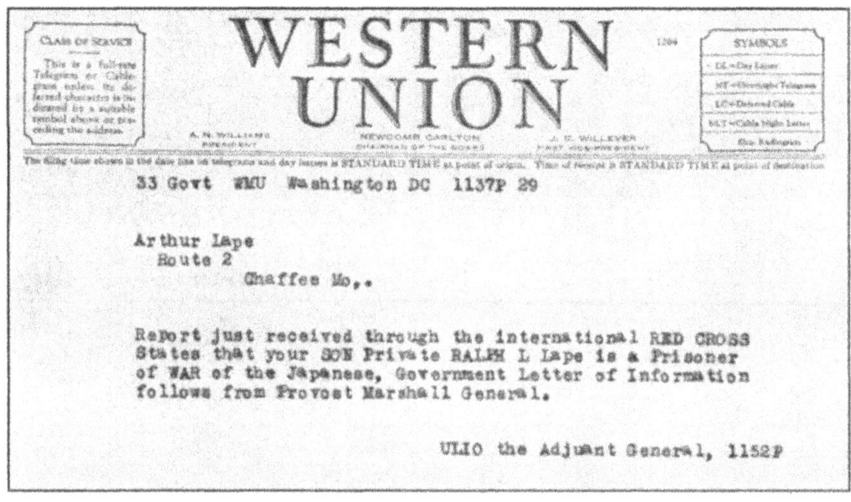

WESTERN UNION

33 Govt WMU Washington DC 1137P 29

Arthur Lape
Route 2
Chaffee Mo.,

Report just received through the international RED CROSS States that your SON Private RALPH L Lape is a Prisoner of WAR of the Japanese, Government Letter of Information follows from Provost Marshall General.

ULIO the Adjuant General, 1152P

Telegram from the Adjuant General.

because I saw it there. It was pitiful. No wonder thought because at this prison the diet was strictly rice. Three small bowls each given at breakfast, lunch, and dinner. Some of the prisoners were lying on bare floors in the barracks were covered with flies. Some were dying, some suffering from uncared for wounds, and many were ill from the lack of food. Many of the men were slapped around by the Japs. On one occasion we stood in the pouring rain for an hour during roll call as punishment. We never were sure what it was that we did. After about a week's stay at this camp we boarded a boat for Japan."

POWs celebrating the 4th of July in Malaybalay Mindanao, PI. It was against Jap regulations and would have meant death if the prisoners had been caught.

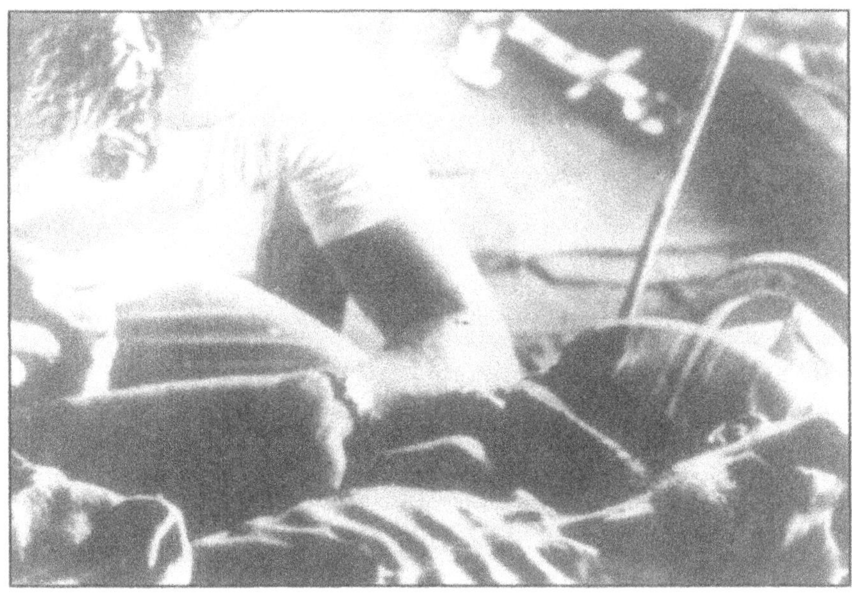

Dying POW in Bilibid Prison.

A Point of Interest

HELL SHIPS

Tattori Maru: 11 dead. Departed Manila October 8, 1942 with 1,202 American POWs. Stops at Formosa, Japan, and arrived at Manchuria on November 11,1942.

Umeda Maru: 15 dead. Departed Manila November 7, 1942 with 1,500 American POWs. Arrived Japan November 1942.

Nagato Maru: 157 dead. Departed Manila November 7, 1942 with 1,700 POWs.Arrived Japan November 25, 1942. 7 died enroute, 150 dying men left on dock were never seen again.

Taga Maru: 70 dead. Departed Manila September 1943 with 850 American POWs. Unknown arrival date.

Shinyo Maru: 668 dead. Departed Zamboanga, Mindanao December 3, 1944 with 750 American POWs. Torpedoed by USS *Paddle* on September 7, 1944 Only 83 POWs survived.

Haro Maru: 39 dead. Departed Manila October 3, 1944 with 1,100 American POWs. Arrived Takao, Formosa October 25, 1944

Arisan Maru: 1,795 dead. Departed Manila October 10, 1944 with 1,800 American POWs. Torpedoed by USS *Snook* on October 24, 1944.

? *Maru*: 1,100 dead. Departed Manila October 16, 1944 with 1,100 American POWs. Torpedoed October 18, 1944 by unknown submarine

Oryoku Maru; *Brazil Maru*; *Enuri Maru*: 1,426 dead. *Oryoku Maru* departed Manila December 13, 1944 with 1,800 American POWs. Sunk by U.S. carrier planes off Bataan peninsula on December 15, 1944. *Brazil Maru* departed Lingayen Gulf December 27, 1944 with the survivors, arrived January 2, 1945. *Enuri Maru* with survivors, departed Takao January 14, 1945. Arrived Moji, Japan January 29, 1945.

THE HELL SHIP TOTTORI MARU
October 6, 1942 -November 12, 1942

On October 6, 1942, Ralph's group of two hundred and seventy-five along with approximately 1,500 POWs from Luzon were crammed aboard the *Tottori Maru*. "The Captain of the ship said that we were not prisoners of war, but guest of the Emperor. 'We are taking you to Japan where we can feed you better because we took a lot of food off of the island of Corregidor,' the Japanese Captain explained. That was a lie because I talked to some guys there and they were down to their last food when they surrendered. We started out of Manila. We were out to sea about three days before we got into Formosa. The conditions were terrible. Below deck it was extremely hot. The men had trouble breathing and several men died from suffocation. The Jap guards passed a bucket around for them to relief themselves and often it was over flowing before it was emptied. We got a small portion of rice while we were on the ship, but it was not near enough to eat.

On the third day just before arriving at Formosa an American sub attacked us. They fired two torpedoes and the Japs managed to maneuver the ship and the torpedoes missed. We landed at Formosa. They took us off the ship and hosed us down with a fire hose. We stayed there for several days waiting on a convoy. The conditions in Formosa weren't much better than the Philippines, but they sure beat the ship. We could get air and we had been washed off even if it was with ice cold water out of a fire hose.

Several days later we boarded the ship again and arrived on November 9, 1942 at Chosen, Korea. Most of the POWs from Luzon disembarked here and were taken to a camp at Mukden, Manchuria. Then from there to Japan. We lost a lot of prisoners. We had been stuffed down in the hole with so many that they couldn't even lie down. We had to carry a lot of them out and bury them at sea. They had canvas bags we wrapped them in and dumped them over board.

Ralph Lee Lape

I was one of the lucky ones on the trip because I got to stay on top of the deck. They had a hog pin with about three hogs in it and that's where I stayed the whole trip until we got to Japan. Once we got to Japan we were passing a large naval base and when we passed it they made all of us go below deck. It wasn't so bad by then because so many men had died that there was a lot of room below decks. There was a lot of room, but the lower decks were horrible. It stunk from men throwing up. Many of the men had dysentery and there was waste everywhere. They made us stay down there until we passed the naval base and then shortly after that those of us that had survived the trip arrived at Tokyo Harbor."

CAMP KAWASAKI

This camp was located about three miles from Tokyo. This camp held American, British, Italian, and Norwegian prisoners.

The living barracks were approximately 18 feet by 75 feet and housed about 120 prisoners. The barracks were built out of wood and covered with shingles or tree bark. Some of the barracks were two-story. Most of the barracks were divided into three sections with each prisoner allowed about 30 by 73 inches for living quarters and stowing clothes.

The floors were wooden in some, but buildings with dirt floors did not have proper drainage which caused flooding when it rained.

During the winter ice would form under the mats in the sleeping area and would have to be washed down by the prisoners during their days off in order to get rid of fleas and lice.

The barracks had a three by three-foot fire pit in the center of a section with a small amount of wood allowed during the evening.

The latrines were in a separate wood building large enough to accommodate 30 men at a time. They were called the straddle trenches. The trenches had no drainage so they had to be dipped out. The was distributed to the country side. The open trench caused flies and maggots to accumulate and they crawled around the building and into the living quarters.

The main diet was rice and barley. It was given to the prisoners in small portions.

A Japanese Lieutenant, Lieutenant Myazaki was often in authority in the camp. Some of the other guards at the camp were Mizuno, Shiozawa, Watanabe-nick named Porky The Pig, Saito-nick named Buck Tooth, Kondo, and Kuriyama.

CAMP KAWASAKI ... *RALPH'S PERSONAL EXPERIENCE*
November 12, 1942-July 25, 1945

"We boarded a train to Kawasaki and walked three miles to our new Quarters at Camp Kawasaki-Tokyo Area Prisoner of War Camp #2. They had barracks there that we stayed in. We had wooden bunks to sleep on. Our food consisted of rice and steamed barley. We were in the camp for about a week when we were assigned work details at the Nippon Steel Mill. The first job that I had was working on the railroad. We made railroad tracks. We were on the tracks with civilians. We worked at this job every day. We would get up before daylight, walk to the plant and work 10 to 12 hours a day, and then return to the barracks. On our first Christmas at the camp the Japs let us take a day off. They allowed us part of a British Red Cross Parcel, an apple, a tangerine, and some cigarettes. Although we did get part of a Red Cross Parcel on occasion the food wasn't enough to compensate for the daily hard labor. By the Christmas of 1943, I had lost 50 pounds. We continued the same routine day after day.

Then on November 1, 1944, a B-29 was seen flying over Tokyo and the first air raid was sounded. From that point on the Americans started flying missions day and night over Japan. They used incendiary bombs and burnt houses and buildings all around. The steel mill had a hospital for the civilians and the hospital had been destroyed. The steel mill was shut down for a while so we were put to work cleaning up the mess after each bombing. One day we were cleaning up the area and a couple of our guys wrote V for victory on one of the walls of the hospital. There were a couple of Japanese that could read English and they told the guards. That night when we got back to the camp the Japanese called all of us out and put us in formation. They made us stand there night and day for three days. A lot of the men would fall. The Japs would come over and use rifle butts and beat the prisoners. After three days the men who wrote the V sign, finally came forward. They were taken out and executed.

The next day we went back to work. Ted Venable and I were working on this railroad and they put this older Jap civilian in charge of us to do some different clean up details. He would take us and tell us what to do and we would do it. He was good to us and we liked

COMMANDANT
NAVY NUMBER 128 (one two eight)
c/o Fleet Post Office
San Francisco, California

1[illegible] DEC 1943

Mrs. Julia Mae Lape
R F D 2
Box 115
Chaffee, Missouri

Dear Mrs. Lape:

This office has been advised that a broadcast by a Tokio radio station on October 14, 1943 contained a message, purportedly from Ralph Lee Lape - U. S. Army Air Corps Private - Interned in Japan.

We are sending this message on to you in the event that you have not received it from any other source. If at any future time we receive additional information through radio broadcasts, we will forward any messages directed to you. We do not have any other contact with prisoners of war.

All requests for information and correspondence relative to Americans, who have been captured or interned by the enemy, should be addressed direct to the Information Bureau, American Section, Office of the Provost Marshal General, War Department, Washington, D. C.

Very truly yours,

JOHN A. GILES
Lieutenant, USNR
Public Relations Officer

DPRO/1
2728-A—S/M Base (128)—6-4-43—2M.

Letter informing parents that Lape has moved to Japan.

A Point of Interest

WAR CRIMES TRIAL

During the war crimes trials a number of those in authority at Camp Kawasaki were tried and convicted. Lt. Myazaki received forty years in prison, Mizuno received five years, Shiozawa received twenty years, Watanabe-Porky the Pig-received forty years, Saito Buck tooth-received thirty years, Kondo received one year, and Kuriyama received life in prison. All were to serve their sentences at Sugamo. By 1958, all the Jap guards were released from prison.

Lape and fellow POWs in Kawasaki Prison. Lape is in the bottom row, third from the left.

him. It was in the winter of '45 and the ovens in the plant were warm. We got our bowl of steamed barley and after that we laid down by one of the stoves and went to sleep. The next thing I knew someone was kicking me. I looked up and it was a high ranking Jap officer that was inspecting the plant. He yelled at us and we got up. They slapped us around a little bit. The old Jap guard was hard hearing and he was a sleep. He didn't hear it. They pulled him up and beat him until he couldn't walk. That was the way that they punished each other. If one of them messed up they would appoint a person with the next highest rank to beat them. Anyway they took us back to the barracks and they made us stand out in front of the barracks. They sent this big Jap down and he started in on Ted first. He liked to use his Judo and he would hit him. He had a big bamboo stick that he was using too. I thought that Ted had more sense, but he was kinda asking for it. This Jap would kick him down and Ted would just jump up and get back in formation. The Jap would knock him down. Ted would get back up and stick that chin out for him to hit him. I told him, "Ted when he knocks you down stay down." Ted wouldn't let him, but after several knock downs he finally stayed.

Then he started on me. He hit me with the stick and used Judo. I went with the hits and he never did knock me down. I think it was because he was tired. Finally, he just walked off. Ted looked at me and said, "I'm better than them damn Japs and I won't bow to them."

At the steel mill we had different officers and the higher the rank the more stripes they had on their caps. This Jap picked me to follow this civilian worker around that had a stelin torch. He showed me how he wanted his torch disassembled and put away. He told me that he wanted me to put it away every time he finished. I did this every day for a long time. Then one day he told me to put the torch up and I started pulling the lines in and rapping them like he told me. I had my back to him and all of a once he started yelling at me and hit me across the back of the neck. It was such a surprise and before I thought I swung and hit him. I stood up and faced him and he started at me. He was a smaller man than I was and I grabbed him by the arms and put my legs together so he couldn't hit me in the groan. There were orders out and

PRISONERS OF WAR MAIL

東京俘虜收容所

FROM #1996

NAME&NO RALPH L. LAPE

NATIONALITY AMERICAN

RANK PVT.

CAMP DISPATCH CAMP NO5 TOKYO AERA

KAWASAKI JAPAN

俘虜郵便

TO TRULIE MAE LAPE

R.F.D. #2 BOX 115

CHAFFEE MISSOURI

U.S.A.

Front of postcard from Ralph Lee Lape while in POW camp in Kawasaki, Japan, dated Dec. 22, 1942.

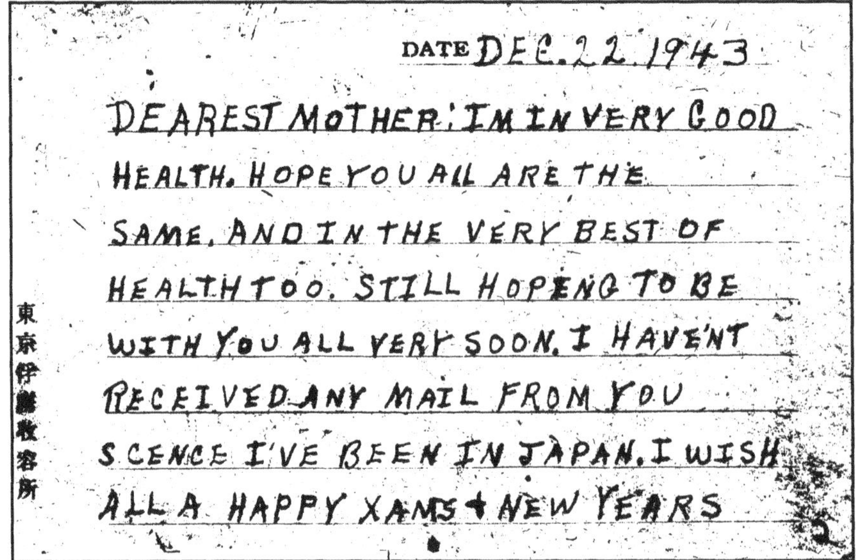

DATE DEC.22.1943

DEAREST MOTHER: IM IN VERY GOOD HEALTH. HOPE YOU ALL ARE THE SAME. AND IN THE VERY BEST OF HEALTH TOO. STILL HOPENG TO BE WITH YOU ALL VERY SOON. I HAVEN'T RECEIVED ANY MAIL FROM YOU SCENCE I'VE BEEN IN JAPAN. I WISH ALL A HAPPY XAMS + NEW YEARS

東京俘虜收容所

Back of postcard from Ralph Lee Lape while in POW camp in Kawasaki, Japan, dated Dec. 22, 1942.

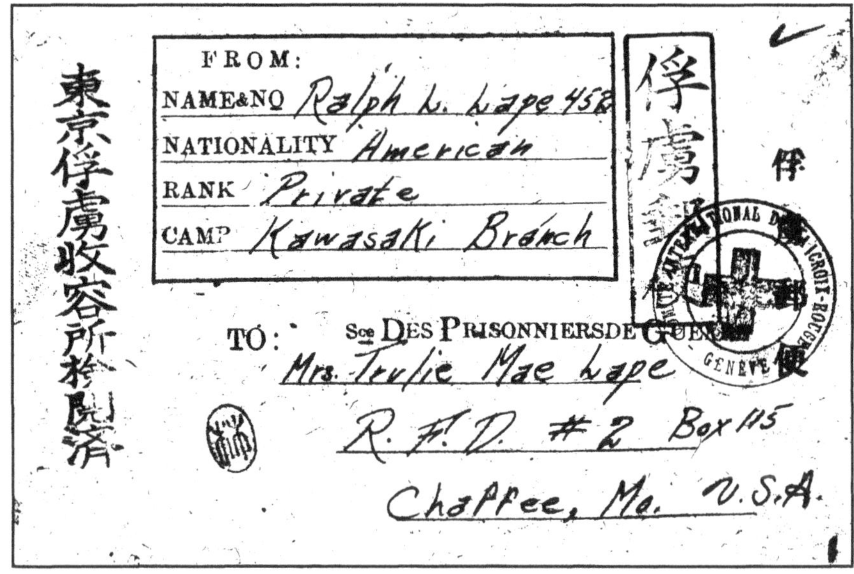

FROM:
NAME&NO Ralph L. Lape 458
NATIONALITY American
RANK Private
CAMP Kawasaki Branch

TO: Mrs. Tevlie Mae Lape
R.F.D. #2 Box 115
Chaffee, Mo. U.S.A.

東京俘虜収容所検閲済

俘虜郵便

Front of postcard from Ralph Lee Lape while in POW camp in Kawasaki, Japan, dated Dec. 19, 1943.

DATE 19 December 1942

Dear Mother:
I am well, and safe in Japan. My health is excellent. I have had no news of the Family since Dec. 1941. How are you and the Family getting along? Remember me to everyone
Love — Ralph L. Lape.

東京俘虜収容所

Back of postcard from Ralph Lee Lape while in POW camp in Kawasaki, Japan, dated Dec. 19, 1943.

placed all over the bulletin boards that if any of us struck a Japanese guard that it was punishable by death. I thought I had had it. There was another Japanese guard that was in the plant that really liked me. Ray Kellem from West Plains, Missouri came over with the guard and they started talking with the boss. They were talking in my favor. They told him that I was a good worker and I didn't cause any trouble. They got him to settle down. When the guard came in the civilian didn't tell the guard. For three days after that I was really sweating it out because I thought they would kill me, but they didn't.

I did see them take a man that had stole some sugar out of the mess hall out and beat him night and day for two or three days. He was an older man like Pappy Nettles and it was really hard on him. His head swelled up and we thought he would die, but he made it.

We didn't get anything to eat but steamed barley and carrot soup. We never got salt so every once in a while we would sneak down and get a bucket of water from the ocean.

When the water settled, we would get the salt from the side of the bucket. It was the only way we had of getting any salt.

The bombing was bad and the Japs started making weapons out of steal for the civilians. They told us that we would all be killed if the Americans invaded Japan. We would never see it. They just simply thought we had to die.

We watched as the planes came over and bombed Tokyo. The Jap guards beat us for it. They were always beating us for something, but they were worse when the bombing started. Then in the middle of April 1945 B-29s flew over our camp area at approximately 6,000 feet and hit Tokyo. It was a large air raid and it knocked out our water and electricity.

DATE APRIL 17th 1944.

DEAR MOM + POP:

I AM ALLOWED ONCE MORE TO SEND MY LOVE AND GREETINGS TO YOU ALL. I AM IN FINE HEALTH AND HOPING YOU ALL ARE THE SAME. PLEASE LET ALL MY FRIENDS AND RELATION KNOW THAT I AM OK. AND HOPE TO BE WITH THEM PRETTY SOON. MOTHER I RECEIVED YOUR PACKAGE ON MY BIRTHDAY AND IT IS THE MOST

東京俘虜收容所

Page one of letter from Ralph Lee Lape while in POW camp in Tokyo, Japan, dated Apr. 19, 1944.

DATE ______________

APPRECEITED THING I HAVE EVER

RECEIVED. "THANK YOU." HOW IS JOAN + THE

REST OF THE GIRLS. I GUESS YOU HAVE

LOT. OF GARDEN STUFF PUT OUT THIS

YEAR. TELL SOME OF THE GIRLS + BOYS

AROUND HERE TO WRITE I WISH I COULD

BE HOME BY XMAS WELL TELL EVERY

BODY HELLO. WELL I GUESS THIS IS ALL

FOR THIS TIME, GOD BLESS YOU ALL.

YOUR LOVING SON Ralph.

東京俘虜收容所

Page two of letter from Ralph Lee Lape while in POW camp in Tokyo, Japan, dated Apr. 19, 1944.

For this raid we weren't beat. The Japs had a better pay back. They gave us the news that President Roosevelt had died. We were saddened by the news, but at the same time we had to laugh to ourselves because the Japs tried to convince us that they were now going to win the war because our President had died. That was a joke.

About a month later, in late May, we had the largest raid to date. There were approximately 600 planes dropped incendiary bombs on Tokyo. The Japs wouldn't let us go to the bomb shelters. Luckily no one in the camp was injured.

In July the camp was hit by heavy demolition bombing which lasted all night. Twenty-two prisoners were killed and our camp was completely destroyed. The entire area was a total mess.

We were moved to another camp."

CAMP NIIGATA

July 1945 -September 1945

"We were moved to Camp Niigata located about 500 miles north west of Tokyo. All we did was unload boats. We had to walk for a mile and a half to work. We unloaded boats all day. The boats were full of food. We worked day after day unloading the food, but we never got any of it.

I never received a beating at this camp. All in all it was a better camp than the first one.

It was getting close to the end of the war and the Japs started thinning out. They begin to lay off of us. When you bragged on one of these guards, they would answer a lot of questions before they thought. They told me about Germany surrendering."

SURRENDER

August 16, 1945

"When the A-bombs were dropped, we didn't know it, but we did know that something had happened. They were always bragging about shooting down planes or something, but one day it was different. The Japs wouldn't even look at us. They looked down and were really humble. Then we found out that they had surrendered."

THE THIRD TARGET FOR THE A-BOMB

Ralph found out when one of the American officers came into camp that he had come close to a brush with death. The officer began his speech by telling the POWs how lucky they were. Ralph didn't take to kindly to it considering he had been a prisoner of war for three and a half years until the officer explained that had the Japanese not surrendered, Niigata had been chosen as the third A-bomb target. Then, he understood the what the term lucky meant.

LIBERATION

Ralph and his fellow prisoners were not liberated from the camp, they just walked out after two American officers arranged their release but never came back.

The Americans marched out of the camp to a train station and demanded to be taken to Tokyo. While disembarking the train, Ralph and some of the other Americans noticed two armed soldiers and a Red Cross girl. Some of the guys ran over and hugged and kissed on the girl. She laughed and understood the men.

Ralph was taken to Yokohama where he was fed, deloused, given medical treatment, and new clothes.

HOME

September 1945 -July 1946

Ralph boarded a C-47 and flew to Okinawa where some of the Japs were still dug in, to Manila because MacArthur wanted all able-bodied men to come back so he could show them that we had taken it back, and then finally returned to San Francisco. A train took him to a hospital in Iowa where he stayed until he recuperated.

He returned to his home in Chaffee, Missouri where he met his wife Diane Miller. Ralph was going to reenlist, but his future wife didn't like the idea. He was honorably discharged in February 1946 and shortly afterward he and his wife Diane were married on July 24, 1946.

EPILOGUE

Ralph and Diane had two boys Steven and Ralph. Ralph worked at the Cape Girardeau airport for a short time and then worked for 36 years on the Burlington Railroad. He retired in 1983. Ralph expresses a deep interest in air planes which in part is shown by the many model planes that he has built and displayed in his home. He enjoys retirement with his wife. The couple just celebrated their 50th wedding anniversary the 24th of July.

Lape and Ted Venable with a Red Cross worker shortly after their release from prison camp.

THE WHITE HOUSE

WASHINGTON

TO MEMBERS OF UNITED STATES ARMED FORCES BEING
REPATRIATED IN OCTOBER 1945:

It gives me special pleasure to welcome you back to your native shores, and to express, on behalf of the people of the United States, the joy we feel at your deliverance from the hands of the enemy. It is a source of profound satisfaction that our efforts to accomplish your return have been successful.

You have fought valiantly in foreign lands and have suffered greatly. As your Commander in Chief, I take pride in your past achievements and express the thanks of a grateful Nation for your services in combat and your steadfastness while a prisoner of war.

May God grant each of you happiness and an early return to health.

Harry Truman

BELATED MEDALS
October 1992

Ralph attended a reunion in Salt Lake City, Utah with the 5th Air Base Group. Forty-seven years after the war, Ralph was awarded the Air Force Bronze Star and POW medal for his service in World War II.

Lape and his wife today.

CHAPTER FIVE

LIEUTENANT THOMAS J. HART
U.S. ARMY

PORT BATTALION G, 5307TH, 475TH, AND 124 CAVALRY L TROOP
CAPTURED DURING AN OFFENSIVE IN BURMA AFTER BEING LEFT FOR DEAD

CAMP HOSI
JANUARY-MARCH 1945
ESCAPED

FIGHTING FOR ONE'S COUNTRY
March 1943

At the age of 17 Tom went to the Army headquarters to enlist in the Army. One of the Army officers wanted to know why Tom wanted to join at such a young age. Tom replied, "because I want to fight for my country." The Army enlisted Tom, but he wasn't allowed to leave for active duty until he turned 18.

On his 18th birthday, in March 1943, Tom received orders to report to Fort Benjamin Harrison in Indianapolis, Indiana for a physical. He passed the physical and was sent to Fort Lawson in Seattle, Washington. They had to clear a wooded area for tents and never did transfer from the tents to the new barracks being built. They completed their training in basic warfare in about eight weeks.

Tom was then assigned to 286th Port Company "A" as a Longshoremen. He was trained in ship repair, loading and unloading ships. "I thought that I was going to carry a rifle all the time, but the only time I ever shot a rifle was on the range during basic, " Tom explained.

"After we completed the training we were suppose to get a 15-day furlough, but instead they shipped our unit to Skagway, Alaska. We loaded pipe for a pipeline and stayed in Alaska for about three months."

In June 1943, Tom's unit returned to Seattle and the men were given 15 day furloughs. After the furlough, he returned and had orders to report to San Francisco where they were to catch a ship that would take us to the South Pacific. They were in San Francisco for a couple of weeks and then boarded the USS *Hermitage* and headed west in October 1943. During the journey across the Pacific Tom would acquire the nickname "Sugarfoot." Tom, an ordained minister, used the word in place of swear words. A few weeks later "Sugarfoot" and his unit arrived in Freemantle, Australia. Tom saw his first kangaroo, enjoyed the white beaches and was entertained by a show of musicians and dancers in the next four days and then it was time to pull out once again.

Thomas Hart

A JOURNEY TO INDIA

Tom's ship was on the high seas for about four days when they developed mechanical trouble. The drive shaft on the ship broke and they coasted into the island of Bora Bora. It took five days to repair the ship. The ship headed for India zigzagging all the way across the Indian Ocean. Tom turned nineteen during this 46-day trip to Bombay, India in November 1943.

Tom and his unit loaded aboard trains and headed for Calcutta, India where the battalion was to work on the docks. When they arrived at the docks, Tom was shocked, " I saw all these men and women walking around with mouths that were as red as blood. I thought there was something wrong with them. This has to be the worse place in the world to be. Later, I found out I was wrong. They chewed a tobacco that had red juice instead of brown. I felt better after that. On the docks we unloaded rifles, bombs, tanks, and ammunition. I never expected to see it again when it left the dock, but I did. The war kept getting worse and worse. By the type and amount of supplies coming in I knew we were going to make an invasion against the Japs in jungle terrain somewhere."

SABOTAGE

There were Jap sympathizers on the docks. They would constantly feed information to the Japanese army about the amount and types of supplies Tom's unit was moving on the docks. They also sabotaged the area as Tom recalls, "I had coolies working for me and I treated them good. They would really work well for me. One day I noticed this Hendo setting on a pallet. I went up to him and asked him what right he had to just set around while the rest of us worked. He said, "Go to hell," in English and when he did he realized he messed up and took off running. I chased him all over the docks and through warehouses and finally with the help of the MPs we caught him. He was a spy for the Japs.

That same night while I was working on the docks, I noticed this crane with a pallet of steel hanging over the dock. The coolies were working under the pallet and I kept watching this pallet. Sparks started flying and the strands on the cable begin to break. Just as the last one snapped I ran over and knocked the coolies out of the way. Had I not, they would have been killed.

The next day they took me off the docks and told me that I couldn't go back on the docks anymore. I asked the Lieutenant why he was doing it to me. He said, 'Sugarfoot, there are spies on the dock and they are out to kill you. I can't let you go back any more.' I was devastated."

MERRILL'S MARAUDERS

Tom was depressed from being relieved of his duties on the docks and his resistance broke down which then developed into a severe fever. After three weeks in the hospital he was assigned to a construction job building barracks. He hated it. Then one day a famous unit was asking for volunteers. "I was walking pass one of the barracks and I noticed a notice on the side of the barracks. It stated that if there was anyone interested in volunteering for the 5307th Infantry, Merrill's Marauders sign here. Well I put my name down there in a hurry. I was the third on the list.

A few days later all the volunteers met in a theater on the base with one of the officers. He told us that if we were volunteer for the Marauders that we would be in combat duty. That it was going to be rough. He gave us one last chance to leave if we weren't interested. A large group got up and left. When the theater cleared there were about 50 of us left. We were told we would have our orders in two days and that we weren't going to receive any training because they needed us right now."

THE FIRST COMBAT
June 1944

"Boy, two days later we had our combat gear and were headed for the train," Tom explained. "My old Lieutenant came up as I was leaving and told me that he would give me a

Sergeants rating if I would change my mind. I told him that I never changed my mind. He offered me Staff Sergeant and that sounded good, but I turned him down. We boarded the train and started across India. Somewhere in India we boarded trucks and finally arrived at our destination. The minute we got to the destination we were being fired at by the Japs. I had an M-1 and cartridge belt and I jumped from the truck. I loaded with a clip and learned how to fire that rifle immediately. It seemed like I was shooting in the air because I had never shot a weapon and I had a talk with my self about settling down and not wasting bullets. We were pinned down by the Japs over night but the next morning they were gone.

We started assaulting the airport the next morning. The Japs were well fortified and we fought for every inch of ground until we finally took the air field. They had torn up the air fields, but we were told that the Combat engineers would come in and fix it.

After we took the air field we were regrouped and they started sending the original Marauders home. There was only about three hundred of us left. We defended the air field and were hit by several suicide planes and constantly had to guard against Jap snipers."

THE MARS TASK FORCE

July 1944 -January 1945

"The 475th Infantry begin to train even harder, to be offensive combat men," Tom said. "Some of us began to move out. Those of us that had been trained by the Marauders had a replacement unit to come in, known as the 124th Cavalry, from Texas.

These men were extremely good with horses, but they had never had any other training. We had mules. The mules were the ones we had unloaded in Calcutta, when I was in the 508th Port Battalion.

The 124th Cavalry knew how to fight like cavalry men, but they knew nothing about the jungles. So, we who had some earlier, bitter experiences in jungle fighting, were dispersed among the cavalrymen and the 475th Infantry.

Maybe these men knew nothing about the jungles, but they were very quick to catch on. The Mars Task Force became even meaner than the Marauders. Those Texans weren't afraid of anything. They were use to snakes and other prairie animals because they were a border patrol outfit from the 56th Cavalry in Brownsville, Texas. Neither group gave up their identity. The 475th Infantry is known today as the 75th Infantry, and the 124th Cavalry still holds its former name the 56th Cavalry Brigade-in Texas-to this day.

The Mars Task Force was made a new unit in July 1944. Mytchinaw had been secured, and now it was time for more jungle combat training. The Japanese were gaining more and ground. General Cheves was our command leader at the time, then came Colonel Hazeltine and Colonel Jefferies. These three courageous men were the ones who thought we were ready to go into combat. They had a lot of faith in the men of the Mars Task Force. May I say, they were absolutely right. By now I was becoming a seasoned combat fighter in the jungles along with the other brave and fearless men in our unit. I believe that we were more deadly than any of the fighting men known at that time.

I was assigned to Troop L of the 124th Cavalry, under the leadership of Captain Thompson. Our troop was known as the front scouts, while the G, F, and I troops of the 124th Cavalry, were the flanks. We all had our particular jobs to do, in our newly organized unit.

Major Blair, Captain Thompson, and Lieutenant Rhoads, were our troop leaders. I was placed in the squad with Sgt. Eggers and Corporal Fields.

I became known as "Padre" because of my past experience of being a minister of the Nazarene faith and I had taken our Chaplain's place on many occasions because he was busy elsewhere, in the fighting, where he was needed most. Chaplain Gump was a very busy man, behind the lines, serving the wounded and other personnel.

The Mars Task Force began to lay down a hard fight against the Japs. In August 1944, a rather light skirmish took place. The Japs were driven back by a surprise attack from F and L troops. It didn't last long, because we were surrounding the Jap forces in small groups, to cut off the supply routes-then taking a little time to mop up the pockets that had been cut off from their main forces. It was very effective, because the enemy would run, rather than fight, and we ran, too-to regroup. The Japs thought that the Americans had regained their combat readiness, when they were able to infiltrate wherever they wanted to.

In December 1944, I was given a field commission as Chaplain, with the rank of First

Lieutenant. This was just before Christmas, for there was no one to offer the Eucharist to the front line combat troops. Colonel Hazeltine said, later, that he went on the performance of duties in the field, and gave the honor of such a promotion when it was clearly necessary to do so.

This new, combined group, would later become known as the Mars Task Force. The name was acquired after a diary was found from a morally wounded Japanese soldier. His diary read, "Their men are all from Mars. They're everywhere. We don't know where they will strike next."

It was with pride that we began the warfare of seek and destroy and run. This was done expertly most of the time. We were trained for this kind of battle fighting. The jungles became our friend, as well as our enemy. The enemy side had the same problems as the Marauders. Pestilence and hunger were taking their toll on the Japs, as much as it was on the Americans.

It was pestilence that was hurting us more than the actual combat fighting, now. The monsoons were hitting us hard. It would rain for days and days and days, then the sweltering heat would hit us. It was as if the lurking jungle was lashing out at us foot soldiers.

On one occasion we camped near a stream. The cobras were thick in the area. We didn't know this until the next day. Dick Thompson and I, who were the BAR men, woke up and while we were shaking the water from our blankets, Dick noticed a cobra was erect and ready to snap at him. We finally got enough courage to get close enough to cut its head off with our machetes. Some of the men weren't so lucky.

We had to stay in this area another night, because we got the word that the Japs were heading our way, and we were to destroy them. The next day we received orders to move out, because the Japs moved in another direction. We were relieved to hear this, for we were anxious to get out of cobra country.

The jungle was an enemy, but also a friend.

We were headed south toward Bhamo, when we were alerted that a company of Japs was secured around the town of Bhamo. We began our cautious way in the jungle. We found several encampments of Japs, and ran each of them out. The jungle hid us from the enemy, and in our training we were to sneak up on the enemy at night, and hit them when least expected it.

Our squad was to secure a Bhuddist Temple that the Japs had made into a fortress. We called for the artillery. Then we made a rush toward the Temple. In the holes that the artillery made in the walls, we were able to throw hand grenades into the Temple. We ran into the Temple when the shooting stopped, but the Japs had left under fire. We secured the Temple and made it safe, without one bullet being fired after we got inside. The jungles helped us achieve our goals most of the time.

Just after securing Bhamo town, we were on a rest period. Tom and I, decided that we would go into town and look around. As we were sightseeing, we got word that we were to pull out the next morning. All men were to report back to their squads at once.

Well, we knew then that something was about to happen. The next morning we pulled out, and we walked for two days-about twenty to forty miles-with hardly any rest. We catnapped at night, and we would get moving before daylight. We were careful not to leave anything uncovered, such as ration containers, chewing gum, wrappers, or cigarettes-because we knew that we were surrounded by Japs.

We went down the mountain, and got caught in the valley-with no where to go. Someone had made a mistake on the map. The Japs were looking down our throats. We knew we had to get back on high country. Desperately, we began to move out with our mules, for they were carrying the ammunition and other materials that we couldn't carry up the mountain stream. Our mules would sometimes slip off the ridges and fall into the water. We had to have them.

Finally, after eight to ten hours of hard walking, we made it to the top. We thought we were safe. We made camp. The order came that no one was to eat or drink anything. No noise was to be made at all. For once, the sounds of the night birds and animals were a blessing, so no one could hear our mules snort. It all blended in together.

We were prepared for the worst to come. It did. F Troop was taking a hard beating. Lieutenant Rhoads was killed and another officer was evacuated. In one second his groin was shot off completely. Sgt. Knight was seriously wounded, and then the fighting stopped.

F troop was completely wiped out, except for about 30 men. They really took a bad beating. The Japs had fallen back into the lower country-but, they were still on one hill. Troop L was to secure that hill. The Japs had just beaten the socks off of F troop, and these Japs were the same bunch that had done it.

We all lined up at the foot of the hill. Every man was to be on his own from here on. Then came the word, "Move out!" It seemed as if the whole world was shooting guns. The heavy machine guns were shooting over our heads. The artillery quit coming in. All you could hear was screaming in warlike fashion-we had American Indians in our unit. We were all fighting with BAR and 30 caliber guns.

All of a sudden the artillery fell on us. The line had to stop, for we had gotten into the sights of a Nambu (Japanese machine gun) the Japs were firing at us. One by one, men began to fall. I noticed Wayne Christman stop. He was by me. He pointed in front of me on the ground. A Nambu was aimed in our direction and the dirt was spitting up toward us. I stopped and zeroed in on the direction from which the bullets were coming, and finally the Nambu stopped.

In the meantime, Tom called out to me to run, because I would get it from the next artillery shell. He no sooner got it out, when I felt something hit me from behind."

We were burying a comrad after he had drowned in a stream. I was officating as the Chaplain.

Crossing the Irawady River on pontoon bridge built by the Engineers.

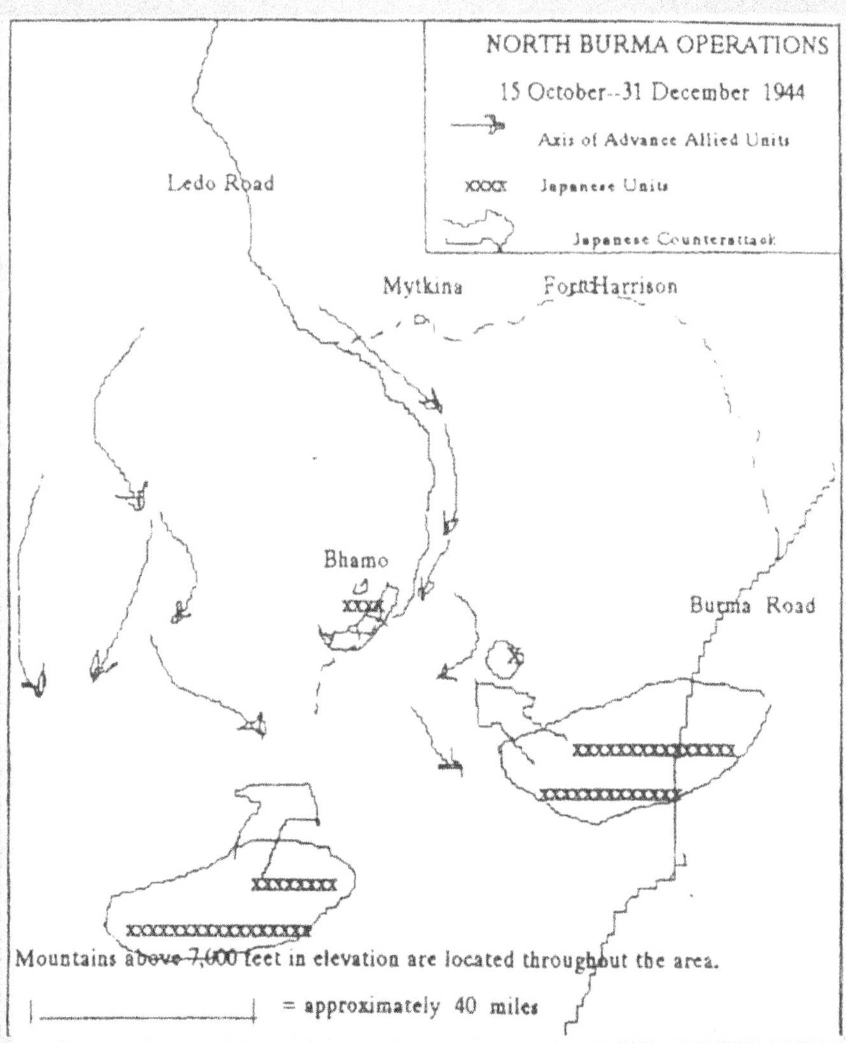
NORTH BURMA OPERATIONS
15 October--31 December 1944
Axis of Advance Allied Units
Japanese Units
Japanese Counterattack
Ledo Road
Mytkina
Fort Harrison
Bhamo
Burma Road
Mountains above 7,000 feet in elevation are located throughout the area.
= approximately 40 miles

"L" Troop was caught in the valley with nowhere to go but up a mountain stream. We were surrounded by the Japs. This is where I prayed for a sign of hope.

Carrying Lt. Knight from Knights Hill down to the covering. He was shot in the groin and died later.

BEING WOUNDED

"As I was lying on the ground being left behind from the main body of my comrades, I was being picked up by four or five men" Tom explained. "They dragged me over my buddy Wackler, who lay dead with his shirt pulled open and at least three bullet holes in his chest. I knew that he was dead.

While I was being carried down the hill, I heard these men talking. They were not using English language. These were Japanese soldiers. I knew then that I had been taken prisoner.

Fear gripped me like nothing in this world before. I wasn't afraid of the men, as much as I was afraid of what they could or would do to me. Many times we had gone through a village where we would see the body of an American soldier hanging from a tree limb. His penis had been cut off, and stuffed in his mouth as he was dying.

A Point of Interest

POWs WORLD WAR II-PACIFIC

	Navy	Marines	Army/Air Force	Philippines
Captured and interned	3,848	2,274	27,465	25,580
Died while POW	901	901	11,107	10,650
Returned to U.S. control	2,947	1,756	16,358	14,930

I could mention other atrocities that the Japs did to the villagers who were sympathetic toward the American fighting men. Inhuman treatment was forced upon our missionaries, also.

Especially bad things were done to the women and girls. The native women were badly treated by the Japanese soldiers. The Japs wanted to win the war, but they never seemed to care how they did it, or how badly others would feel about the Japanese soldiers and people. They wanted to be superior in every way, above other people. They had no friends among the villagers.

So, my greatest fear about my captors, was what they would do to mistreat me."

A PRISONER OF WAR . . . *TOM'S STORY*
January 1945 -March 1945

"I was thrown to the ground and kicked and beaten with rifles. My head was hurting so badly. I kept feeling a strange sensation in my chest. It felt like fire coming into me. Finally, they quit their play with me. I was told to stand up at attention. I tried to stand, but every time I would fall again. Then, someone would hit me again. I tried it five times, then I prayed to God for extra strength to be able to stand up. I got up the strength that I needed, and stood at attention the best way I could.

One officer came up to me. He slapped me across the face. I became very angry. That anger that built up inside me was my salvation. For the first time in my life, I began to hate violently. Fear and hate gripped me so hard, that I was afraid I would lose control.

The officer noticed that my chest had been bleeding. Even I didn't know this. He tore my shirt open. I had a piece of shrapnel penetrating my chest bone. He hit that piece of metal with his hand, to see if he could shove it further into my body. I stood there in fright, knowing that he wanted me to fight back, or faint, or to die. Instead of crying out, I prayed for God to let me not feel the pain. I was talking to Jesus Christ the whole time. Somehow, I felt no pain at all, as the officer tried to push the shrapnel through to my inner chest wall. The piece of metal would not move.

He asked me my name. I gave him my name and serial number-but not my rank-because I had just been awarded my cross as a Chaplain, and was made a 1st Lieutenant. I thought I had lost my cross. I never felt in my pocket for it. He took my dog tag, that had been pinned to my shirt.

I thought that it was funny that I did not have it around my neck. I never gave it another thought because I didn't really know what had happened to me. All I could remember was, that I was tumbling in the air before I lost consciousness on the battle field.

As I stood in front of these men, I felt that I was losing consciousness again. I felt hungry, and I was hurting in my head and chest. I must have passed out then. When I awoke, I found myself in a dark, boarded room. I could barely look through the cracks of the wall. I knew that I was a prisoner at that time. I heard men talking. As they got closer and closer, I knew I was in for a beating. I had heard that the Japs did this sort of thing to all their prisoners.

I began to pray for courage and strength. At that moment I felt a sense of strength and power move over me. I was certain that it was the peace of God, with the power of his spirit, coming to me in a place where there was no peace. By the time the soldiers came in the door, I was standing at attention and was saluting them as they walked in. They knew, then, that I was able to be interrogated.

I lost all track of time and days. Nothing seemed important, only to be prepared to live and not to die. So I kept this in my craw all the time, live man live!

Then the officer in charge came to see me. He could speak good English. He said he was my friend, and that he went to college somewhere in California. I didn't know much about California, but I made a small smile. He took it wrongly. He hit me in the face. I was a boxer before I entered the Army, so I could take a good punch. It didn't even bother me.

The officer asked me my name, rank, and serial number, and what outfit I was with. I gave him my serial number and name only-I told them no more, regardless of what they did to me. It is true that when you were a prisoner of the Japs, you were mistreated badly. That's saying it mildly!

I was told that I would be taken from the dark place. They took me in front of the Jap soldiers, so everyone could see an American in captivity. Then I was put in a place that had some more light. This was when the interrogation really started. I was to sit at a table with my hands downward on the top of the table.

They asked me questions about my outfit. When I refused to tell, they would hit my hands with the butt of a rifle. I would see blood begin to spurt from my fingers and knuckles. No one will ever know how much it hurt. I would not give in and tell them anything. Then, they would pierce my fingers with pieces of sharp bamboo sticks. Oh! how that would hurt, where I was already hurting so badly. Finally, I would pass out and they would leave me alone for days.

The officer came into the place, and said to me, 'I see you didn't die after all. You must be a miracle man.'

I said nothing at all. He went out. I knew that he was going to try, again, to kill me. I knew that I had to escape quickly now. I had watched my captors very closely, and observed that around late afternoon everyone would be silent. That time of day, hardly anyone was around. It must have been a rest period for the Japanese."

THE ESCAPE

"I called for the officer to come and see me. The guard got an officer who could understand English, but he could not speak it. I asked him to come closer to me-that I would tell him all that he wanted to know. He smiled and came near me.

For the first time, I knew that I was going to kill, because that is what we were trained to do. I grabbed him, then, with my badly bruised arms and hands. I destroyed him. I hid him in the dark park of the Basha. I began to laugh and cry at the same time, hysterically. I couldn't keep quiet. I yelled and screamed and cried and laughed until I got hold of myself and began to pray for forgiveness.

I felt easier then, and began to relax. I knew I had to get away quickly, now. I kicked a loose board, that I had located earlier, and crawled out of the hole to get outside. Just then, a guard saw me. I had to kill him, too. I got on my hands and knees and crawled along the line of escape that I had planned while in the Basha.

When I got to the jungle, I felt safe. But I knew that there had to be booby traps, so I watched for them-closely. When I found the traps, I stepped carefully over them, and I was free.

I was soon more deeply into the jungle, and felt free in every way. Now I had time to heal myself. I had a chance to forget my experiences as quickly as possible. I had only the jungle to worry about now. It was better than being afraid that I was going to die in a prison camp."

SURVIVAL IN THE JUNGLE

"After my escape from the Japanese, I began to roam in the jungle in the day, and find open country to sleep in the night. I wandered and wandered until I began to get my bearings, I had to decide where and what I must do in order to survive, because I was getting extremely thirsty and hungry. I thought I would die of starvation or thirst. I had no sense of time and days. One day and one night never made any difference to me. If I would happen to wander near a village I would run away, because I was afraid of being captured again. So I stayed in the jungle all the time.

I thought only of survival. I needed a place to live that would be as safe as possible from the elements of nature. So I decided to build me a tree house. While I was wandering around, I found a machete and trench knife that I could use for tools, as well as for weapons.

I looked for a good tree that had the right kind of limbs for a tree house. When I found the perfect tree, I began to cut bamboo trees and split the bamboo in order to make the floor of my house. In doing so I found that the bamboo had pure water stored in the fourth section from the ground. It was cool water and tasted good. So I drank water until I nearly burst.

I got awfully sick after that, but I think I drank too much to start with. I would tie the end of the vine around one piece of bamboo and then make a cross bar. Then I would tie a piece at a time, until I made my floor complete.

I then wondered how I was going to get it up the tree. This stumped me. I thought that I should have built it in the tree in the beginning. I didn't want to take it apart, so I figured a way to get it up the tree.

I cut a large vine, and climbed the tree. I looped the vine over the limbs on which I wanted my house to be. Then, I tied one end of the vine to the floor, and pulled on the other end until I got it higher that where I wanted to place it. I fastened the loose end to a small tree. Then climbed to where I was going to set the floor. I managed to swing it over the limbs, and let it fall into place.

I left my machete on the ground. I had to shimmy down the tree, then climb back up the tree, and start all over again. I swung the floor back and forth until I had the thing in place. At that time, I swung my machete and cut the vine. The floor fell perfectly into place. Then I secured the floor to the limbs with a vine. I just sat there, admiring my new home.

I didn't know where I was, or why I was there, only that I had left prison camp. I began to drink my water more slowly at this time, and rest up after a hard day's work. I sat and said to myself, "I will finish the house tomorrow."

As I sat there, it began to get dark. The night birds and animals began to get noisy. The monkeys were jumping from one limb to another. I hadn't noticed that I was being watched by the monkeys or the birds. There they were, looking at their new neighbor, who had just moved in. So I began to talk to them right away.

The moon got bright. It was shining through the leaves above me. The night sounds of the jungle made me very sleepy. I forgot about the Japs, and prayed my prayers. The Japs had taken my Bible, that I carried in my shirt pocket. My mother had given it to me, when I left for the service. I could still pray and quote from memory. I felt safe, and fell sound asleep.

I was awakened when something touched me the next morning. I jumped up and scared the biggest monkey I had ever saw up close. When it screamed, it scared me. I thought I would die from fright. Soon, composure came back and I realized I was in good hands after all. I sat there wishing that the monkey would come back. He did. We were both more careful the next time not to scare each other.

As the morning went along, I was getting hungrier by the minute so I thought I would climb down from my house to find some food. I'd remembered, in jungle training, that there was food to eat, such as roots, berries, and wild lemon and banana tree. I heard a familiar noise like a jackal growl. I climbed back up the tree and looked down and sure enough there were two jackals looking up at me. They thought they had their breakfast, but I didn't think so. The monkey, who was watching, began to jump and scream and the other monkeys came and the noise was terrific. Then the two jackals left and I knew the monkeys were running after them.

I waited and waited until every thing got quiet again. I climbed down and started looking for berries or nuts or anything that was edible, but it was to no avail. I found nothing to eat. Boy, I was hungry. So I began to pray that God would feed me. The day went by because I didn't feel like building the roof on my house. I was too weak to do anything.

About evening time, I heard something like a hissing sound in the tree next to mine. I looked around and saw the biggest snake I'd ever seen. He was about 4 inches in diameter. He looked like he was a mile long. I didn't see the end of the tail.

Nothing can hurt you, no creeping thing can harm you, and many other psalms and prayers-that I cannot now recall- came to my mind in a flesh, in just a few seconds.

I thought I would break the silence, and called him Buck. I told him to stay where he was, and I wouldn't bother him. All of a sudden, I felt something touch me in the back. There his tail was. I looked at him and told him that he could keep his tail-if he didn't harm me.

It was getting dark, and I was afraid to go to sleep with Buck around. I stayed awake as long as I could, but then I finally passed out from exhaustion.

I woke the next morning. The monkeys and buck were still there. There was no problem.

I ventured down the tree, to see where the monkeys were getting the food they were eating. I went into the brush with them. Sure enough, they were eating berries. I sat at the bush and ate berries, for what seemed like an hour, I thought I was filled up, and my hunger went away. I came back to the opening, knelt on the ground, and raised my arms up toward heaven. I gave God thanks for the animals, for my snake Buck and for my food.

I fed Buck by throwing my knife and hitting a wild boar. Buck seemed to want to stay around. I didn't mind it after a while, because I had heard that a python will keep other snakes away. God sent me both protection and food.

One day, the monkeys and birds really were restless. I could see the birds fly straight up into the air. The monkeys were jumping up and down and screaming. I remembered that was the way they did, when we would enter in the area. Someone was coming.

I jumped down from my tree house, and ran for the jungles. I was glad I listened, because there was several men coming through the jungle. I figured that they were Japs. I lay in the brush-even stopped breathing-until they left. That was much too close!

I made another hideout on the ground, so that if this happened again, I would be hidden and safe. When I came out of my hiding place, I saw Buck all curled up in my tree house. That's why no one bothered to see if there was anyone around. So Buck saved me again."

FRIENDLY HANDS

"Each day, I would cut through the jungle to see where I was. It seemed that an eternity had passed. I heard motors running. I came running back home, and was scared. I thought that someone was coming after me. When I noticed no one came, I ventured every day closer and closer to the sound. I saw a truck going down a road. I got closer so that I could see who they were. I saw a star on the side of the truck and I knew they were Americans.

I ran madly toward the road. I was waving my hands and screaming to the top of my voice for them to stop. They wouldn't stop until the last truck and the driver got out and asked who I was. I fell to my knees and began to cry out loud. The officer came to me and asked who I was. I told him my name, rank, and serial number. I told him I was a Chaplain and was an escapee from the Japanese. He couldn't believe it.

He told me to get in the back of the truck. When I did, I fell on the floor exhausted. It was getting along in the evening and I asked the men in the back where they were headed. They wouldn't answer me at first. They questioned me about my looks, where I had been, and how I got all the dried blood on me.

I didn't know I was in that condition. They said my hair and beard were matted with blood and dirt. I didn't believe them. Finally, we got near an airport. They took me into a building where there were nurses and doctors and other medics. It was near dark.

I was taken to a room that had cement tubs, or something like that. One man had me undress and get into the dark water. This felt so good to me. It was the first bath I had had for a year. I was so thankful. He asked me how I got so beat up, but I never said anything except it was rough.

He tried to shave me, but my beard was too thick. He tried to use the hair clippers. They pulled too badly, so he got some nurse's scissors, and cut my beard and hair with those. Finally, he was able to shave me. He cut my hair with clippers. My face and head was so swollen, that he was afraid to cut my hair very close. Then, the doctor gave me a good physical.

I had to stay in the hospital until they released me to go to Kunming, China. My body was full of lice and other scaly things. My feet were rotten with jungle rot. I wasn't sure how long I had been in the jungle. I know for at least 92 days, for each day I made a mark on the tree. I don't know the number of days that I was unconscious, but those days were obviously not counted. Never-the-less, I lived through it all: dysentery, malnutrition, dehydration, and all."

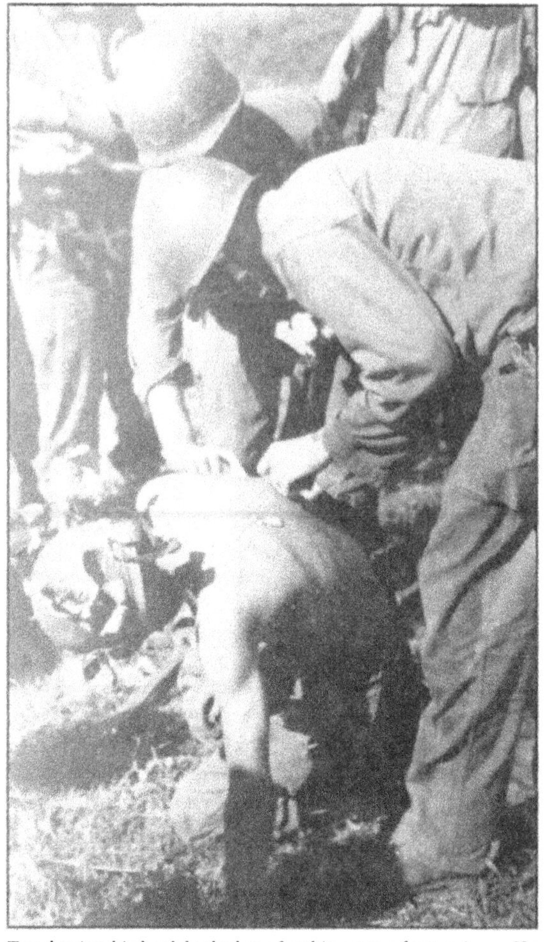

Tom having his back looked at after his escape from prison. He was stabbed in the back by a Jap bayonet. He was picked up by a truck convoy on the Burma Road.

KUNMING, CHINA

After a couple of weeks, Tom boarded a C-47 for India. He stopped at Kunming, China for a period of time and enjoyed the culture and traditions of the people of the land. The visit was not without problems however because it was during the time that the communist government was taking over China. The Inland Mission station had to put up a wall around their compound to protect the American missionaries. Tom did what he could to help until he finally was assigned to a General Hospital in India.

HOME

Tom made it home and was discharged on November 5, 1945. Four days later he married Betty Craig. The couple had three sons Joseph, Jerry, and Jim. All three served in the armed services and two, Jim and Jerry, served tours in South Viet Nam. His oldest son Joseph served in the Navy. Tom became a United Methodist Minister in 1954 and served the Lord in Indiana and Illinois for 40 years.

FORTY YEARS LATER

For thirty-six years Tom was troubled by nightmares about combat in World War II. He was repeated told that the cause was stress unknown. In 1982, Tom suffered a heart attack with the same diagnosis, stress unknown. Tom requested hypnosis therapy from the Veterans Administration to determine the causes of his stress.

The hypnosis uncovered the memory loss suffered by Tom for the past forty years. He had had a complete loss of memory of the experiences he had had in combat, as a POW, and the survival of the Jungle. Through therapy he was able to recall and relieve the stresses from his World War II experiences.

On October 5, 1985, forty years after his return to the United States Lieutenant Colonel John Hays, commander of the 3rd Battalion, 130th Infantry awarded Tom the Bronze Star, World War II Medal, Good Conduct Medal, and the China Service Medal for his service.

One wintery day in February 1985, Tom had his picture taken in the local newspaper while distributing food to the Senior Citizens. An old friend Loren Thomas who served with Tom in Burma and was on the hill the day that Tom was wounded saw the photo in the paper. Both men were living in the same town. Loren had thought that Tom was dead because he had seen him hit and he had been left for dead. Tom called Loren. Loren said, "This can't be Sugarfoot, because Sugarfoot is dead."

"We made an appointment to meet," Tom explained. "Immediately, we recognized each other. After thirty-eight years of thinking I was dead, I suddenly became alive."

Tom Hart and Loren Thomas in 1984.

CHAPTER SIX

PRIVATE FIRST CLASS JOHN MCLAUGHLIN
U.S. ARMY

COMPANY E 325TH GLIDER INFANTRY
CAPTURED IN ITALY

PRISONER OF WAR
SEPTEMBER 1943-FEBRUARY 1945
STALAG IIB-STALAG VIIA-STALAG LUFT III

GLIDER INFANTRY TRAINING AND NORTH AFRICA
December 18, 1942

John was inducted in the Army on December 18, 1942. He completed three months of training at Fort Bragg, North Carolina as a Glider pilot with the Glider Infantry Training.

Regiment. On April 9, 1943, shortly after his training the unit was shipped to Casablanca, North Africa. They were there for a few weeks before the unit was moved. According to their leaders there was no other way to get to the location but by gliders because there were no trains and it was to far too be trucked. So they flew in the gliders with no real idea where they were headed. During their training they had only flew short distances for thirty minutes at a time and this trip lasted for hours with the gliders going up and down fighting the turbulence. All of the pilots got deathly sick. They landed once only to find out that they were in the wrong place. They resumed their flight and finally landed at the destination. A group of squad tents lined up under Olive trees in the middle of the desert. They still didn't know where they were at, but they would stay at this location until September 1943.

THE INVASION OF SICILY
September 1943

John's unit was sent to the seaport of Bizerta, North Africa. That's where they saw their first action. The Germans hit them with an air raid that lasted for hours. The unit never received any casualties, but the Germans did. They lost a lot of planes.

John's unit stayed at the seaport for a couple of weeks and trained everyday. John knew they were getting ready for an invasion. "We finally learned that we were going to invade Sicily (an Island between North Africa and Italy)." John recalls. "The paratroopers always went in before us so they could clear the way for the gliders, otherwise we would be in trouble went we landed. One day the paratroopers took off and the next morning we were suppose to go in by gliders. The next morning right before we were to leave they cancelled the invasion. I found out later that the Air Force had messed up.

John McLaughlin

They had a certain flight pattern they were suppose to take, but instead they flew right over the Navy who was bombarding the shores of Sicily. The Navy had orders to fire on any aircraft in the area and they shot down most of our own planes killing most of the paratroopers.

A couple of days later we landed in LCIs (landing craft). The Germans had already pulled out from Sicily and were setting up a front in Italy. We were in Sicily for about two weeks and then we got the word that we were going to invade Italy.

They had invasions on the east side and at Anzio beach. We boarded LCIs and landed at a beach that had already been taken by the Americans. We were at the wrong place so we got back on the boats and finally landed with the main invasion. The beach head was pretty much taken. The Germans had pulled back into the mountains. We had this real tall mountain and we had to climb it. The Germans had their front line set on the top of this mountain. It seemed like it took us two days to get to the top. We had all this equipment to move and we were carrying a lot of individual equipment too-rifle, pack, ammunition. By the time we got to the top of the mountain we were totally exhausted. Our outfit was in chaos. Part of the men got separated. We lost our lieutenant. When we got set in on the front line our platoon sergeant took charge."

THE STAND OFF AND CAPTURE
September 1943

The unit had moved to the top of the mountain to relieve the Rangers. They had been there for a while. They were trying to take the Germans out so the other units could move down the mountain, but the Rangers couldn't move them. "The Germans had their top SS troops on the front," John explained. "They were tough. We took the Ranger's positions late in the afternoon and the Rangers pulled back. I was in the first platoon, the first squad. All the time that we had been in training our squad had been on the point so I knew where we were going to be. There were seven of us on point, four of us were in one foxhole and three in another. I was in the back one from the sergeants place. That afternoon the sergeant told us that there was going to be a artillery barrage by the Germans. We were to cover over our foxholes the best we could. We crawled around and got as much wood and stuff to cover us as possible. The next morning they opened up with all they had. They really plastered us. The third platoon, I heard later was almost wiped out. The Germans had moved up on us while the artillery barrage was going on. They pinned us down. We ran out of water and food. Our company couldn't get any water or food up to us. We were there for three days pinned down. On the fourth morning the news came down for us to withdraw. We had been the first in and we knew we would be the last out. When the other units withdrew we were suppose to receive cover fire so we could withdraw. We waited all day and realized that the unit had pulled back without us. We were pinned in the holes the rest of the day and that night. The fifth morning the sergeant decided that we should surrender. The sergeant had a white handkerchief and he waved it. I watched until he crawled out of the hole and I crawled out of mine. For years after we surrendered I wondered if we did the right thing, but I guess I wouldn't be here right now telling this if we hadn't, but who knows."

THE FIRST DAYS AS A PRISONER OF WAR
September 1943

"The Germans took us down the mountain to a village that they had occupied," John said. "The whole village was in shambles. Artillery was still coming in and our planes were strafing. We were in as much danger as we had been when we were up on the hill. We had to take cover in ditches and under bridges with the German guards. We were under fire the whole time we were there. They made us clean up a sugar refinery. We were scooping up brown sugar and pulling it in sacks. We found out what it was and we started loading up our pockets with sugar. We hadn't had anything to eat and it was good. Food from the time we were captured became a problem and remained a problem the whole time we were prisoners. We didn't get much to eat.

THE TRAIN RIDE

After about three days they started marching John and the rest of the prisoners. They finally got to a railroad yard and like most prisoners they would have the experience of riding the forty and eights. "That's when the punishment started for me," John explained. "They loaded us on boxcars like cattle. There was at least a 100 men in each boxcar. They had two petitions with a door in the middle and barbed wire on each side of the petition. The prisoners were on each end of the car with the guards in the middle of the car. We must have been on that train for two weeks. We went the whole length of Italy and Germany. They gave us a loaf of bread and some water a couple of times while we were on the train and one can of dog meat. That's what it looked like but I don't know what it was. How we survived that I don't know. We were stacked in there like hogs.

They stopped the train a lot, but they only let us off one or two times. If you had to pee, you did it in the floor. If you had a bowel movement you were in trouble. It really got to smelling by the time we got to where we were going. I remember one time when they stopped the train and let us out to use the bathroom. I ran into one of the guys that was in my foxhole, his name was Browning. We were squatted down taking a dunk. It was dark. All at once I heard him whisper, Mack I think I found potatoes. He had been digging around and had sure enough found some potatoes almost matured. We dug up the potatoes and eat them dirt and all. We stuck as many as we could in our pockets.

When we were almost to Germany we started getting hit by our planes again. They bombed every night and every day. We were in a railroad yard. They hit us with B-17's. I have never felt so helpless as I did then. The Germans would stop the train and take cover, but they wouldn't let us out of the boxcars. I felt like a trapped animal. These attacks happened several times, but luck for us we were never hit."

STALAG VIIA

Stalag VIIA was located in Bavaria northeast of Munich and one kilometer north of Mooseburg.

The camp was situated in a flat area surrounded by hills. The camp three main compounds which were in turn divided into small stockades. The Nordlager held new POWs, the Suedlager held Russians, and the Hauptlager held all other prisoners including Americans. The compounds were surrounded by barbed wire with several guard towers scattered along the perimeter.

The barracks were wooded buildings divided into two sections divided by a center room used for washing and eating. The barracks had a water faucet, water pump, and some tables. The prisoners slept on triple deck wooden bunks and mattresses filled with excelsior. By the end of the war, the men per barracks increased from 180 to 400. Men slept on the tables, floors, and ground.

The men were given Red Cross parcels to share. In addition, their daily diet consisted of spinach-type greens or barley soup. Five men shared one loaf of bread. The POWs did receive potatoes on occasion and some margarine.

The general condition of the clothing was poor. Although the Red Cross provided some supplies it was less than adequate. Most POWs wore the clothing they were captured in throughout the duration of their imprisonment.

THE ARRIVAL AT STALAG VIIA
October 1943

"We finally arrived at Stalag VIIA" John said. "It seemed that this camp was a holding place for all prisoners. There were French, British, Russian, and Americans. I spent four days in a little room about 6 foot by 6 foot with nothing but water waiting to be interrogated, but they never asked me much. I didn't know anything anyway. Then I was in the camp with everyone else. I met Henry Leg. He had been shot down in 1942. I had been walking around for about two days. Nothing to eat, nothing to smoke. All at once I spotted this guy. I thought I knew him. I followed him into the latrine and finally I said aren't you Henry Leg. He turned and looked at me. We couldn't believe it. We were from the

A Point of Interest

THE GREAT ESCAPE

The prisoners of Stalag Luft III begin digging three tunnels code-named Tom, Dick, and Harry. The theory for digging three tunnels at the same time was that if the Germans found a tunnel of the size of these tunnels they would most likely not look for any other tunnels because they would not believe that more than one tunnel could be dug at a time. Each tunnel was 30 feet below ground to foil the sound detectors. Harry-336 feet long when finished-was the tunnel used for the escape. On March 25, 1944, 76 men escaped. Hitler was so infuriated by the mass escape that he ordered approximately 5,000 Germans to search for the prisoners. All were caught within two weeks except for three men who made their way back to allied units. The gestapo took fifty of the prisoners into the country side and mowed them down with machine guns. They also shot three German civilians from whom the electrical wire was stolen by the prisoners to light up the tunnels.

same home town and had run around together when we were home. It was a real morale booster.

We budded around together the whole time we were prisoners. He took me to his barrack and gave me some of his cigarettes. Boy, I would take two or three drags off of them cigarettes and they were gone."

STALAG LUFT III

Stalag Luft III was located in a pine woods at Sagan, 168 kilometers from Southeast Berlin. There were six compounds three occupied by Americans and three occupied by British officers. The compounds were divided into 15 buildings or block houses. The barracks were one-story hutments with 12 rooms in each house. Each house held 80 to 110 men. The bunks were wooden double deckers.

The food consisted of soup, barley bread, and Red Cross parcels. It was only adequate because of the supplements from the Red Cross.

Treatment in this camp was excellent as compared to other prison camps until March 1944. Fifty British officers were murdered after they escaped from the prison camp. This escape became known as The Great Escape.

STALAG LUFT III THREE WEEKS LATER
November 1943

"We stayed there for three weeks and then they started separating the guys," John explained. "They took all of us that were airborne troops and set us to an officers camp, Stalag Luft III. Why I don't know, but we were really lucky because it was one of the best camps in Germany. That's where I got my first Red Cross box. We ate most of what we got, but we would save back some food so we could pitch in when we got new prisoners.

We had all kinds of technicians in the camp and they put radios together by bribing guards with cigarettes and D-ration bars for radio parts in return. We had radios and got the news all the time about where the front was. We would meet about every three days in one of the barrack and one of the guys would watch for the German guard. If he saw them coming he would yell "Tally Ho".

We also had an escape at this camp. They started a tunnel under a bunk bed in the barrack next to the fence. The beds were three tiers high. They would take the bed boards and the straw out of the bottom bunk and start digging. The dirt was carried out in their trousers. They would tie their pant legs some way so that when they got outside they could let the dirt fall while they walked around. It was sandy and they could get rid of dirt like hat.

A Point of Interest

ESCAPE

There were more than 91,000 Americans captured by the Nazis from 1942 to 1945. Of those only 737 prisoners of war successfully escaped.

They finally got the tunnel dug out and a bunch of them escaped. The Germans came in one morning and lined us up and started the count. This German officer told us that there was an escape, but they had caught all the prisoners or killed them. We didn't believe the Germans, but we never saw any of them again. This was later to become known as the Great Escape."

After that the Germans found three or four more tunnels. They run water in them and caved them in. After that they started sabotaging our Red Cross packages. They would punch holes in every can of meat we would got which caused the meat to spoil. They told us that it was to keep us from saving up the meat for escape, but I believe that they did it for revenge. It made it a lot worse for our food supply because we couldn't ration it out and make it last for a month until we got another package."

STALAG IIB

This camp was located one and a half miles west of Hammerstein on the east side of the highway leading to the city.

The camp covered 25 acres and was divided into four compounds. The compounds were separated by barbed wire fences while the entire camp was surrounded by two barbed wire fences. The 1,000 American POWs occupied 5 one-story buildings. The barracks were over crowded with three tier bunks, POWs sleeping on tables, chairs, or on the floor.

Red Cross parcels were distributed, but the German rations consisting of hot water for breakfast, water soup for lunch with six or seven small boiled potatoes per man, and three slices of heavy black bread for dinner were insufficient.

The Germans issued no clothing at all. Prisoners wore the same unwashed clothing they were captured in for the duration of their captivity.

The military intelligence department claimed this camp to be one of the worse in Germany. Treatment of the prisoners was generally bad with eight Americans killed while on working parties.

DOING TIME IN STALAG IIB
Fall 1944

"Sometime in the fall of 1944, they took all the enlisted men except for the sergeants and moved us to Stalag IIB," John continued. "We went out on work details in this camp. I worked each day in some sort of working party until the winter and then I got assignment to a working party that was located outside the camp."

A SPECIAL WORKING PARTY
Winter 1944

"During the winter they took 13 of us and loaded us on a train again," John explained. "This time the ride wasn't as bad because we weren't as crowded. They took us to an evergreen forest to cut trees. We cut the trees down and trimmed them into six foot logs for mine props. It was really bad by then. It was really cold and snowed all the time. It was rough working out in that kind of conditions. All 13 of us stayed in a little building about 14 feet by 14 feet. We had a little stove that we could heat water and that was about it. We still got our Red Cross boxes once a month. The Germans gave us potatoes, turnips, and a ration of barley bread.

We were there for a few months and then in the distance we begin to hear the artillery fire on the front lines getting closer. We could tell by the way the Germans were talking that the Russians were moving fast. I found out later that the Germans would stop the American push and the Russians would advance. When they stopped the Russians the Americans would advance. But the Russians were on the move."

THE MARCH BACK TO STALAG IIB
February 1945

The Germans started marching John and the other prisoners back to Stalag IIB later one afternoon. It was a difficult march fighting the cold and the snow. "I don't know how far we walked, but it started snowing hard," John recalls. " It got knee deep. Some of the guys took off out of the column and got away. Most of us decided not to run because we knew the Russians would be there soon and we didn't want to take a chance on getting shot.

We finally got to this big house. The Germans were all old and they were about played out. They said that we could stay there that night. We had loaded all of our food when we started out and we still had some of the Red Cross packages left. We had coffee, too. We told the women in the house to heat us up some water and we dumped a can of coffee in there. They liked to went nuts. They hadn't tasted coffee in years. They really enjoyed it."

THE GERMAN SOLDIERS SURRENDER
February 1945

"After a while, German soldiers started straggling in wounded and shot up." John said. "There were about six of them. They were young and they got with the old guards we had. They decided that they would be better off if they surrendered to us. They came in and told us that they were going to surrender to us and they gave us their guns. For some reason they thought that we could keep them from the Russians, but there was no way we could do it. We couldn't take them anywhere because our front was hundreds miles away. So what we did was put them in a room by themselves.

The next day we made contact with the Russians. We had met this young Polish civilian who could speak German and English. We found some paint and painted American flags on the back of our field jackets and then walked out to the front to meet the Russians. We had the Polish guy to translate for us and told them that we had these German soldiers as prisoners in the house. They went into the house and got the Germans and that was the last that we saw of them."

LIBERATION AND THE MARCH FOR RUSSIA
February 1945

"By now there was only six of us left," John continued. "We were in bad shape again. The Russians were our allies, but you wouldn't know it by the way they treated us. They took everything we had except for a little bit of food we had left from the Red Cross packages. They never gave us any food or transportation back, but they did assign a soldier to go with us. I don't know what rank he was, but he carried a sub-machine gun with him and he couldn't speak English. The farm where we were at had some horses and a two seated buggy. So the six of us and the Russian started out in this buggy toward Poland. We stopped at several houses on the way and got something to eat. I don't know how many days we traveled, but we wanted to get to a Russian officer so we could get some help. Some one who could speak English. All this Russian wanted to do was to find something to drink and get drunk. Finally, got in Schwaback, Germany and we found a headquarters with a Russian officer. He got us a truck and got us on our way.

We started out across Poland toward Russia. We rode for days. We didn't get any food and had to stop along the way and get food from civilians where we could. We went through Warsaw and I will never forget the looks of that city. It had a million population and there wasn't one building standing in that place. The Germans had come in and took it from Poland. The Polish counter attacked and took it back from the Germans. The Germans took it again and then the Russians came in and took it from the Germans. There were no bridges across the river. Nothing was standing.

One town we were in I saw hundreds and hundreds of Jews that had been liberated from a concentration camps everywhere. They were in the stripped uniforms. You could see the terror on their faces from the atrocities they had experienced. The only others that I ever saw with that look were Americans brought in after the Battle of the Bulge. They were the most pitiful looking human beings that I had saw. There were pictures that I saw on television of people in the holocaust being thrown in the graves and these guys looked almost that bad. You could see every bone in their body. We all got together and got them some food. The Germans were smart and they knew that 106th Infantry Division because they were new. There was one guy that was in a foxhole about froze to death. All at once the Germans were all over them. He had the same feelings that I had. Did he do the right thing by giving up. We told him not to ever say or feel that way again. He had no choice if he wanted to live."

ODESSA, RUSSIA AND AMERICAN TROOPS
March 1945

"We crossed Poland and went into Russia," John continued. "We got to the seaport at Odessa, Russia. I never really felt secure or liberated until I started seeing the big white stars on the American trucks. We found the Americans and an officer talked with us for a while and then they fed us and we were issued new clothing. I had on the same shoes that I had on when I was captured. That is what was left of them.

A few days later they put us on a boat and we crossed the Black Sea and went to Naples, Italy. We stayed there for a while and got medical attention."

HOMEWARD BOUND
May 1945

A couple of months later they put John on a boat and a couple of weeks later they landed in Massachusetts. "The whole time I was a prisoner I was hungry' John said. "I dreamed of food all the time. The one thing I dreamed of most was fried eggs. When I got to my home town, there was probably a shortage on eggs because that's what I ate for days. They sure were good."

EPILOGUE

John was discharged and returned to his home in Mt. Vernon, Illinois. He met his wife Norma Stewart and they were married in 1947. They lived in Illinois all but two years which were spent in Everett, Washington where John worked at a lumber mill.

John and his wife raised four children Danny who died in 1975, Vicky, Scott, and Mark. They have two grandchildren John and Ambre both Vicky's children and two great grandchildren Alec and Gage.

On April 11, 1996 John passed away. As his wife told me he was anxious to see this book. I am sadden by his death and that he was unable to see his story and to read the stories of his fellow ex-prisoners of war. However, I am grateful that he was willing to tell his story so that people can read about the sacrifice that John and men like him made to pave the way for us to live in the greatest country in the world.

CHAPTER SEVEN

STAFF SERGEANT R. L. HULSEY
U.S. ARMY AIR FORCE

8TH AIR FORCE 93RD BOMB GROUP 409 TH SQUADRON CAPTURED AFTER BEING SHOT DOWN OVER SOLINGEN, GERMANY

PRISONER OF WAR
DECEMBER 1, 1943-MAY 4, 1945
STALAG 17B

A VOLUNTEER SETS ARMY RECORD
August 1940 -July 1942

On August 6, 1940, at the age of 18 Russell Hulsey joined the Army. He was a volunteer, patriotic, and by all means ambitious. He completed basic training, Gunner School in Nevada, and Armor School in Denver, Colorado. During that time his motivation and leadership qualities repeatedly placed his performance far above his fellow soldiers. One promotion after another finally led him to the rank of Staff Sergeant. It also led him to a unique title. At the age of 19 he became the youngest Staff Sergeant in the U.S. Army.

Russell was in a training command until late 1942. By now the war was in full swing and the young Staff Sergeant wanted to do his part. He volunteered for combat duty and was sent to Tuscon, Arizona and then to Biggs Field at El

Russell Hulsey

Now 31st Says It Has Youngest Staff Sgt.

By William Graffis

Before the 28th School Squadron "blows its top" about having the "youngest staff sergeant in the United States Army," and before they challenge any other outfit in this matter of who has the youngest staff sergeant, they'd better move over into the right side of the tracks and talk to the boys in Flight 3 of the 31st School Squadron.

Pride and joy of the 31st is Staff Sergeant Russell Lee Hulsey, age 19, quite a bit younger than Sgt. Donald M. Schultz, Flight 18, 28th School Squadron. While Sgt. Schultz will be 20 in December, Sgt. Hulsey has until June 9, 1942, to reach the ripe old age of a double decade.

A native of Dupo, Ill., Sgt. Hulsey has been in the Army since August 6, 1940. Formerly attached to the Seventh Air Base at Scott Field, Sgt. Hulsey transferred to Jefferson Barracks Sept. 1, 1940.

Usually a complacent individual, Sgt. Hulsey is quite rightfully a little up in the air about this 28th School Squadron claim, especially when he recalls those pleasant days when he was in the permanent personnel of the 28th.

The son of Mr. and Mrs. George Hulsey, Sgt. Hulsey starred on the Dupo Community High School basketball quintet for three years as a forward. After graduation

Hulsey's crew in North Africa, 1943. Standing left to right: Glennister-Eng. Brann-Radio, Lt. Wilkenson-Bombardier, Lt. Thomas-Pilot, Lt. Soliski-Copilot, Lt. Golisch-Navigator. Kneeling left to right: Lt. Check-Flight Surgeon, Halapy-Right Waist Gun, Mapes-Tail Guns, Hulsey-Left Waist Gun, Zimmerman-Tunnel Gun.

Toro. Upon completion of his training he was sent overseas to a B-24 heavy bomber group.

COMBAT DUTY
July 1942-December 1943

In July 1942, Russell was shipped to Europe as a replacement crew for the 8th Air Force 93rd Bomb Group of the 409th Squadron based at Hardwick, England. Then for a while his unit was based in Bengazi, Libia and went on several missions in North Africa and other areas in support of the 9th Air Force.

In 1943 a new policy was implemented for the air crews. Completion of 25 bombing missions was a ticket back to the United States. Very few men or crews completed that many missions because of the intense Nazi anti-air defense. For example, in October 1943, the 8th Air Force lost so many planes that bombing raid were suspended during that month. In November they resumed the raids. Russell like most of the airmen, wanted to complete his 25 missions and go home, but this time his decision to volunteer would work against him. "I was assigned to the Topelo Lass and got sick during one of the bombing raids. I wanted to make the mission up in order to get my 25 missions so I volunteered to go on a bombing run with another crew. On December 1, 1943, we took off with a bombing mission to hit a steel mill over Solingen, Germany. At 1:00 P.M. we were flying at 18,000 feet when we were hit with flak. We had to leave the formation with one engine on fire. We dropped below cloud level and were attacked by German fighter planes. One of the gunners was killed during the attack and the plane was severely damaged. The pilot could not control the plane and I was forced to bail out. It was the first time that I had ever bailed out of a plane. I had never gone through the training for it back in the States. As I jumped, I looked up and the plane blew up above me as I fell through the clouds. It was snowing and very cold. As I hit the ground, I could hear dogs barking. The visibility was poor and I had no idea where I was. I gathered up my parachute and hid it in a hay stack. I found a couple of trees with moss growing on them. I had learned that it grew on the south side of the tree so I could determine my direction from that. I found a road and begin walking west. Late in the evening after hours of walking I came to some crossroads and noticed a country church. I wanted to get in out of the cold for the night so I decided that this would be a good place to stay. I went inside the church and laid down on the floor at the front pew. About thirty minutes later I heard the door open and someone walks into the church. My heart almost stopped, I was so scared, but I found out that it was an elderly lady that had saw me go into the church. She couldn't speak English so she motioned for me to follow her. She took me to her house and put me in her basement. It was just getting dark outside."

Imogene

THE CAPTURE
December 1, 1943

In a short time the basement door busted open only this time Russell wasn't as lucky. "I was in the basement for about one hour when German soldiers busted in the door," Russell explained, "Someone had spotted her helping me and reported it to the Germans. They shot her and took me to a small building in the village where they kept me over night. The next morning they took me to a grade school and paraded me in front of the school children. They told them that I was one of the American gangsters that were destroying their country.

Later that day they put me on a train and sent me to Frankfort, Germany. I was interrogated there. They asked me about my training, how many planes were in our group and where we were stationed. All I would give them is my name, rank, and serial number. I had put a picture of my girlfriend in my billfold to carry with me. One of the guards going through it, found the picture and asked me who it was. I told him that it was my girl friend and that if I made it back to the states I was going to marry her. He said, "if I had someone that pretty waiting on me I would want to keep the picture. He stamped the back of the picture and gave it to me. I still have it today."

FORTY AND EIGHTS

Forty men and eight horses would be a load for the Germans, but not the American POWs. They were crammed on the boxcars to the point that they couldn't set or lay down. They rode for days without food, little water, and with no provisions for relieving themselves. Russell recalls the experience. "After the interrogation they placed me and other prisoners on a train and transported us to a prison camp. We were on the train for several days before arriving at the camp. All together it had been approximately two weeks since my capture and during that time all I had to eat was dark bread and water. For the next several days it wouldn't get any better. The train was packed with no room to lie down. One corner was used to relieve ourselves and we got no food. After several days we arrived at Stalag 17B near Krems, Austria."

STALAG 17B

Stalag 17B was located 85 kilometers west, north of Vienna, Austria. The first American prisoners to arrive at the camp was on October 13, 1943. From that time until April 1945 there was a steady input of prisoners which reached approximately 4,300. The camp consisted of 12 compounds, five of them for Americans, the others for Italians, Russians, French, and Serbs. Each compound had four double barracks, 40 feet wide and about 130 feet long, constructed on piling 25 to 36 inches off the ground. Each barracks was divided by a washroom which was divided into three partitions. Each washroom had 24 water faucets but usually only three of the six worked. When the faucets broke the Germans refused to replace them, using the excuse that the Americans broke them in an effort to

A Point of Interest

HOGAN'S HEROES

During the 1960s the television series HOGAN'S HEROES hit the air. The hit comedy series portrayed prisoners of war in Nazi prison camps. The setting was based on Stalag 17B.

Stalag 17B in 1944. Photo was taken by a prisoner who had obtained a camera and smuggled it into camp.

hinder the German effort. There was never any hot water to wash clothes or to clean the Barracks. Water was turned on one hour in the morning, at noon, and in the evening. The water situation was very poor and there was never enough water for the three hundred men in the barracks. By the end of the war conditions became even worse. The barracks were built to house approximately 240 and by the end of the war there were at least 400 men crowded into each barracks. There were two barbed wire fences surrounding the camp and watch towers equipped with machine guns at strategic points.

LIFE IN PRISON CAMP
December 1943-April 16, 1945

About a month and a half before Russell was captured and sent to Stalag 17B the first Americans were sent to the camp. The POWs found filthy barracks loaded with bedbugs, fleas and other varmints. The Nazis had made no attempt to clean or to delouse the living quarters before the prisoners arrived. The bunks had large masses of lice eggs and bedbugs, and the prisoners never got rid of the lice and other varmints during the time the camp was open. The Nazis claimed they could get rid of the lice by shaving the prisoners heads so the lice could not breed in their hair. They shaved their heads in the middle of winter with below zero temperatures. The majority of the men had no caps to cover their bald heads. They added delousing showers by the time Russell arrived. "The first thing that they did was to run us through a delousing area. They made us take all of our clothes off as they ran us through the showers. Then they shaved out heads and took us to the camp.

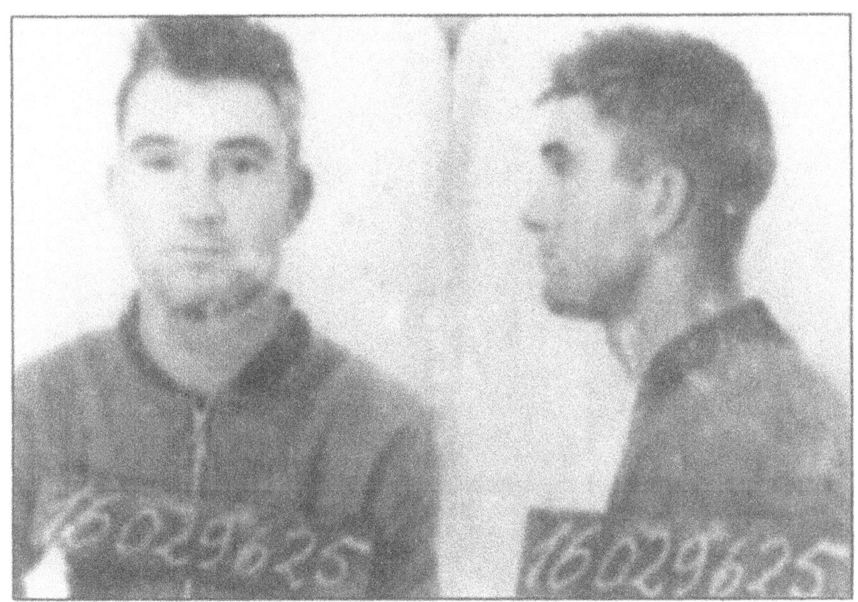

Russell Hulsey in prison camp.

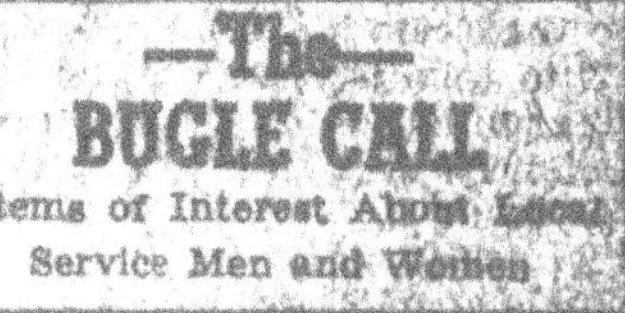

—The—
BUGLE CALL
Items of Interest About Local Service Men and Women

Mr. and Mrs. George Hulsey this week received direct word from their son, S|Sgt. Russell Lee "Bobby" Hulsey, who is a prisoner of the Germans after being shot down while participating in a bombing raid over German-occupied Europe.

The letter which they received reads in part as follows:

"Am a prisoner of war somewhere in Germany. Am feeling fine and in the best of health. Please don't worry about me, as we are being treated very nice. Tell everyone hello for me. You can give my thanks to anyone connected with the Red Cross, as we can see what a wonderful job they are doing over here. Write to my commanding officer and let him know I'm okay. Please don't write to me as we don't have any address here yet. Will write as often as I can. Mother, please don't feel bad about all this, as it is the way I wanted it to be. I want to be happy here. So you be happy and help me [illegible]

There was a total of about 4,000 American prisoners in this camp. They kept us locked in the buildings most of the time and on a few occasions turned their police dogs loose on us in the barracks because they were concerned that we would attempt to escape."

Russell, as many of the prisoners did, became victim to the sub-zero temperatures with a frost bite to both hands. The barracks weren't heated and there wasn't anything to burn for heat in the sub-zero temperatures. The Nazis issued two thin cotton blankets to the men. There was a stove in each barracks but no coal was ever furnished. The only heat generated was by the 300 prisoners in the barracks. Often prisoners slept two and three together in a bunk to stay warm.

During the 18 months that the prisoners were in the camp they received five showers. When the showers were given four or five men at a time had two to three minutes under the water tap. By the time half of the men had showers the hot water was gone and the remainder had to take showers in ice cold water.

There were never enough eating utensils for the men. They were issued a bowl and spoon. If the bowls were broken, they were never replaced. The utensils weren't that much of a problem because there wasn't that much to eat as Russell explained, "we didn't work, but we didn't get much to eat. As high as 17 men had to share a loaf of bread. Of course the Germans didn't have anything to eat either so it was difficult to provide for us. They made rutabaga soup, dehydrated cabbage, and sometimes we got half

A Point of Interest

TIN CANS

Prisoners in Nazi prison camps used the tin cans from the Red Cross parcels they received to make spoons, knives, cups, bowls, and trays for eating. They also used the tin cans for repairing beds or to repair holes in the barracks to keep out the cold or patch barracks roofs.

rotten potatoes. The soup and cabbage often had bugs and worms in it. We did get a few Red Cross parcels and some clothing, but for the most part food was very scarce. They would line us up and when we got the Red Cross parcels they would take a bayonet and punch holes in the cans so that you had to eat every thing right then. They did that so we couldn't store the food for an escape.

The prisoners spent much of each day waiting on time. One of the things that gave hope and raised morale for the prisoners during these times was mail. Each prisoner was allowed to write and receive mail. Russell wrote to his family and let them know he was a prisoner of war and insured them he was okay. He also wrote to his girlfriend, Imogene.

The prisoners also used their creative abilities. Prisoners painted pictures made from anything they could get their hands on. Some of the paintings were on paper and some were painted on the walls. They even made up their own Christmas cards during the second Christmas in the camp.

Christmas passed and day by day the prisoners endured the hardships as prisoners of war. Then in April 1945, Russell and the other prisoners who dreamed of the day the war would end begin to realize that their dream was about to become a reality. The Russian front was moving closer. The guns could be heard at night. They got closer and closer each day and then one morning the prisoners were called into formation. The Nazis told them, "we are leaving the camp."

THE MARCH
April 8, 1945-April 26, 1945

On April 8, 1945, 4,000 of the prisoners began a 18-day march. The march covered 281 miles and ended at Braunau, Austria. The marching column was divided into eight groups of 500 men with an American leader in charge of each group, guarded by about 20 Nazis guards and two German Police dogs. They averaged 20 kilometers each day and at night they stayed in barns, open fields, and along side of the road regardless of the weather conditions. Russell recalls his memory of the march. "They moved us out of the camp on April 8, 1945 because the Russians were moving in. We walked 281 miles in 18 days. We went through a little town called Braunau, Austria which is Hitler's birthplace. During the march we saw hundreds of Jews marching the opposite way we were going. If they fell out of line, the Germans just shot them like cattle. I saw them shoot several of them. The Americans didn't drop out. We had groups of five hundred and if someone got in trouble everyone else stepped in and helped. We had American planes coming over dropping leaflets telling us who they were and to stay together not to try to escape because they were going to get to us. They put us in groups of five hundred about twenty minutes apart and we walked from daylight till dark. We just stayed on the side of the road or in a field at night. We went across some mountains and we were higher than the clouds at one time during the march. We reached Braunau after 18 days and we couldn't move any further because we were sandwiched between the Americans to our front and the Russians who was coming up to our rear. The Germans took us into a nearby woods and left us."

Kriegsgefangenenlager

Postkarte

90

Miss Imogene Harris

Gebührenfrei!

Absender:

Vor- und Zuname: S/Sgt. Russell L. Hulsey

[Ge]fangenennummer: 100467

[La]ger-Bezeichnung: M.-Stammlager Luft 3

[Deut]schland (Germany)

043

[C]ENSOR

Empfangsort: East St Louis

Straße: 430 Mildred Avenue RR-1

Land: Illinois U.S.A

Landesteil (Provinz usw.)

Front of postcard from Russell to Imogene while in Stalag 17B, dated Dec. 12, 1943.

Kriegsgefangenenlager

Datum: Dec-12-1943

Dear Imie-

Am feeling fine and am in as good a condition as the last time you saw me. Can only write 2 letters and 4 cards a month so you won't get much mail from me. I can recieve as many as are sent to me. My address is on this card. Think of you all the time.

Love
Russell

Back of postcard from Russell to Imogene while in Stalag 17B, dated Dec. 12, 1943.

Dec. 15 1943

Dear Imogene—

Hope this letter makes you feel a little better. As I guess you are pretty blue at the present time. Am feeling fine and am looking forward to the day I will be home. Is pretty cold around here and we have had snow on the ground for quite sometime. After what I have went through all ready, I guess I will live through this also. You always said I was lucky and I guess I am. I sure would like to ~~have finnished my missions~~, but it was not for me to do, I guess. We were shot down Dec. 1, so I never got to recieve any Xmas boxes at all. Last year I never got any, so it will be nothing new. Honey I can write 2 letters and 4 cards a month, so one is for you and the other for mother. We can recieve all we want, only it takes about 5 months to get them, so write plenty. The boys mother who sent the purses to you, has a son and he is with me. I thought I was going to let my hair grow, but they changed my mind here as they cut it very short. Write soon, say hello to your mother & Dad.

Love
Bobbie

Letter to Imogene from Russell while at Stalag 17B, dated Dec. 15, 1943.

Dear Imogene -   Dec-25-43

Honey, As I can't be with you this xmas, Am writing you this letter And thinking of you And of the day when we will spend Another xmas to-gether. Our xmas was very white, As we had plenty of snow on the ground. We also had church services xmas eve at midnight. Most of the barracks have xmas trees And the fellows made all the decoration's out of soap. About the only the we don't have on them is lights And xmas packages. The camp I am in is made up of American Airmen only. Most of the fellows feel lucky to be here, so every one does his best, to things As Nice As possiable. I had mother buy your xmas present, so I hope you like it. she wrote me what she got, but As I couldn't see it, I don't know much what it looks like. I hope you got word, that I was O.K before xmas As I know everyone would feel much better. Don't have Any more space so write A Nice long letter. Love Russell

Letter to Imogene from Russell while at Stalag 17B, dated Dec. 25, 1943.

Kriegsgefangenenpost

Postkarte

SO

An

Miss Imogene Harris

Gebührenfrei!

Absender:

Vor- und Zuname: Sgt. Russell Hulsey.

Gefangenennummer: 100467

Lager-Bezeichnung:

11043 M.-Stammlager Luft 3

Deutschland (Allemagne)

CENSOR

Empfangsort: 430 Mildred Avenue - R.R. 1

Straße: East St. Louis - Illinois

Land: U.S. America

Landesteil (Provinz usw.

Front of postcard from Russell to Imogene while in Stalag 17B, dated Feb. 16, 1944.

Kriegsgefangenenlager, Datum: Feb. 16, 1944.

Dear Imogene As we received only one letter form this month to write Am sending you a card. Skip. Am feeling fine and thinking of you most of the time. Is plenty cold here and has been snowing for three days. Honey hope I have a letter from you when you receive this. Love Bob.

Back of postcard from Russell to Imogene while in Stalag 17B, dated Feb. 16, 1944.

Kriegsgefangenenpost

Postkarte

An

Miss Imogene Harris

Gebührenfrei!

Absender:

Vor- und Zuname: S/Sgt. Russell Hulsey.

Gefangenennummer: 100467

Lager-Bezeichnung: Stalag 17B

Deutschland (Allemagne)

Empfangsort: 106 Nelson Ave. R.R. 1

Straße: East St. Louis - Illinois

Land: U.S. America

Landesteil (Provinz usw.)

U.S. CENSOR 11035

Front of postcard from Russell to Imogene while in Stalag 17B, dated Feb. 15, 1945.

Kriegsgefangenenlager

Datum: Feb. 15-45

Dear Imogene — Some mail came into camp yesterday but I didnt get any. Am looking fore some, with pictures of you. When this bunch of fellows get home, things are sure to happen. As we have been out of circulation for about two years. In bed at 9:00 P.M. every night. Take care of yourself, and hope it won't be long. Love Bobbie.

Back of postcard from Russell to Imogene while in Stalag 17B, dated Feb. 15, 1945.

A painting of the Tupelo Lass done by a POW in Stalag 17B.

Front of Christmas card sent to Imogene from Russell.

Inside of Christmas card sent to Imogene from Russell.

CAMP 17-B

Towns we went through on our walk across Austria

Kaems
Renburg
Senftenburg
Ludendorf
  One day 4/8/45 (out)
Himberg
Muhldorf
  One day 4/9/45 (out)
Freistitz
Heiligeblut
Streitrofesen
Poggstall
  Two nights 4/10-11/45 (barn)
Laimbach
Hirschenau
Isperdorf
  One day 4/12/45 (factory)
Sarmingsten
St. Nikola
Stamden
Grein
Klamm
  Two nights 4/13-14/45 (barn)
Baumgartenburg
Mitterkirchen
Naarn
  One day 4/15/45 (barn)
Au
Mouthousen
St. Georgen
Luftenberg
Steyregg
  Two days 4/16-17/45 (barn)
Plesching
Linz
  (Crossed Danube River here
  north to south)

Wilhecing
  One day 4/18/45 (out)
Alkoven
Fraham
Horsling
  One day 4/19/45 (barn)
St. Thomas
Prambachkirchen
Michaelbach
Potting
Neumarkt
Widldorf
Kallham
  Two nights 4/20-21/45 (barn)
Erlach
Riedau
Taiskirchen
Anolrichsfust
Aurolzmunster
  One day 4/22/45 (out)
Eitzing
Mairing
Ranzing
Surten
Freiling
Seinberg
Durtcham
Altheim
  Two nights 4/23-24/45 (barn)
St. Peter
Haselbach
Braunau
Randshafen
Inn - Salzuch Blick (out) 4/25/45
  Wood, war was over; rain,
  cold as hell

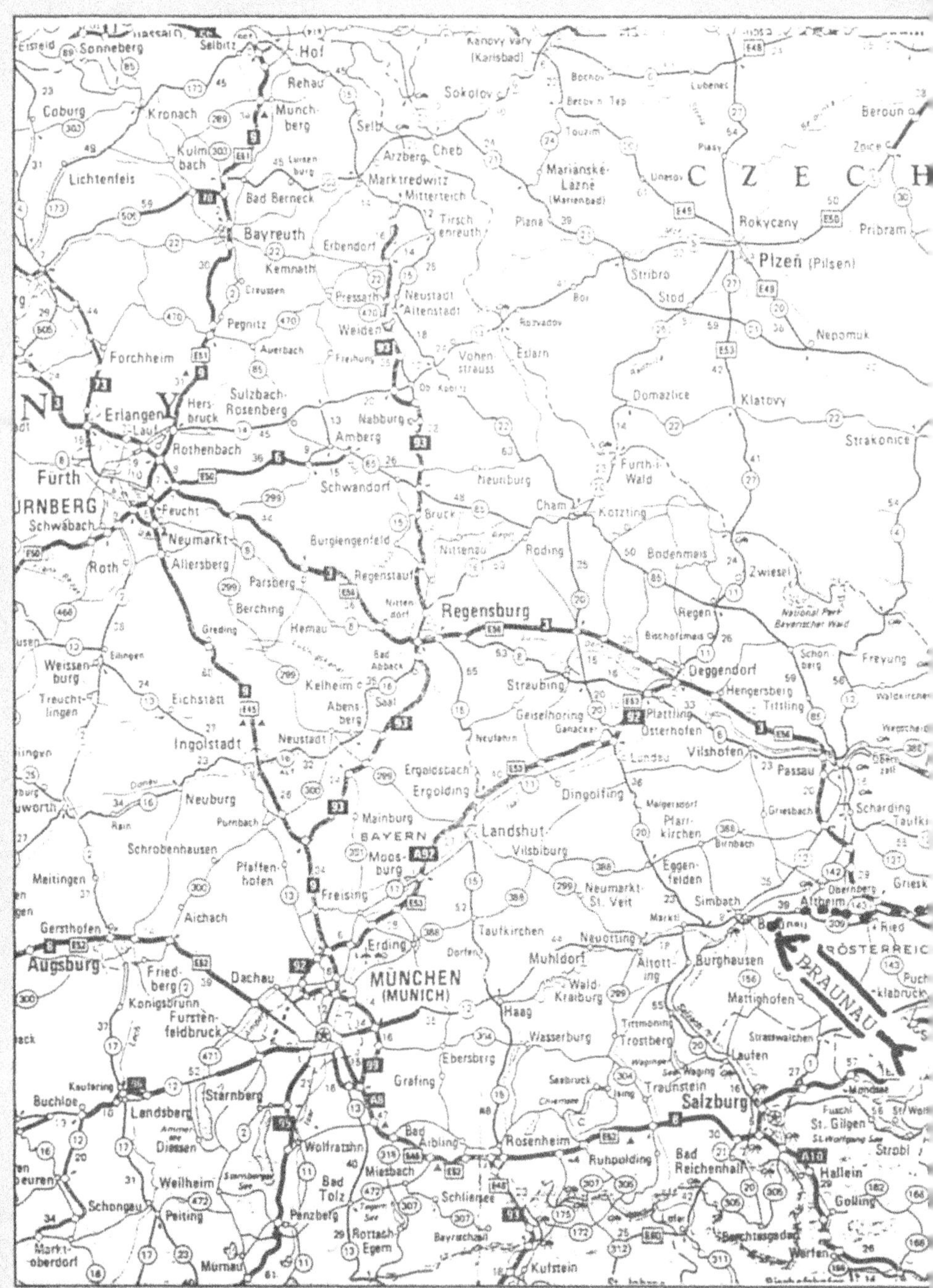

Sonneberg
Selbitz
Hof
Karlovy Vary
(Karlsbad)
Coburg
Kronach
Rehau
Münch-
berg
Sokolov
Beroun
Kulm
bach
Selb
Lichtenfels
Arzberg
Cheb
Marianské
Lazne
(Marienbad)
C Z E C H
Marktredwitz
Mitterteich
Bad Berneck
Tirsch
enreuth
Planá
Rokycany
Pribram
Bayreuth
Erbendorf
Plzeň (Pilsen)
Kemnath
Stribro
Stod
Pressath
Neustadt
Altenstadt
Pegnitz
Weiden
Nepomuk
Auerbach
Vohen-
strauss
Eslarn
Forchheim
Sulzbach-
Rosenberg
Domazlice
Klatovy
Erlangen
Hers-
bruck
Nabburg
Amberg
Rothenbach
Strakonice
Furth
Schwandorf
Neunburg
Furth-i-
Wald
NÜRNBERG
Feucht
Bruck
Cham
Kotzting
Schwabach
Neumarkt
Burglengenfeld
Roding
Bodenmais
Zwiesel
Roth
Allersberg
Nittenau
Regenstauf
Parsberg
Regensburg
Regen
Berching
Hemau
Greding
Weissen-
burg
Kelheim
Deggendorf
Freyung
Eichstätt
Abens-
berg
Straubing
Hengersberg
Treucht-
lingen
Geiselhöring
Plattling
Osterhofen
Ingolstadt
Neustadt
Vilshofen
Ergoldsbach
Ergolding
Passau
Neuburg
Dingolfing
Landau
Rain
Schrobenhausen
Mainburg
BAYERN
Landshut
Pfarr-
kirchen
Schärding
Pfaffen-
hofen
Moos-
burg
Vilsbiburg
Eggen-
felden
Meitingen
Neumarkt-
St. Veit
Freising
Simbach
Aichach
Gersthofen
Taufkirchen
Erding
Neuötting
Burghausen
Ried
ÖSTERREICH
Augsburg
Fried-
berg
Dachau
MÜNCHEN
(MUNICH)
Mühldorf
Altött-
ing
Königsbrunn
Fürsten-
feldbruck
Wald-
kraiburg
Mattighofen
BRAUNAU
Haag
Wasserburg
Trostberg
Laufen
Ebersberg
Grafing
Traunstein
Buchloe
Landsberg
Starnberg
Salzburg
St. Gilgen
Diessen
Wolfratshn
Bad
Aibling
Rosenheim
Ruhpolding
Bad
Reichenhall
Strobl
Hallein
Weilheim
Bad
Tölz
Miesbach
Schliersee
Golling
Schongau
Peiting
Penzberg
Rottach-
Egern
Berchtesgaden
Markt-
oberdorf
Murnau
Kufstein
Werfen

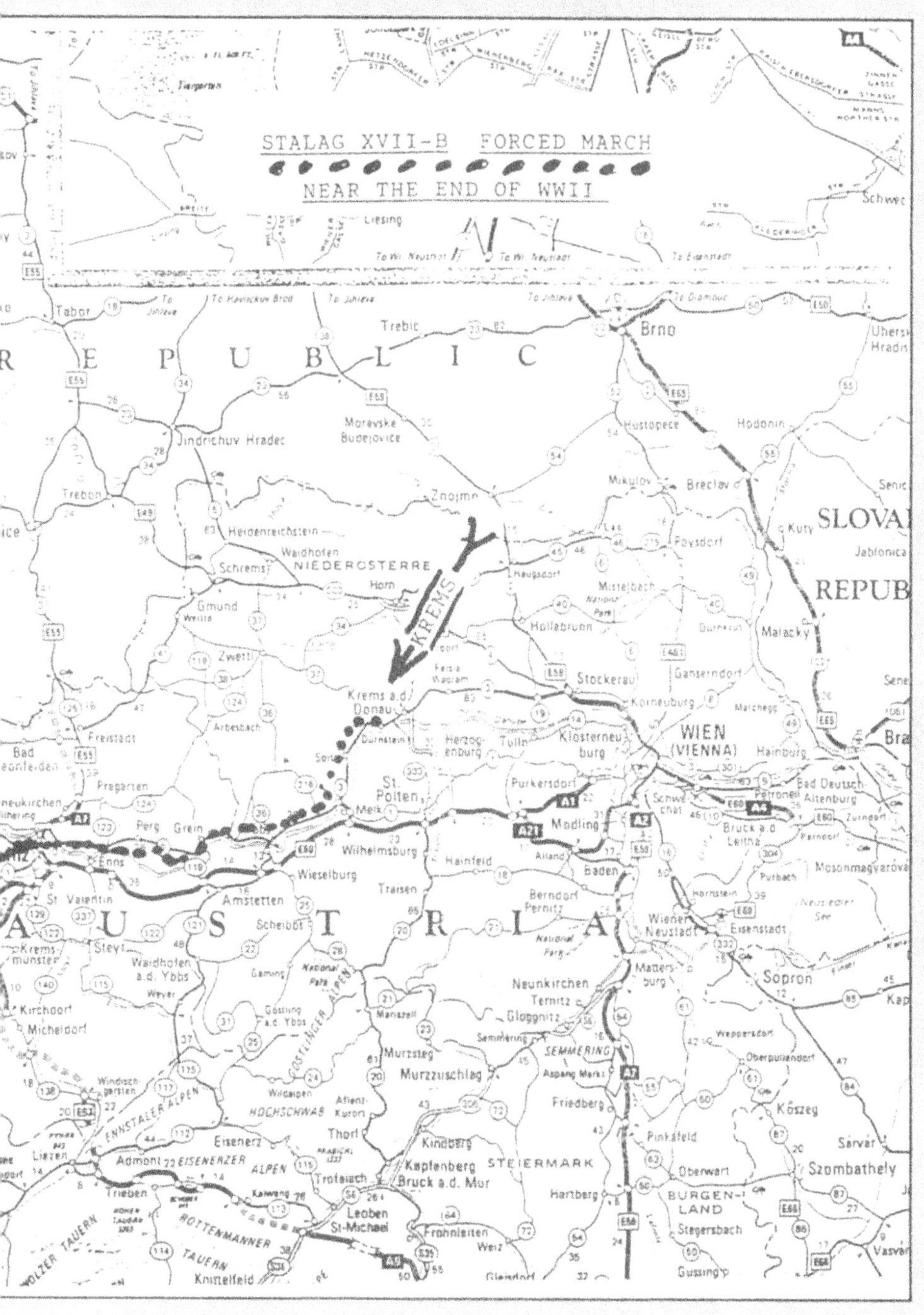
STALAG XVII-B FORCED MARCH
NEAR THE END OF WWII
REPUBLIC
AUSTRIA
KREMS
Krems a.d. Donau
WIEN (VIENNA)
SLOVAK REPUB
NIEDEROSTERRE
STEIERMARK
BURGEN-LAND

LIBERATION
May 4, 1945

"Across the river Patton's 3rd Army was set up," Russell said. "We were sandwiched between them and the Russians so the Germans put us in some big woods and left. The next day on May 4th, Patton's units came across the river and found us. When Patton's Army came through, they were moving fast. They dropped guns and ammunition and told us to take care of ourselves. They left a couple of officers in charge of us and left. We were there for about three days and we roamed the countryside looking for food. Three days later they moved us to an air field and put us on C-47's. We flew to Camp Lucky Strike in France. We were there for about three weeks. We were given medical treatment, new clothes, and plenty of food. I was fortunate compared to many of the prisoners because I only suffered from some frost bite to my hands and my weight loses was about ten pounds. Many of the prisoners never made it back and many of those that did suffered much worse than I did."

HOMEWARD BOUND
June 12, 1945

On June 12th Russell boarded the USS *All American* bound from the United States. Russell set foot on American soil a couple of weeks later and headed for home on a thirty-day leave. After reminiscing with his family he headed to his girlfriend, Imogene's house. They spent much of his leave together and then after thirty days he received a letter from the Army. " I was to report to Florida for recuperation. The letter stated that if you are going to bring your wife you better let us know. I wasn't even married. I told Imogene that if we were going to get married we better do it now because the government was going to pay our way to Florida. We got married and went to Florida. A few weeks later I went to Chicago and was discharged on September 24, 1945."

EPILOGUE

In June 1946 Russell took up Heating and Air Conditioning as a trade and worked in a family business until he retired. Russell has never forgotten his experiences in the war and made an effort to find out about the other men he served with. He found out that only four

Russell Hulsey on the march.

A reunion with his crew. Hulsey is in the bottom row on the left.

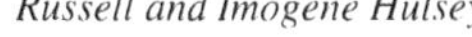

Russell and Imogene Hulsey

Julie, their daughter.

of the ten man crew in the plane he was shot down in made it out of the plane alive. He never knew any of the crew because it was the first and only time he flew with them.

Hartis Hamilton engineer on the plane, one of the four survivors, contacted Russell in 1984 and they met in Dalton, Georgia 41 years after they were released from Stalag 17B.

Russell did make contact with some of the crew of the Topelo Lass. Russell is a member of the American Ex-Prisoners of War and has attended several of the POW reunions.

Russell now enjoys retirement and golf with his wife Imogene in Calvert City, Kentucky. They have a daughter Julie Alles who lives in Texas and works as a Clinical Dietician. Russell said that a couple of years back he got a letter from the government ordering all ex-POWs to report to the VA hospital for medical screening. "I went to the VA and set with these POWs most of the day. I had a little trouble with my frost bite after the war and although I had perfect teeth when I went into the service they were taken out at an early age after the war because of the vitamin deficiency caused by a poor diet in prison camp. But as I sat there I looked around and there were men there with arms and legs missing. Others couldn't walk. I thought about it and I got up and left. Those fellows needed help not me. I felt good and I was healthy. I felt lucky that I had both legs and arms and my health. I have never been back since."

CHAPTER EIGHT

TECHNICAL SERGEANT GORDON K. BUTTS
U.S. ARMY AIR FORCE

451ST BOMB GROUP (H), 725 BOMB SQUADRON
15TH AIR FORCE
SHOT DOWN OVER MOSTAR , YUGOSLAVIA
DURING AN AIR RAID

PRISONER OF WAR
APRIL 17, 1944-MAY 7, 1945
STALAG LUFT III, STALAG VIIA, AND STALAG XIIID

PRE-WAR ENLISTMENT
October 29, 1940

Gordon enlisted in the U.S. Army at South Bend, Indiana, on October 29, 1940. He was sent to Fort Benjamin Harrison in Indianapolis for his basic training. After his arrival by bus he received his first Army meal-a bologna sandwich and a glass of milk.

From Fort Benjamin Harrison Gordon was sent to Maxwell Field in Montgomery, Alabama where he was introduced to what would become common place-six man G.I. tents constructed with wooden floors and frames. He was also introduced to southern style cooking. One morning at the mess hall Gordon covered his cream of wheat with sugar and milk. It was grits.

For the couple of years Gordon was sent to a couple of bases in the south before embarking on a troop ship for several ports in Central America; debarking at Rio Hata, Panama to build a technical school to train aircraft mechanics; and working as a clerk in the inspection division at Albrook Field near Panama. The major turning point in Gordon's career came in October 1942. He heard about an Air Cadet examination that was being given and anyone could take the exam. He was told that he couldn't pass the exam by a buddy because it was designed for college graduates. Gordon was a high school graduate with six months business college. He took the exam anyway and passed by one point. Then after passing a battery of physical and physiological exams, Gordon was on his way.

Gordon Butts

Gordon begin flight training at Harlington, Texas and washed out of flight school. It was the low point in his career. He was given a choice of Officer training in the infantry or Corporal in the Army Air Corps. He chose the Air Corps.

Gordon trained for the next couple of months before being assigned as a Gunner on a B-24H and heading for Europe.

HEADING FOR EUROPE
December 1943

As of December 1943, the group started overseas. The ground support personnel of the group went by ship. Each individual aircraft was to fly by itself to Africa.

Gordon's group flew to West Palm Beach, Florida, stayed a couple of days then to Puerto Rico. They landed on the south side of the island. The next day to Georgetown, British, Guyana. Then to Belem, Brazil. The next day to Natal, Brazil and all Gordon could remember is flying over jungle. They stayed three days in Natal and Gordon spent most of the time checking over the aircraft, mainly the four engines. He took off all of the engine covering to check and make sure nothing on the engine was rubbing against another part. As Gordon said, "I don't swim so I didn't want to ditch in the ocean."

The group took off in the early morning, over the Atlantic headed for Dakar, Senegal, West Africa. The navigator gave the crew an ETA (estimated time of arrival) and he was within ten minutes of the time. They were ten minutes early, and glad to have made it over 2,000 miles of ocean. They had an extra rubber gasoline tank in the bomb bay, but had not had to use it.

When the airplane landed Gordon heard the loudest noise, he thought something was wrong with the plane. It was the metal lattice runway they were landing on. These are metal pieces hooked together to provide a hard landing surface. Each piece was about twenty inches wide, about ten inches long, and hooked together. They were used in most of the fields the crews were to land on.

They stayed at Dakar until all our group was in Africa. One day while the crew was training word came down that one of the planes had lost some engines. The plane was about five miles out from the base. "We watched for them and could see the plane coming in on one engine and a prayer. The runway was cleared and it came straight in. We never thought the plane would make it, but it did," Gordon explained.

Most planes had a picture and a name painted on their plane and the crew that brought the plane in on one engine was an exception, but not for long. They named their plane Three Feathers. There was a whiskey named Feathers so the crew painted a young lady holding a bottle of Three Feather Whiskey.

One other time while we were at Dakar Gordon found out that the President was in the area. "President Roosevelt returned from a meeting with Churchill and boarded a cruiser in the bay," Gordon recalled. "I had binoculars and watched the President being put aboard. I didn't know he couldn't walk and was in a wheel chair. I didn't know because the news reporters always took photographs of him from the waist up and they never wrote about him being in a wheel chair."

As time went on Gordon's crew decided that they wanted a picture and name painted on their plane. "We met and chipped in $10.00 to get the job done," Gordon said. "After several days of discussion among the crew the pilot finally decided we had discussed it enough and named the plane "Honeychile."

From Dakar Gordon's crew flew to Marrekeck, Morocco. On the flight they had to fly over the Atlas mountains. While flying over the mountains our carburetors on a couple of the engines iced up, Gordon said. " We turned the deicers on and the engines quit missing just about the time that the wings started icing up. When the wings ice up they loose their lift. The deicers on the wings which are located on the leading edge of the wing and move in and out to crack the ice were turned on, and the ice was removed. It was a busy time for a while.

On the early part of the trip we flew over the Sahara desert at about 100 feet, looking for a B-24 that was missing, but we saw nothing.

Years later the plane was found and the story was in Life magazine. They found no bodies, and the plane was in good shape. It had landed but not crashed. Another mystery."

Gordon's stayed in Marrekeck until an air field was captured in Italy and they could fly in. Marrekeck had a population of over 100,000 and was a tourist vacation spot before the war. There were major hotels and many gambling casinos. " I saw my first French Foreign Legion soldier there. When they would enter a cafe, they would stop and salute, then enter. This is in case there were any officers in the cafe."

There was actually two parts to the city, an European section and a native section, called

Gordon Butts

B24H

Medina. The native section was off limits to G.I.'s. "Being the good G.I. that I was I wanted to see why we shouldn't go in," Gordon explained. "The native section was a walled city with large gates. The gates were closed at sundown. I went to the native part of the city and stayed to long. I was caught in the city when the gates closed. What to do? How to get out? I saw a cart pulled by a load with hay. Most of the moors could speak some English. I stopped the cart and asked what he would charge to take me through that gate. We settled on $10.00 and he hid me under the hay. He took me through the gate, without trouble. The best $10.00 I ever spent because I didn't want to loose my stripes."

In December of 1943, Gordon's crew moved to Italy. They landed in Gioia Del Colle, Italy. They had tents, open mess hall, tent showers, and a wash bench with cold water faucets. It is cold in December in southern Italy.

THE FIRST MISSION

"Our landing strip was again steel grading linked together, Gordon said. "We flew a few practice missions and was ready for combat. Our first mission was on the coast of Fier Radar station on the coast of Albania. We were excited and a little afraid. We circled a few times trying to find the target. We had no flak and saw no fighters.

Now we were combat wise, we thought. No fighters, no flak. Why? We missed the target by five miles and had dropped the bombs in an open field. Mission one was over and only 49 to go."

A SERIES OF MISSION

The next missions were at radar stations, a marshalling yard (railroad yard), then a mission to support troops. The Honeychile ran into flak but had very little trouble with fighters.

Mission number six was to support the ground troops at Anzio. They had a lot of flak and a few fights, but they were not hit.

Mission number 10 they bombed a marshalling yard and then a Messerschme Aircraft Factory in Regensburg, Germany. This was the toughest mission for the Honeychile up to that time. Gordon's group led the mission with 40 aircraft. They flew without fighter escort. They were attacked almost continuously by the Luftwaffe ME 109s aircraft (German Air Force) and there was intense anti-aircraft flak from batteries near the target. During the aerial battle their gunners shot down 16 ME 109 fighters, but we lost six B-24s.

"I shot down my first ME 109 on this mission, Gordon said. "The 109 tried to fly up and through the formation. I was manning the top turret. When I saw him he was about 150 feet from us. I could see the pilot in the cockpit clearly. I fired. Other planes in the formation saw the plane explode. You had to have verification from other crews to claim a kill.

We were so beat up after landing at Foggia Air Field in Italy, about 50 miles from our home base, that night I couldn't sleep. All I could think about was the pilot's mother. War is hell.

I had another experience with 109s later. We were on a mission and there must have been a squadron of them.

In your turret you have two 50 caliber machine guns. In order to charge (load) the round (cartridge) into the barrel, you pull a cable with a handle on it, then let go. This puts a round into the chamber and you are ready to fire. My left gun jammed and would not fire. The right gun quite firing. I tried to charge the right gun and the cable broke. Each gun has a sear pin. It is a safety device, the end of the pin sticks out about three quarters of an inch. I reached down and got a spent casing and stuck it into the sear pin and pulled. I was able to charge the gun so it would fire, I continued to fire one gun for the rest of the fight.

When we landed I tried with one hand then with both hands to charge the gun. No luck. This shows what you can do when your adrenaline kicks in during a fight."

The next mission the Honeychile hit Foulon Sub Pens in France, then a marshalling yards in Northern Italy. The yards were in a valley and the sky was black with flak bursts. They received some flak damage, but nothing serious.

Our next mission on March 15, 1944, they bombed the city of Cassino, Italy. The German ground troops used an old church ruins to dig in. Only part of the group dropped bombs because of cloud cover. This turned out to be a difficult time for Gordon. " We were over the target and I was told to go to the back of the plane, the bombardier had opened the bomb bay doors, Gordon said. "Since I had to walk through on the cat-walk I closed them. I just got in the back of the plane and the bombardier let the bombs go. The bomb bay doors were closed and the bombs took the doors with them. I still had to walk back to the cockpit and my turret. All I could see was open space and the earth below.

As flight engineer you never wore a parachute, just a chest parachute harness. If you wore a parachute you could not get around inside the plane. I hung on to the bomb racks and walked the catwalk back to the cockpit.

I thought I would catch hell when I got back to base, but no one said a word, about the doors. The next morning we had a set of new bomb-bay doors and was ready to go again."

From March 7th to April 4th of 1944 Gordon's crew flew a mission about everyday, unless they were grounded for repairs. They bombed a variety of targets in Rumania, Austria, Italy, Budapest, and Hungary.

The morning of April 5th, 1944 they found the target was to be Ploesti Oil Refineries in Rumania. This was the most heavily defended target in Europe. This refinery provided the greatest source of fuel for the German war machine in Europe. The Germans were determined to protect it, and keep it operating. The last raid on Ploesti had been in August 1943. The mission was to go in at ground level. General Brereton, the commander of the mission told the airplane crews that they expected 50% lose of planes. The crews were not happy.

The loses were not quite that high. Of the 177 planes that went in, 54 failed to return. "The Air Corps felt if only 5% of the planes were lost on a raid, it was a successful mission. But, the catch was that you had to fly 50 missions to go home. Fifty missions at the 5% rate is 250%, what chance did you have to come home," Gordon surmised.

"What actually happened in my squadron, the 725th, was that one full crew of ten, and four other crew members from other crews got home. Of course what keeps you going was that it wouldn't happen to you, just the other crew," Gordon explained.

"We lived in a tent city separate from the ground maintenance and other personnel. In April every crew around us had been shot down. We were a jittery crew.

In crews shot down some of the men who bailed out were captured and became POW's. If it was going to happen, we hoped this is what we could do.

The next mission was going to be the big one, Ploesti.

We all knew what had happened on the last raid. This was the Groups 24th mission and our 20th. Only 30 more to go. The only thing that we felt good about was we were going in at 20,000 feet and we felt we had a chance. This was a major effort, several groups from Italy would be bombing the target from different directions. We expected a rough fight and it happened, many ME 109 fighters on the way to the target and more fighters as we came off the target. While over the target, major flak. We received flak damage, but it could have been worse. I shot down two ME 109s on the raid, one going into the target and one coming off the target.

We lost four B-24s over the target. For this raid we received a second Presidential Citation. One of the things most people don't realize is the ways the Germans air force attempted to shoot us down. We were bombed while in flight from German aircraft dropping bombs into our formation from above. This was not very effective. We did fear having ME 109s around with rockets trying to hit us. I only saw two bombers hit with rockets, they exploded on contact. The Germans would flip in back of our formation, out of range of our 50 caliber machine guns and lob rockets into the formation. This was scary, but again not very effective."

After the Ploesti raid the Honeychile made raids on marshalling yards in Yugoslavia and Rumania, and an airdrome in Hungary and Rumania. It was a busy time in April 1944, four targets in four days.

MISSION 23-THE LAST BOMBING RAID-*GORDON'S STORY*
April 17, 1944

"Dawn April 17, 1944 another raid. This one was to bomb the Belgrade Zemun Airdrone, Yugoslavia. This was the Groups 29th mission and our 23rd.

It was a normal mission to the target, some ME 109s on the way and some flak over the target. We were hit by flak. We had bombed at 20,000 feet and was letting down to about 14,000 feet over the Carot Mountains in Yugoslavia. The mountains were about 10,000 feet. Intelligence had not told us that the Germans had 88mm anti-aircraft guns on top of the mountains. We were literary flying down their barrels. They opened up and we were hit. The first hit was on number three engine. This is the engine that has the main hydraulic pump which enabled the pilot to control the aircraft.

At this time I am standing between the pilot and co-pilot. I saw the pilot go through the regular check of all controls, no response, the bail out order was given.

I had my chest parachute harness on. I hooked on my chute, checked to make sure the two snaps were secure and got down off the main flight deck to the deck below. That was the last thing I remember. I think the airplane exploded and blew me clear. The next thing I remember was floating in space with my parachute open. What made the chute open, I do not know. Maybe the explosion, opened it. I may have had a reaction, for we often practiced bailing out, after a mission, when we landed and stopped rolling. It will always be a mystery why more didn't get out. There were four men in the tail of the plane, the tail gunner and back turret gunner bailed out. The last thing the two men remembered was the two waist gunners fighting over who would open the bottom escape hatch. I often wondered why they didn't go out the open waist windows. Of the ten men in the plane three bailed out, two of the four in the tail and one, myself in the cockpit end of the plane, the rest went down with the plane."

THE CAPTURE

"On the way down I was machine gunned by a ME 109. The silk of my parachute was full of holes, but I was not hit. I landed in a tree my feet were about three feet off the ground. A German soldier came over and pointed a Lugar at me and said in broken English, "for you the war is over," I agreed.

S/Sgt Sanborn and S/Sgt Tittle was on the ground when I landed. We were all taken to a jail in Mostar.

The flying crews never wore a gun or knife into combat. Why wear a gun, if you bailed out were you going to fight the whole German army with one gun? If you had a gun and landed among civilians who had shotguns, pitchforks, and clubs were you going to win the fight with them?

It was better to be taken to a POW camp, where they had a guard you and feed you. In POW camp your chances of survival was better."

THE JOURNEY TO PRISON CAMP

"We were in jail in Mostar for three days. We were interrogated. We had been trained only to give name, rank, and serial number. That's what we did. After I was interrogated, the German Captain told me more about our group then I knew. He knew our group by our crashed plane.

When our group had flown about 15 missions one of the tail gunners bailed out over Germany. We were told later that he was interrogating downed airmen at a interrogation center in Germany. I would say he was a spy.

We were taken to Sarajevo. There was a large German garrison there. In the jail we would watch the new German recruiter learning to march and do the goose-step.

Our jail was okay, food fair, but we could bathe and wash our clothes. We had only our flying suite. At Sarajevo the three of us were put on a train with three guards.

On the train we went through many towns and cities we had bombed. A grand tour at German expense.

The next stop was Budapest, Romania, we stayed there a couple of days, then to Vienna, Austria.

Here we were held in the mess hall at an Army camp. We slept on the floor. We had been given two German Army blankets, one to sleep on and one to use for cover."

STALAG LUFT III

"Our next stop was at our POW camp at Sagan, called Stalag Luft III. The camp was situated in a pine-wooded area out of the city of Sagan. It is in Northern Germany near the old Polish border. There were four compounds of American Army Air Corps prisoners, three of Royal Air Force officers (British, Australian and Canadians). Each compound had 15 buildings. Ten were barrack or blocks each housing 80 to 110 men. The high rank officers had 2 to 4 men per room, normally there were 10 men to a room. The blocks were one-story much like the barracks we had in the U.S. Beds were double decker bunks.

When we entered camp the prisoners lined up on each side of the road looking for some from their old outfit. I found no one from our group.

We were taken to the supply building and issued new clothing. The clothing had been sent here from Switzerland where supplies had been stockpiled. The uniforms were enlisted men's uniforms, even though this was an officers camp. They issued us one overcoat, one pair of gloves, one pair of wool trousers, one belt, one G.I. blanket, two German blankets, one blouse, two pairs of winter underwear, one sweater, one cap, two wool shirts, two pair of socks, one pair of high top shoes, and four handkerchiefs.

I was assigned to the enlisted men's room in a block. All the men were Sergeants, for all air crews were Sergeants. They were expected to take care of the block-clean the bathroom, which only had sinks and stools, clean the hall. We were dog robbers, officers could not work. This was the reason that the camp had to have some enlisted men.

I was lucky to end up in an officers camp. In the enlisted men's Stalags the housing conditions were bad, and the food poor, not that ours was good.

I was assigned to a room of ten men. Two men did the cooking, two men did the dishes, and cleaned the room. Each man was responsible for his bunk and surrounding area. Sometimes duties were rotated. The rest of the men were assigned to block duty.

After I had been there a few days I was assigned to the compound's first aid room. I had had some Red Cross courses in first aid, before joining the Army.

There were no doctors in the compound. In the center compound was a hospital manned by German, American, and British doctors for seven compounds of men.

If we couldn't take care of a patient we sent him to the compound hospitals.

There were three of us manning the first aid station.

All new prisoners coming into camp, if they were wounded or ill were examined by us, if necessary were sent to the hospital.

The Germans furnished very few medical supplies, what supplies we had we received from the Red Cross. In 1944 we received some much needed Sulfur powder. We mixed this with iodine and this made a paste that we could put on wounds and cuts. It worked.

Sanitation was poor. Bathing facilities were extremely limited. In theory the camp shower house could provide each man with a three minute shower weekly. If we got one a month, we were lucky and it was with cold water.

I was housed in the west compound. Our American Senior Officer was Colonel Darr H. Alkire. His duties were to run the camp and he was our contact with the German Luftwaffe, who ran the camp. Again we were lucky to be held by the Luftwaffe rather than the German Army.

The camp was operated like a military base. We had appel (roll call) twice a day, morning and evening. In some cases there were special appels, example, would be when they wanted to search the blocks. There were guards stationed in guard towers armed with rifles and machine pistols. The guards were fourth class troops, either peasants or too old for combat duty, young men convalescing after long tours of duty or wounds received at the front.

While we were in the camp they had no contact with POWs.

In addition to uniformed sentries, soldiers in fatigues hid under the blocks, listening to conversation in the block, looking for tunnels and making themselves generally obnoxious.

Occasionally the Gestapo descended upon the camp for a long, thorough search. The only way we could get back at the guard was passive resistance at appel. Instead of falling in, we milled about, smoked, failed to stand at attention, and made it impossible for the Germans to take a count. This was not done often, for they would bring in German regular soldiers with rifles and machine guns.

There was an escape committee operating in the compound, and men did escape. Any individual that wanted to try an escape had to have permission of the committee.

The Germans did supply some hot food about 1,900 calories a day. While this was insufficient, what they provided was mainly brown bread and potatoes, and meat three days a week, vegetables twice a week, and watered down soup on alternate days. To supplement the German food we received Red Cross parcels, most were American, some British, and Canadian. This was food like we had at home and greatly appreciated. These parcels came out of Switzerland and were delivered to the compounds in G.I. Army trucks. These trucks were driven by Swiss civilians. We were to get one half parcel a week, but as the war went on the normal rations were a half parcel every other week. Some of the items in the parcels were Spam, corned beef, salmon, cheese, dried nuts, crackers, Klim (powdered milk), orange powder, liver paste, and a chocolate bar. The chocolate bar became money, if we wanted to trade with anyone for something, the question would be, how many bars of chocolate for the items.

Each compound had an athletic field and volleyball court. POWs built a theater, the materials furnished by the Germans. Musical instruments were brought in by the Red Cross from Switzerland, and several orchestra and choral groups were formed.

There were bridge tournaments and a school was sit up to teach a wide range of cultural and technical subjects, named by the former teachers.

The Germans and the officers that ran the camp wanted to keep the men busy for morale purposes. Busy people don't cause trouble and try to escape.

The sports equipment was provided by the Red Cross. There was a library which is where I spent my time. I was lucky because I had a job at the first aid room. I worked six mornings a week and part of the afternoon at the aid room. Some of the times I would take patients to the central hospital which gave me a change of pace.

Most of the prisoners were interested in keeping in shape. The most common exercise was to walk the compound circle. Starting from the outside guard fence, there were two more barbed wire fences, which had coils of barbed wire between them. Then inside of the prison was a space of about ten feet wide which was a no mans land. If you were in this area you could be shot. Just in front of the no-mans land was the walking path which was about five feet wide. Wide enough room that three people could walk abreast. There was always people walking, except at night. At night we were locked in our block. If you went out you could be shot.

Walking the path was interesting for often you would find fresh dirt on the path. This was a clue that some one was digging a tunnel. The tunnel diggers would carry the dirt from the tunnel in their pockets or small bags and dump it on the path. We would never ask about the dirt.

Of course the Germans also watched the new dirt on the path. So the hunt would be on to find the tunnel. This was the camp from which the British soldiers attempted escapes in the film, "The Wooden Horse." They were caught as they came out of the tunnels and shot. The ashes were in urns in the Central Hospital, as a reminder not to try to escape.

In April when I arrived some of the blocks were planting gardens, with seeds sent from home. Fresh vegetables would be a welcome addition to our diet.

We did receive some mail from home and packages could be sent every three months. I received one package while at Sagan. My mother said she had sent three.

These packages were often pilfered. We could send one letter a month, my mother did receive some letters. All mail was read and censored by the Germans.

The International Red Cross made all the extras we received possible. To a man we gave thanks to them.

One day when we were walking the circle a twin engine German fighter flew low over the camp.

It made a lot of noise, but no propellers. What made it fly? Then we realized this was the knew jet fighter the ME 262 the Germans were building. They started production too late, to make a difference, thank God.

There was always a friendly discussion between the fighter pilot and the bomber crews. It went like this, fighter pilot, "You bomber crews shot me down. I was looking for protection for I was having trouble, when I got in formation, you shot me down. The answer, "You pointed your nose at us, we had a standard rule, if any plane pointed his nose at us, we shot it down." This friendly, I hope, discussion could go on for days.

The reason for this discussion was that the Germans had rebuilt some of the American fighters from the planes that crashed. They would come up and get into the formation and fly with us. Then all of a sudden they would kick their rudder and start firing.

Whenever a fighter came into our formation we always trained our guns on them.

Another reason I was glad I was in an officers camp Stalag Luft III was because the guards were from the Luftwaffe, the German Air Force.

We knew from the radio broadcasts mainly the BBC (The British Broadcasting Corporation) picked up on our canary. (The canary was an illegal radio in the American compound.) In a room next to the first aid station was a map of Europe. The map would show where the Germans battle lines were. On the same map the Americans would put on a line where BBC and the Allies said the battle lines were. The Germans would come each day and look. They knew there was a radio in camp. They searched for it. Sometimes I think they didn't want to find it. The canary was never a topic of conversation in camp. It was understood you did not ask questions. Just enjoy the map. The lines were (put up with yarn and pins) that the Russian Army was not to far away.

The big question was would the Germans move us out before the Russians captured us."

THE MARCH TO NURNBERG
January 25, 1945

"We received the answer at 2100 hours (9 P.M.) on January 25, 1945. All compounds received German orders to move out on foot within 30 minutes. Colonel Alkire had told us two weeks before to be ready to move on short notice.

In knotted trousers used as packs and make shift sleds we packed clothing and all the food we had. The Germans issued one Red Cross food parcel per man. We abandoned books, letters, camp records and took our overcoat and blankets and left.

By 2400 hours (12 midnight) all men, except some that couldn't walk, marched out into bitter cold and snow in a column of threes. Destination unknown.

Our guards from the camp went with us, they carried rifles and machine pistols.

We marched all night, fifty minutes of marching and ten minutes break, every hour.

German rations consisted only of black bread and margarine obtained from horse drawn wagon-the camp kitchen.

Each compound marched separately, each could tell a different story.

We slept in unheated barns, empty factories, and on the ground. After the first 24 hours we were given a thirty hour rest for recuperation. I am not sure where we were at this time or where we were going. The guards from the camp were old men and had trouble keeping up.

The G.I.s told the guards that they would carry there rifles for them, they knew we couldn't escape in this kind of weather.

At the first river we came to, we dumped all the rifles in the water. We had some very angry guards. We had a good laugh."

THE FORTY AND EIGHTS

"Later we were loaded on unmarked 40-8 freight boxcars, 50 men to a car. They locked the doors.

We were in the boxcars for three days and nights with no water and no sanitation. One corner of the car was reserved for a toilet area. But who could go in a corner with 49 men looking on.

Our greatest fear was that our train would be strafed by our P-51s or P-47s. At that time of the war the fighter planes were sent out to shoot up trains or any other target of opportunity.

The 40 by 8 means forty men or eight horses. Fifty men in the car made it crowded. There were four boxcars of prisoners. An the third afternoon we de-trained at Nurnberg.

After being in the boxcars for three days we needed to relieve ourselves. Having no place to go, the guards kept us together in the marshalling yard, we looked at each other took down our trousers, squatted down and let nature take its course. What a relief. Some picture, 200 prisoners getting relief."

STALAG XIIID

"Conditions at Stalag XIIID at Nurnberg were deplorable. The barracks had recently been inhabited by Italian POWs who left them filthy.

There was no room to exercise, no supplies, nothing to eat out of, and practically nothing to eat, for no Red Cross parcels where available upon arrival.

The German rations were 300 grams of bread, 250 grams of potatoes, some dehydrated vegetables and margarine. A few days after our arrival, Red Cross parcels started to arrive by truck.

Toilet facilities during the day was satisfactory, the only night latrine was a can in each sleeping room. Many of the men now had diarrhea, the can had insufficient capacity, so the floors was soiled very soon.

The barracks were not heated. The morale of the prisoners dropped to its lowest ebb."

THE MARCH TO STALAG VIIA
April 3, 1945

"At 1700 hours (5 p.m) on April 3, 1945 we were told to evacuate the Nurnberg camp and march to Stalag VIIA at Mooseberg.

The Germans agreed that the Americans would take over the march. The Americans were responsible for preserving order, and that we would march only 20 kilometers a day, about 12 miles.

On April 4, 1945, each POW received one food parcel and we started south. While we were marching through a marshalling yard near a highway, some P-47s dive bombed the yard. Two Americans and one British soldier were killed, three others were wounded.

The next day a large replica of the American Air Corps insignia was placed on the road with an arrow pointing in the direction of the march. This ended the bombing of the column.

Many of the men were very weak and had difficulty keeping up. This is when we started the flying wedge. The weaker prisoners were aloud to drift back through the column as we marched.

Then a group of the stronger prisoners would take the weaker prisoners to the front of the column, during the ten minute break. This was repeated every hour.

Colonel Darr H. Alkire was now in charge of the column, he was an excellent officer and was responsible for many of the improved conditions during the march.

The German guards were aware of how close the American Army was, and this helped.

Even though the Americans were in charge the guards went with us. On the third day of this march diphtheria broke out among the men in the column. Since I was the medic, I did what I could, which wasn't much.

A couple of days later I had the disease. I could hardly talk, my throat was beginning to close.

We were camping near a barn. I climbed up into the hayloft. I thought I had had it and the hay was a soft place to lay. Later in the day I heard Colonel Alkire asking were Sergeant Butts was at. They told him in the hay loft. He shouted for me and wanted to know what the problem was. I crawled out to the opening and tried to answer. He couldn't understand me, but realized I had caught the diphtheria. He said to lie down and stay there.

We had been getting Red Cross parcels on a regular bases for we were near The Switzerland border. Since Colonel Alkire was in charge he told the German Captain that we needed more Red Cross parcels, now. The German Captain called Switzerland to send a truck load of parcels right away.

The truck was there the next morning. They unloaded the parcels and told the driver to take me to the column ahead of us, for there was a doctor with the column.

This was what the driver did. When we got to the column, they found the doctor . I had worked with him at Segan, he had been stationed at the Central hospital. He asked what was wrong and when I tried to answer he knew.

In his medical bag he had some diphtheria serum and he gave me 1,000 units and told the driver to take me to Stalag VIIA. It was down the road about 20 miles."

STALAG VIIA

"When I arrived at Mooseburg they put me in a barracks. This was where they dumped all the sick prisoners. There were no German or American doctors, no medical personnel at all. I don't remember much for the next few days. I had gone into a coma and just laid in my bunk. An Army Corporal took care of me as I came out of the coma. He fed me, gave me water, and looked after me. I don't even know his name.

The sanitation was unbelievable. When I was able to move I would crawl to the latrine. The latrine had a sloping floor, with holes in the floor. The holes took care of the human waste. There were no stools or sinks. When finished, I would crawl back to my bunk. I was very weak.

This nameless Corporal saved my life. This was near the end of April. General Patton's 3rd Army and the Germans fought a battle with the camp in the middle. Bullets flew like mad in the barracks. A British soldier in the bunk next to me was killed in his bunk, by a

Stalag VIIA shortly after the prisoners were liberated.

stray bullet. It hit him in his mouth and came out the back of his head. We had talked and he told me he didn't want to go home. He had been captured in North Africa."

LIBERATION
May 7, 1945

"From the barracks we were taken to an evacuation field hospital for seven days. The rule was that after seven days you had to move up to another hospital. I was the last one to leave from my old barracks. At that time I was paralyzed in both legs, arms, and throat and I was down to about 105 pounds.

From the evaluation hospital we were flown out on a C-47 hospital plane. We were on the ramp waiting to get on the runway. The first plane took off, the second plane taxied to the runway, it tried to take off and crashed at the end of the runway. We taxied to the runway and took off through the smoke of the crashed plane. I was afraid, for the last time I was in a plane, it went down.

They took me to a hospital in Reims, France where I stayed for a few weeks. I begin to get stronger.

The next stop was Camp Atturbury near Franklin, Indiana, at Wakeman General Hospital. At Wakeman I was given a lot of vitamins and all the food I could eat.

I was a RAMP (Released Allied Military Personnel) and treated very nicely. When I started to walk and could move around I went down to the recreation room to watch a ping-pong match.

I noticed a young lady, also in hospital clothing. I asked if the chair next to her was taken and she said no. This was the beginning of a life long experience. She was a WAC recovering from a appendix operation. We were married in the hospital chapel on September 7, 1945."

EPILOGUE

Gordon and his wife just celebrated their 50th wedding anniversary. They have three children: Karen Lee, Thomas Brooke, and Donna Lynn, and six grandchildren: Thomas Brooke, Christopher Brian, James Michael, Steven Todd, Jamie Nicole, and Caitlin Brooke.

Gordon was discharged with 100% disability, which was reduced to 60% and is now at 10%. He then earned a BS, MS, and EdD from Southern Illinois University, where he taught for 33 years. Gordon and his wife now enjoy their retirement and grandchildren.

CHAPTER NINE

SERGEANT WILLIAM C. BRADLEY
U.S. ARMY

88TH DIVISION COMPANY F 351 INFANTRY DIVISION
CAPTURED WHEN HIS OUTPOST WAS
OVER RUN IN ITALY

PRISONER OF WAR
JULY 27, 1944-MAY 1, 1945
STALAG IIIA AND IIIB

THE BEGINNING
March 1943

In March 1943, the war was going full blast. Bill was raising heck with his parents to let him join the Army because he already had two brothers in the war. Bill was a basketball player in his senior year of high school. His team was expected to win the state championship that year, but those hopes were diminished when they lost the regional tournament. The next day Bill quit school and joined the service. Over the next couple of days he went through a physical and was issued uniforms. Then Bill and a trainload of new recruits headed for Fort Jackson, South Carolina. They were forming a new unit-the 106th Division. Over the next several weeks Bill trained, was promoted to Corporal and put in charge of a 12 man squad, and won several boxing matches in golden gloves.

A few weeks into training his unit was sent to Tennessee for maneuvers. His squad was dropped off in the Tennessee hills and told to find their way back to the unit. They were to use their compass for direction. Bill and his squad were goofing off when Bill realized he had lost his billfold. He had to have it back because it had several photos of girls that he felt he couldn't do without. The whole squad back tracked looking for the billfold, but they didn't find it. It was the next morning when they found the road leading back to their unit and hitched a ride from a chow truck. They hid behind the pots and pans until they got to their unit. Their Lieutenant was mad. Bill claimed that they had been lost and showed the Lieutenant a broken compass. Bill had busted it against a rock to use the broken compass as an excuse for being late. That night Bill was in a foxhole thinking that he had fooled the Lieutenant. It was raining hard. The Lieutenant came by about midnight and ordered Bill and his squad to report to the medics tent. The whole squad was given shots for overseas duty and the next day they were on a train for the east coast. "They say we all have a double some place, Bill said. "We were on the train headed for Baltimore, Maryland. A kid was sitting across from me and I looked at him, then he would look at me. It was like looking in a mirror. We just set there looking at each other. Finally, I broke the ice and asked him where he was from. He had a southern draw. His name was Charles Burrow from Greensboro, North Carolina. He must have gotten killed because I wrote to him several times after the war and never got a letter from him. I just took it for granted that his folks if they got the letters just didn't bother to answer because he was dead. But, I never saw him after we left the train.

After four days we arrived at Camp Meade and stayed over night. The next day we moved to New York City and boarded the aircraft carrier USS *Carr*. It was real nice going over. We had the run of the ship-movies every night. We zig zagged all the way over because we had a German U-boat following us. There were destroyers with us and the ship tracked the U-boat on radar. But, it never did attack.

Several days later we arrived at Casablanca. Meanwhile, my brother Buzz was in Italy. He had already went through the African campaign. The Stars and Stripes came out with several stories that there was going to be a big boxing match in Algiers. I read the story and it read that Bradley was going to be pulled back from Italy to fight in this tournament. I went to my Lieutenant and got on my knees and begged him to let me go to Algiers for a couple of days to watch my brother fight. We were only about a hundred and fifty miles from the place. He wouldn't let me. He said that we were on strict orders to be here. He expected us to be called at any time to back up the 35th division at Anzio. Buzz made it to the championship rounds. He lost to a Frenchman by the judges split decision.

Buzz went back to the front lines at Anzio. We just knew that's where we would end up because that's where the big push was going on. We were going to movies every night. Had a bunch of trouble with some Lieutenants one night. I had been drinking two or three beers, the first alcohol I had ever drank, and myself and a bunch of drunk Sergeants set right in the middle of some officers at the movies. We were carrying on and this Colonel came down and told this Lieutenant to help us back to our tents. We said that's okay we can make it. We didn't have any rank insignias on and they never did know we were enlisted men.

We used to listen to Berlin Sally almost every night. She played music for us and we liked to listen to it. She kept us up on the war and of course she always let us know that we were listening. Then early one morning we loaded aboard British ships. It was about one in the morning. We knew that we would dock where the fighting had finished and move in land from there. We sailed out into the middle of the Mediterranean and sailed around for a couple of hours and landed right back where we had taken off. We thought what in the hell is going on. They loaded us and told us to go back to our tents, but not to unpack. We went back to our tents and the next morning Berlin Sally was on the radio, "Well boys, we had a party for you last night and you didn't show up. We sure missed you. Did you have a nice ride?" She asked.

Finally, we did ship out and landed in Naples. We were there about two weeks. I got to box one more time. An English Lieutenant and I had a match. I beat him."

Bill Bradley

BILL BRADLEY ACE SCRAPPER, 10TH DIVISION

One of Flashiest Lightweights at Fort Jackson, Sports Moc-mentator Says

A picture of the fighting dough-boys team that carried the Lions of the 10th Division to the championship at Fort Jackson, has reached here, along with a comment on the fighting ability of Bill Bradley, son of Harry Bradley of Murphysboro. Bradley is pictured in the end position, second row of the team of ten fighters.

The Fort Jackson boxing team is admittedly one of the strongest in the country.

Sports comment on Bradley said:

"On of the flashiest lightweights seen at Fort Jack- n is Private First Class William Bradley, hard-hitter from Murphysboro, Ill. Bradley's specialty is dazzling his opponent with flurries of head and body blows, and then applying the K. O. tough. He's a good looking kid with an over-abundance of courage.

"Bill se s up ny course they want, wheth r it a toe-to-to slugging, or the sc ntific hunt and peck stuff. Of t fights prior to his induction, Br ley won 48 and lost 10. Twen- seven of those victories were knockouts. He has fought only five times as a soldier, marking up four wins and one loss (They still talk about that one). Three of his wins were by knockouts."

Bill and his brother, Buzz (Buzz was slightly wounded in battle in Sicily according to reports) got their baptism of fire in the fighting ring down at St. Andrew's gym here. Their training there, it happens, have taken them a long wa for popularity in the armed se

Sgt. Clarence Bradley, Professional Featherweight Champ of Fifth Army

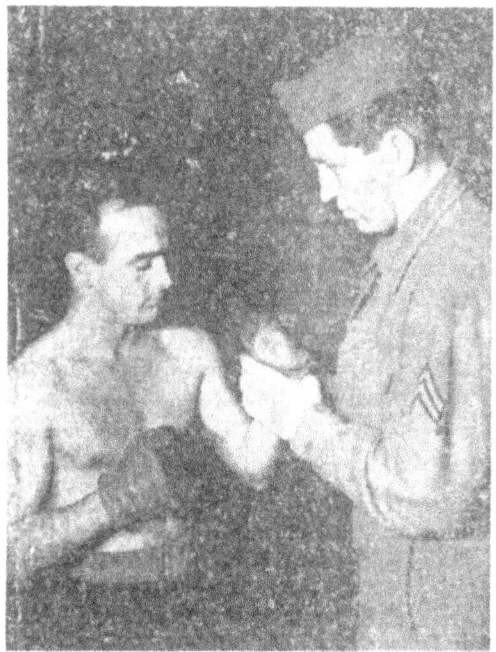

WITH THE FIFTH ARMY, ITALY—Having just won the professional featherweight boxing championship of the Fifth Army, Sergeant Clarence Bradley, left, gets his gloves dusted off while training in Italy for the coming campaign in Africa, where he will contend against champions of all other major army and naval units in this region for the North African theatre of operations title. His manager, on the right, is Dan McKenzie, son of Mr. and Mrs. John McKenzie, 224 Fifth street, south, Virginia, Minn., who first undertook Bradley's management while they were stationed in Ireland. McKenzie has held numerous Golden Gloves championships, including those of Minnesota and the Iron Range. Bradley's parents are Mr. and Mrs. Harry Bradley, 440 North Ninth street, Murphysboro. Fighter and manager alike serve with the 34th Infantry Division.

Young Bradley got his ring legs down in St. Andrew's gym along with a number of likely local boys who went in for the Golden Gloves bouts.

He and his brother, Bill, starred in local boxing for two years or more and Bill knocked the boys around in the training camps in the Carolinas while Clarence made headway for the Fifth Army Crown.

MILFORD & BILL BRADLEY
Hello boys: Happy New Years
And good luck
AUNT MAMIE

Sgt. CLARENCE 'Buzz' BRADLEY
Hello Buzz. Whereever you are
a Merry Christmas and Happy New
Year. God bless you and good luck
AUNT MARIE

"Buzz" Bradley "was robbed," in the conventional ring parlance, of the championship of the Inter-Allied Boxing tournament held in Africa.

* * *

That is the substance of a letter received this morning by The Column, from Dan J. McKenzie, who signs himself as the trainer of the Fifth Army team, for which "Buzz" fought.

* * *

"Buzz" himself hasn't let out a single squawk, and he probably won't. He isn't that kind of boy. But apparently, judging from the trainer's letter, it really was a very close battle, and "Buzz" probably had the edge, because he was the choice of the referee, no other than Jack Sharkey, although the judges picked his opponent as winner.

* * *

But here is the letter of the trainer:

Italy, March 17

"Dear Editor:

" One of the most unpopular decisions handed out in the recent North African held Inter-Allied Boxing Championship tournament, was that which was given against Clarence "Buzz" Bradley, a Murphysboro, Illinois fighter. Bradley, according to the fistic experts at the ringside, took all three rounds in his bout with Rene Pons, French ex-amateur champion.

* * *

"The boys fighting in the professional featherweight class, engaged in a thriller that had the service and civilian fans in a continuous uproar from the opening bell to the finish of the last round. The American scrapper scored with ease, punches with both hands to the head, which had his French opponent rocking from the effects. Pons used a good left hook to the body as his main weapon, but good as they were, the plan to slow Bradley was over-ruled by the latter's fine fight.

*

"As Pons would score with his left Bradley retaliated with two, and three lefts and rights to the head. In close quarters, both men fought like tigers, and much to the delight of the crowd who soundly applauded the fighters efforts. It went on like this for the three rounds, and Bradley easily looked the winner, though he had to fight hard for what would have been his decision. Then came the announcement that Pons was the winner. The gallery, after cheering a bang-up scrap, reversed their voice and soundly booed the verdict of the judges, while the Referee (Jack Sharkey) saw Bradley ahead by a good score. This was one of the many undeserved verdicts throughout the tournament.

Dan J. McKenzie,
5th Army Team Trainer"

WILLIAM C. BRADLEY PROMINENT IN BOXING FOR FORT JACKSON

"Buzz", the Other Fighting Bradley, Comes Through African Campaign to Swim in Sea

Private First Class William C. Bradley, formerly of South Twentieth Street in this city, is now a member of the 106th "Lion" Division boxing team at Fort Jackson, S. C.

Bradley contributed many points which enabled his division to win the recent Fort Jackson boxing tournament, according to the public relations office there.

He fights in the light heavyweight class, and of 5 bouts, he has engaged in during his army career, Bradley has won four and lost one. Of the four bouts won, he has registered three knockouts.

The 106th, being a young division, has not fought any off-post contests, but with the spirit and talent shown by it during the Fort Jackson tournament, challenges are due to fall in line.

"Buzz" Bradley, the other fighting son of Harry Bradley, is having a little fun somewhere in Africa, according to a recent letter. "Buzz" asked his folks at home not to worry about him, said he had come through the African campaign without a scratch, and that presently he was doing a little swimming in the sea and some boxing—"just resting," he said.

And as that was the first word from "Buzz" in quite some time it was cause for jubilation at home.

HEADING NORTH TOWARD GERMANY

"The next day we moved out," Bill said. "They walked us through the mountains and through these tunnels that go all the way out into the valleys. There we got out first taste of seeing dead people. Just as we came out of this big tunnel there were bodies every place. Burned, bloody men, women, and children. They hadn't had a chance to clean them up. They were turning black and we got the first smell of death. We finally realized we could get killed.

We walked all night and finally got close to the front lines. We got our first taste of gun fire when a German plane spotted us and started firing at us. We got off the road and hid in the trees. Then we got hit by 88 millimeters. After the shooting stopped we gathered up on the road and they broke us up into companies. I was assigned to company F. I met the 1st Sergeant and he had us to dig fox holes.

The war at that time was being fought by small groups. Thirteen or fourteen man squads were going out on patrol, setting up ambushes, and then returning to the lines. I was on a patrol everyday for three months. I had a lot of them at night, to. I had rather go on a ambush patrol than anything because we could lay down and rest and hope we didn't see anything.

At this time, my brother Buzz and I were writing letters to each other. I was getting mine. I found out that his unit was right beside ours, the 34th, the 88th, and the 45th. We were in he middle of them. I asked my Lieutenant if I could get a couple of days off to go find my brother. I told him that he was in the 34th Artillery Division and they were behind us so he had to be behind the lines. I didn't know it, but he wasn't behind the lines. He was a front observer for them and was out in a jeep ahead of the company spotting targets. Buzz had gotten one of my letters and asked the Colonel to find me and bring me up to him. The day that he talked to my commanding officer was the day I was captured. He told the colonel that I was missing in action. At he same time, Buzz had run over a land mine and was seriously wounded. When the Colonel returned, he got word to Buzz that I was on a mission and they couldn't turn me loose. It wasn't until after the war that we learned what had actually took place.

I did find out that he had been wounded though, while I was on patrol. We were out on patrols all the time and I actually begin to feel safer on the patrols than I did with the company because the Germans were always throwing artillery on us. The Germans and the Americans were about a mile apart and in between was no mans land. The Lieutenant called me up for a midnight patrol. We were going out to set up an ambush. I got the boys lined up for the patrol.

Each time we were going out on an ambush I would take the B.A.R. (Browning Automatic Rifle) from this little Mexican and give him my M-1. I would position myself in the middle of the squad with strict orders not to fire until the B.A.R. opened up. We were laying out there that night and we could hear someone coming through the hedgerows-coming from the German direction. It was pitch black. We were in some bushes behind a little hill and they kept coming. Then we could hear them talking. We couldn't understand what they were saying, but they were talking in English. Then when they got almost to us and I was ready to jump up and open up with the B.A.R. About that time one of them fell over a wire and let out with "Son of a Bitch." That's what saved them because I jumped up and they yelled hold your fire. It was a squad from the 34th division. They had gotten lost. Buzz was from the 34th and I asked them if they ever heard of him. They said they had and that they had got to see him box a couple of times. When they found out that he was my brother they told me that he had been wounded, but they didn't tell me he was wounded badly. I just took it that he would be all right.

The farmers in the area built beautiful country homes out of stone. We were sent out one day to one of these homes. It was a big two-story home with a full basement, big yard around it. The people that owned it had fled to the mountains until the war bypassed them. But, orders were to set up an observation post. We were to report back everything we saw. We were about a half mile from the Germans and we could see them moving around. That night I guess the Germans saw us because we laid out around that house till almost day light. I passed the word that we were going back into the house. I told them that I would go in first and if everything was all right I would wave them in. There was a basement door that I went through into the basement and there was nothing in there. I waved at the guys and they came out of there positions one at a time and nothing happened. All thirteen of us got in that house and all hell broke loose from both sides. The Americans and the Germans were both firing artillery at us. The 88 rounds were just bouncing off of the stone walls of the house. So we went into the basement to wait out the bombardment from both sides. While we were down there I found a vat of wine and we started drinking it. Three hours later the bombing stopped and needless to say we were feeling pretty good. I told the guys we better get out of there and back to the company. We had to let them know that we couldn't stay there with both sides bombing us,. We started out on the opposite side of the house. On the side facing the 34th division. We were on this hillside overlooking another little valley and we saw a big German tank getting down beside one little building and two Germans were setting down beside one little building and two Germans were setting out on the ground eating and drinking and we saw two other Germans shining on the tank. And out I front of them I could see seven or eight Americans crawling on the ground in the leaves sneaking up on them. I said lets just stay here and watch this. We had a ring side seat. So we laid down about three hundred yards from them and watched. Pretty soon the Americans got up on them. They threw a hand grenade in the tank and blew it up. The Germans come running up this path right at us. So we just laid there and when they were close I jumped up and told them to put their hands up. They didn't understand English, but they dropped their rifles and put their hands up. I told the guys we will take these guys back to the company. We did and when we got back the Lieutenant said that we couldn't keep them with us because they didn't speak English. He told me to have someone to take them back to the rear so they could be interrogated by an interpreter. This little Mexican that we had jumped up and said, "I will take them." He wasn't gone fifteen minutes and we heard that B.A.R. fire a couple of burst. He took them over the hill and shot them. Everybody knew what he had done, but he claimed that they had been taken off his hands. There was nothing else said about it, but he didn't escort anymore prisoners."

THE STAND OFF AND CAPTURE
July 25, 1944 -July 27, 1944

Bill told the Lieutenant that he spotted a house that was right down on the river 40 yards from German lines. There was about a four foot ditch with a sandy bottom between the unit and the house and on the opposite side between the house and the Germans there was a levy built right up to the windows. Bill thought that it would be a great place for a outpost. "He told me to set it up," Bill explained.

"About seven that night we headed out. We came up the ditch toward the house and just before we got there we could see a light flickering. So we stopped and waited until about five in the morning. We still didn't know who was there, but I told my guys we were going to by-pass and go on. So we did and we were able to get in the house without being spotted. The next morning we found out that the flickering was coming from an old Italian and his wife who had been camping in the area. They walked right by the house and over to the German side. A couple of days later the old man spotted our telephone lines and told the Germans we were in the house. We had been watching them and reporting back everything we had seen. As a matter of fact the Lieutenant had sent an artist out to draw a sketch of the river and the area where the Germans were located. They checked the ditch bottom to see if it would hold a tank.

After a couple of days we were running low on C-rations and I sent one of my men back to the company to get re-supplies. I told him that I would walk back a little ways because about half way back to the company area there was a orchard. It had some fruit and I was going to pick some for the squad. I didn't even take my cartridge belt with me-just my rifle and helmet. I walked back with him to the orchard and I told him what to tell the lieutenant and he went on his way. That's the last time I saw him. I found out later that after we had been captured he was assigned as the new squad leader and was killed.

I started back to the house. There was a shed a little ways from the house. It was stored full of furniture. I had a kid there as a guard and when I came by he was leading back against the building in a chair. He was asleep. When I came by him, I didn't bother to wake him up. About fifteen yards to the right of the shed was a hay stack and I had two men there. The Mexican was watching the Germans and reporting back to the company by phone. I was carrying a helmet full of apples; I had a rifle slung over my shoulder; and I wasn't paying attention to anything as I walked toward the house. I got about even with the shed and all hell broke loose. There were four Germans standing by that hay stack and they opened up with burp guns. I just froze. I didn't even see'um till the first shots. I threw them apples up and run around the shed. They never touched me, but I could feel the air of the bullets. God was with me because they were only ten yards from me when they opened up and I was right in the open.

After I got around the shed I could peak out and see that there was a squad of Germans behind the other four. They all hit the ground. They weren't sure when they approached if we were there, but they had followed the phone line up to where they saw us. They had cut the line. I yelled at one of the men in the house and told them to get on the phone to call the company and let them know that we were being hit. He yelled back and said that he had been trying.

One of the boys in the house opened up with the B.A.R. on the Germans and they scattered. They were on the opposite side of the shed so I decided to go through the shed and to the corner of the shed to get a few shots. When I got there they really opened up on me. I went back the other way and got to the other corner of the shed. I decided that I was going to make a dash for the house. I told the B.A.R. to cover me. I looked around the corner and not ten feet from me was a German Captain and a regular soldier setting up a machine gun. I didn't have any grenades with me or I could have got them, but it was a good thing I didn't because the German Captain kept me from getting killed. I took off for the house and I heard someone right on my heels. I turned and looked over my shoulder and it was this German Captain chasing me and firing his pistol. When he shot I would zig then zag. His gunner was firing a trail on both side of us all the way to the house. He couldn't shoot me because he was afraid he was going to hit the Captain. When I got to the door, I turned and fired a couple shots at him from the hip. He fired and hit me in the shoulder before he turned and started running. If I had been aiming I would have hit him, but I was excited and firing from the hip. I made it into the house and he made it back to the machine gun.

I looked around and other than the guy on the B.A.R. nobody was around. I went down into the basement and eleven guys were on the floor asleep. I kicked them and told them to get up. I just knew the Germans were going to blow the place.

We got up to the windows and was firing at the Germans. While this was going on we would hear someone run up this cobble stone walk I front of the house. They would stop, and then pretty soon they would run back. What was happening was this German Captain was running up the sidewalk and throwing a grenade in the basement. Why he didn't throw one up on the floor where we were is beyond me, but I told one of the guys that I would fix him. I had thirteen grenades piled under this window and I wanted until I heard him run up and stop and then I would drop a grenade out the window. Nothing would happen. I did that thirteen times and not once did the grenades go off. The Germans had such a concentration of fire on the house that I knew we were all going to be killed if we didn't surrender. We signaled to them that we wanted to surrender and were instructed to come out of the house one at a time. When I came out the door I figured out what had happened to the thirteen grenades. There was a cistern right below the window where I was dropping the grenades. I had dropped everyone of them in the cistern and they were below ground when they were going off.

I found out after the war that our company had just been assigned a new Captain. He was the reason we had been captured. When the 1st Sergeant found out that we were being hit he wanted to take a platoon and get us out. The new Captain said, "No." He called the battalion commander and told him that the outpost had been wiped out and he was going to establish a new one. Two hours later we were still fighting.

Anyway, this German Captain came running up to me. There was a dead German laying there and he tried to get me to pick him up. I told him I couldn't because I was wounded. A couple of the other guys picked him up and the Germans took us across a creek into a small village where there were four or five houses. We stayed there for about five hours. They put us in a room right next to a room where all the of the German commanders would meet to make out here battle plans. The Germans hadn't checked me very well because I still had a grenade. We had been told that the Germans were not going to take any prisoners because they had heard our division wasn't taking any prisoners. I told one of the guys that if they were going to shoot us we were going to take some of them with us.

They came in and took one of the men into the room where all the commanders were at. They started questioning him. He didn't know anything so they asked him who was in charge. He told them Sergeant Bradley. They came into the room where we were and started asking for Sergeant Bradley. After they called my name several times I finally stood up. I still had the grenade under my shirt. When they took me into the room I stood at the end of the table and saluted them and they saluted back. I had already decided that if they started to shoot me I was going to drop the grenade in the middle of the table. They told me to sit down and I did. They started questioning me. He asked me about crossing a railroad that was near our company position. I told them that they knew we had or we would still be on the other side which would be where our company was located. I told them I didn't know because I hadn't seen them for a week. They kept it up for a while and then finally sent me back with the other guys.

They took our billfolds and mine had a lot of clippings in it about the boxing tournaments and pictures of my girlfriends. They kept them and sent them back to the rear echelon. I didn't know it at the time."

BILL BRADLEY IS REPORTED MISSING IN ACTION IN ITALY

Not Heard of Since July 27; Cpl. Bradley, Like Brother, a Real Sportsman

Cpl. William C. Bradley, younger brother of "Buzz" Bradley, recently wounded in action in Italy, has been reported missing in action since July 27, according to an official telegram to his mother, Mrs. Toleta Bradley, South 9th street, Murphysboro.

The message under date of August 17 read:—

"The Secretary of War desires me to express his deep regret that your son, Corporal William C. Bradley, has been reported missing in action since 27 July in Italy. If further details or other information is received you will be promptly notified.

"ULIO, the Adjutant General."

"Fighting Bill" Bradley they called him here and in the army camp ring games, when like his brother "Buzz" he stood up with the best of the boys of his class in the squared ring.

The Bradley boys came through the St. Andrew's Gym; in program four square and liked by everyone for their sportsmanship.

Harry Bradley, the father, and the mother are to cling to the hope that the "reported" missing in action message may later be changed to a happier conclusion.

BILL BRADLEY IN NAZI PRISON CAMP

Had Been Reported Missing Since July 27 In Action In France

Official word reached his relatives here Monday that William Bradley, one of the "fighting Bradleys" of the war camps who graduated from St. Andrew's gym prize ring, is in a German prison camp.

Bradley was reported missing since July 27 in action in Italy. His brother "Buzz" earlier was reported wounded in action and is now reported recuperating in a hospital.

Oct. 2, 1944

Dear Mrs. Bradley

On a shortwave broadcast from Germany there was a message for you from your son. Dear Mom. I am a prisoner of war in Germany ~~but~~ don't worry, contact local Red Cross about address and sending packages. Love Bill.

Not knowing if you heard this broadcast I took the liberty to forward the message to you.

Sincerely

Mrs. George L. Collins
42 Lexington Ave
Providence, R. I.

CPL. BILL BRADLEY IN OK MESSAGE TO RELATIVES

Provost Marshal General's Office and Three Civilians Tell of Broadcast From Germany

Mrs. Harry Bradley, mother of Cpl. Bill Bradley, some time ago reported missing in action, received this message October 3 from the Provost Marshal General in Washington, D. C.:

"Following enemy propaganda broadcast from Germany has been intercepted. Quote, I'm a prisoner of war in Germany. I am ok so don't worry. I'll write more soon. Tell all hello for me, especially Dottie Love Phil. Cpl. Phil Bradley. Unquote. Pending further confirmation this does not establish his status as a prisoner of war. Stop. Additional information received will be furnished. Stop.

Lerch Provost Marshall General

Cpl. Bradley's father here, reporting this message, said "Phil" as broadcast undoubtedly should have been Bill.

The father produced as confirmation of this a letter from Mrs. J. D. Howard of Raonoke, Va. to Cpl. Bradley's mother here. It said in part that she had just picked up a short-wave broadcast from Germany. There was a message from Cpl. Bill Bradley, 36740172. Mrs. Howard repeated the message as reported by Washington, except that she used the surname Bill instead of Phil.

"Mrs. Howard's letter clinches it," the father said today. The number she gave is Bill's number. I wouldn't take a hundred dollars for that letter."

The Bradleys also have received three postcards from persons who heard the broadcast. They are from Mrs. W. C. Dannemann, New York; Mrs. C. P. Skilton, Carbondale,

THE JOURNEY TO STALAG IIIB

July 1944

"They started marching us to the rear," Bill explained. "We stopped at this little town. There was German activity-tanks and troops moving everywhere. They threw us in a little town jail. They took one of the guys out to question him and he told them that I was in charge and they came and got me immediately. I went into these officers quarters and there was a big fat German officer setting there. He got real friendly, offered me coffee and cake. I took them because I was getting real hungry. Then he started asking about that railroad and location of the company. I told him I didn't know where they were at. He said, "I see you did a lot of fighting. How would you like to fight Max Schemeling?" (German Heavy Weight Champion of the World.) He said before I got a chance to answer, "You were in quiet a fight down at Fort Jackson." I thought how in the hell does he know that. Then it dawned on me. He had my billfold. I said, "how about I get Joe Lewis to fight Max?" He got a big laugh out of that. He told me he could have me shot. I told him I knew it, but there wasn't much I could do about it. He sent me back to the little jail. We had the best meal we would have that night. They brought us in some beef stew and gave us a loaf of black bread. I couldn't stand the smell. I took one bite out of it and threw it over in the corner of the cell. A German soldier told me I better save it because I would think it was cake in a couple of days. So we wrapped it up and kept it. The German guard was right because we didn't get any thing to eat for the four days.

THE FORTY AND EIGHTS

They took Bill and the other prisoners down to the train depot. There were prisoners of war setting all around the place. They were packed on the boxcars like cattle. There was no food and little water given to them for the next four days. They sat between each others legs and anyone having to relieve themselves did so in a helmet and passed it to the man next to the air vent. Four days later the weary POWs arrived at Stalag IIIB.

STALAG IIIB

Stalag IIIB was located near Furstenburg southeast of Berlin.

The camp consisted of four compounds separated by barbed wire fence. The Americans were located in one compound and housed in wooden barracks. The barracks housed about 80 to 100 prisoners in each house. The barracks had no heat. POWs were given one blanket to sleep with. The double wooden bunks had straw mattresses which were infested with fleas and lice. The windows were broken and the roofs leaked.

The food distributed by the Germans was inadequate. It consisted of potato soup, barley bread, and coffee. The POWs diet was supplemented with Red Cross parcels.

THE FIRST DAYS IN THE CAMP

"The first guy I saw was my old squad leader from Fort Jackson, John Hally," Bill recalled.. "I was lucky I knew him because we shared everything in the prison camp. His folks would sent a parcel every week and we lived on it. What was his was mine and the same with me. The Germans usually took half of the goods, but they didn't his. On the other hand my folks sent a parcel every week and I never got a one of them. Between that and the parcels that the Red Cross sent we made it.

German guards would come in about once a week and shake us down. They would bring in these medal detectors and check the area. They found a few rusty nails, but that was about all. We had this interrupter by the name of Ralph Hill. He was from South Carolina. He was a Staff Sergeant and had been a prisoner for three years. Everyday they would come in and take a few of us from each barrack outside to cut wood. Most of us didn't have much clothing and it was really getting cold. We came back in off of this work detail one day and we had received field jackets from the Red Cross. This German SS officer came into the camp and was going to take all of these jackets back to the front for the German soldiers. They were really hurting. It was the coldest winter they had since 1888. It got 30 or 40 below zero. This building we were in didn't have any heat. The wind would blow through it like it didn't have walls. We would huddle together and sleep in the straw trying to keep from freezing to death. There was 98 of us in the building so we did pretty good. We had to take turns. One time your butt would be against the wind, next time it was someone else's turn.

They had just come into our barrack and lined us up against the walls. This German officer would come around and point his finger right in your face. Are you the one that got the food? Were you the one outside? "No sir!" We would answer. It was just a game with them. Well, the word got out that the SS was going to get the field jackets. The Sergeants in each barrack sent orders for us to tear up the field jackets. This SS officer went to all 18 barrack and lined the men up trying to find out who tore up the jackets. There was only one jacket left and this Sergeant was wearing it. He had just come in from the field and he didn't know what was going on. He walked in and this SS officer told him to take it off. He looked around and saw the pile, then he looked at the officer and said "No sir." The SS officer ordered one of his men to shoot him if he didn't take it off. A German soldier stepped up and stuck the rifle in his belly. The Sergeant stood there for a minute and then took it off. He ripped it up standing there with the German soldier aiming at him. The SS officer started yelling and cussing and walked out. He never did do anything to the Sergeant."

A THIEF AMONG US
December 1944

"We had this Sergeant from the 106th division that was brought into our camp, Bill said. "We had been saving all of our cigarettes for Christmas. We were going to have a fire all day. We were going to set around it and sing Christmas carols all day. We had saved 28 packs of cigarettes to buy coal from the German guards. We woke up about two days before Christmas and all of the cigarettes had disappeared. When we went out for formation one of the guys told the 1st Sergeant that our cigarettes were missing. He went to the German guard and asked him to hold the men outside while he went in to do a search. The guard agreed and the 1st Sergeant, myself, and a couple of other guys went in and found all 28 packs in this new Sergeant's blanket. We had a kangaroo court. Stealing is one thing that you didn't do. You could steal from the Germans, but not from your buddies. We all got together and it was decided that we were going to beat the shit out of him and throw him out into the snow. They also decided I was to fight him. They got some tape for my hands and a pair of leather gloves from the Germans. When we started this guy came at me like a mad man. He was swinging and it was obvious he didn't know how to fight. I bent down under and came up with a couple of upper cuts. I knocked two of his front teeth out the first punch. He had guts though because he just kept coming. I knocked him down four times and he would just keep getting up. Finally, I said that's it. I quit. One of he guys threw a bucket of water on him and they put a sign around his neck that read, "I am a thief, I stole from my buddies." Then two of the prisoners got him by each arm and marched him through all 2800 men in the prison camp. After that none of the prisoners would let him come into their barracks. That night it started snowing. We always went outside at night to watch the planes bomb Berlin. We were only 50 miles from there and when they bombed it always lite up like a Christmas tree. We went out and this Sergeant was leaning up against this barrack. He was shaking so bad the snow was shaking off of him. I told one of the guys that he was going to freeze to death if we didn't bring him in. So we took a vote, went out and got him, and threw him in a bunk. Everybody threw blankets on him until he warmed up and then we left him with his own blankets. After that we all forgot about it."

A GERMAN POKER PLAYER
January 1945

Prisoners did have some recreation and sometimes with the enemy as Bill recounts. "There was a little German Sergeant that was recuperating from a wound he received while on the Russian front. He loved to play poker. The Germans had American cigarettes that they had taken from the Red Cross packages and this German Sergeant would come in each day with a carton of cigarettes. We would play with him. Let him win a few hands and then take him for the big pot. He always came with a carton of cigarettes, but he never left with any. He would get up and say, "see you tomorrow." We were about to get kicked out of this place because you could hear the Russians in the distance, but just before we did he came in and wanted to play. He was playing poker and got to bragging about how great a soldier he was and how many Russians he had killed before he got wounded. He said, "you know when I go back to the front I want to go to the American lines. I want to kill some Americans." When he said that I grabbed his pistol out of his holster, pulled the clip out of it, and threw it out in the snow. He looked at me, his face was red, and started calling me all kinds of names in German. He stormed out of the barrack and was on his hands and knees in the snow looking for his pistol. We were all at the windows laughing at him. He found it, slammed it in his holster, and took off out the front gate. Two days later that little fart was back again with another carton of cigarettes ready to play poker. Everybody was quiet when he walked in because we didn't know what he would do. He stopped and looked at us and said, "Ha, you guys thought I couldn't take a joke. Come on lets play poker." Two hours later he left without any cigarettes."

FAMILY PHOTOS

Prisoners of war clung to anything from family or home. It was a symbolic gesture of hope that someday they would be free men, but sometimes as Bill recalled it wasn't the best for morale. "Most of the guys had pictures of their wives and girlfriends tacked up on their bunks. After the Battle of the Bulge there was a kid from the 106th division given a bunk and after two or three days he tacked a picture of his girl on this bunk. Two bunks over there was an identical picture. Both of them had dated the same girl before they left New York. When we got back we found out that there was a whole pack of these women that were marrying GIs before they were going overseas to collect insurance money when the GIs were killed. It was a game."

BRIBING THE GERMAN GUARDS

"We could get the German guards to do anything for American cigarettes," Bill said. "You could have got a free trip across Berlin if you wanted it. But, I traded cigarettes with them and they would turn their heads long enough for me to sneak out of the compound and over to a Italian camp where I could get food. The Italians liked the chocolate bars from the Red Cross packages and I would trade them for potatoes and other vegetables. Then I would bring them back for us to eat. I got caught several times. Each time you got caught you were suppose to do five days in the hole. It was a little outhouse like building made out of blocks. It had a little stool in it. You couldn't lay down and stretch out. You could set down and stretch a little, but you had five days in there with a piece of bread and a glass of water a day. I had twenty-five days coming. They never did get any food from me because every time they would catch me I would throw the food over as I lifted my hands. One of the other guys would get it and take it in the barrack for the other guys. It was a standing rule in the camp for food always goes back to the hands of the original hands that it came from. So far, I hadn't done any time.

Then Phil Weatherall got caught and had five days to do. When I had signed the little black book I had signed right under Phil's name. So I knew when they took him for his five days I was next. For the next five days I saved a little food to take with me. They brought Phil back and I knew I was going the next day. I rolled my blankets up and hoped that I could bribe the guard with cigarettes to let me have them. You could easily freeze in this weather. The next morning this German Sergeant came in and I was sure he was after me. By now we could really hear the big guns of the Russians. They were really close. When he walked in I started walking toward him with my cigarettes and he stood there looking at me. Then he said I have orders for you men to pack up anything that you want to take with you. We are leaving in an hour."

THE DEATH MARCH TO STALAG IIIA

March 1945

"About an hour later we started on a march. I never saw so many prisoners of war in my life. We were all congregating and heading toward Berlin to Stalag IIIA. The Germans would let us stop on the side of the road every four or five hours and catnap for five or ten minutes," Bill recalls. "The guards were getting a ride in between us every hour. They were the old guard. One man about every five hundred yards. We could have easily killed them, but there was no place to go. The snow was several feet high. I tried to run it one day to chase a jackrabbit I saw, but I couldn't get through the snow. So we walked and walked. The sergeant that had stolen from us passed me on the march. I will never forget the look on his face. He didn't even know who I was. He walked as if he was in a complete daze.

The worse thing that I saw on this trip was some SS troops that were moving as we were. They were moving some young Jewish boys all 13, 14, or 15 years old. We were laying over in this ditch one day and these German officers come riding through on Clydesdale horses. They were running these fifteen Jewish kids. All of them were dressed in stripped uniforms. These kids were run out. The Germans pushed them over to the side of the road and just came along and shot each one in the back of the head. It's the worse thing I ever saw. We couldn't believe this went on.

We went on through this little town there were bodies along the road where the Germans had shot kids and Jewish prisoners. They didn't fool with the Russian prisoners either. I saw a lot of Russian prisoners alive, but all of them had a arm cut off. The Germans maimed them on purpose so they couldn't hold a rifle again. But some of them did hold one again and escaped. I saw a lot of Russian soldiers murdered by the Germans.

The Germans had the gas chambers. I went through one of them, took a shower, and then stood outside getting dressed while I watched them run 15 Jewish kids in there and gas them. Right after that they ran about 10 Russian soldiers in and gassed them too. As they were throwing them out the door I turned to one of my buddies and said, "damn I'm glad they pushed the right button while we were in there." There are a lot of people that say these type of things didn't happen. But I saw it. And what little I saw was nothing as to what went on.

We marched right through one beautiful town that hadn't been touched by the war. It was a very clean town. One of the prisoners commented on it. We just couldn't believe that it was that clean in the middle of a war. We spent four hours in the town resting and one of the guards ordered us to get in this garage and rest. We went in and laid down. We could see him out front marching. About midnight we heard the door squeak and someone came in. We thought it was the guard, but it was a old German lady. She had a couple loaves of bread. It was probably the only food she had in the house and she shared that with us.

We left the next morning and walked by a big garrison where the SS troops took their training. It hadn't been hit by the bombing yet either. Finally, after seven days of marching we arrived at Stalag IIIA."

Wednesday, February 14, 1945
THE DAILY-INDEPENDENT Murphysboro, Illinois

Germans Moving War Prisoners To East Of Oder

WASHINGTON, Feb. 13—(UP) —The Germans are moving all of their war prisoners to interior points west of the Oder river, the state and War Departments announced today.

The announcement said that American prisoners formerly held in eastern Germany are being relocated, but relatives should address mail to their last known addresses pending further information.

Camps being moved or already moved were in East Prussia, Poland, and that part of the German province of Pomerania east of the Oder. They included Stalag Luft IV, Stalag II A, talag II B, Stalag III B, and talag III C.

Prisoners in Stalag Luft III, the announcement said, are being moved to the southwest. Those in northern Silesia are being taken to the northwest. Prisones in southern Silesia are being moved southwest across Bohemia.

Among those being transported to the southwest, the announcement said, are Americans who were in Stalag VII B and Stalag 344. Officers from Oflag 64 are being sent to Stalag III A at Luckenwalde, betwegen Berlin and Leipzig.

"The destination of the other prisoners has not been confirmed," the announcement said. "Information concerning the relocation of prisoner of war camps is constantly being received.

Kitchen at Stalag IIIA.

STALAG IIIA

Stalag IIIA was located at Luckenwalde a few miles south of Berlin.

This prison camp was divided into compounds separated by barbed wire. The Americans were located in two of the compounds housed in wooden barracks. The barracks had no heat. Some prisoners received blankets, but because of overcrowded conditions many did not. The bunks were wooden triple deckers.

The food consisted of soup, steamed barley, barley bread, and coffee. Red Cross parcels were shared by POWs.

Close to the end of the war many prisoners were forced to sleep in make shift tents which were located in the open fields near the camp. The conditions then worsened.

CROWDED CONDITIONS AT STALAG IIIA
April 1945

The Russian and American front lines were moving rapidly. They begin to sandwich the Germans and as fronts moved closer the Germans would evaluate one prison camp and move the prisoners to another camp. The result was overcrowding. "There were prisoners everywhere and there was no more room in the camp," Bill said. " So they put us out in a great big field with one strand of fence around it. We could walk right through it. You would see a guard every so often, but we weren't going any place we were so beaten down.

In spite of our situation every night while we were there we had a dice game. The old German guards loved it. They would bring in cigarettes, roll the dice, and some of them would even bring in blankets at night and shine lights on them so we could play.

After a couple of days we were staying in big tents. They had four or five of them put up, but it still wouldn't hold all of us. I was lucky enough to get to stay inside the tent. They had straw on the ground for us to sleep on.

After a few days we could hear the guns getting real close. I had my talk with the former world champion Max Schemeling. He said that he would like to come back to America. He had come to the camp in a new suit that he had bought while he was in New York. He said that he had been in the German Paratroopers and was wounded in Poland. They discharged him after that. I found out later that they had sent him there to see if he could find out any additional information. The Germans wouldn't give up. They were trying to find out if we had any secret weapons and the war was only a few days from being over. They just wouldn't admit it or accept it."

LIBERATION DAY
May 1, 1945

"The next morning about 4 A.M. it got real quite," Bill continued. "It was so still it woke me up. There wasn't a gun firing anywhere. During the night the German guards had

Kitchen at Stalag IIIA.

Tent area at Stalag IIIA.

all taken off. We didn't even know it. There was a great big woods over from the camp and four or five of the old German guards had run over there and hid. Right at sunup we could hear the tanks coming. We thought it was Americans, but it was the Russians. They came swarming in. They had their women and children with them. The first thing we saw was a big Sherman tank bust through the front gate come rolling up there and stopped. There was a Russian woman who jumped down off of the tank. She had to have cleaned up before they came in because she was so white. She had shoulder length black hair. It glisten in the sun. She was dressed in white and had a forty-five pistol on each hip just like Patton. She looked us over, jumped back on the tank, and waved them on. Right behind them came the rag tag army Russian soldiers, children pushing wheel barrels full of kitchen utensils. We really had a meal.

Myself and some of the other guys took off up to Hitler's mansion because we knew there would be food there. I took a couple of P.38 pistols off the wall. They were special made with pearl handles. They were stolen later when I was returning home.

For a couple of days we were in the camp and one day a Russian Lieutenant came up and asked us if we were hungry. We told him we were because we couldn't get filled up. He took us up to this beautiful home owned by a German Aristocrat. There was a old man and woman in the house. They even had a servant. This young Russian guy didn't even knock he just walked in and motioned for us to come in. The old man and woman was just sitting down to a great big meal. You could have fed twenty people with what was on the table and there was just two of them. The Russian officer told us to set down and eat. We started to set down and this old German man jumps up, "nicks, nicks!" (Get out in German.) This Russian Lieutenant jumps up and walks over to this old man and points his finger in the old mans face and told him to set down. We ate like kings. The Germans hadn't eaten while we were there, but there was plenty of food left. I stood up when we were finished and told the Russian we were ready to go. He walked over and picked up a turkey leg and started eating on it. This German came at him again. The Russian pushed him back into his chair this time. Then he walked over took hold of this table and turned it up side down. Then we left."

HEADING FOR AMERICAN LINES
May 3, 1945

Bill and a couple of his buddies took off the next day because they decided they weren't going to sleep in prison camp anymore. They knew there was a motel in a near by town because Bill had been by it a few times. There was a big army factory that made ammunition at the edge of this town and they heard that the Russians had been moving prisoners in there. There was an estimated 40 to 50 thousand of them that had been put in there within the last week. "We walked over to this motel," Bill explained. "We were the first Americans to come into the town. I guess most of the Americans were afraid to leave the prison camp because of the Russians, but we were at the point that we didn't care. This old man came out and he begged us to stay there. He told us they would put us up. We didn't know it at the time, but if you were there first it was yours. The Russians wouldn't come in.

We stayed and that night we were sound a sleep and about one in the morning someone started beating on the door. I went to the door and there were two Russian soldiers that come to the door. They had come to see what they could find. Both of them were drunk. One had a bottle of vodka in his hand. He would take a drink and then hand the bottle to the other soldier. One said, "Ah, Americans. Have a drink." I took the bottle, stuck my tongue down on the bottle, and acted like I took a big drink. "Thank you comrade," I said and handed the bottle back to him. They just walked off and never bothered us again.

The next morning we were sitting outside and we could see down in the valley where this big factory was located. We could see the German prisoners standing around the building and in the yard. The Russian guards were out in the yard walking around. Then all of a sudden every building blew. Gas, flames, and black smoke came gushing out. The Germans prisoners came running out with their clothes on fire. Many of them ran to the fences and tried to climb over, but the Russians shot them. We found out later that there was at least 35,000 Germans killed. The Russians had set the place. It was pay back time."

ARRIVING AT THE AMERICAN LINES
May 6, 1945

A couple of days later the trucks came for the prisoners. "We caught the last truck out," Bill said. "After a three or four hour drive we stopped at a big air base that the Army had set up in at Hilderberghausen. We stayed there for a day and then they flew us to France in a C-47. We landed in Paris and I rode under the Arc De Triompe and out into the country to Camp Lucky Strike. At Lucky Strike they fed us boiled chicken everyday. We got new clothes. We saw movies every night. That lasted for about a month."

Richard Hamilton, a member of the color guard at American Legion Post No. 95 of Vandalia, bows his prayer offered at the Veterans Day program last Fri gion Home.

HOMEWARD BOUND
June 1945

"Then we loaded aboard ship," Bill continued. " My shoulder had completely healed until I decided to box one of the heavy weights on the ship. I had intentions of being a professional boxer. After the match I tore the shoulder up again and the healing had to start all over. When we landed in New York I was sore. I couldn't hardly move my shoulder. I got home and went to the old house where we lived. My parents had moved and it just so happened that the mailman lived next door to the old house. I went to the post office and the mailman was there picking up his mail. It was 4 A.M. I said do you know where my parents live. He knew me right away and said, 'Yeah, get in the truck I will take you home.' He pulled up in front of the house and said, "you live here." I said, "I guess I do." My old dog was laying on the front porch. He was fifteen years old and he died the day after I got home. The first person I saw when I came into the house was a little fat guy laying on the bed. I though who in the hell is that. It was Buzz. Mom and dad heard me open the door and came running out. All my brothers and sisters came in and we had a good homecoming."

DUTY AT A GERMAN PRISON CAMP
September 1945

After 90 days at home Bill was sent to San Antonio, Texas. The Army made a big mistake as Bill explained, "there was a prisoner of war camp there holding German soldiers. They made a mistake of putting a bunch of ex-prisoners of war in charge of them. They told us we only had to guard them a couple hours at a time. We started pulling our guard duty. They told me to go down and get three of four of them to go empty the garbage cans. I asked where I was suppose to check out a gun. They said that I didn't need a gun. "I do if I am guarding prisoners." They sent me down to ordnance and I was issued a sawed off pump shotgun and a .45 pistol. The Germans had got the word that we were there to guard them and they were on there best behavior. When I went to get them I told them not to utter a word, I would be right behind them. I walked them in the alley ways for four hours and they didn't say a word.

The next day the Germans were complaining about the steak they had been given because it was to tough. They had put a kid on the machine gun corner that had had a rough time in the Nazi Camps. The Germans had beat him and almost killed him once. These German prisoners came out and started raking their tin cups on the fence in protest of the steak. "We want better food. We want better food." This kid told them once to get back in the barrack. The Germans started throwing their tin cups at him. He opened up on them with the machine gun and killed six of them. The next

Post 95 honors Veterans

Friday program includes 2 POWs

By RICH BAUER
Managing Editor

"On this day, we gather ourselves together to honor our veterans," Greg Lay, commander of Crawford-Hale American Legion Post No. 95, said Friday morning. "I wonder where we'd be today without our veterans.

"If there were no veterans, there'd be no one to fight the wars. I wonder where we'd be," he said during the Veterans Day program at the Post No. 95.

Lay then explained what America would be like today if its people had stepped forward to defend their country. "We'd be living under Communism, under Hitler, under Sadaam or under any of these types of government.

"I think we as Americans need to look around us and see what we've got and the freedoms we have...and truly give credit and honor to those who made it possible – the American veterans," Lay said.

Special guests at the program were three local residents who served in the armed forces during World War II – Bill Bradley, Harold Miles, Miles Filer. The program included speeches by Bradley and Miles.

Filer's experiences in World War II – which included a term as a prisoner of war – were related by the emcee for the program, Vandalia Mayor Rich Walker, who also talked about two other local veterans.

Those veterans – Duane Tedrick and his brother, the late Dwight Tedrick, combined for about 60 years of service to their country, Walker said. "Seldom can a single family boast of such dedication and service," the mayor said.

Bradley, who also was a prisoner of war, told how a number of his experiences were like those portrayed on the old television show, "Hogan's Heroes." But it was not an easy time for him or his family.

Bradley was one of three brothers who served in World War II.

"For 25 or 30 years I didn't realiz how much grief my parents wer through with three of us over ther (in another country)."

That came to light, he said, a his son went off to fight in the Viet nam War.

Friday's program also include

Please See VETS, Page :

Photo by Rich Bauer

Bill Bradley, a World War II veteran who was a prisoner of war, was among those speaking at the Veterans Day program held last Friday morning at Crawford-Hale American Legion Post No. 95 of Vandalia. Seated behind Bradley in the photo are Farrell Gruenbaum of the Legion Auxiliary (left) and Russell Hewitt, Post 95 chaplain.

day all ex-prisoners were moved. That never even got in the papers. It was hushed up."

DISCHARGE FROM THE ARMY
November 1945

They transferred Bill and the other soldiers to California. While Bill was there he boxed a few times. He met a girl there and dated her for a while and then they transferred him to San Francisco to guard the dock gates at Alcatraz. After a month he was discharged on November 23, 1945.

EPILOGUE

Bill came home and joined his brothers as a student at McCarthey College. They all became high school teachers and coaches. In 1984, he retired, but continued to substitute teach and referee basketball games. Bill married Kathleen Ketti in 1946. She passed away in 1955. He remarried in 1956 and was divorced in 1986. He had three sons Craig, Bruce, and Keith. Also, two daughters Cindy and Sandy and fifteen grandchildren.

Bill resided with Flo Allen in Brownstown from late 1986 until his death on May 29, 1996. One friend said of him, "He instilled in thousands of students the importance of country, patriotism, and the trials of war. Many students came from afar to attend his funeral. He couldn't have possibly realized how many lives he touched."

CHAPTER TEN

SERGEANT WM. ROBERT CARR
U.S. ARMY

398TH BOMBER GROUP, B-17 GUNNER
CAPTURED AFTER BEING SHOT DOWN ON A BOMBING MISSION OVER GERMANY

PRISONER OF WAR
AUGUST 4, 1944-APRIL 26, 1945
STALAG LUFT IV

A CALL TO DUTY
September 1942

Bob Carr was excited when he entered the U.S. Army on September 10, 1942. He always had an interest in flying and he received orders for the Glider program. After his basic training he was transferred to Texas for 30 hours of glider training, but to Bob's surprise after he completed the training the Army decided to disband the glider program. They said they didn't need any more Glider pilots. "The Army gave me a choice," Bob explained. "I could be discharged and drafted later or I could take my choice of training as a crew member for a B-17. The training would consist of radio or engineer school. I chose radio school and was shipped to Rapid City, South Dakota. I wasn't the best radio operator, I could only take on 20 words a minute and I got beat out of a spot by a man who could take 22 words a minute.

Then they sent me to gunner school in Yuma, Arizona. I had to take training as an aerial gunner. I was then sent to Rapid City where I was assigned to a crew. I was there for about six weeks and then sent by train to the east coast and we shipped out a few nights later. The next morning we were in a large convoy.

THE FIRST MISSION

Bob and his crew landed in Liverpool, England on July 14, 1944 and were assigned to the 398th Bomb Group 601 Bomb Squadron Group. The crew trained for about two weeks and in their newly assigned B-17 the Hells Bells. Then as Bob tells us the Hells Bells and crew got their first mission. "My first mission was on July 28, 1944, Sourbergenon, Germany. It was rough but we made it through all right. We didn't have any Mesersmitdt after us, just flak for the anti-aircraft guns. There were a few planes that went down in our group, but we didn't take any hits at all. The next two days were bad weather so we didn't fly."

William Carr, 1943.

THE SECOND MISSION

The second mission they weren't as lucky. "Our next mission was scheduled for August 3rd" Bob explained. "It was over Holle, Germany. Our navigator got wounded on this

Top-turret gunner Harry Goldstein of the Bronx, New York. Top gunner was also B-17's crew chief, responsible for proper functioning of the aircraft from the engines to armament.

Waist-gun positions, with gunners dressed for high-altitude flight. Suits were electrically heated and oxygen was supplied through face masks. Side windows are open so that the waist gunners may command all lateral approaches to their plane. Temperatures in this position were at high altitudes as low as 40-degrees below zero.

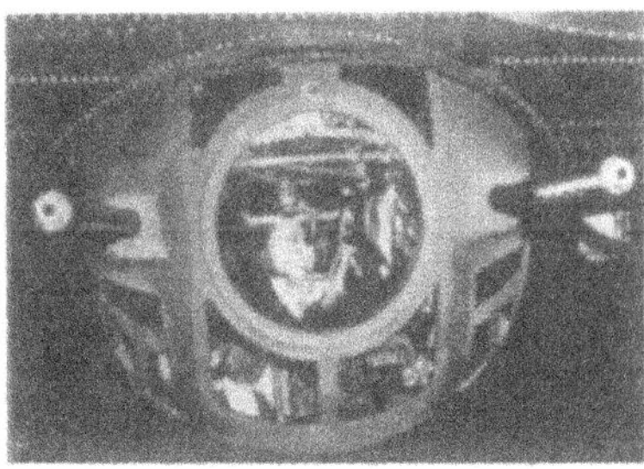

A ball-turret gunner (who was, of necessity, not a large man) in a position curled up inside the belly turret. With his left eye peering through the sight he controlled the movement of the guns by hand and by foot pedals.

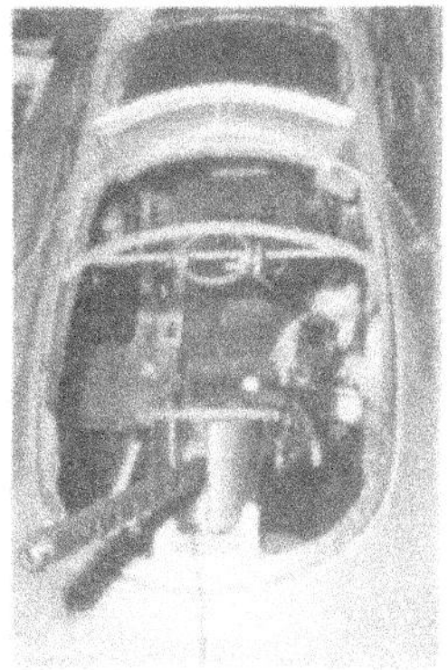

mission and on our return we had to break formation going back. There was an ambulance waiting when we got back and I thought, well we won't fly tomorrow. I was wrong."

THE THIRD MISSION

Bob was wrong about having a mission the next day, but being wrong wasn't the worst of it. It would be the last mission he would fly in the war. "We had a mission on August 4th and were flying over the Baltic. We acted as if we were going further over the Baltic, and flew past the target then made a right angle turn and came back in over the target. Things were uneventful until after we dropped the bombs. One of them hung up. We worked on it and got it to drop. About that time some flak hit us. I was unclear as to the damage and all

SGT. W[illegible]M CARR
OF NEAR CENTRALIA
MISSING IN ACTION

Sergt. William R. Carr, 25, son of Mr. and Mrs. Robert D. Carr, Route 2 Centralia, is missing in action over Germany, his parents, learned in a telegram from the War Department Saturday evening. He is thought to have been on his first bombing mission. He went overseas in July trained as a ball turret gunner.

He graduated from the Centralia Township high school in 1938.

He is the only son of Mr. and Mrs. Carr. They also have a daughter, Margaret, whose husband, Pvt. Virgil Crenshaw is in England.

MISSING IN ACTION—Sergt. William R. Carr, son of Mr. and Mrs. Robert D. Carr of Route 2, Centralia, has been listed as missing in action over Germany. He was trained as a ball turret gunner in the Army Air Forces.

I can remember is what the radio operator said, "that sounded like a bunch of rocks being thrown on a tin roof." Immediately we were on fire and the left Tokyo tank was burning. The pilot called me on the radio to see if I could see anything underneath because I was in the ball-turret. I couldn't see anything, but the decision was made to drop down to 10,000 feet from the present 24,000 to see if we could put the fire out. We dropped down and got the fire out. The pilot then discussed with the navigator if we should try to fly across the Baltic Sea to Sweden. It was about 74 miles, but it was across water so they decided not to chance it. Shortly after that, the fire alarm went off again and orders were given to bail out. I had put my parachute under my left arm in the gun turret that day so I decided to bail out from that position. It was an uncommon way to leave the plane and as I started out I caught my side pockets on the plane and had to climb part way back in. Then I jumped. As I was falling, I watched the plane head out over the Baltic Sea and take a nose dive. The fall was uneventful, but as I got close to the ground I could see people coming from all directions. When I landed, I was trying to take my parachute off."

THE CAPTURE
August 4, 1944

Continuing, Bob gives his account of his capture. "One of the home guards, a man about 45, was riding his bicycle across the field as fast as he could. When he got up close to me, he said, "Pistola, Pistola." I said, "No." He pointed a pistol at me. About that time two Polish farmers came up carrying pitch forks and pointing them at me. The home guard ran them off. I found out later that there was a reward of 10,000 marks for any capture.

He then took me across the field to his house. It only had one room, but the most amazing thing to me was that the door to the house led out to the chicken house and the chickens could walk in and out of the house freely. I was standing in the room watching his wife and two daughters take the parachute apart for the silk material. Then all at once a hand grabbed me from behind and threw me out into the yard. It was the Burgermieister of the town. He was very anger. He started hitting me and asking me questions in German. I didn't know any German so I couldn't answer him. He beat on me for a while and then he started taking all my clothes off. He found an escape kit in one of my pockets. It had maps, money, and some food. I had forgotten about it coming down because I saw all the people gathering before I hit the ground. Anyway, he went ballistics and started beating me again. He took me into town and had me stand in the road as he took the rest of my clothes off except for my briefs. There were women standing all around me. Then one of the home guards came up and he got into an argument with the Bergermieister. They were face to face yelling at each other. I don't know what was said, but my guy won because the Burgermieister gave me my clothes back and I got to get dressed again."

THE JOURNEY TO PRISON CAMP

"The home guard took me down a little trail through the woods to a road that led to another town," Bob said. "We were doing all right for a while and then we passed a guy on the road who was carrying a shotgun. He stopped the home guard and they started talking. They got into an argument and I thought I was going to get the worse, but soon the home guard motioned for me to start walking. We continued on and as we would pass farm houses people would come out and take turns hitting me with their fist. I got smart and started putting myself between the home guard and the people until we finally reached the town. The Germans had knocked out the side of one of a basement wall in a house and used it as a holding place. That's where they put me and to my surprise part of my crew was there. It wasn't long until a bus came and got us.

We went by a B-17 crash site. The pilot of the plane was still laying out in the field. People were going up to the body and kicking the body just to see if it would move. One of the captured crew members from that crew told us the pilot had held the plane steady until all the members could bail out. I couldn't believe the unconcern that the people had that were kicking at the body. They were full of hate.

Soon we arrived at the air field. Once again I had to take my clothes off. The Germans went through them and asked a lot of questions. I had to strip all the way this time and because I had been circumcise they wanted to know if I was Jewish.

We stayed the night and the next day they loaded us on a train. It was a passenger train and there were German soldiers on the train going home on leave. They didn't pay much attention to us. They were all happy I suppose because they were going home. We passed through Berlin and unfortunately for us we did so right after a bombing raid. We had stopped at the train station and had to get off the train and walk to another train a couple of blocks from where we were at. There was a crowd gathered and they were throwing rocks. The soldiers were protecting us, but just as we got to the other train one of the Nazi officers came up and hit one of the pilots in the face. I'll never forget what the pilot said, "You son-of-a-bitch if I get lose I'll come back and bomb you again."

One of the guards handed the radio dispatcher that was on my train a satchel to carry and one of the civilians tried to grab it out of his hand. Just about that time we were starting to board the train and a man was standing on the platform beside us. He could speak English very well and he said, "You bastards. You dirty bastards."

The radio operator looked at him and said, "Blow it out your ass."

THE INTERROGATION

The Germans brought all the American pilots through Frankfort for interrogation. Bob was no exception. "We arrived in Frankfort, Germany and they took us off the train. There was a bus to take us up to the interrogation center, but our bus was too small and we had to walk. The German Sergeant was pressing us hard and some of the guys had shrapnal wounds so they couldn't go any faster. He seemed to be pretty good until he had an audience and then he had to show his authority. Once no one was watching he would let up on us.

We arrived in late afternoon. I got my picture taken and then they took me for interrogation. I gave my name, rank, and serial number and that was all. They told me they were going to give me some food in a little bit, but I didn't get any food that night.

The next morning they gave me a slice of bread and some peas. They interrogated me again. Because I had been separated from my crew, they thought I was a P-38 pilot instead of a B-17 crew member. There had been some P-38's shot down in the area. We went back and forth for a long time me giving my name rank and serial number and them asking about being a P.38 pilot. This went on for about three days and the last person that interrogated me was a Nazi Major. He asked me about my position and I gave my name, rank, and serial number. Then to my surprise I learned that he knew all about my crew. He named each position on the plane and even knew the crew members by name and position. I respected him for one thing. He knew that I was in the ball turret, but he wouldn't make me say it."

WAR DEPARTMENT
THE ADJUTANT GENERAL'S OFFICE
WASHINGTON 25, D. C.

bJ

IN REPLY REFER TO:
AG 201 Carr, William R.
PC-N ETO156

20 August 1944

Mr. Robert D. Carr
Rural Route #[illegible]
Centralia, Illinois

Dear Mr. Carr:

This letter is to confirm my recent telegram in which you were regretfully informed that your son, Corporal William R. Carr, 16,121,910, Air Corps, has been reported missing in action since 4 August 1944 over Germany.

I know that added distress is caused by failure to receive more information or details. Therefore, I wish to assure you that at any time additional information is received it will be transmitted to you without delay, and, if in the meantime no additional information is received, I will again communicate with you at the expiration of three months. Also, it is the policy of the Commanding General of the Army Air Forces upon receipt of the "Missing Air Crew Report" to convey to you any details that might be contained in that report.

The term "missing in action" is used only to indicate that the whereabouts or status of an individual is not immediately known. It is not intended to convey the impression that the case is closed. I wish to emphasize that every effort is exerted continuously to clear up the status of our personnel. Under war conditions this is a difficult task as you must readily realize. Experience has shown that many persons reported missing in action are subsequently reported as prisoners of war, but as this information is furnished by countries with which we are at war, the War Department is helpless to expedite such reports. However, in order to relieve financial worry, Congress has enacted legislation which continues in force the pay, allowances and allotments to dependents of personnel being carried in a missing status.

Permit me to extend to you my heartfelt sympathy during this period of uncertainty.

Sincerely yours,

J. A. ULIO
Major General,
The Adjutant General.

A Point of Interest

PRISON SLANG IN THE STALAGS

GOONS - The name the POW's gave to the guards and staff in their respective prison camps.

FERRETS - The name for the German guards who roamed the camp's interior searching for escape attempts or contraband.

GOING INTO THE BAG - A British slang term for being taken prisoner.

ROUND THE BEND - A term for a POW that was experiencing psycho neurosis (irrationality or depression). Initially a British term adopted by the Americans.

THE TRAIN RIDE

"The next day we were sent by train, 40 and 8s, to Stalag Luft IV in Poland," Bob said. "The train ride took five days. We got little food and no water. The conditions were terrible. There was no room to lie down. Men had to set between each others legs. There was no place to relieve yourself so men were relieving themselves in a helmet and passing it across from prisoner to prisoner until the prisoner by the vent could dump it. The smell was unbearable. On several occasions they stopped in larger towns in the marshalling yards for bombing raids. They locked us in the train. Every bomb they dropped we thought was going to drop on us and they came close enough that we had flak hitting the top of our car. It took five days to get to the prison camp, but it seemed like five years."

STALAG LUFT IV

Stalag Luft IV was located at Gross Sycrow, Pomerania, 20 Kilometers southeast of Belgard. This prison camp did not open until May 12, 1944. The barracks were wooden with insufficient ventilation. Bathing facilities were inadequate. The toilet facilities consisted of a row of toilets and a open pit behind the barracks. The barracks were surrounded by barbed wire.

A PERSONAL ACCOUNT

The adjustment to prison life was a shock for American prisoners of war. Especially pilots whom often just days earlier were living a relatively normal life other than the bombing missions. Bob recalls the experience, Stalag IV treatment was very rough. When our planes came over, the Nazi guards would go ballistic. They would make us go inside the barracks. We weren't supposed to look out. One of the guys got close to a window and saw the guard aim at him just as he ducked. The window was shot out. I was there until February, and I got one shower. We got one piece of bread a day and soup once a day. The Red Cross sent us packages which helped. The packages were supposed to be for one person, but four of us had to share one package.

Each morning we were required to fall out in front of the barracks. Sometimes they would pick at random one barracks and trash it. They would throw everything out in the middle of the floor and when you went back in you had to find your things. They claimed they were looking for a radio.

One day a group of four German planes came over. All at once one plane took a nose dive and crashed into the ground near the camp. The Nazis went nuts again and made all of us go inside. They started test firing their guns which made us really nervous."

DEAR MOM & DAD AUG 21, '44

I GUESS BY NOW YOU KNOW THAT I AM ALL RIGHT. I AM NOT WOUNDED IN ANY WAY BUT HAVE ONLY GOD TO THANK FOR THAT. THE FOOD IS NOT BAD AND SO FAR WE HAVE PLENTY OF CIGARETTS. I HOPE THAT YOU ARE ALL WELL AND DID NOT HAVE TO WORRY TOO LONG ABOUT ME. WE GET TO WRITE TWO LETTERS AND FOUR POST CARDS A MONTH. WE RECIEVED OUR FIRST RED CROSS KIT AND IT HAD JUST ABOUT ALL THE TOILET ARTICLES I NEED IN IT. THE CLIMATE IS NICE AND I AM GETTING A NICE SUNTAN. I BELIEVE YOU WILL BE ALLOWED TO SEND ME A PACKAGE SO, SEE THE RED CROSS AND FIND OUT WHAT YOU CAN SEND AND THE BEST WAY TO SEND IT. TELL EVERY ONE THAT I AM O.K. AND TO KEEP UP THE GOOD WORK. I KNOW THIS HAS BEEN A LOT OF WORRY BUT EVERY THING IS GOING TO BE ALL RIGHT. KEEP SMILING!

ALL MY LOVE

Bill.

Letter sent from William Carr to his parents while he was at POW camp dated Aug. 21, 1944.

Kriegsgefangenenpost

Mit Luftpost

Postkarte nach U.S.A.

RM 40 Pf

GEPRÜFT

An

MR ROBERT D. CARR

Gebührenfrei!

Absender:

Vor- und Zuname: SGT. WILLIAM R. CARR

Gefangenennummer: 4030

Kriegsgefangenenlager der Luftwaffe Nr. 3

Bezeichnung:

Deutschland (Allemagne)

Empfangsort: CENTRALIA, ILLINOIS

Straße: ROUTE #2

Land: U.S.A.

Landesteil (Provinz usw.)

Front of postcard sent to Robert Carr from William Carr while he was at a prison camp dated Aug. 28, 1944.

Kriegsgefangenenlager

Datum: AUG. 28, 1944

DEAR FOLKS. I AM STILL FEELING FINE AND THERE IS PLENTY OF FOOD FOR US HERE. I DO HOPE YOU ARE ALL WELL AND NOT WORRYING ABOUT ME BECAUSE EVERY THING IS OK. KEEP UP THE GOOD WORK AND WHEN THIS IS OVER I WILL BE HOME. Love Bill

Back of postcard sent to Robert Carr from William Carr while he was at a prison camp dated Aug. 28, 1944.

(Revised 1 August 1944)

HEADQUARTERS ARMY SERVICE FORCES
OFFICE OF THE PROVOST MARSHAL GENERAL
WASHINGTON 25, D. C.

PARCEL MAILING INSTRUCTIONS

Parcel label, W. D., P. M. G. Form No. 19, shall be pasted securely on the outside of the Prisoner of War parcel.

The contents of the parcel must be listed on Post Office Department Custom Declaration, Form No. 2966, at the time of mailing. Should this form not be available at your local post office, the contents of parcel should be listed on plain paper and attached to the outside of parcel. NO POSTAGE IS REQUIRED FOR MAILING PRISONER OF WAR PARCELS.

Articles bearing such slogans as "FOR VICTORY BUY WAR BONDS" or any other war slogan expressing assurance of victory should not be included in Prisoner of War parcel as the German Government has threatened to confiscate all parcels containing such slogans.

SIZE AND WEIGHT OF PARCEL:

a. Weight of parcel, when packed, must not exceed 11 pounds.
b. Dimensions of parcel shall not exceed 18 inches in length, nor 42 inches length and girth combined.
c. Parcel should not be sealed and should be so wrapped that postal inspection of contents may be easily made.

The current Export Bulletin of the Foreign Economic Administration provides that gift articles for export shall not be packed in (1) glass containers, (2) hermetically sealed, vacuum or soldered tins, or (3) collapsible tin tubes (such as shaving cream or tooth paste tubes).

Be sure and detach parcel label, W. D., P. M. G. Form No. 19, at the perforation attaching it to the two tobacco labels, W. D., P. M. G. Form No. 26, before pasting it on parcel. (See tobacco mailing instructions for using tobacco labels, Form No. 26, and tobacco order, Form No. 26A.)

No substitutes nor additions to items listed below are permitted in Prisoner of War Parcels and, if included in such parcels, will be removed by the postal censors.

The signature and address of sender must appear in ink in the space provided on the parcel label.

LIST OF PERMISSIBLE ITEMS WHICH MAY BE INCLUDED IN PRISONER OF WAR PARCELS

SMOKING ACCESSORIES

Tobacco pouches
Pipes
Cigarette holders (except paper)
Cigarette cases (nonmetallic)
Pipe cleaners

TOILET ARTICLES

Washing powder
Medicated soap
Bath soap
Towels, bath and face
Mouth washes and dentifrices, (non-liquid)
Wash cloths
Shoe-polishing cloth
Toilet kits
Tooth powder (in nonmetallic containers)
Tooth brushes
Shoe brushes
Combs (nonmetallic)
Brushes, scrubbing
Hair brushes (nonmetallic)
Clothing brushes
Safety razors
Safety razor blades
Shaving brushes
Nonbreakable shaving mirrors
Talcum powder (in nonmetallic moisture-proof containers)
Styptic pencils
Shaving soap cakes and powder
Small metallic mirrors
Women's toilet articles except liquids (in nonmetallic moisture-proof containers)
Cleansing tissues
Toilet paper
Camphor ice (cardboard containers)
Sanitary supplies for feminine hygiene
Orange sticks

ITEMS FOR CHILDREN

All kinds of clothing and shoes
Crayons
Small indestructible wooden toys and games

SPORTS AND GAMES

Playing cards
Backgammon
Checkers and other similar board games
Chess
Cribbage
Puzzles and games
Chinese checkers
Ping pong or table-tennis sets
Soft balls
Baseballs
Medicine balls
Footballs
Softball or baseball gloves
Poker chips
Dice
Dominoes
Horseshoes
Miniature bowling
Miniature golf
Jump rope (individual type)
Boxing gloves
Soccer ball
Volley ball

LIST OF PERMISSIBLE ITEMS WHICH MAY BE INCLUDED IN PRISONER OF WAR PARCELS—Continued

CLOTHING

Athletic clothing and shoes
Socks
Sock supporters
Belts
Shirts (regular Army or Navy if prisoners of war)
Slacks (regular Army or Navy if prisoners of war)
Underwear
Gloves
Handkerchiefs
Mufflers
Sweaters
Shoes
Shoe laces
Insoles
House slippers
Overshoes (rubbers)
Bathrobes
Pajamas
Nightgowns
Suspenders
Neckties (only service ties for prisoners of war)
Bathing suits
Women's wool hose
Officers' blouses
Overseas caps
Women's blouses
Skirts
Dresses
Ribbon

MISCELLANEOUS ITEMS

Single blankets
Chewing gum
Shoe polish in tins
Toothpicks
Nail clippers
Wallets
Mending kits
Small scissors
Sewing kits
Shoe repair leather and nails
Buttons (nonmetallic)
Hair clippers
Vitamins in containers of cardboard, plastic, or other unbreakable materials
Safety pins
Standard phonograph records and needles
Watches (low priced)
Eyeglasses (securely packed)
Service insignia (for prisoners of war)
Religious emblems
Fountain pens
Pen holders
Pen points
Pencils
Water color paints
Oil paints for artists
Paint brushes
Glue (powdered)
Small musical instruments
Rulers
Hair nets and pins
Knitting needles (nonmetallic)
Crochet needles (nonmetallic)
Crochet thread
Knitting yarn
Elastic
Pillow covers and pillow slips
Table scarfs
Sheets
Rugs
Cooking utensils
Iodine crystals
Sponges (except rubber)
Pans, baking
Dishes, pudding
Openers, can
Boilers, porridge, double
Whisks, egg
Jugs
Pans, frying
Dishes, vegetable, with covers
Spoons, serving, table and tea
Ladles
Cloths, dish and drying
Forks, dinner
Shakers, salt
Pots, tea and coffee
Plates, dinner
Colander
Plates, pie
Kettles, tea
Bowls
Bowls, coffee
Mugs
Bowls, mixing
Kitchen and eating utensils, not of glass or other breakable materials

(IMPORTANT NOTICE.—In order that food items reach their destinations in good order, it is essential that they be strongly packed in moisture-proof containers. This is particularly necessary in the shipment of such items as powdered milk, sugar, cocoa, etc.)

FOOD ITEMS

Processed American or Swiss cheese (must be packed in cellophane and cardboard containers)
Dried prunes, raisins, or apricots, peaches, and apples (in 1 pound or ½ pound cellophane packages)
Dried soups (in cellophane bags)
Bouillon cubes (¼ pound)
Meat extracts, dried (¼ pound)
Cereals of the whole grain variety as the oatmeal and dark farina type, or vitamin-fortified white grain cereals (cardboard containers)
Nuts—only pecans, Brazil nuts, or peanuts in shell or salted (cellophane bags or cardboard boxes)
Rice (1 pound in cellophane or other transparent paper package or cardboard boxes)
Plain or chocolate powdered malted milk in press-in top tins not in excess of 1 pound
Malted milk tablets in press-in top tins not in excess of 500 tablets
Hard candy
Sweet chocolate in bars, hard—no soft centers—not to exceed 2 pounds
Candy bars
Dried cocoa
Dried vegetables in cellophane or cardboard packages
Onion flakes
Dried noodles, macaroni, or spaghetti in cardboard boxes
Baking powder
Fruit cake, in commercially packed cardboard containers
Biscuits, cookies, and crackers (1 pound in cardboard containers)
Coffee in plain bags not in excess of one-fourth (¼) pound
Tea, bulk (loose), in bags or cardboard boxes, not in excess of one-half (½) pound
Postum (in press-in top tins or cardboard boxes)
Nescafe (in press-in top tins or cardboard boxes)
Ovaltine (in press-in top tins or cardboard boxes)
Cocoa in press-in top cans or cellophane bags not in excess of one-half (½) pound
Sugar in paper bags or cardboard boxes not in excess of 1 pound.
Saccharin
Seasoning materials, except pepper
Banana flakes, dried ripe bananas, and similar products
Roasted soy beans
Dried figs (in cellophane packages or cardboard containers)
Dates (in cellophane packages or cardboard containers)
Meal, flour, or various mixes to be used for baking or cooking such as Bisquick, gingerbread mix, pudding mix, muffin mix, pancake flour
Precooked beans
Powdered eggs
Powdered milk
Garden seeds
Dried pudding

25-11825-20M

A Point of Interest

AIRMEN OVER EUROPE

From 1939 to 1945 during bombing raids over Nazi occupied territory 150,000 allied airmen were killed. Another 45,000 were captured and approximately 6,000 were shot down and evaded capture.

Gefangenen Gazette

SPECIAL SUPPLEMENT TO
PRISONERS OF WAR BULLETIN

Published by the American National Red Cross for the Relatives of American Prisoners of War and Civilian Internees

Washington, D. C. — September 1944

Col. Delmar T. Spivey, senior American officer at Stalag Luft III, sent to the editor of PRISONERS OF WAR BULLETIN a complete file of the *Gefangenen Gazette* from October 15, 1943, to April 9, 1944.

Gefangenen (Prisoners') *Gazette* is produced, by hand and typewriter, three times weekly, with a Sunday supplement of colored cartoons, by American airmen-prisoners at the Center Compound. When sending the file, Colonel Spivey wrote:

Credit for this paper is given to 2nd Lt. Ronald T. Delaney, who, under most adverse circumstances as to material and subject matter, has shown persistence and initiative to a commendable degree.

There are some 1,500 young American airmen at Luft III, and the articles and cartoons in the *Gazette* throw a vivid light on camp conditions and on how the men there are temporarily adapting their lives to an atmosphere that must be completely alien to them.

It is unfortunately a physical impossibility to make the complete file available to all families of the men at Luft III, and to the many other families of American prisoners of war who would surely find it intensely interesting. PRISONERS OF WAR BULLETIN, however, has prepared this special supplement made up entirely of extracts, drawings, and cartoons, taken more or less at random, from the *Gefangenen Gazette*. No editing has been done here, but, of course, every issue has to be approved by the German commander before it goes on the camp bulletin board.

Stalag Luft III, which, like all other camps for airmen, is under the control of the Luftwaffe, is probably the best established camp for Americans in Germany. Enlisted men in the Stalags, and especially on work detachments, have much less opportunity for study and play than officer-prisoners have.

GILBERT REDFERN, *Editor*
Prisoners of War Bulletin

ABANDONING CAMP
January 1945

In early 1945 the Russian front was moving fast. It was closing in on the prison camp, and as many of the camps did, they moved the prisoners. Bob recalls the evacuation, "About the middle of January we started hearing artillery fire in the distance. It was the Russians making a drive. The Germans told us to get our stuff together, that we were going to move out. We would walk about 10 or 15 Kilometers the first couple of days. They always tried to keep us in a building of some kind and one of the nights, that building happened to be a chicken coop.

We all got lice really bad. We would try to sleep for a while before the lice woke up and started moving. When they did move, they would bite, and we had red splotches all over our bodies.

We walked and walked. When we would come to a larger town, we would see the tin foil on the ground where our planes had dropped it to mess up the radar. We had also been told not to talk to the civilians. These people had been in war for at least three years before we had gotten into it and many of them had either been bombed or had family killed in the war and may retaliate against us. As a result, the guards said they would not be responsible for our safety if we spoke to anyone.

We weren't getting much to eat. Bread and water was about it. One day we were on a break standing at the side of the road. It was in the Baltic area, and it was wet and muddy. This man came by in a carriage with horses. It looked like something that you see in the south during the 1800s. He had been wounded and was on his way home. He said something to the people that was with him, and they dropped some of the potatoes on the ground for us. We had them that night.

I had a bad case of dysentery. It's hard to explain how you had to drop your pants in the middle of a town or where other people were at to relieve yourself, but there was nothing else you could do. There was a Canadian doctor that was in our group, and he sent word down the line to eat charcoal. I got sticks and built a fire. I ate the charcoal. It was easy to do because I was hungry. It stopped the dysentery. I found out later that it was a common way to relieve dysentery in the States. The air raids were getting closer all the time. Some of them were our own planes. Then we begin to see our observation planes. We started walking in PW formation to let them know we were prisoners of war. We thought we were doing pretty good. A formation of B-29s came over, and I looked up. I thought that looks like a pretty good formation. Then I noticed that the bomb bay doors were open, and I saw these little dots dropping. I realized that they were bombing. A building near where we were at was hit. The building had been a storage building for captured materials that the Germans were keeping. Each of us got a bayonet, and I put mine in my coat. I carried it for the remainder of the war.

Occasionally, we would hear planes firing in the air, but all we could see were vapors, then a parachute where a pilot was coming down.

We knew that it was about over when we started coming by houses with white bed sheets hanging out their windows."

LIBERATION
April 26, 1945

"About a day before we were liberated, we had a change of guards," Bob explained. "The old guards had sometimes been bad, hitting on us and so forth, so they gave us a new guard that walked with us for about a mile, and some of the British that had been captured for up to four years began to take the rifles from the guards. We walked to the lines and were liberated on April 26, 1945 at Bitterfield, Germany. We walked across the bridge at Bittersfield. My feet were bloody from the shoes that I had been wearing. They didn't fit. We went to an aid station and they cleaned me up. We were really hungry. I had lost about 35 pounds. I can remember this big pile of K-rations, and we were trying to get through this fence to get to them. This major came along and got on top of them with his pistol drawn to keep us from getting into them.

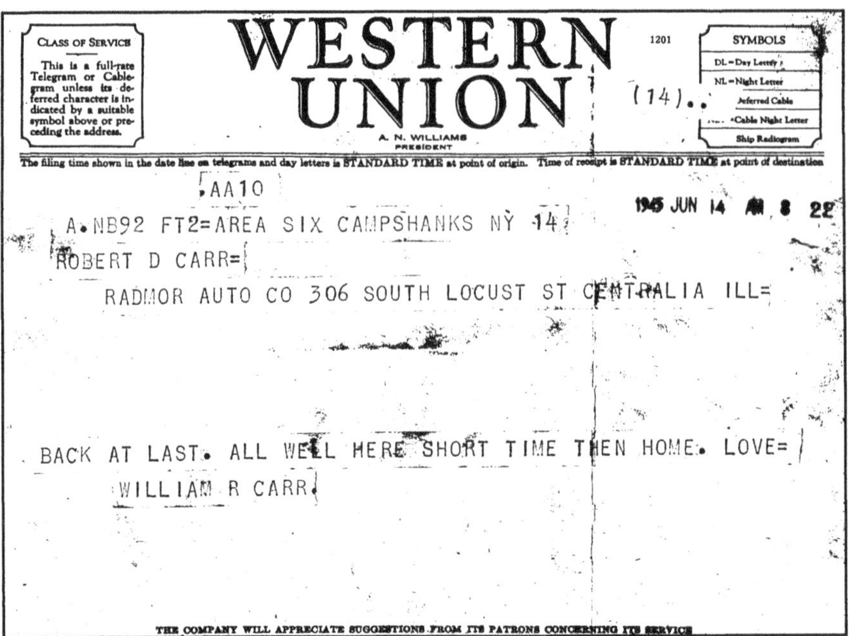

WESTERN UNION

A. N. WILLIAMS PRESIDENT

CLASS OF SERVICE

This is a full-rate Telegram or Cablegram unless its deferred character is indicated by a suitable symbol above or preceding the address.

1201

SYMBOLS

DL=Day Letter

NL=Night Letter

Deferred Cable

Cable Night Letter

Ship Radiogram

The filing time shown in the date line on telegrams and day letters is STANDARD TIME at point of origin. Time of receipt is STANDARD TIME at point of destination

(14)

AA10

1945 JUN 14 AM 8 22

A.NB92 FT2=AREA SIX CAMPSHANKS NY 14

ROBERT D CARR=

RADMOR AUTO CO 306 SOUTH LOCUST ST CENTRALIA ILL=

BACK AT LAST. ALL WELL HERE SHORT TIME THEN HOME. LOVE=

WILLIAM R CARR

THE COMPANY WILL APPRECIATE SUGGESTIONS FROM ITS PATRONS CONCERNING ITS SERVICE

Bob and Veneta Carr

Later, we moved to Holle, Germany, and I had a chance to take KP. I found some fresh cans of fruit and some condensed milk. I ate and drank, and they stayed down for about ten minutes. I was really sick. It took a few weeks to get my system use to the proper diet.

A couple of days later they put us on a DC-3 and flew us to Camp Lucky Strike in France. We were fed everyday three or four times a day until we were sent home."

HOMEWARD BOUND
May 30, 1945

On May 30, 1945 Bob and several thousand other ex-POWs boarded a troop ship and headed for the United States. About two weeks later on June 13, 1945 they arrived at New York Harbor. Bob took leave at home, returned to the Army for the rest and recuperation, and a few months later on October 29, 1945 was discharged from the Army.

EPILOGUE

Bob went to work for Linkon Auto Supply which at the time had one store. Thirty-seven years later when he retired, they had grown to 28 stores. He was the branch operations manager when he retired. Bob met Veneta shortly after his discharge, and they were married on June 30, 1945. They had three sons William, Richard, and Michael. He and his wife now enjoy their retirement.

CHAPTER ELEVEN

STAFF SERGEANT EDWIN DOUGLASS JR.
U.S. ARMY

COMPANY F 35TH DIVISION 134TH INFANTRY REGIMENT
CAPTURED IN NANCY, FRANCE

PRISONER OF WAR
SEPTEMBER 11, 1944-APRIL 21, 1945
STALAG XIIA, IIIC, AND IIIA

THE BEGINNING
August 1942

America's involvement in World War II was eight months old in August 1942. Induction centers were full of young men being enlisted to fight the Axis powers. They came from the cities, small towns and rural farm areas all over the U.S. On August 17, 1942, Edwin Douglass, a farm boy from Southern Illinois received his induction notice. He was to report to the induction center at Scott Air Force Base for entry into the Armed Services. After a complete physical he was sent to Camp Wheeler, Georgia for 13 weeks basic. Then to Camp Meade, Maryland for further infantry training. It was getting close to Christmas and Ed wanted to go home. Ed was short of money he explained, "It was during Christmas and we were drawing for six day leaves for Christmas. It was toward the end of the month when I drew mine and I was broke. I went to this buddy of mine that I had went through training with. I told him that I was broke and I needed money to get home on. He asked how much and I told him I could make it on $20.00. I can still see him pulling that money out of his pocket. I thanked him and turned to walk off. He asked me if that was enough. Before I was able to go, the furlough was canceled and I took him his $20.00 back."

Right after Christmas they shipped Ed's unit out to California by train. He ended up in F Company of the 134th Infantry Regiment, but only after a mishap or two. "We were going through Texas on the train and we picked up a load of medics," Ed said, "We found out that we were supposed to go to the Quartermaster's battalion but they had a mix up. The medics went to the Quartermaster's battalion and they sent us to the 134th medic's battalion. We spent the night and the next morning we were milling around when a T-4 came strolling through. He asked us how much medical training we had. We had this old Sergeant that had been busted back at Camp Meade. He spoke up and said, "Medical training Hell! I wouldn't roll a pill for no son-of-a-bitch. I'm Infantry! After that they sent four or five of us at a time to different companies. That's how I ended up in F Company."

Edwin Douglass Jr.

F Company was sent to Camp Roker, Alabama, Tennessee maneuvers, and then Camp Buckner, North Carolina. "That's where the really rough training started," Ed explained. "Two weeks in the Virginia Mountains and then we boarded the USS *Eugene Anderson* for Europe. We ate twice a day and they had to feed twenty-four hours a day because they had so many people on the boat. It was crowded and we had to take baths in salt water. I was looking forward to seeing land, soon."

THE LANDING IN EUROPE
May 12, 1944 - September 10, 1944

Ed's unit landed in Saint Ive, England, on May 12, 1944. For the next few weeks the infantry unit trained daily. Then on July 5, 1944, the 134th Regiment landed on Omaha Beach. "We never even got our feet wet," Ed explained, "everything had been cleared for us in the D-day invasion. Our first real big objective was Saint Lo, France."

The 134th hit Saint Lo on July 14, 1944. For the next 14 days the men took the town block by block, building by building encountering snipers, machine gun nest, and Nazi artillery and tank fire. Finally, Ed's unit seized the on July 27, 1944.

After another 45 days of fierce fighting, the 134th regiment had taken Mortain, Montargis, Troyes from the Nazis and on September 10, 1944 were on the outskirts of Nancy, France.

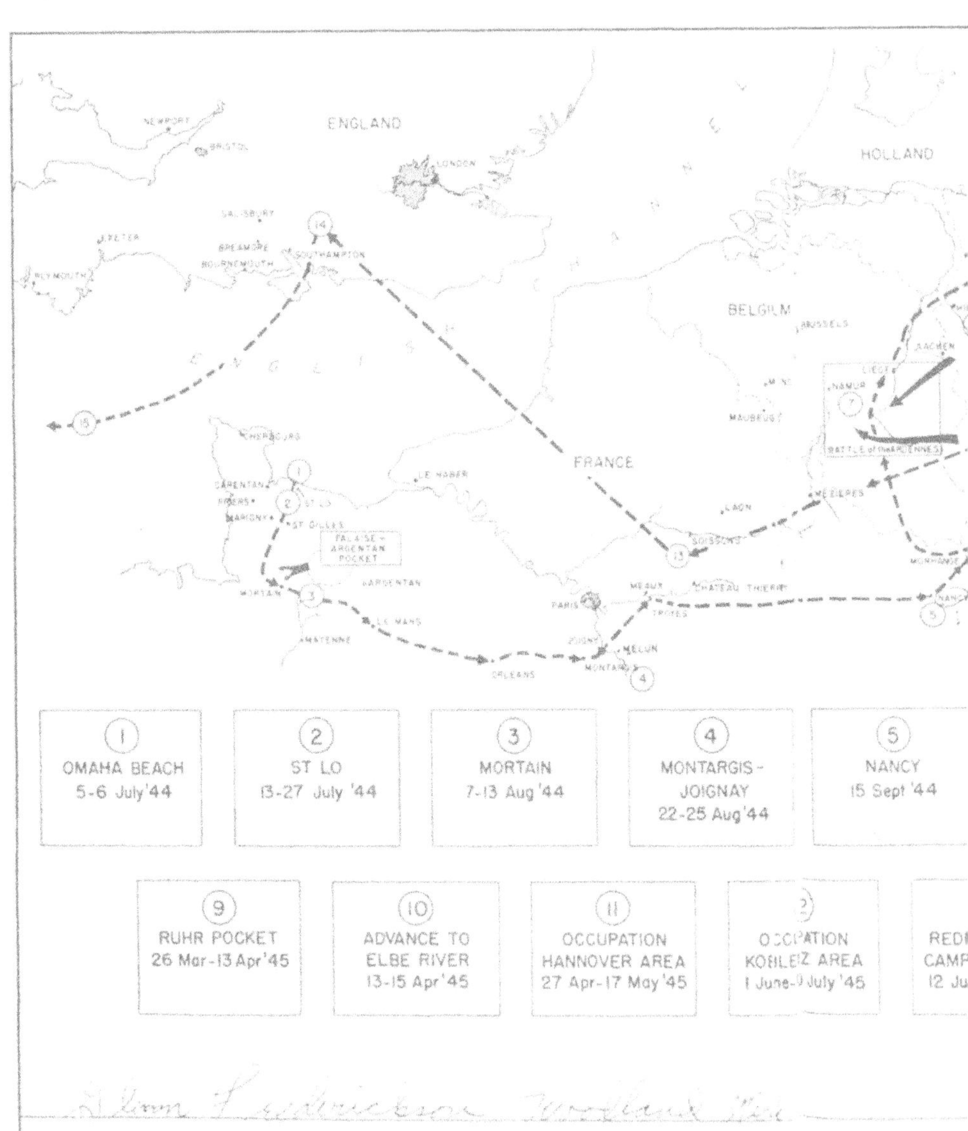

THE BATTLE AT NANCY, FRANCE
September 10, 1942

As the preparations were made to take the town of Nancy, France orders were given to E Company, F Company, and part of G Company of the 2nd Battalion to cross the bridge into Nancy. Ed was assigned to F Company and he and his fellow soldiers started moving at 2200 hours. Although the unit took heavy casualties, within an hour the companies had raced across the bridge. It appeared that the strategy was working until the Nazis figured out what was going on.

The Nazis began to bring in heavy concentrations of artillery. Although the American units ordered tank destroyers and another platoon to the scene they arrived too late and the Nazis counterattacked.

The 3rd Battalion was ordered down to cross the bridge. They were halted along the road however, when continuous fares and endless mortar and artillery shells marked the bridge. The 3rd Battalion commander made his way toward the bridge in an attempt to locate the 2nd Battalion. He found the command group of the 2nd Battalion in a culvert beneath the approaches to the bridge. Medics were working on the wounded, soldiers worked vainly to keep the communications lines open, officers screamed into the telephones to make themselves heard above the bursting shells which were landing all around them. The intensity of the fire made it impossible to move much less cross the bridge.

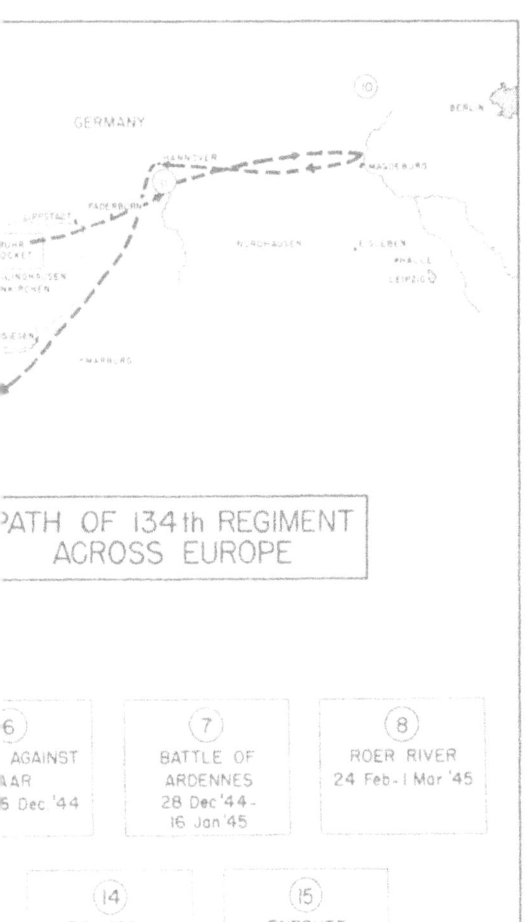

Then at 1:30 A.M. on September 11, a tremendous explosion shook the ground. Ed and the men of the 2nd Battalion knew immediately that what they had feared most had just become a reality. The bridge had been blown and they were cut off. Nazis screaming "Heil Hitler!" closed in. Now with their backs to the river, the lack of communications, the lack of contact, the lack of visibility, and the presence of the German tanks without antitank defense was all too overwhelming. Ed was wounded, but the pain from the wound was nothing compared to yearning in his stomach for Ed had never given up at anything. Now he realized, he had a choice. He could surrender or die. There was no other choice.

THE CAPTURE
September 11, 1942

Ed's personal account, "I think the Germans blew up the bridge. There were a lot of men that didn't get across the bridge, but those of us that did just had to roll in on the bank of the river. The Germans were in front of us and they rolled tanks in behind us. We were trapped. Orders came down to surrender.

We threw our guns down and came out from behind the banks. We were lined up and we wanted to smoke. This German is standing there with his gun and he pulls out

A Point of Interest

PRISONERS KILLED IN AIR RAID

In late December 1944, sixty American Officers in Stalag XIIA were killed during an American B-29 air raid on Limberg. Stalag XIIA was located only 600 yards from a Marshalling Yard (railroad station) which was the intended target.

his cigarettes and wanted to trade one of his for an American cigarette. I didn't really want to because I had tried one of the German cigarettes before and I didn't like them, but I traded with him anyway.

A short time later they took me back to an aid station for a hip wound I had received. The Germans had a tent set up and they were bringing German soldiers in as well as us. They finally got around to taking the shrapnel out of my hip and we went to a small hospital somewhere around Nancy, France. We met this French orderly that had learned English from a book. He was really good at it and he came up one day and wanted to know what bullshit meant. He said that he could find bull and he could find shit, but he couldn't find bullshit. We told him it was slang.

STALAG XIIA
Third Week Of September 1944

Ed was in the hospital for about a week before the Nazis shipped him to Stalag XIIA. The camp was located just 600 yards from a marshalling yard (railroad station) in Limburg, Germany. This transit camp fluctuated from 1,500 to 4,000 prisoners depending on the time period of the war. The barracks were one story approximately 40 by 130 feet, each containing ten rooms leading from a central hallway running lengthwise with the building. Most barracks had no furniture, but those that did had a small stove, a table, and a few stools. Bunks were stacked six high and each room, approximately 15 x 23 feet was designed to provide for 16 men. In the latter part of the war as the prison population increased, men were forced to sleep on the floor or ground, in some cases with nothing but straw as a bed. The bedding was louse infected and all the prisoners suffered with body lice. The roofs leaked, windows were broken, lighting was inadequate, and there was no heat in the barracks. There was one cold water tap located in a building used for a latrine. The walls and tools in the latrine were covered with feces. The prisoners made fruitless efforts to keep the area clean, but because all the prisoners suffered from dysentery it was impossible to control their bowels.

The food was inadequate. The diet was bread and soup. Most of the prisoners averaged 900 calories or less a day. As Ed explained, "the Germans never mistreated us as for as beating us, but we didn't get much to eat. We got a Red Cross box that four of us had to share. It is what kept us alive. The package had nine packs of Old Gold cigarettes in it and I got them all because the other guys that I shared with didn't smoke. Later I traded the cigarettes for food."

Ed was at Stalag XIIA for a few days then he was packed onto a train with hundreds of other prisoners. He had no idea of his destination.

THE FORTY AND EIGHT BOXCARS
September 1944

The main transportation of American prisoners was by rail. The 40-8 boxcars were the most common. The 40-8 referred to by the Germans meant forty men or eight horses. For the prisoners it was much worse. Prisoners were packed into the boxcars so tight that they were unable to set or lay down. The cars were sectioned with men at both ends of the

Barracks at Stalag XIIA

Straw floor at Stalag XIIA

boxcar, separated in the middle of the car by barbed wire and an armed German guard. The floors of the cars were often covered with horse manure mixed with straw. When men could set or lay down they had no choice, but to lie in the manure. The men would travel for days without food and water. The trains would not stop between destinations and when they did most of the time the prisoners were not allowed off of the trains. Prisoners had to use one corner of the boxcar for relieving themselves. The conditions after days of traveling became deplorable. Ed's personal account of the trip from Stalag XIIA to Stalag IIIC on a forty by eight, "We were in Stalag XIIA for a few days and then they loaded us aboard forty and eights for another camp. We were packed in the train so tight that you couldn't roll over without the help of your buddies. We were fed bread once in the four or five days that we were traveling. No water.

Several times we stopped in rail stations and the Germans would leave us on side rails with other detached rail cars. When our planes bombed they would leave us locked in.

We saw a lot of damage, but were never hit.

Many of us had relieved ourselves in one corner of the boxcar. I was lucky, but many were not. They suffered from bad cases of diarrhea and could not control their bowels. As a result, many relieved themselves standing in place. The conditions were unsanitary and the smell became unbearable after a few days with the crowded conditions in the closed in boxcar."

STALAG IIIC
October 1944 -February 1945

After five days aboard the 40-8 boxcars, Ed and the other prisoners arrived at Stalag IIIC. Stalag IIIC is located at Altdrewitz in the northeast part of Germany. The camp was designed much like the other Nazis Stalags as Ed explained, " I begin to catch up with the guys that I had been captured with. There were six of us in the barrack. It was really getting cold and we did get a small ration of coal, but it wasn't enough. The barrack had double floors so we burnt the wood from one of the floors.

We had a wash house with water pipe that stuck up out of the ground. When it got cold the Russians got horse manure and packed around the pipe so that the pipe wouldn't freeze. It worked because we had water all winter.

Our latrine was an open pit behind the wash house.

During Christmas 1944, they issued a Red Cross box that had boned turkey and the trimmings. Some of the boys saved potatoes out of their rations and we put on a good feed. It messed some of them up. They had got so much rich food that I saw some setting on the stool and throwing up at the same time. I didn't get sick, but I was lucky.

A few days later one of the guys thought that he was over the diarrhea and stood up and let a fart. He shit all over his self. We all laughed, but inside it wasn't really funny.

I walked outside after the feed and light a cigarette. This old German guard was walking the post between the barrack. He was old enough to be my father. I had a full belly and was feeling pretty good it being Christmas and all. He looked over at me and put his fingers up to his mouth. I took one of my cigarettes and light it. I handed it to him and he carried on for an hour over that cigarette."

A couple of months later the Russian front moved closer and closer. The Germans decided they would have to abandon the camp. Ed was on the move again.

THE MARCH TO STALAG IIIA
February 1945

The Nazis picked about thirty of the prisoners including Ed and marched them into Altdrewitz. "They put us in a basement of a house overnight," Ed said, "While we were there the Russians came into the town with tanks and shot the place up. The next morning the German soldiers were coming through picking up the dead soldiers, throwing them on the back of trucks and moving on. They made us help. We took a door off of a house and used it as a stretcher. We would put as soldier on it and carry the body to the truck. This old Germans soldier on the truck would grab them by the hair of the head and pull them up on the truck and stack them. This German lieutenant came and got us and took us around the corner of this house to pick up a soldier. He was really shook up. He was shaking his pistol at us and spoke perfect English. He looked at us and said, "why in the hell did you Americans come over here and fight Germany. Why?" We never gave him any trouble because he would have shot us if we had.

After that they marched us toward Stalag IIIA. There were a lot of refugees on the road. Most were Germans running from the Russians. We would stay in barns, houses, and basements on the way. On a couple of occasions we slept on the ground. We didn't get much to eat. One night while we were in this barn I got to looking around and found a carrot bed. We had all we could eat that night.

The next morning I got up and was rolling my two blankets up. As I made each roll, I would put a carrot in the blanket. Some of the other prisoners said that they would kill me if I got caught. I said I may as well be killed as starved to death. We started out that morning. The sun was coming up and it was pretty warm. I reached back and got a carrot and the one of the other guys said, "hey Doug give us a carrot." I said, "if I am going to get shot over them I'm going to eat them."

STALAG IIIA

February 1945- April 21, 1945

After traveling for about a week Ed and the other prisoners landed in Stalag IIIA at Luckenwalde. "It was a big camp," Ed explained. "It was crowded too. We had to sleep on a concrete floor for about two weeks and then there were a few empty beds. They had made the bunks six high. It was better sleeping except for the body lice. We were infested with them.

They fed us soup once a day. Sometimes all it was was hot water. We used it to take a bath with instead of drinking it.

We used to make a blower. We would take a flat board, one milk can with the end out of it would be laid down and make a fan. It was used to cook with.

The Russians were treated a lot worse than we were. They carried dead out of their compound every day. They just starved them. We had grass soup one morning. None of us would eat it. This Russian came over by our barracks with a pot. We would just pour the soup in his pot as we passed. He was happy as could be. The Russians would go out and

Outside living area at Stalag IIIA.

work. They would steal what they could and bring it back to the camp for trade. We traded, but the most valuable item was cigarettes. You could have bought your way out of camp with enough of the cigarettes."

Each night the artillery fire in the distance signaled to the prisoners that the front was getting closer. Then on April 21, 1945, Ed woke up in the early morning. It was quite. The artillery fire had stopped. He and the other prisoners walked out into the yard and found that the Nazis guards were gone. They were silent as they looked at each other, but they all knew that they day that they had prayed for had finally came. The end of the war.

THE LIBERATION
April 21, 1945

Ed's account of liberation day. "The Russians finally came in with tanks and knocked the fence down. They left an old truck and told us if we couldn't go eat now it was our own fault. We went out and found some live stock and started doing our own butchering. The Russians came with their women. When they weren't shooting, they were setting on these Sherman Tanks we had given them with their women drinking vodka. They were drunk yelling and laughing.

We went into the Russian compound and it was amazing. They were starving to death in those compounds, but they had drawn some of the most beautiful pictures on the walls that I have ever seen.

When those Russians got out and went to town there

Barracks at Stalag IIIA.

Kitchen at Stalag IIIA.

were some Germans really hurting. They were out for revenge. We were around the camp for a few days and their weren't any Americans coming around so a couple of my buddies and I took off on foot. We finally caught up with some GI trucks and they took us to an air field. We boarded C-47s and were flown to Camp Lucky Strike in France. I had lost 38 pounds."

HOMEWARD BOUND
June 1945-October 31, 1945

On June 6, 1945, Ed boarded a boat for home. "They assigned several of us to CP duty just as soon as we took off," He explained. "We got back in the storage room and I noticed a gallon can of pineapples. I thought I haven't had them in a long time and I opened them and started eating. Some of the other guys opened different cans they liked and they ate. The officer in charge never said a word, although we weren't supposed to do it. One day he came in and we told him that it had been the best assignment we had ever had in the Army. He just laughed.

When we got back to the states I finally made it to Chicago and got 60 days leave with orders to report back to Texas. I found out that my folks had thought I was dead. A while after I had been captured, they got a telegram from the war department that I was missing in action. Then a little later they got a letter that I wrote from Stalag IIIC. Well, when the Russians were coming and they took the 30 of us out into that little town, the Russians attacked. Although we were taken onto Stalag IIIA the rest of the Camp had been liberated by the Russians. I didn't know it, but my cousin was in the camp, was liberated and got home long before I did. My folks let him see the letter and he told them that he had been in the camp. There were a lot of the prisoners that had been killed. They then thought I was one of them. They sure were glad to see me."

EPILOGUE

Ed was discharged in California, returned home in Illinois, and begin to farm. He has been farming ever since. He married Beth Florence Hale and the couple have two sons Frank Lee and Harold Ray. Beth passed away and Ed remarried, to his present wife Maxine.

Ed belongs to the 134th World War II Association and stays in contact with his former service buddies. Recently, he attended a 50-year union in Garden Dale, Texas where he met with many of the men that he fought within Europe and lived within the Nazis Prison Camps.

Douglass at reunion with fellow ex-POWs.

CHAPTER TWELVE

TECH SERGEANT THOMAS HAROLD BOARDMAN
U.S. ARMY AIR FORCE

96TH BOMB GROUP 413TH BOMB SQUADRON CAPTURED DURING A BOMBING MISSION OVER GERMANY

PRISONER OF WAR
SEPTEMBER 13, 1944-APRIL 26, 1945
STALAG LUFT IV

MARRIAGE, THE DRAFT, AND THE ARMY
February 1943

World War II affected the lives of everyone, especially young men. Such was the case for Harold Boardman. The war was in full swing and so was Harold when he was drafted in the U.S. Army in February 1943. It was just two months after he was married and two days after his 19th birthday. He was sent to Shepard Field, Texas for basic training and then to Larado, Texas for Aerial Gunnery training. In January 1944, Harold went to Sioux Falls, South Dakota for radio training. After several months of training, he was classified as a radio gunner for B-17s.

THE FLIGHT TO ENGLAND
April 14, 1944 -May 1, 1944

On the morning of April 24, 1944 in questionable weather the Harold and his crew took off across the United States headed for the east coast. Flying at the assigned 13,000 feet the crew crossed the United States and continued over the Altantic ocean. A few days into the flight the crew landed in Iceland to discover that the land was nothing but a lot of rocks with no trees.

After a night's rest they took off for Prestwick, Scotland. On May 1, 1944 in a hazy afternoon the crew landed in Scotland. The crew signed some forms, collected their gear, and were taken by truck to Glasgow Railway Station. After a few hours of waiting they boarded the train for a long ride. Hours later the crew arrived at Stone, England where they stayed for ten days waiting on assignment.

During the wait Harold and his fellow crew members were taken to an assembly center where they were allowed to review daily bombing missions statistics and records. It didn't take long for Harold to realize that you would have to be very lucky to complete the 25 missions required before you got a ticket home.

Thomas Harold Boardman and his wife.

Boardman and crew.

The assignment finally came in. Harold and his crew were being assigned to the 96th bomb Group of the 413th Bomb Squadron.

THE FIRST MISSION
June 7, 1944

The weather was on the crew's side on the first mission as Harold explained. "Our first mission was the June 7th the day after D-day. Because of weather conditions we really didn't accomplish very much. Our bomb group had been called back, but we didn't get the call back and flew over France by ourselves. We were lucky it went without incident and returned safely. The only good thing about it was that we got to count it as a mission."

THE NEXT 17 MISSIONS
June 11, 1944-September 12, 1944

Throughout the summer of 1944 Harold and his crew completed 17 more missions in France and Germany. They covered a gamut of targets from anti-personnel missions in support of troops, oil refinery complexes, to engine factories. One raid however, is pressed in Harold's memory. "The worse raid that I went on was over Paris. We were bombing a Standard oil plant on the outskirts of Paris. For morale reasons our bombing route was issued by the Air Force. We couldn't release our bombs by radar so we had to do a visual bombing raid at 17,000 feet. When we finished the bombing raid we turned and flew over the heart of Paris. We lost half of our bombing group after we released our bombs. The Germans had some expert anti-aircraft gunners and they really were good. I did three bombing raids over Berlin and expected a good defense there, but it was nothing compared to what we got over Paris."

MISSION 19-THE LAST MISSION
September 13, 1944

"We flew often with overcast skies," Harold explained. We were not any safer when they used radar to shoot at us, but it made us feel better to have cloud cover between us and the enemy. On our 19th mission we were over Ludwigshaven, Germany and the clouds dissipated. It was about 12 noon when we moved over the target and there was a clear view of everything. They walked right across our wings with anti-aircraft fire and knocked out three engines of our four. It put us out of the formation and we stayed in the air for about 30 minutes and almost made it to France. The 3 engine caught on fire and we bailed out at 13,000 feet. I always wanted to meet the instructors again that gave us the training on parachuting. They always told us to turn on our stomachs. When I jumped from the plane I realized I was on my back with my head down. I spent a few minutes trying to turn over and after the third time I looked down and I could see the trees. I pulled the cord and the chest cute I was wearing opened just as natural as could be. Had I been like they said, I should have been the shute that would have opened in my face. I have always wondered why they told us that.

B-17 on a bombing mission. Taken from Boardman's plane.

We landed right in the middle of a German Infantry division. They were digging in to stop the advance by the Americans. I hit about thirty feet from the top of this hill. I hid my parachute and ran to the top of this hill. When I got there I realized we were right in the middle of a German Infantry unit. I just set down. A few minutes later a German soldier came up and wanted to know if had a pistol. By good advice we didn't carry our guns and were taken prisoner right away. I told them no."

A POW. . . *HAROLD'S STORY*
September 13, 1944 -April 26, 1945

"The Trauma of being a prisoner was a real adjustment. One day you are living a half way normal life with the exception of the combat missions, a comfortable bunk, plenty to eat and then the transformation to a status of POW is startling.

They loaded us aboard trucks with a 15 year old armed guard and we headed for Frankfort. The kid was scared to death and so were we. We were afraid that they were going to hit a bump and his rifle was going to go off. We made it though. In Frankfort they interrogated us first. They knew everything about our crew and really didn't push for to much information. After the interrogation they lined us up against a wall outside and took some newspaper shots."

THE TRAIN RIDE

"Then they put us on a train. I was on it overnight and stopped the next day at a temporary camp. Then after about four or five days later they put us back on the train. Before hand they put me in charge of the prisoners. They wanted me to sign a paper that we wouldn't escape. I told them that I wouldn't do it. I found out from one of the guys that they would take our shoes if I didn't sign it. Winter was coming on and I thought about that and the fact that we didn't know where we were going. Then I thought about it and wondered what in the hell would they do if we did try to escape. It was silly to worry about it and I signed it.

We were on the train for seven days. The conditions were terrible. First of all, the boxcar was suppose to hold 40 men and we had 80 jammed in the boxcar. There was a small air vent at each end of the boxcar so the air was tight. Mine had to set between each others legs and any one that had to relieve themselves had to do it in a helmet and pass it back until the man next to the air vent could pour the contents out of the helmet. The floor

A Point of Interest

PSYCHOSIS

Many of the prisoners of war have stated that the cause of psychosis for prisoners of war was not the cold or the lice or the lack of food or being liberated or the fact that a prisoner had to sit on a toilet while 3,000 men watched, but the anxiety suffered from not knowing what was going to happen to them from one day to the next.

had horse manure and straw on it and combined with that, men who had diarrhea, the close quarters, and no ventilation to speak of, things got real foul smelling. We got very little water or food during the trip. By the time we arrived at the prison camp it seemed like the trip had taken a year instead of seven days."

LIFE IN PRISON CAMP

"The camp had a psychopath for a leader. Young Nazi Marines ran the first prisoners by bayonet and dogs from the train to the camp, three miles away. They bayoneted over a hundred prisoners although they did not kill any. They also turned the dog loose on us.

I was a prisoner for three days before I could eat. We got a hard black bread to eat. You could slice it paper thin and it would stay together. Some said it had aspestia powder in it and some said it had saw dust in it. I couldn't eat for the first three days and three days after I was liberated I couldn't eat, but in between it was okay.

After a few weeks in the camp any food begins to taste good. The only thing on your mind is food. I ate bread and soup with an occasional potato peel in it. On February 26, my birthday, I had one raw potato to eat. Potatoes and the barley bread were the only solid food that the Germans gave us. The margarine was remarkable. It stayed together regardless of the temperature I don't know what it had in it but it spread better than our butter. The guy next to me was always talking about what he wanted to eat when he was released. It was a fried egg with a Hershey almond bar on the top. That use to drive me crazy thinking about that, but I never did try it when I got out.

The barracks had no heat so we were issued one blanket to fight the cold. It wasn't enough, but better than nothing. We wore the same clothes the duration of our captivity and they were never washed. We had no bathing facilities at all. We were covered with lice and fleas. It was just a miserable experience."

THE MARCH
January 1945

"In January 1945 the Russians broke through the lines about 15 miles from our camp. We were roused out of our bunks and given the news that the next day that the Russians would be in the camp and the Germans would be gone. We were excited, but warned not to get excited to soon. Two hours later we were called out again. His time the Germans informed us that we had a few hours to pack our belongings. The next morning they moved 7,000 of us out of the camp.

We marched south for three months. We were strafed by our own aircraft a couple of times until they realized we were POWs. After that they would tip their wings as they few over.

We would sleep in barns, fields, and on the road as we moved. We didn't get much to eat as we moved. About the same diet as camp-bread, water, and watery soup.

My feet were swollen and covered with blisters from the walking. My boots and socks were wore out and that didn't help, but I was better than some. Several of the men couldn't walk because they were so weak. We helped them along and we didn't lose a one.

We were lucky compared to the Jews. No matter what direction we seemed to be walk-

A Point of Interest

HYDEKRUG RUN

In the Summer of 1944 the Russians liberated Stalag Luft VI. The Germans moved the airmen from the prison camp ahead of the Russians. The POWs were loaded aboard a German ship, the *Masuren*. For days they were kept below decks in horrible conditions. When the men arrived at their new destination they were taken onto the dock and hand cuffed in pairs. A German Captain gave the order for the POWs to run. Under guard by Nazi Marines armed at fixed bayonet with Alsation Hounds they chased after the POWs. Many of the prisoners, because of their physical and medical conditions, were unable to run and often fell. The men hand cuffed to them were forced to carry them on their backs. When the run was over there were over 150 POWs who had sustained bayonet wounds, dog bites, and broken legs.

ing they were always walking in the opposite direction. They wore stripped clothing. Those poor people were walking skeletons. Many were too weak to continue walking and the others were too weak to help them. The Nazis would just shoot them."

LIBERATION
April 26, 1945

"Three weeks before we were liberated they switched guards and they were much more civilized to us. For two or three days we could hear small arms fire. We were now moving at night and staying up in barn and fields during the day. The Americans were dropping pamphlets telling the Germans to surrender. They had had orders to kill all the POWs but the infer structure broke down to the point that they knew there was no use.

We got to this little town and we turned into this town and there was a American soldier standing at the edge of town. He had a uniform on with the neatest creases in it. A pencil mustache and a machine gun laying on his lap. I knew then we were liberated. I had so many lice on me that I could have fallen and they would have carried me the last mile. We got across this river and everybody was throwing their blankets down. I threw mine as far as I could and then found out we were gong to stay there for the night. There were hundreds of us looking all around for our blanket rolls. I found mine and forgot that I had a couple of souvenirs in it-A German beer mug and bayonet."

CAMP LUCKY STRIKE

We slept on the straw that night and the next morning they took us by truck to Halle. They had provisions set up for 3,000. There was 15,000 of us. We stood in line for something to eat all day. I had lost 60 pounds in prison camp and now I was back on my prison diet. I was standing there six deep at least another four hours before getting anything to eat. This guy popped out of the tent and said I need 20 men for KP duty. I shot out of that line and was right there. He took us inside and we got to eat before we started. Then all we did was start unloading truck after truck of C-rations that they were taking inside and cooking. After a couple of hours of that I thought we need to give someone else a chance. I stuff my legs and pockets full of C-rations. I couldn't bend my legs when I walked out of the tent. I didn't have to go to the mess hall.

I had received a shrapnel wound in my left leg and I got treatment for it. Then a short time later we got the word we were going to go home."

Boardman at a 1992 Reunion. Left to right: Norm Thye, Thomas Boardman, Al Preston, Donald Wagner and Adam Klosowski.

HOMEWARD BOUND

It took us about two weeks for Harold and the other soldiers to cross the Atlantic. "When we pulled into New York Harbor on June 29, 1945, it was one of the most beautiful sights I ever saw," Harold said. "I was glad to be home."

Harold was on leave for 60 days and then returned to camp. On October 29, 1945 Harold was honorably discharged from the service.

EPILOGUE

Harold returned to Sikeston, Missouri where he became a Certified Public Accountant. He and his wife Caretta had four children Brenda in 1946, Michael in 1948, Marcus in 1953, and Kevin in 1958.

In 1968, Michael was killed in action in South Viet Nam.

Harold says that he thinks a lot about his past experience as a POW. "I would not want to go through the experience again, but I have always considered the men that were captured by the Japs as the real prisoners of war."

CHAPTER THIRTEEN

2ND LIEUTENANT CARL W. REMY
U.S. ARMY/AIR FORCE

8TH AIR FORCE 95TH GROUP 336TH SQUADRON
CAPTURED DURING HIS SECOND BOMBING MISSION OVER GERMANY

PRISONER OF WAR
SEPTEMBER 28, 1944-MAY 1, 1945
STALAG LUFT I

DEFERRED FOR TWO YEARS
October 1942

In 1942 Carl had two years of college under his belt at Oklahoma University. The war was going strong and a program was offered to college students to allow them to finish college before going into the service. A student could enlist in the reserves and get a two year deferment to finish college. Carl and a bunch of his buddies joined and were sworn in the Army/Air Force reserves in October 1942. All their papers were stamped "Deferred for Two Years" in big red letters. Four months later they all got orders to report for active duty. He went to Wichita Falls, Texas for basic training, then to college training detachment at Saint Marcas, Texas, for officers training. From there he was shipped to West Texas State Teachers college for aviation training. After completing this training he was sent to California for cadet school. After several other training schools, Carl became a B-17 bombardier. He was now qualified to locate and mark targets, test and inspect the equipment, and in an emergency was trained to navigate by means of dead reckoning pilotage. Then he was given orders for England.

A FLIGHT TO ENGLAND
September 1944

"We took the new B-17 from the east coast and flew it to England. It was pretty exciting flying over the North Atlantic," Carl explained. "We flew inside of Greenland and landed in Iceland for an overnight stay. Then the next day we flew to England.

We had a lot of training on formation flying and simulated bomb dropping, but that was it."

THE FIRST MISSION
September 27, 1944

On September 27, 1944, Carl's crew flew their first mission. It was on the main river near Frankfort, Germany. It was a milk run, there weren't any fighters to deal with. In England the crews flew their first ten missions in the first ten days. That was a wake up call at 1:30 in the morning and taking off about daylight and heading for Germany.

THE LAST MISSION. . .*CARL'S STORY*
September 28, 1944

"On September 28th we were up and at it again. Our mission was the Merseburg Oil Refinery which was deep in Germany. This was the 25th time this place had been bombed. We took off early and formed up above the clouds and headed for Germany. We cleared our guns over the English Channel. We were near the target about 11 A.M. We made the turn and began the long bomb run at an altitude of 27,000 feet. The accuracy of the German flak batteries was uncanny even though we were five miles high with a cloud layer under us. Besides the ordinary 40 and 88 millimeter stuff there was a terrifying rocket, which left a dense black exhaust trail all the way up and then exploded leaving a black ball of smoke giving the thing the appearance of a giant cobra.

Being a deputy-deputy (lead bombardier), I had the bombsight set up, but since the clouds did not break, I knew it would be a PFF (Path Finder Flight) run, so I turned the sight off and glued my eyes to the bomb bays of the lead ship a few feet above and ahead of me.

The idea is, of course, for the entire group of planes to drop its bombs at the instant the lead ship does.

The flak gunners simply seemed to have our number. When it bursts so close you can hear it inside the plane and can see that the black puffs have wicked, fiery, orange centers, that's damn close!

A flak suit can't be worn over a parachute, but with all that stuff hitting us, I felt inclined to wear my chute anyhow, so I just kind of draped the flak jacket over my shoulders. As I crouched there with the bomb release button in my hand I could hear the showers of flak bursting against the ship. The near misses tossed the ship around, and after one of them burst almost in my face, there was a hole in the plexi-glass right in front of me. I knew I wasn't hit and I glanced back at Swann, the navigator, and saw that he was okay.

That was only the beginning. For the first time in my life I was earnestly praying. I was concentrating on the bomb bays of the head ship but that didn't keep me from knowing what was happening to our ship. Two engine was hit and began to wind up to a high pitched scream. Heath, the pilot, fought the controls and did an excellent job of holding formation. Flak literally rained through the nose creating a fine mist of glass particles and dirt from the floor boards. The tail-gunner reported that both handles of his guns had been blown off by flak that ripped through both sides of the armor-plated tail, but he wasn't touched. The waist-gunner reported flak holes in the waist, but he was okay. The ball-turret was blown to hell. Lucky for the ball turret gunner that he wasn't in the turret. The glass was shattered in the top turret but the engineer, Younts, was busy elsewhere. After a close burst at twelve o'clock high, Heath told Eastman, the co-pilot, to take over the controls. One fragment had knocked Heath's helmet askew, broken his goggles and inflicted a wound over his right eye. Then a burst over the right wing blew holes in the wings and four engine; flak shattered the pilot compartment glass.

Heath and Younts, the engineer, were trying to feather two engine which was still running away at a terrific speed causing the ship to shudder. Runaway engines sometimes throw their props, and that screaming propeller a couple of feet to my left was a real concern.

Finally, after an eternity, I saw the bombs leave the lead ship, and instantly I hit the bomb release at 1205. Lights flicked off on my control panel indicating all bombs dropped, but when I said on interphone, "Bombs away," the armor gunner, Curtis, reported one five hundred pounder had hung up. At the same time we veered sharply in the turn off the target catching hell from the flak worse than before. Our crippled plane lost speed and altitude wondering crazily around the sky. The interphone crackled and popped and I couldn't understand what was being said. We couldn't keep up with the formation, and Heath and Eastman were working hard to keep from being rammed by the on rushing groups of bombers behind us.

There was another B-17 badly hit careening crazily around the sky leaving a trail of smoke. It finally leveled out and disappeared in a southernly direction. The pilot was probably trying to make Switzerland; a greater distance than France. I've always wondered how that crew made it.

Heath ordered, "Prepare to bail out." As if I wasn't ready. Eastman radioed the lead ship of our group telling them we were okay, but bailing out. There lead navigator acknowledged, "Good Luck." Then we were all alone over Germany.

I told Curtis, the armored gunner, to kick out that hanging bomb. He's a well-trained boy and did it with ease, even waiting for the proper moment when he thought he could splatter a small German village below. He certainly got a big kick out of personally bombing Germany.

We dropped lower and lower - easy prey for German fighters, and there was no sign of an American fighter. Eastman was radioing over and over for "Little Friend" (P-51s) to come and help us. Our fighters usually protected lone, crippled bombers.

We were out of the flak by this time. There were no fighters - just us. At this time it began to soak in that we probably wouldn't get back to England. My main reaction was that this can't be me in an airplane that's going down in Germany. This must be a picture show. This sort of thing happens to other guys, but not to me. I must be dreaming, I'll awaken in a minute—wonder what mom'll think—I told Betty I'd be home for Christmas—dear God.

But I wasn't dreaming. Heath said to throw everything that could be torn loose out of the ship in order to lighten the load. I remembered the story of the guy who bailed out in order to lighten the plane enough for his buddies to fly home. He was brave.

Out went guns, ammunition, flak suits, and among other things thousands of dollars worth of radio equipment. The navigator kept his G-box (Bomb Sight Equipment) and I kept the bomb sight.

The fatally hit four engine caught fire and Eastman feathered it. By transferring all the fuel from two engine, Eastman was able to stop the runaway two engine, but it was still windmilling-holding us back.

Eastman was still calling for fighters. We were dropping fast, and Swann was fighting maps and instruments trying to plot us a flak-free course to the Alsace in France. He measured distances to Switzerland, Sweden-too damned far.

Heath again ordered the crew to get ready to jump. Swann reported that at our present rate of descent we'd be on the ground before we ever reached France, so Eastman dropped flaps, and we mushed along at stalling speed, 100 mph, and started holding an altitude of a little over sixteen thousand feet. My hopes soared till Swann told me we were bucking a head wind of over 60 miles an hour. Then I knew we'd never make it. The straining one engine and sputtering three engine would never get us there.

Fighters were dog-fighting about three miles to our left, and a little later some P-51s came to escort us.

We were still mushing along on a prayer when the ball gunner reported that three engine was on fire, so Heath said he guessed it was time to jump. As Heath feathered three engine, the interphone went out and we went into a shallow dive. I thought the pilot and co-pilot must have jumped out, so I ripped off my oxygen mask and other entangling equipment and scrambled past Swann up to the pilot's compartment to find them still there looking scared. There were holes in the wind shield and both Heath and Eastman had little holes in their jackets and were covered with plexi-glass dust. Heath, with a little blood trickling down his forehead was smoking and gave me a faint smile. Eastman looked cool and collected. Heath said, "Goddammit, we've had it," and told me to go around the ship and tell every man that if he wanted to bail out, go at once, but that he, Heath, was going to land the ship and all who wanted to stay could do so.

I didn't have to make up my mind. I was staying for sure. I'd heard too many true stories of how lone airmen, parachuting into Germany were beaten, pitch forked, burnt in oil, dragged behind a truck, castrated, and I figured we'd be a little safer all together.

I crawled back down in the nose to find Swann still working on his maps. It was hard making him understand we were positively going down. He seemed kinda numb or something.

We made our way back to the radio room and Carlsen, the radio operator, said he would stay with the ship. Curtis, the armored gunner, and Shull, the ball gunner, said they would rather crash land. With the ship diving, interphone dead, and his guns knocked out, the tail gunner, Goodshed, was still at his position just like the hero in a movie. I had to send Shull back to get him. While Younts cranked the wheels down (no electrical power) the rest of us popped chutes and prepared padding in the radio room for the crash.

Meanwhile, we had broken through the overcast and were at a very low altitude. Heath, suddenly worried that Swann and I were still in the nose, sent Eastman down to see. He barely made it back to his seat - didn't even have time to fasten his safety belt for the landing.

I looked out of the little radio room window and saw that the terrain was very rough and wooded. But Heath picked a field, circled and went in for a landing. Suddenly a brick house and a telephone pole loomed up ahead, so straining one engine with our last surge, the plane cleared the obstacles and I felt the wheels touch ground on the plowed hill side. Eastman immediately cut all power, and as we bucked along the rough field, the plane suddenly swerved and I felt Swann lying on top of me. He, too, thought we were nosing over. That swerving was when Heath skillfully maneuvered the plane to miss a German girl working in the beet field.

We finally rolled to a stop with the plane smoking and steaming like a tea kettle, oxygen hissing and two engine on fire. I felt that I couldn't get out fast enough because the plane was due to blow any second. So everyone in the back ran down the waist and jumped out the back door. It was 1305.

I fully expected a reception of swarms of Germans, but the peasants working in the field where we landed just stared or kept on working. The navigator, gunners, and I ran about a hundred feet from the plane while big Heath dropped out of the nose escape hatch. Eastman didn't appear for a few seconds and with the pilot's compartment filling with smoke, I was afraid we'd have to go in and drag him out. But he soon came out. When I first saw him, he had a big flak hole though the right shoulder of his jacket, and I thought, "God, he's been hit!" But I was mistaken. He hadn't been wearing his jacket, but just put it on before he jumped out of the plane.

About that time my nervous tension relapsed and I felt weak as a kitten. Tears came and I wanted to break down and cry hard. But then I looked at Big Heath and he had big tears too, so we all laughed instead. Rather hysterical, I suppose.

It dawned on me why no Germans were bothering us. Our American P-51s were flying patrol over us occasionally letting go a burst of machine gun fire. You might call it local air superiority.

I had just decided to go back to the plane and set off a fire bomb to completely destroy the ship, when one of the P-51s made a pass at our B-17 shooting at it. Obviously, he intended on destroying it, so we had to get out of there at once. I still had my chute harness on, and wired to it were my escape shoes. We all started running over the hill, and I skinned out of my chute harness leaving my shoes - my first mistake.

We made it to the woods and ran a little ways into the wooded area. It was afternoon and we found a low spot in the woods. There were a lot of leaves on the ground and we pulled them up around us to hide until dark. Then when it was dark we started walking. We had maps and few rations that we were suppose to ration out over a few days. We ate it all right then.

We could hear Germans or somebody in the woods and we were afraid they were going to get us, but they didn't. We evaded them all night. We left the woods the next morning at 0500 stopped on a hilltop and stayed under cover until nightfall then we walked night. By then we all had colds and were extremely tired. We were walking along this road about 50 feet apart and a German armored column came down this road. We all sought cover in the ditch. After they passed we couldn't find all of the men. They were so tired they had fallen asleep as the Germans were passing."

THE CAPTURE
September 30, 1944

"On the third day we didn't much give a damn. We were so tired and hungry we were walking on the road in daylight. We even passed some people that were uniformed and gave them a Heil Hitler. We got to the small village of Herbstein, Germany. To go around the town would have been so rugged because it was semi-mountain country so we had gotten by with so much we would walk through the town. There we were in American flier uniforms. We got most of the way through and then got surrounded by the Folksstrom (The Old men Peoples Army). They took us to the courtyard and lined us against the wall. They operated the bolts of their guns. We were standing there with our hands up and thought they were going to shot us, but they didn't. Instead they searched us and then took us down to the woods at the edge of town. We were sure they were going to shoot us then, but they had taken us down there to use the toilet. Then they brought us back and put us in the Herbstein jail.

We were then moved by train to Geissen Prison where they had a dungeon in one of the buildings and they put us there for the night."

HEADQUARTERS ARMY SERVICE FORCES
OFFICE OF THE PROVOST MARSHAL GENERAL
WASHINGTON 25, D. C.

11 November 1944

RE: 2nd Lt. Carl W. Remy, O-772 733,
United States Prisoner of War,
Interned by Germany,
International Red Cross Directory,
Geneva, Switzerland,
Via: New York, New York.

Mrs. Wayme L. Remy,
1717 NorthWest 20th Street,
Oklahoma City, Oklahoma.

Dear Mrs. Remy:

The Provost Marshal General has directed me to inform you that the above-named has been reported interned as a prisoner of war as indicated.

The report received did not give his camp location. This conforms with the usual practice of the German Government not to report the address of a prisoner of war until he has been placed in a permanent camp. Past experience indicates that his camp address may not bereported to this office until one to three months have elapsed from the time he was first reported a prisoner of war.

Pending receipt of his permanent address, you may direct letter mail to him by following instructions in the inclosed mailing circular and by addessing him as illustrated above.

Sincerely yours,

Howard F. Bresee

Howard F. Bresee,
Colonel, C.M.P.,
Assistant Director,
Prisoner of War Division.

Incl:
Mailing Circular.

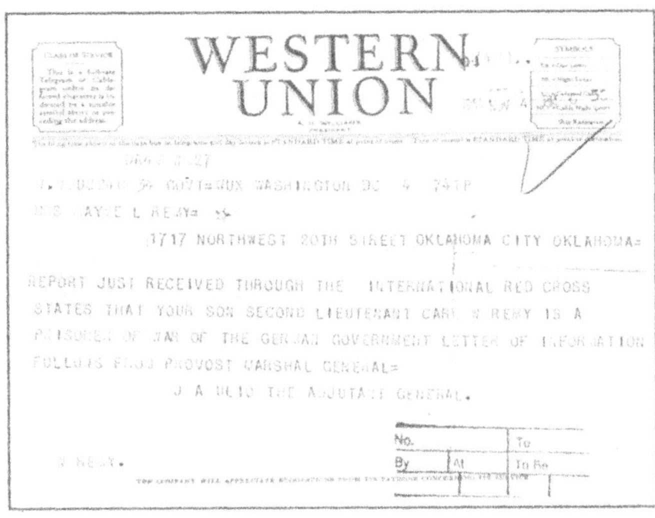

WESTERN UNION

DR4? 8 27

REPORT JUST RECEIVED THROUGH THE INTERNATIONAL RED CROSS STATES THAT YOUR SON SECOND LIEUTENANT CARL W REMY IS A PRISONER OF WAR OF THE GERMAN GOVERNMENT LETTER OF INFORMATION FOLLOWS FROM PROVOST MARSHAL GENERAL=

J A ULIO THE ADJUTANT GENERAL.

1717 NORTHWEST 20TH STREET OKLAHOMA CITY OKLAHOMA=

THE INTERROGATION. . .*FRANKFORT, GERMANY*

"Sometime the next morning they boarded us on the train and we went to Frankfort, Germany. We spent the night in solitary then they took us to an interrogation center the next day. We got a little soap and water, but not much at all to eat. They took me in for interrogation. The Nazis officer told me to answer just three questions and you will get to see the Red Cross, get some warm food, and even go to bed and get some sleep. The first question was, "How was your armament for your new tail gunner?" I told them that I had no idea. They knew our target was Merseburg. The second question was, "could you see the target?" I told them I didn't know because we dropped on radar anyway. They brought some pictures in and showed us a photo of the tail section of our plane. A photo of a woman that was suppose to have been killed by the P-51 strafing. They knew the bomb group. They knew my mothers maiden name. I didn't tell them anything and I didn't get to see the Red Cross or get any food or any sleep. I don't think they ever asked the third question."

THE PASSENGER TRAIN

They put us on a passenger train and we moved out. After a while we came up on a passenger train that had been bombed by American Bombers. It was terrible. There were women and children that had been killed and they were trying to get them off the train. There was blood everywhere. The German guards took us off the train and marched us around the wreckage and we were almost mobbed by the German people. But we got on another train and we finally reached Stalag Luft I at Barth, Germany."

STALAG LUFT IV

Stalag Luft IV was located at Barth, a small town on the Baltic Sea. The camp consisted of three compounds each encircled by barbed wire. Some buildings were divided into small rooms holding four to ten double deck bunks, while others were partitioned into larger sections holding 24 twin-tier bunks. The heating, lighting, and ventilation were adequate. By the time the camp was liberated there were 7,717 American POWs and 1,427 British POWs in the crowded camp.

STALAG LUFT I. . .*DOING TIME*

"We started our hitch in the POW camp," Carl said. "The camp is right on the Baltic and the Baltic Sea is kind of warm which helped in the winter.

We were not tortured. We were not forced to work. We never got out of the camp for anything. The food in the morning consisted of grain cereal, we made our own lunch from Red Cross packages, and in the evening rutabagas and potatoes.

When we started out there were about 12 to 15 men in a room that was about 20 feet by 20 feet. In the end we had 24 men in the room and there were triple bunks all away around and out in the center of the room.

There was very little to do. We had a library and could read all we wanted. If your not getting nutrition a lot of people would get headaches. I was one of them so I couldn't read much. I didn't want to exercise either because I wasn't getting enough to eat. I had lost about 20 pounds.

We fell out for a head count twice a day. We would line up out in front of our barracks and the Germans would come by and count heads. I will never forget there were 158 of us and the German would come by and say IN Nune id dock funic (158 in German Language). They would do these head counts everyday to see if any body had gotten away. During the seven months that I was there no one escaped or tried to escape. Because everybody knew the war was going to end and that it was just a matter of time. We got in the camp in October 1944 and the Americans were already at the Rhine River. So we were just going to wait it out.

We weren't sure if we were going to get out alive because we had heard about the Nazis killing POWs so much and especially Jews. We would get a shower once a month. They were nice. It was warm water. They would turn the water on for a minute and we would lather up. Then they would turn it on another minute and we would wash off. But, then after the war hearing about how they did the Jews made me wonder just how safe we really had been.

We had one barrack in the camp that was just Russians and they never would let them out. They were the meanest people I have ever heard of. The Germans would sent the dogs in after them and they would just kill the dogs.

If the Germans wanted something changed in the POW camp they would issue a order to Colonial Packer and if it was reasonable he would issue orders down the line and get the change made. If he thought it was unreasonable he would refuse and they would put him in solitary confinement. That's where he stayed most of the time."

THE DIARY

On May 1, 1945, when the prisoners woke up there were Americans in the watch towers. The Germans had begged to be taken prisoner, but they were told to get the hell out and they just left the camp. The prisoners had no reason to leave the camp since they really didn't have any place to go. Carl kept a daily diary of the events that followed:

APRIL 30, 1945-Everybody is nervous. Himnler, the Nazi Butcher Boy, visited the camp. Half the German guards left the camp last night. It's rumored that the rest will leave tonight. The Germans plan to take 1,500 POWs and go west to escape the Russians. The Germans have been destroying the air field and flak school-big demolition explosions all day. Early in the morning we began digging networks of trenches around the barracks for protection. Used tin cans, knives, and sticks for tools. We completed trenches by nightfall and dived into them at every explosion. German strafing expected. Russians now 20 miles away. Civilians stealing Red Cross food. At midnight, all Germans left the prison camp.

MAY 1, 1945-All Germans except five left for U.S. lines. A major and German staff stayed as our POWs. Our American Colonel Zempke now in charge of camp. Camp life as usual. Still confined for safety. Russians now less than ten miles. The battle can be heard. Germans still blowing up own equipment. All shops in Barth closed. Barth citizens passively awaiting Russians. They say "no resistance." We have plenty of food. Russians should be hear today. I Hope! This is the strangest, most precarious predicament I have been in for seven months. Here are 9,000 POWs unguarded on the Baltic coast in Nazi Germany. Four miles to the south of us is a German air field swarming with all types of German planes. Then a little south of there the Germans and Russians are fighting. I never could understand this prisoner of war idea. We are now free men. Aren't we fair game now? There are four armed parties of around 50 (Kriegies). They've taken over the flak school, Barth Power System, and the air field. The Germans cleared out of the air field before the American Kriegies arrived.

10:00 P.M. MAY 1, 1945-Advanced Russian Patrol arrived at this camp! Only two Russians. They say the main body of the spearhead is about five hours behind. Be here about dawn. Burgermeister in Barth who has been cooperating with us committed suicide. His life wasn't worth a dime.

MAY 2, 1945-Situation is still a very confused state. The two Russians who got here last night arrived drunk with women in a confiscated German automobile. They said the rest of the army is drunk and ought to be here soon. This POW camp is still pretty well under control. MPs have been appointed from our numbers and we are still prisoners-of our own guard. There are almost no weapons in camp. I feel pretty helpless. About 50 American ex-POWs armed with a few old rifles went south to try to contact higher Russian authorities. They were disarmed, "captured," and returned by the Russian Shock Troops. Another body of Americans that had taken over the Barth Air Field were handled likewise by the Russians. Another party of Americans and British from here struck out for Rostock which is probably by now in Russian hands. The air field is very heavily mined. More and more Russian troops are arriving in parties numbering five to fifty men. One Russian tank driver wanted to run his tank through the camp fences and liberate all the prisoners so they could sack the town of Barth.

Two Russian Colonels arrived here at 3:30 P.M. They told one of our American Colo-

8)

THE GREATEST DEBATES FOUGHT IN BULL SESSIONS

RESOLVED THAT:

I WE COULD HAVE STAYED OUT OF THE WAR AND STILL SURVIVED. (CON)

II RUSSIA WAS PREPARED FOR THE WAR. (PRO)

III RUSSIA WILL ATTACK JAPAN. (CON)

IV AN AIRCREW MEMBER SHOULD MARRY REGARDLESS OF THE DEFINITE PROSPECT OF BEING SHIPPED OVERSEAS IN A VERY FEW MONTHS. (PRO) (LATER-CON)

V IN THE GAME OF BILLIARDS, ENGLISH CAN BE IMPARTED TO THE OBJECT BALL. (PRO)

VI B-17'S ARE BETTER THAN 24'S. (PRO)

VII THE TWO END LEGS OF A POOL TABLE WILL LEAVE THE FLOOR FIRST WHEN A SUFFICIENT UPWARD FORCE IS APPLIED TO AN EXACT CORNER. (PRO)

VIII IN A "NO LIMIT" POKER GAME, A SKILLFUL PLAYER WITH AN AVERAGE RUN OF CARDS WILL WIN OVER A LESS SKILLFUL BUT VERY LUCKY PLAYER

9

OVER A CONSIDERABLE LENGTH OF TIME. (CON)

IX YOU CAN GIVE YOUR OWN CAR A BETTER GREASE JOB THAN A SKILLED MECHANIC. (CON)

X ANY KIND OF A STANDARD COLLEGE EDUCATION IS A GOOD THING FOR A GIRL. (PRO)

XI RESOLVED THAT OVER 70% OF THE FEMALES OF MARRIAGEABLE AGE ARE VIRGINS.

XII MR. CHURCHILL WAS RIGHT IN HARPING ON UNCONDITIONAL SURRENDER IN THE EARLY PART OF THE WAR. (CON)

XIII THE WAR WILL BE OVER BY CHRISTMAS. (1944) (PRO)

XIV A PRUNE IS A DRIED PLUM AND NOT A DRIED PRUNE. (PRO)

(37

THE BEST JOKES

Old Jim Bailey had played poker Saturday night until the wee hours, and the next morning he was in church, dozing as was his usual habit. The preacher was getting pretty tired of Old Jim's sleeping through the sermon Sunday after Sunday. So the preacher thought of a way to embarrass the man. In the middle of the sermon, he said, "We will now have a prayer. Brother Bailey will lead us." When Old Jim heard his name his head jerked up, eyes popped open, and he cried, "Lead? Why, hell, I just dealt!

A wealthy girl out of an Eastern College for the summer vacation went abroad for a few months. In Italy, she met a 'handsome young Hindu named Yogi'. Until this time she was a virgin, but she decided she might as well have a little fun, so she slept with him. By and by, she had to return to school and

16) PERSONAL PARCEL
REC'D APRIL 29, 1945 (PROBABLY MAILED DEC. '44.
WELL PLANNED - EXCELLENT CHOICE

F. E. A. LICENSE "G-PW-2"

POSTAGE FREE
FRANC DE PORT
GEBUHRENFREI

LABEL ISSUED TO:

CENSOR

Sender—Expediteur—Absender | Label Transferred To:

PRISONER OF WAR PERSONAL PARCEL—PRISONNIER DE GUERRE
COLIS "PERSONNEL"—KRIEGSGEFANGENSENDUNG

FROM:
MRS. MAYME L. REMY, G 39377
1717 NORTHWEST 20TH STREET,
OKLAHOMA CITY, OKLA.

FOR:
2ND LT. CARL W. REMY,
U. S. PRISONER OF WAR #6150,
STALAG LUFT #1, GERMANY.

W. D., PMG
Form No. 19

VIA NEW YORK, N. Y., U. S. A.

CONTENTS -

6 HANDKERCHIEFS
1 PR. HOUSE SLIPPERS & CASE
BOX ROSE TALCUM
1 MENTHOL STICK
HARMONICA WITH CASE
BOX CLICK BLADES
TUMS
FEEN-A-MINT
50 ASPIRINS & ST. JOSEPHS
2 BOXES COUGH DROPS
2 BOXES POMADE

3 SMALL HERSHEYS
1 SM. ALM. HERSHEY
2-6.7 OZ. S. AMER CHOC.
1 PORTION NESTLE'S DRINK
1 BIT-O-HONEY
1 LARGE HERSHEY
2 BOXES VITALETS (1 PC. GONE)
2 BAGS DRIED APPLES
1 BAG APRICOTS
3 BOXES PUDDINGS
2 LARGE KRAFT DINNERS

1 BORDENS MINCE MEAT
DECK CARDS
35 SACCHARIN TAB
SOAP
SEWING KIT

Feb. 26, '45

(FROM GOODSPEED, TAIL GUNNER)

Dear Remy,

To answer the most interesting question put forth — Hell Yes! I'll go on that three week drunk with you and the "Big Wheel," providing of course, that the both of you behave as officers and gentlemen (Ahem!) should. Now for the rest of the boys. We were stationed at Stalag Luft #4. This camp was approximately 90 mi. N.E. of Stettin and was built in a manner very similar to this one. Prior to my departure the entire camp was preparing to evacuate whenever the Russian advance warranted. Consequently, I am of the

(2)

opinion that the fellows were forced to march out, which, by the way, isn't a very pleasant prospect. In answer to your question concerning food — my dear friend, at no time have I sat down to a meal and risen with a full belly, except possibly at Xmas time. By the way, I am led to understand that you are as plump as a ripe melon. Evidently Kreigie life agrees with you! (How about cutting me in on your rackets!)

As I said before, Shull is in excellent condition even to the extend of having his head shaved,

(3)

undoubtedly believing that this will forestall baldness. It led to many laughs I'll garrantee you that. Curtis was in his glory . . . teaching the gullible English chaps how to play poker. It was quite amusing to watch him swindle those bumptious asses. Carlson was living in a room with Polish chaps. There generosity was amazing. Yoonts was taking Kreigee life quite hard, consequently, we all endeavered to cheer him up.

Hell! no, I haven't received any mail, although, some fellows who were shot down after me have received mail.

Good luck,
"Speed"

From: Donald C. Goodspeed
West Compound 3
Blk. 11, Room 13

To: Carl W. Remy
North 2
Blk. 9, Room 6

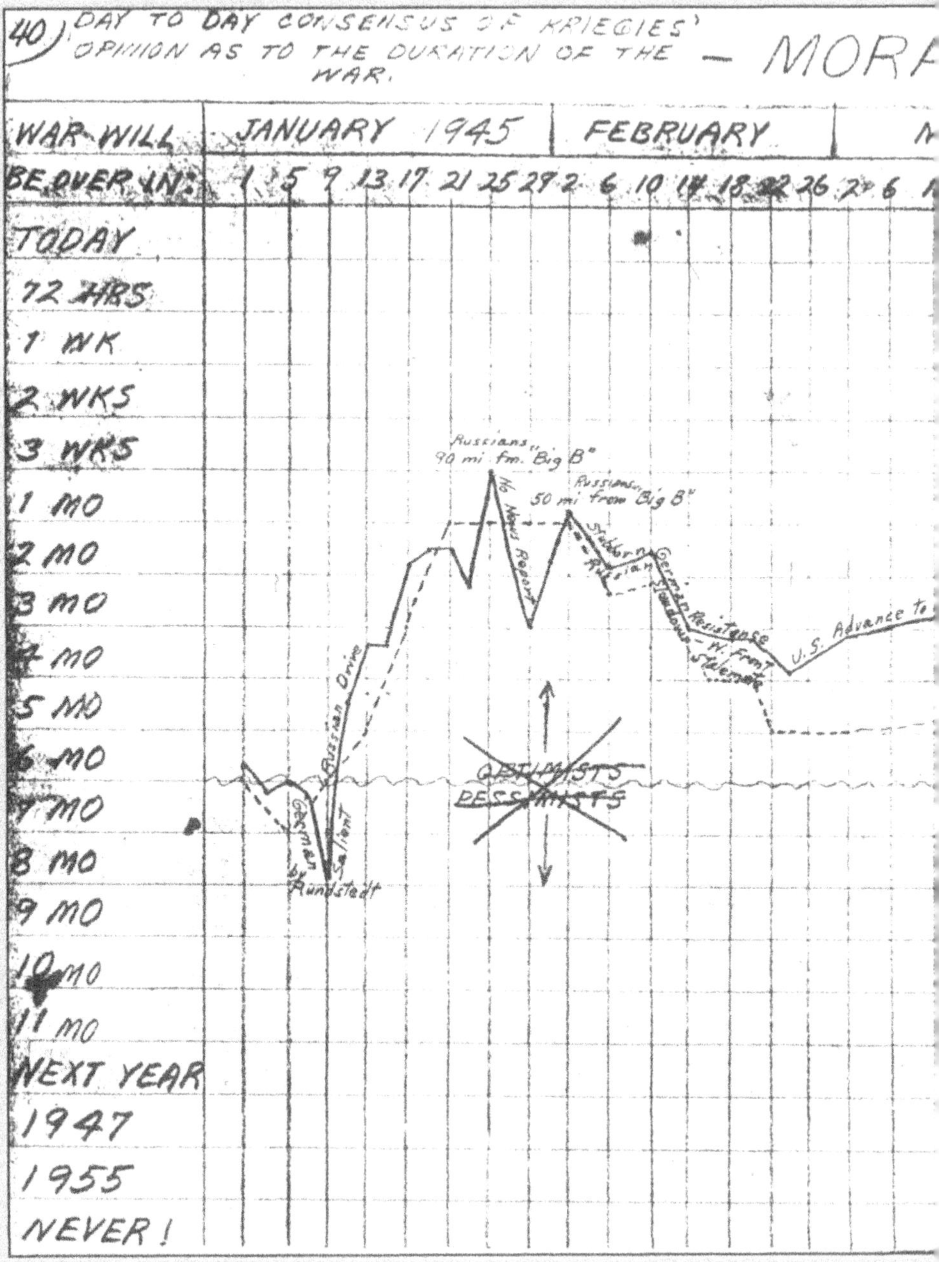

40) DAY TO DAY CONSENSUS OF KRIEGIES' OPINION AS TO THE DURATION OF THE WAR. — MORA

WAR WILL BE OVER IN:	JANUARY 1945	FEBRUARY	M
	1 5 9 13 17 21 25 29	2 6 10 14 18 22 26	2 6
TODAY			
72 HRS			
1 WK			
2 WKS			
3 WKS			
1 MO			
2 MO			
3 MO			
4 MO			
5 MO			
6 MO			
7 MO			
8 MO			
9 MO			
10 MO			
11 MO			
NEXT YEAR			
1947			
1955			
NEVER!			

Russians 90 mi fm. "Big B"

No News Report

Russians 50 mi from "Big B"

Stubborn Russian

German Resistance

Slowdown W. Front Stalemate

U.S. Advance to

Russian Drive

German Salient by Rundstedt

OPTIMISTS

PESSIMISTS

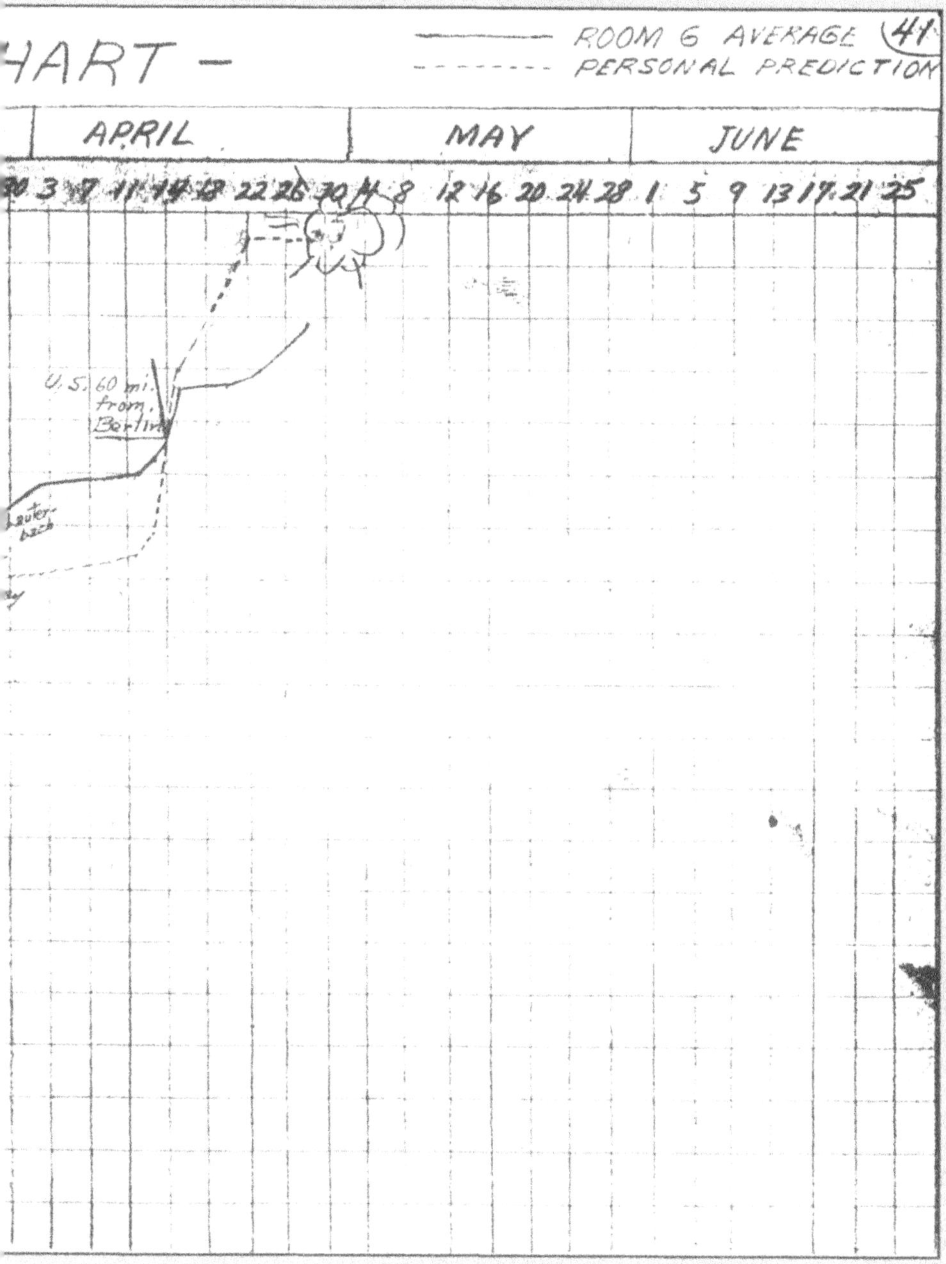

HART –

——— ROOM 6 AVERAGE (41)
- - - - - PERSONAL PREDICTION

APRIL	MAY	JUNE

30 3 7 11 14 18 22 26 30 4 8 12 16 20 24 28 1 5 9 13 17 21 25

U.S. 60 mi. from Berlin

Lauter-bach

nels that he should be happy and overflowing with joy to have been liberated by the Russians. To keep the Russians in good humor, the Colonel started hugging and kissing and crying over them. They were satisfied.

But they weren't satisfied for long. These two Russian Colonels said we shouldn't still be behind barbed wire, but should be out raising hell. Our commanding officer, Colonel Zempkes, said , "No!"; the Russian Colonel leveled a gun at his head and said, "yes, you will tear up the prison camp."

So the camp went stark raving mad. 9,000 ex-prisoners tore down the barbed wire and guard towers with their bare hands. These Russians we were dealing with, were not the crack Russian spearheads but the Terror Troops which fan out and create havoc demoralizing the Germans. Human life-their own and anyone elses-is worth nothing. I could hear shots all over the place. In a few seconds, the entire camp was emptied. I went over to the German Flak school. This establishment is huge and modern covering about a square mile. Civilians and French and Polish ex-Prisoners had been through the place before me. The Germans had blown up part of it-mainly radar equipment, and the civilians finished off the rest. There were millions of fur coats, boots, and jackets stored there and still undamaged. There are no young German males left, and the few old men along with the women and children were living in the Flak school buildings setting up housekeeping.

There were a lot of the Polish, French, and Russian whores living near the Flak school. There are always a lot of these captured women near German soldier concentrations. The Germans believe a mistress is necessary for morale. Some of these women were nice looking and apparently of high class. This may seem like a mess of senseless scribbling, but the way things are happening accounts for it. I wonder if I'm losing my mind. I went on into the outskirts of the town of Barth. The civilians were white and trembling-scared senseless of the Russians and afraid but to a much lesser degree of us. Russians were shooting and raping civilians for no reason at all. In one spot I saw three women, a child, and a baby, all with their brains blown out. I saw the little white baby buggy near the dead woman, and wondering where the baby was, I drew back the little pink coverlet over the top, and saw a little soft, fat, German baby, all tucked in, in a little lace nightie. The only thing amiss was that his brains were blown all over the little white pillow.

I was almost sick and returned to camp. The Germans murdered Russian women and children, so why shouldn't the Russians do likewise?

At about five o'clock, the Russian told Colonel Zempkes to have the prison camp ready to move out by six o'clock. Colonel Zempkes said, "no," that we would wait for Americans to fly us out. The Russian drew his pistol, and said, "you will move!" So we began a mad scramble to roll packs and get ready. We were each given three Red Cross parcels, 33 lbs. of food. Then Colonel Zempkes pulled a fast one on the Russian. He passed the word around for everyone to scatter out all over the countryside so that the confusion would be so great the Russians couldn't move us. You see, the Russians had no definite plans. They just wanted to see us out and free, so we could go along with the Russian Army to loot and raise hell.

I was in town again and got a close-up of the Russians fighting man. They were all drunk and I was kissed and hugged till I was weak. There was a Russian woman soldier with a huge machine gun slung over her back. She stopped me an since I understand a little German and no Russian, and she spoke nothing but Russian, I was unable to give her much help. Later I saw her again and she asked, "American Flieger?" I said I was. All the Russians wanted to give us a bottle of whiskey. Americans were stealing and getting drunker than the Russians. They didn't exactly steal; they just asked the trembling German civilians for cars, bicycles, motorcycles, etc., and the Germans fearing for their lives, gave up everything.

German men in civilian clothes came up to the camp gate begging to be taken prisoner. They were ex-German guards who fled this camp last night. We turned them away. Let the Russians get'um.

Only three or four miles from here by the side of a munitions factory there was a concentration camp full of Poles, French, Jews, and German political enemies. Til today this camp had no knowledge of the existence of that camp.

Tonight two more Russian officers arrived. They belong to the follow-up, consolidation armies. Things are beginning to calm down. These newer arrivals promised Colonel Zempke that we would not have to move out of here, but could stay a limit of ten days which should give the American authorities time to evacuate us.

Colonel Zempke issued an order that no ex-POW is to leave this camp on his own. However, he said no men were leaving in droves. I think it's two dangerous. Five men in this camp have been killed already

MAY 3, 1945-We had roll call at 0700 and we are confined to camp. Colonel Zempke gave a talk and said that any man who leaves camp now will be charged with desertion. He said that this area is now under Russian Martial Law and they shoot and ask questions later.

Shots can still be heard all over the place. Occasionally a machine-gun burst out.

Ex-POWs are still leaving for American lines in spite of the order against it. MP lines have been placed around the peninsula, but this afternoon I saw the departing men going out of here by boat on the west side of the island. I don't blame them. I'm about ready to get the hell out of here too. The Russians don't give a damn about us, and we can't seem to contact the Americans. What I want to do is go home. I'm sick of mad Russians and dead people. Americans are even going to attempt flying a German JU 88 to American lines. God help the guy who tries it.

A friend of mine in camp was in town last night and in his wanderings ask a German civilian for some whiskey. The German showed him a cellar full of it, then departed. The American jerked the cap off one of the bottles and spilled some of the liquor on the back of his hand. He was treated for bad acid burns. There was much cheering upon hearing Hitler is dead.

MAY 4, 1945-We have the run of the peninsula, but can't go into Barth. More Americans have been killed some by mines. Many are still leaving for home. I am undecided.

More concentration camps have been uncovered near here by us. There was a horrible underground section containing many dead men and women of many nationalities. Some were in such bad shape they can't be removed. They won't get well. There were underground chambers which are flooded to kill the occupants. There are also electrocution chambers. Many hospital cases were brought over here to our POW hospital. The inmates look like the starving Greeks I used to see in the newsreels. Around 7,000 of these prisoners have been located.

The air field has been completely cleared of mines and bombs. Some British Major defused about 250 vibrator type bombs without an accident.

Shots and explosions can still be heard.

The Russians say we should be in mourning for President Roosevelt. They say that tomorrow everyone will wear a black band on his left arm. I'm damned disgusted at being pushed around by the Russians. Two Russian Generals are coming here tomorrow to inspect the joint. I hope they like it. It's deplorable. The latrines are full and overflowing all over the compound. You have to watch your step or you'll be walking in the refuse where guys have relieved themselves.

I saw about twenty German civilian woman and children fleeing from Barth. There were little kids barely walking with packs on their backs.

MAY 5, 1945-I could still hear plenty of firing across on the islands this morning. The two Russian Generals came and departed. I went over on the bay and saw many Americans still leaving this place. I'm thinking of going myself. Why don't they get us out of here? At about noon another high ranking Russian General came. He was a big rough looking brute with a chest full of medals. It is rumored that F/M Montgomery is supposed to fly here to confer with him.

All the big dogs in our camp had dinner today with three Russian Generals. One of the Generals is Russia's #2 man. He told in detail about the battle of Stettin. Right into the middle of this came an American jeep with a Major, Captain, and a Sergeant from General Simpson's 9th U.S. Army. They drove from the other side of Rostock. The Russians had a whole slew of newsreel cameraman here, and they say the news of this camp will be in the newspaper in the U.S. tomorrow.

It is a fact that F/M Montgomery will visit here tomorrow. Also, Russia's #1 General. We have plenty of good food here. I haven't eaten a tenth of mine.

Colonel Zempke said we'd probably start leaving here tomorrow-probably by air.

MAY 6, 1945-This camp has become a big side show for the military bigwigs to come and look at. I'll probably be sitting in this damned hole for weeks to give everyone a chance to look at us. Any ex-POW pulling out from here now faces a charge of desertion. But

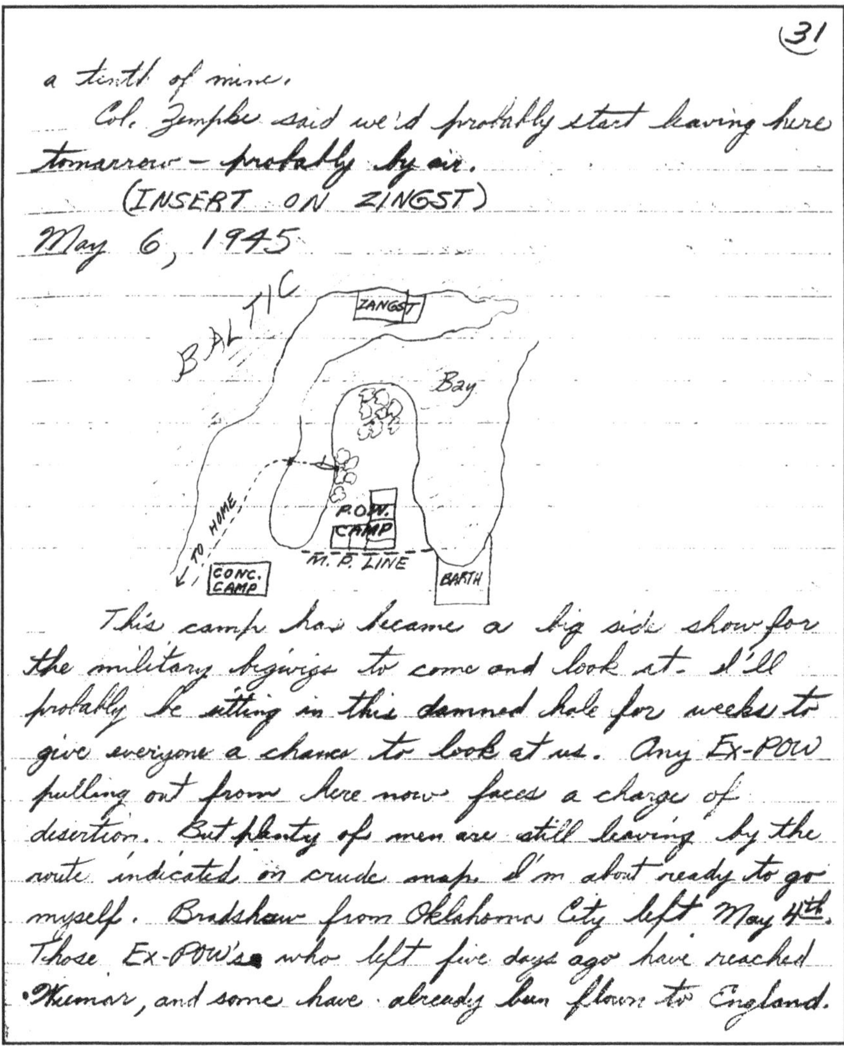

(31)

a tenth of mine.

Col. Zemke said we'd probably start leaving here tomorrow – probably by air.

(INSERT ON ZINGST)

May 6, 1945

This camp has became a big side show for the military bigwigs to come and look at. I'll probably be sitting in this damned hole for weeks to give everyone a chance to look at us. Any Ex-POW pulling out from here now faces a charge of desertion. But plenty of men are still leaving by the route indicated on crude map. I'm about ready to go myself. Bradshaw from Oklahoma City left May 4th. Those Ex-POW's who left five days ago have reached Wiemar, and some have already been flown to England.

plenty of them are still leaving by the route indicated on a crude map. I'm about ready to go myself. Bradshaw from Oklahoma City left May 4th. Those ex-POWs who left five days ago have reached Wiemar, and some have already been flown to England. I feel damned silly sitting here. I was over on the bay and heard shots and screaming over on the other peninsula. The Russians are still raising hell.

I estimate that 2,000 men have left walking home.

I have come to he conclusion that one of the main reasons we are still here is the diplomatic screw-up. I guess the Russians just hate to see us leave.

More about the concentration camps-Those unfortunate souls have been penned up for over five years. The men and women living together indiscriminately, so there are little three year old bastards that haven't been outside the barbed wire enclosure.

F/M Montgomery did not arrive and probably never will. That was just another line of bullshit out by this command. It's no wonder discipline is so poor and nobody believes anything.

MAY 7, 1945-More Russian Generals today and the place is lousy with little uniformed Russian "Boys" on bicycles with machine guns on their backs.

The Russian USO put on a show for us. The band played stinking long haired junk, but we laughed and cheered because every bandsman had a machine gun slung over his back.

MAY 8, 1945-I took a Cook's Tour today of the Barth area. As we marched through the town the Barth citizens lined up four deep on the sidewalk. Most of them stared, but some of them smiled and spoke. All the German babes are eager to sleep with Americans. One of the reasons for that is they believe this would keep them from being raped by the Russians. They're sadly mistaken. We, also are Russian prisoners, more or less.

The Russians are getting a little more organized now. They herded 50 head of ex-German milk cows through the camp gates. We are to butcher them. I think this is unnecessary. The Germans are going to starve anyhow. Nothing can avert a famine.

The Germans are hoping that the Americans are going to be occupation troops here. Another thing they are sadly mistaken about.

Over at the Barth airfield I went through a jet plane assembly plant. Very interesting. The Germans even use foreign labor for this. All the plants have charged barbed wire around them. I also looked over some JU88's, FW 190's, and other planes. The Germans left the field and hangars intact. Very little destruction by them.

Some ex-POWs from here are shacking up with German Fraws in town. There are many beautiful German women, although most of them are fat, straw-haired, round faced, rosy cheeked; what I mean is Nicht S.A.

There is no sign of our getting taken out of this damned place. It's worse sweating this out than when the Germans had us.

By the way, I heard today the war's over. So what?

MAY 9, 1945-The Allied High Command offered Colonel Zempke, commander of this host, 600 DC-3 transport planes and 500 G.I. trucks. He turned them down! I can't imagine what's in his mind. It is he who's imprisoning this camp now. The Russians wanted to evacuate us one week ago.

Hank Strunc, who speaks Bohemian quite well, and I were touring numerous concentration camps, today. Germany is actually just one big concentration camp. Every factory has it's own forced labor. Before actually seeing these people live under such horrible conditions I didn't believe the stuff about Germany. But it's all true only more so.

In one of the camps I conversed with some Polish and Rumanian Jews. We were able to convey thoughts using broken German, Russian, and English. They had been doing hard labor for five years on rations of one eight of a loaf of bread one bowl of thin soup per man per day. Their average weight was about 80 pounds-arms and legs like broomsticks. Their limbs were bent from hard work without enough food, and broken from beatings. They ripped open their shirt fronts and tapped their concave chests explaining, "Kaput", meaning destroyed. They were rotten with T.B. and they themselves realize they can't live long.

They told us of working carrying dirt at a dead run on their shoulders. When they would slow down, the Germans would beat and whip them. All of them wanted to shake our hands, so we made for the nearest soap and water after departing.

There were many new and old graves-and some being dug, all around the outside of the barbed wire. The Jews being buried with the Star of David and the other nationalities with a cross.

All around the town of Barth I was able to recognize several ex-wermacht troops in civilian clothes. Most of these characters were faking a limp or arms in slings.

One of the French prisoners expected to be put to death any time, so upon being liberated by the Russians, he made his way directly to the German vaults where records were kept. There he discovered some very interesting facts about the future of the American officers of this camp, Stalag Luft I. Now the following is strictly rumor, but the Germans have done a hell of a lot worse. He said that in the month of March, the Nazis had definite plans to cremate some or all of the airmen at this camp, and then send the ashes back to the states in retaliation for the bombing of German cities. He said they went so far as to ship a great number of gas chambers up here for the mass execution. Now this could be true, because the Germans did send the ashes of 100 airmen to the Protection Powers in Switzerland some months ago.

You know, it is a strange coincidence, they almost starved us in the month of March.

MAY 10, 1945-General Eisenhower says to ex-POWs, "Standby!" Colonel Zempke says, "I'll get you to your doorstep in the very near future." Last week he said he hoped to have us on our way by the day before yesterday. Allied officers visiting here from the U.S. lines say, " Nice camp you have here." No sign what so ever of getting out of here.

MAY 11, 1945-I am still standing by. I could kick my rear for not walking out of here a week ago like 750 who did.

I went swimming today in the Baltic, pretty cold.

I was swimming again late this afternoon and fishing, too.

Night-Got good news at 10:00 P.M. Evacuation planes are due here tomorrow or day after (Sunday)! The order of leaving is (1) sick and wounded (2) British personnel (3) North I compound (4) North II(me) (5) North III (6) Staff Personnel. I think I'll do damned well to get out of here by Wednesday. I'll go to a French Port, probably, and then by boat to USA.

Three men slipped out of camp and tried to sail to Sweden in a 32 foot sailboat, but the Russians intercepted them in the Baltic and riddled the boat with shore batteries. The three men were returned here safely.

MAY 12, 1945-At reveille this morning it was announced that B-17s would begin to arrive at Barth Airfield for our evacuation by 2:00 P.M.

Surely enough, at 2:00 P.M. sharp, two B-17's were sighted. They landed and at about 2:30 PM, two C-47's came in. After that three more squadrons of 17's arrived making a total of 40 planes for today. 900 men are to fly to Paris this afternoon. I'll probably go out tomorrow, because a Brigadier General arriving in the lead ship said, "he expected to finish the job tomorrow."

Planes loaded are leaving every few minutes.

MAY 13, 1945-Mothers Day-Sunday-Boarded a B-17 at Barth Air Field at 12:15 P.M. Arrived at 4:00 P.M. 8 km. south of Laon, France. No fear of flying, no air sickness. Transported by G.I. semi-trailer truck to a tent city. Supposed to get showers, delousing, and new clothes.

MAY 14, 1945-Leaving here at 8:30 to board a ship at LaHaure. Flying to La Haure on a C-47. We didn't get showers at the last camp nor did we get clothing. I had a G.I. breakfast, more than I could eat, consisting of eggs, oats, white bread, coffee, jam, peaches, and pineapple juice. I hadn't tasted eggs, white bread, or peaches for eight months. Then at 8:30 A.M. I boarded a G.I. semi-trailer which took me to the train station in Reims-so we didn't fly to La Haure after all. Our second meal today was in the afternoon.

This train is of old German coaches. We are traveling just as crowded with less rations than when the Germans transported me to prison. It seems we've gone all over France, and still we're some one hundred miles from the coast. I'm filthy dirty not having bathed since prison. If I didn't have lice, I have them now!

In the evening we stopped in a marshalling yard where a tank car of French wine was parked. Someone pulled the drain plug, so the thousand odd men had wine. It was lousy stuff. In every station the French girls are all eager to kiss Americans.

MAY 15, 1945-In the middle of the night we were detracted in the marshalling yard, and left there all night. Everyone's in a pretty bad mood. About half the train has the G.I.s. It was damned cold all night, so we built bonfires along the tracks. I got a couple hours sleep on the ground near the fire. The reason for the delay was that the French train engineers got drunk, so the ex-POWs drove the train and blew a cylinder out.

We finally pulled out and arrived at St. Valery, France on the coast at 4:00 P.M. Got out to the camp on G I trucks and sweated a shower, clothes, and food line till 8:00 P.M., and at that time (30 hours without food), I finally got an improvised meal comparable to Stalag times. I crawled into bed on a canvas cot in a tent with a blanket and blanket sleeping bag for cover and was uncomfortably cold all night.

MAY 16, 1945-Awakened at 6:00 A.M. to find I had caught cold because of insufficient bed clothing. My clothing consisted of only a GI fatigue suit undershirt, shorts, socks, am shoes, I allowed Strunc, my bunk mate, to lend me a jacket he brought along from Stalag I. I stood in line so long in order to get breakfast that I did not go to noon chow.

MAY 17, 1945-There are thousands and thousands of liberated POWs here, so it will take me a long time to get out. There are lots of German POWs here also working in the camp. These Germans are a very scared bunch. They willingly work like mad. They are guarded by large Negroes who carry their automatic rifles unslung-fingers on triggers. I can guess easily what's going on in the minds of these German POWs. With the discovery beyond all doubt of the innumerable atrocities to American POWs, they're scared to death that they'll receive the same. The rats are pampered in the ETO as they are in the States.

In the evening, Strunc and I walked over to the Atlantic Ocean about four miles from here. Although D-Day was almost a year ago, this entire coast including towns and villages was so heavily minded and destroyed in the bitter struggle which ensued in this very area that it is still uninhabitable. There are mines and booby traps in every room of every house, and all over the beaches and countryside lie unexploded shells and mines. Roads are the only safe places. Pieces of ships, life jackets, and ammunition litter the beaches.

A carton of cigarettes can be sold to the French for 500 franks ($10.00). A shot of whiskey costs 25 franks (50 cents). All French kids can speak American to the extent of, "gum, cigarettes, and aviator."

No sign of getting out of here.

Finally Carl was put on troop ship and sent us home. He arrived on June 20, 1945.

"It was a wonder day that I will never forget," Carl recalls. "The entire crew got home alive. The pilot visited me some and the co-pilot wrote to me. Now it is hard to believe that about half of them are dead. When I think of them I think of them as young men. People don't realize that these were 19 or 20 year old kids flying these bombers. Most people think men flew these bombers. We were kids."

Lieut. C. W. Remy

Lieut. Carl William Remy, son of Mrs. M. L. Remy, 1717 NW 20, has been liberated from Stalag Luft 1, where he has been a prisoner since Sept. 28, 1944. His mother has received two V-mail letters from him in France where he is awaiting shipment home. He states he is in good health and expects to arrive home the last of June.

EPILOGUE

On October 30, 1945, Carl married his wife Betty. On November 23, 1945, Carl was discharged from the Army. He finished his degree and the couple raised two children, a son Steven and a daughter Suzanne Ware. Today, Carl continues to works full time as an Electrical Engineer in Metropolis, Ill. The Remy's celebrated their 50th wedding anniversary October 30, 1995.

Left to right: Suzanne Remy Ware, Carl W. Remy, Betty Taylor Remy and Stephen T. Remy.

CHAPTER FOURTEEN

CORPORAL KENNETH M. SMITH
U.S. ARMY

COMPANY H 423RD INFANTRY REGIMENT 106 DIVISION CAPTURED DURING THE BATTLE OF THE BULGE

PRISONER OF WAR
DECEMBER 19, 1944-APRIL 2, 1945
STALAG IXB

A DAY IN INFAMY
December 7, 1941

Ken's story begins on a Sunday afternoon December 7th, 1941 as a sixteen year old boy. It was a beautiful day. Ken and his brother came into the house and from the look on their father's face the two brothers knew something serious was going on. Ken's father was listening to the old Zenith six volt battery operated radio. He told the boys that the Japanese had just attack Pearl Harbor and told them to set down and listen to it because it was going to affect all of their lives. "I don't know what happened to me at that moment, but I can remember it as if it was yesterday. I knew I would be in the military as soon as I was old enough. I wanted to be.

I was 16 and had already quit school and I worked for a oil contractor. I worked most of the time until my 18th birthday which was January 25, 1943. About a week later I went to the draft board and told them that I wanted to be in the next bunch that was going in. In March they called me up. I wanted to go in the Marines. They sent me to Chicago for my physical and told me then that the Marine quota was full. I asked for the Navy and I got orders for Scott Air Force Base. I thought well that won't be to bad to be in the Air force and after I got to the base I got another set of orders and two days later I was headed for Fort Jackson, South Carolina for Army Infantry. They were just activating a knew division. The 106th Infantry division."

TRAINING WITH COMPANY H, 423RD INFANTRY REGIMENT
March 1943

Ken was assigned to a heavy weapons unit H Company 423th Infantry Regiment. He felt fortunate to be in a newly formed unit because for the most part everyone was equal. Basic training was a little more demanding than Ken thought it should be. " I was fighting the system for about the first three weeks because I thought it was a little tougher than I wanted," Ken said. "I had a platoon Sergeant, Sergeant Webb. He called me into his office one night. He said he wanted to talk to me. He told me that I was just going to make it harder on my self by rebelling and talked with me for a long time to try and change my attitude. I am glad he did because I did change my attitude and at the end of training I was promoted to Corporal."

Orders came down that a number of men were going to be taken out of the outfit and sent overseas as replacements. Ken had enlisted to fight and he volunteered to be a replacement, but they turned him down. Instead he went into advanced training and finally ended up in the Tennessee mountains on maneuvers. Ken was ambitious and an excellent soldier, but once again he ran into trouble. He and a Lieutenant got into a disagreement and in the end Ken was busted back to Private.

AWOL

It made Ken so mad that he went to a bar, got drunk, and went over the hill. "I had some friends in Indianapolis and I went and stayed with them, Ken said. "I worked for thirty days driving a truck for Roadway Express under my friends name and social security number. After that I went back home in Mt. Carmel, Illinois. The Chief of Police saw me and told me that if I didn't get out of town he was going to arrest me because he had a warrant. I left town and went back to Indianapolis. Three days later I was walking down the street and I saw a Mess Sergeant from H company. The unit by now had moved to Adaberry near Indianapolis. I asked how things were going. I knew I had to go back, but I didn't want to be caught. I still felt a duty to my country, but I had made a mistake and I didn't know how to correct it. I decided that I would turn myself in to the company hoping that it wouldn't be as bad on me. I caught a bus back up to Adaberry and walked into the barrack. The first sergeant was setting behind his desk and I said, "First sergeant I want to turn my self in." He looked at me and said, "Smith, my ass bleeds for you." Then he told me to go over to a certain barracks and we would take the matter up the next morning.

The next morning the company commander called me in. He had all my records. Up to the time that I went over the hill I had a good record. He wanted to know what made me do such a thing. I probably wouldn't have done it if I hadn't been drunk, but he told me that he would have to court martial me. He would go as light as he could. I had a special court martial and I got six months at hard labor and loss of two-thirds of my pay. They took me back to the barracks. I didn't have any gear and I was waiting for them to take me to the stockade. About two hours later the run came over and took me to the Captains office. He had all my records out on his desk and he went over some of them. Then he saw where I volunteered to go overseas. He asked me if I still wanted to go. I told him that's what I joined the Army for and he told me that he was going to send me as a replacement. He would suspend my sentence, but I would still lose my pay. I was relieved and went back to the barracks still under armed guard. A short time later he called me back to his office. He told me there was a problem that he couldn't send me overseas without a furlough. I swear to God five days later I was home on leave.

When I got back my orders were delayed and I was sent to work in a motor pool. I worked there most of the summer and by Fall we got word that the entire unit was being shipped overseas. We had some proficiency test that we had to take. The Captain came and got me and wanted me to take a squad for the test. We had our water cooled machine guns and the way it worked we would set up fire at targets until we were told to advance. We did this in three stages. I wanted to do something for the Captain since he helped me and I worked my butt off. We got the highest score and that was the end of my motor pool days. I was back in the infantry as a gunner."

CROSSING THE ATLANTIC
October 1944

On October 8, 1943 Ken and his unit left Indianapolis by train and two days later they were in Massachusetts. Then after eight idle days on October 16th they boarded a train to New York Harbor and boarded the Queen Elizabeth. Five days later they had crossed the Atlantic and landed in Scotland. October 24th they boarded a train for a trip to Totington, England where they stayed until November 17th.

BORN, BELGIUM
December 1, 1944 -December 15, 1944

On December 1 the 423RD loaded aboard LSTs and started across the English channel. The LSTs returned to England a short time later however because of engine trouble. Five days later repairs were complete and the unit crossed a rough English Channel and landed in France on December 5th. They were trucked from there in open trucks in the rain and four days later made it to Born, Belgium. Company's G, H, and Headquarters Company remained in Born while Companies E and F were moved to the near by village of Medell. These companies were in division reserve. The rest of the outfit had moved up on the Siegfried Line.

Thinking the Ardennes was the least likely spot for a German offensive, American Staff Commanders chose to keep the line thin, so that the manpower might concentrate on offensives north and south of the Ardennes. The American line was thinly held by three

A Point of Interest

BATTLE OF THE BULGE
FACTS

1. During the Battle from December 16, 1944 to January 25, 1945 the weather was the coldest and snowiest "within memory" in the Ardennes Forest area.

2. The 106th Infantry Division alone suffered 416 killed in action, 1,246 wounded and 7,001 missing in action at the end of the offensive. Most of these casualties occurred within the first three days of battle, when two of the division's three regiments were forced to surrender.

3. The surrendering of 7,001 men of the 106th Infantry Division was the largest single recapitulation since Bataan.

4. At Malmedy 86 American prisoners were lined up in a field and murdered by SS troops. The Malmedy Massacre was the worst atrocity committed against American troops during the course of he war in Europe.

5. In its entirety, the Battle of the Bulge was one of the worst battles in terms of losses to the American Forces in WWII.

divisions and a part of a fourth, while one division remained in reserve. As Ken recalls it was a big mistake, "even in training today a infantry division is only capable of covering over a three mile front. The 423rd regiment alone was covering a seven mile front. One battalion in the 424th was in reserve in another nearby town. The 422, 423, 424 regiments were covering a 26 mile front of the Siegfried line. There hadn't been any action in that area in weeks. During the time from December 11th to the 16th 1944 it was obvious that there was a big build up going on behind the German lines. Reports were going back hourly about what was going on, but it was all being ignored."

The battle that was to begin on December 16th was Hitler's last big gamble. He sent three powerful German armies plunging into the semi-mountainous, heavy-forested Ardennes region of eastern Belgium and northern Luxembourg. Their goal was to reach the sea, trap four Allied armies, and impel a negotiated peace on the Western front.

BATTLE OF THE BULGE
December 16, 1944 -December 19, 1944

DECEMBER 16TH

At 5:30 A.M. on December 16th the Germans started their offensive across the rough forested and rocky terrain. It was bitter cold. Snow mixed with rain was falling from the overcast skies. The 423RD regiment was right in the middle of it. The first German outfit that hit went around the unit. "We were ordered to move up and set up a defense to secure the roads north and east from Schonberg, Germany," Ken recalls. "We did and were set up on the roads by the evening. The calvary and engineer units that had positions at Andler and Auw begin making a fast withdrawal. They were moving from the north headed toward Sohonberg.

DECEMBER 17TH

Early in the morning Ken's unit begin to receive heavy resistance. "We lost a lot of men that day. We were ordered to move up the road and support 589th field artillery battalion which was under heavy attack. Their trucks and guns were stuck in the mud and the Germans were going to overrun them. So we attack and got all of them out with everything but two guns. By that time we had lost communications with the division. We were trying to get the artillery unit back to St. Vith, Belgium but every road we tried was either too muddy or filled with German tanks.

Somewhere between Auw, Germany we were trying to break through the German Lines. We were moving down a very muddy road. We just had a few rifleman with us because everything was in chaos. No one knew what was going on. The front of our column hit strong resistance and we were ordered to get off the road. My platoon Sergeant, Sergeant Webb told me to take two men and check out these two houses that were along the road, to see if there were snipers in the houses. The European's build their houses with a barn in one end and living quarters on the other. We went through the barn and there were cattle in the barn. We went into the kitchen and the stove was still warm, but there was no one around. The house was clean and neat. We went up stairs. There were big beds up stairs. They were neat and the floors were shiny. I was a farm boy and the house reminded me of home. The guy with me said he was going to lay down on the bed and I told him that if he did I would shot him. He looked at me really funny when I said that I guess I had a serious look on my face, but we did leave the house as we found it.

We went back to the road and we could hear real heavy fighting ahead of us. We went on down the road with our squad jeep and we got about a half mile down the road from the house. We went around a slight curve to the right and there was a open field to our left. And a wooded area on our right. This Lieutenant that I had had trouble with in Tennessee was now the executive officer of my outfit. He came and got me and told me to set up my machine gun along this fence row about two hundred yards from where we were located. There was a open field in front and a wooded area behind that. There are Germans back there. I was there for just a few minutes and I saw that there was about a platoon of Germans grouping together along the edge of the woods. I waited until they got in place and I opened up. I think I got most of them. I emptied a two hundred and fifty round belt. There was a lot of yelling and screaming going on. Then a mortar shell hit out in front of me about fifty yards. It didn't do any damage, but I knew what was coming. A few seconds later there was one landed just behind me and it must have been a concussion shell because I didn't get any shrapnel, but the concussion almost knocked me out. I picked the gun up tripod and all and headed for the jeep. The column was just starting to advance ahead. The jeep was full so I threw the gun on the tongue of the jeep. We took off and myself and the gun fell off when we hit a bump. I hit hard and I really hurt my shoulder. I was lucky though because a few seconds later the jeep was hit and everyone in the jeep was killed. Then the Germans started pushing the column back. We couldn't hold them so we moved back where the houses were we had checked."

DECEMBER 18TH

By the morning of the December 18th Ken's unit was being attacked from both sides. The fighting was fierce and the casualties were high. They moved into the Ardennes forest and lost contact with the Germans. That night they bedded down in the forest. It was bitter cold. Heavy snow mixed with rain fell from the skies. But, Ken and his fellow soldiers exhausted from three days of fierce fighting paid little attention. They laid in the mud all night trying to sleep.

THE CAPTURE
December 19th

As daylight broke on the morning of December 19th Ken's unit came under heavy artillery fire. "It was tree burst," Ken recalls. "It was terrifying. Men were getting killed everywhere, just blown to bits. We had joined with the 422th division and the commander had already sent a delegation to the Germans to surrender. Our Colonel told the commander that he didn't have the authority to surrender his unit. We were going to fight our way out. We thought we could but we would never have made it and because the commander of the 422 outranked the colonel he had to surrender. He did tell us though that if any of us wanted to try and get out that we could. Myself and eight other guys took off through the woods toward the artillery because we figured we could run under it before we could run away from it. And we did get out of the artillery fire. We ran through the woods for about two

American POWs captured during the Battle of the Bulge. Photo taken by the Germans.

miles and felt like we could get away. We came upon this road and I found out later that it was a road coming directly out of All, Germany which was one of the main roads the Germans were using. We came up on this road and as for back as you could see there were troops, tanks, and horse drawn artillery. Anything you could think of. We were laying there trying to figure out what we should do when a German motorcycle with a side car on come wheeling up. A German officer stood up in the side car and spoke perfect English. He told us we were surrounded if we didn't come out of there they were going to blow us out.

We found out later they had a 20 millimeter gun trained on us down the road. By now I had lost my machine gun. I had picked up a M-1 rifle, three rounds of ammo and three hand grenades. We had Lieutenant Thomas with us and he asked us what we wanted to do. The majority wanted to surrender, but I didn't want to. I had my gun aimed right at this German officer's head. I wanted to blow his head off and to this day I wish I had. We surrendered. Lieutenant Thomas kept saying 'don't Smitty, don't Smitty'. We threw our weapons down and walked down the hill with our hands up. It was the saddest day of my life. That wasn't what I joined the Army for. It was just a absolutely horrible experience to do that. They marched us down to the road. There were a few other prisoners down there. They didn't search us, but they told us to empty our pockets. We started throwing the stuff in our pockets on the ground. I still had three hand grenades in my pocket and I threw them down. They immediately picked them up. I threw a can of c-rations on the ground and they got them. The only thing I had left was a pocket full of T-berry chewing gun and Chesterfield cigarettes. I had forgot that I had therm. I had gotten them the day before when I was looking for a pair of boots when we were still on the jeep. I had gotten into this duffel bag looking for the boots and I found a carton of Chesterfield cigarettes, a box of T-berry chewing gun and a fifth of scotch whiskey. We had drank some the night before and then finished the rest of it the next day going through the woods. I had forgot about the cigarettes and chewing gum but they let me keep them. We started marching down the road and every once in a while we would pick up more prisoners as they were captured and assembled in different areas. By nightfall there was over 500 of us. We knew then that it had been a major offensive. We walked way into the night. We finally stopped and I laid down in the ditch. It was muddy and snow was on the ground. I reached in my pocket and discovered that I still had a hand grenade in my pocket. I talked with a couple of the other prisoners and asked what we were going to do. One suggested

A Point of Interest

NAZI CONCENTRATION CAMPS

Many Americans taken prisoner of war during the Battle of the Bulge were sent to three Nazi death camps: Stalag IXA near Zigenheim, IXB near Bad Orb, and IXC at Berga and Elster. The largest single group were members of the 106th and 28th Infantry Divisions.

On Christmas Day, 1944, the first of 800 men arrived in boxcars at Stalag IXB. The Germans separated the Jewish-American soldiers at Stalag IXB and moved them with many non-Jewish soldiers at Stalag IXC in Eastern Germany, which was part of the Buchenwald Death Camp. The Americans were put to work 14 hours a day drilling a tunnel for a rail line. Guarded by the SS, many were beaten to death and few returned home.

that we wait until a car full of German big shots came along and throw it on them. We figured that we would get a bunch of people killed doing that so we finally decided we would dig a hole and bury it. That's what we did."

THE JOURNEY TO PRISON CAMP
December 20-24, 1944

The next day, December 20 the prisoners walked all day and that night. They arrived at a small village that night. They stayed in a bombed out building for the night. The Germans gave them one small two inch square biscuit. That's all they had eaten since the day before they were captured.

The next day the POWs walked 18 kilometers to Geraldsden, Germany. It seemed a lot longer," Ken explained. " There they loaded us on boxcars. There were 70 men in each boxcar. Not enough room to sit down. If you sit you had to sit between someone elses legs. Before the train moved out one of the German soldiers yelled out "escape". He opened fire knowing the boxcars were packed. One soldier was killed. Then we moved out. When we had to relieve ourselves, we went in a helmet and it was passed to someone on either end of the boxcar where it was dumped out of the air vent. It got pretty rank in there. We had been loaded on the 22nd and on the night of the 23rd we were sitting in the railroad yard at Limberg. A plane came over and dropped a incendiary bomb. We had a pilot on our car and he told us that we were really in for it because that was just a sight for the bombers to follow. He was right because shortly they bombed us. We were lucky our car wasn't hit, but there were some killed. The next morning I don't know how they got that railroad repaired but they did and they pulled us out of there. We would go a little ways and stop. A little further and stop. Then after four days we arrived at Bad Orb.

STALAG IXB

The prison camp was located in Hessen-Nassau region of Prussia, 51 kilometers northwest of Frankfort.

Approximately 290 to 500 men were assigned to a barrack. The barracks were one-story wood and tarpaper types divided into two sections with a washroom in the middle. Washroom facilities consisted of one cold water tap and one latrine hole emptying into an adjacent cesspool which had to be shoveled out every few days. Each half barracks contained a stove. Throughout the winter the fuel ration was two arm loads of wood per stove per day, providing heat for only one hour a day. Bunks, when there were bunks, were triple deckers, arranged in groups of four. Three barracks were completely bare of bunks and two others had only half the number needed. As a result 1500 men were sleeping on the floors. Some bunks had mattresses and some barracks floors were covered with straw. The straw was used in lieu of toilet paper. The outdoor latrines had approximately forty seats which was insufficient for the needs of 4,000 men. Most prisoners received one blanket, but because of overcrowded conditions supplies ran out and several hundred of the prisoners had no blankets. All the barracks were in poor condition; roofs leaked; windows were broken out; lighting was either unsatisfactory or lacking completely. Only a few barracks had tables and chairs. Every building was infested with bedbugs, fleas, lice, and other vermin.

STALAG IXB. . .*KEN'S PERSONAL ACCOUNT*
Christmas Day 1944

"On Christmas day we arrived at a little town of Bad Orb, Germany. Unloaded off the train and started walking up this little mountain road and finally arrived at Stalag IXB.

We stood outside in the rain and cold until each one of was interrogated individually. Although we didn't give anything other than name, rank, and serial number there was no need in getting smart with them because they already knew everything they needed to know about us. One of the things that I remembered during training was that if we were captured it was still our duty to do what we could to cause trouble for the enemy. If we could do something to keep one extra man busy that would be one that couldn't fight. I always kept that in mind and I was sort of mouthy anyway."

THE ESCAPE PLAN

"I behaved for a while and then me, Bobby Lee, and a couple of other guys started planning an escape. It didn't seem like it would be hard to get out of the place. Every night before they would lock us up in the barracks they would line us up in rows of fives and count you off. I figured we could cause some confusion in the count for a couple of days. We figured that we needed to get someone out at night so we could see what was going on and then plan our escape. Myself, Lee, and another fellow were elected to crawl out under the barracks. The barracks were about three feet off the ground and skirted with 12 inch boards. We got under the barracks and the guys messed up the count. The Germans finally got tired of messing with the prisoners so they let them go back in the barracks. That night we found some places that looked pretty good for escape. Some of the places didn't look like they would be much digging to get under the fence. There was a barbed wire fence, about ten feet of rolled wire and then another barbed wire fence. We figured we could make it if we could figure out where the guards were at.

Well, someone must have been offered extra food and believe me there wasn't much of it because we were found out."

THE BEATING

"They took our whole group of sixteen men and put us in a little building. It was used as a recreation building where they could play some games. We had to sleep on the floor and branded as troublemakers. When an American died we were made to bury them. They also made us cut wood for the German quarters across from our camp. One day we were cutting wood and this German officer came by and was yelling at us. I never even looked up from cutting wood and

Cartoon drawing of Stalag IXB by Bob Leaf.

POWs at Stalag IXB.

American Red Cross Card

said, "You Kraut eating son-of a bitch." One of the other German soldiers could speak English real well and he told the officer what I said. The German officer said something to the other German soldiers and the next morning I woke up in the barracks badly beaten. I mean real bad. I couldn't hardly move for about three days. I thought I was going to die. My chest hurt so bad. I had broken ribs and I was badly bruised, but I survived.

We were kept in this barracks for the duration. We had some more burial details and had to cut some wood, but I never talked much after that."

RATIONS

"Every morning they would bring us a big container of coffee. It was hot water with a little color in it, sometimes more than others. Some guys used it to shave with. It really wasn't good to drink, but it was hot and I drank all they gave me.

At noon they would give us a bowl or can of soup. All I had to eat out of was a tin can I got out of the garbage. I had whittled a spoon out of a piece of wood.

At night they would give us a loaf of German black bread which was divided between seven men. Each day a man would take turns cutting the bread. The guy that did the cutting

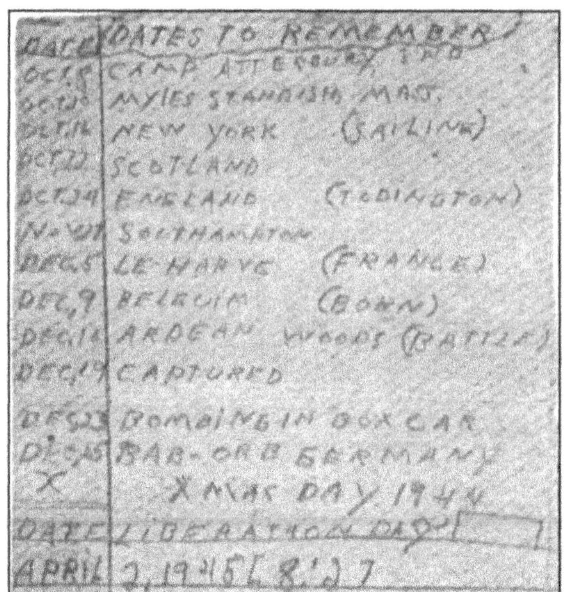

DATE	DATES TO REMEMBER
OCT [illegible]	CAMP ATTERBURY, IND
OCT [illegible]	MYLES STANDISH, MASS.
OCT [illegible]	NEW YORK (SAILING)
OCT 22	SCOTLAND
OCT 24	ENGLAND (TEDINGTON)
NOV [illegible]	SOUTHAMPTON
DEC 5	LE HARVE (FRANCE)
DEC 9	BELGUIM (BONN)
DEC 16	ARDEAN WOODS (BATTLE)
DEC 19	CAPTURED
DEC 23	BOMBING IN BOX CAR
DEC 25	BAD-ORB GERMANY
X	XMAS DAY 1944
DATE	LIBERATION DAY
APRIL	2, 1945 [8:27]

Dates to remember.

got the last draw. Each day some one else took a turn. You also got the crumbs, but you had to be careful not to make too many crumbs or you would be accused of being too messy. It is humorous now, but it was serious then. I weighed about 160 pounds when I was captured and at the end of 105 days and that's after I had been eating good for a week I still only weighed 94 pounds."

LIBERATION
April 2, 1945

Ken and the other prisoners in the camp were liberated on April 2, 1945. "There were a lot of English men in the camp," Ken recalled. "There were a lot of them in bad shape. They wanted to be moved out of the camp first. By the fourth day we were still there although we were eating pretty good. A medic came in one day and said isn't anyone sick. We looked at him and said isn't everybody. He told us that if we wanted to get out of the camp before the English we better get sick. That day every American prisoner got sick. They moved us out by truck to a open field where they had open showers set up.

You could imagine how the body lice were in this place. We had long handles on and part of the past time was to pull your underwear off and turn them inside out pop the big body lice. You could imagine the odor on them after a while. We had fleas, lice, and crabs. We went through the showers and took our underwear and burned them. Then they gave us new clothes. Then we were put on C-47s and send to Camp Lucky Strike in France."

CAMP LUCKY STRIKE

Ken and his fellow prisoners arrived at the camp looking forward to good food and lots of rest. However, their stay started with a tragedy. "The first day that we were there a fellow that I knew by the name of Warren went by a Red Cross set up for coffee and donuts. He didn't know when to quit. The donuts ruptured his stomach and he died. After all that he had went through to die over a doughnut," Ken said.

After about ten days of medical checks, good food, and rest Ken was heading home.

HOMEWARD BOUND
April 22, 1945

On April 22 Ken boarded the USS *Argentina* and head for the United States. Thirteen days later on May 5, 1945 the ship landed at New York Harbor. As they went down the plank the only people that were there were the Red Cross ladies with boxes of ice cream.

"We went to Camp Kilmore, New Jersey and de-programed," Ken explained. "We were suppose to forget all about what happened to us. Then they give us a partial pay and 60 days furlough. Why they did that I don't know. There wasn't a man in that outfit that was physically fit to go on furlough. I look back on it now I wasn't ready to meet my family. I got on a train and went to South Chicago and met my sister. We went out to the house and they had a big party planned for me. I had worked in Chicago and had a lot of friends there. We had the party and I drank a lot of whiskey and it almost killed me. Everyone wanted to talk, but all I wanted to do was to put it behind me.

Two days later I came home. Mary, my girlfriend, was waiting on the curb for me. We had planned on getting married if I made it back. Two weeks later on May 20, 1945 we were married.

DUTY IN SAN FRANCISCO
May 1945 - November 1945

Ken went back to Florida for rest and then he was sent to Texas. "While I was there I was a chauffeur for this Captain," Ken said. "One day he told me he had a deal I might be interested in. They needed a chauffeur in Chicago. If I wanted it he could get it for me in three days. I had a sister in Chicago and it was pretty close to home so I told him I would take it. Three days later I had my orders only it wasn't in Chicago it was San Francisco. My wife was pregnant and the doctors advised her not to go. So I went. I was one of only three men there that had been overseas and I was treated like royalty. I would go pick up a new car and report the Admiral's office. If he had some place to go he told me, if not he dismissed me for the rest of the day. I didn't go back to the motor pool, I toured San Francisco. It was great. On November 25, 1945 I was discharged and went home."

LIFE AFTER THE ARMY. . .*KEN'S STORY*

I went to work here in the oil fields in Mt. Carmel. Worked hard and tried to get ahead. Mentally all screwed up. I drank way to much and made life miserable for myself and my wife. It seemed like everything that I did was a failure. Everything went back to being a POW. People around me didn't help. I had comments about how I was a coward and gave up without a fight. It really hurt. It still does today, not as much but it still does. Even my own family made comments. They didn't know the circumstances. You couldn't hardly get away from it.

Ken and Mary in their wedding picture.

We were both working and we really didn't know what we wanted to do. So In April 1951 we had saved up $400.00. There was an oil field booming in Wyoming and I knew some guys that went out there. One day I came home from work and I told her we are going to Wyoming and start over. We hooked that big old trailer we had to that little car and five days later we made it. I wouldn't do that today for anything.

I never discussed the war or that I was in it. We worked and moved a few times. Then I went to work for a construction company. In two years I was the superintendent. I

Ken and Mary at their 50th wedding anniversary.

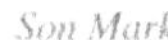

Son Mark

Daughter Pam

IXB barracks in 1995.

Ken standing in the spot where he was beaten after capture in 1944.

worked there for seven years and made good money. I finally became a whole distributor for Chevron Oil Company. In 1982, I retired and came back to my hometown Mt. Carmel, Illinois.

FIFTY YEARS LATER

Ken didn't attend an Association meeting until 1988. He had a great time and after that became more active in veterans' associations. Then an amazing thing happened. Some German soldiers who fought in the Battle of the Bulge contacted the editor of the 106th Association magazine. They wanted to have a reunion with some of the soldiers from the 106th division. In September 1995, 16 veterans and their wives returned to the battlefields in Belgium. Ken was one of those veterans. "We had a great time. I got rid of a lot of ghosts, Ken said. "We were going down the road and wasn't sure where we were. I looked up and I said I have been in that house. One of the guys looked up and said you got to be crazy. I said no and he stopped. It was the house we had gone in 50 years ago. I went to the house and a young lady answered the door. I went in and it was just like it was that day we had been in it, I couldn't believe it.

I took a photo at the point where I was beaten by a German soldier. We walked the route and reminisced with the soldiers that were once our enemy. The war was history and the fact that we were once enemies was history also. By the end of the reunion there was a bond among us. No one said it, but we could all see it in each others faces."

Jupp Steinbuchel in Ardennes in 1944.

Jupp Steinbuchel, circa 1995.

Jupp Steinbuchel in Charkow/Russland 1943.

Jupp Steinbuchel at 1995 reunion with the 106th Infantry.

CHAPTER FIFTEEN

SERGEANT ALVEL L STRICKLIN
U.S. ARMY

301 INFANTRY REGIMENT 94TH DIVISION
CAPTURED DURING THE BATTLE OF THE BULGE

PRISONER OF WAR
JANUARY 21, 1945-APRIL 25, 1945
STALAG XIIA AND XC

FROM FARM BOY TO SOLDIER
March 1943

Alvel was working on the farm with his father when he turned 18. The war was going full steam and like all young men his age he had to register with the draft. He registered and two months later he was drafted. Alvel went to Camp Grant, Illinois for training and several others and finally ended up in Texas with Company A 301 Infantry. His unit went through combat infantry training and then on August 6, 1944 his outfit was shipped to Europe.

NORTHERN FRANCE AND BELGIUM
August 1944-January 21, 1945

Alvel and his unit fought day to day for four months against heavy German resistance through Northern France. After three Bronze Battle Stars and four months of fighting A company 301 Infantry stopped near Belgium. The Battle of the Bulge had begun on December 16th in the Ardennes region of eastern Belgium. Their goal was to trap the Allied Armies and negotiate a truce on the Western front. Even though the German Offensive achieved total surprise to the Americans their goal fell short. All the Germans accomplished was to create a bulge in the American line. Three days after the offensive began the American stand off along with reinforcements insured that the Germans would fall short of their goal. By Christmas day the Germans had not even met their interim objective which was reaching the sprawling Meuse River on the fringe of the Ardennes. What the Germans did accomplish was to expend irreplaceable men, tanks and material.

THE CAPTURE
January 21, 1945

Four weeks later, after grim fighting in bitter cold and snow, with heavy losses on both sides, the bulge ceased to exist. The Germans had still not given up. Alvel and his unit were in the trenches trying to advance. "The Germans were firing directly at us with 88s and we couldn't move," Alvel recalls. "We were in the Monkey Wrench woods. We were taking a lot of direct fire and the casualties were mounting. It was dark and the finally the orders came down that we were to surrender. We learned later that it was the German's 11 Panzer division. We threw our guns down and the Germans took us out to a road. We were told to empty our pockets. I dumped everything I had on the ground and Germans soldiers came by and took what we had. Then they took us one at a time before some officers and they interrogated us. All I gave was my name, rank, and serial number. I just pretended I didn't know anything else they asked.

The next day we started on a march. Each time we went through a village they would stop and call all the village together. They would applaud because we were prisoners of war. We were lucky compared to many. On the march several times I saw groups of Jews being marched in the opposite direction that we were going. Several times I saw them fall because they were so weak they couldn't walk any further. The Germans would just shoot

A Point of Interest

BATTLE OF THE BULGE

FACTS

1. More than a million men, 500,000 Germans, 600,000 Americans (more than fought on both sides at Gettysburg) and 55,000 British participated in the battle.
2. Three German armies, 10 corps, the equivalent of 29 divisions participated.
3. Three American armies, 6 corps, the equivalent of 31 divisions participated.
4. 100,000 German casualties, killed, wounded or captured.
5. 81,000 American casualties, including 23,554 captured and 190,000 killed.
6. 1,400 British casualties, 200 killed.
7. 800 tanks lost on each side, 1,000 German aircaft.

them like dogs. They would just leave them lay and continue on. We walked for the next two weeks until we arrived in Limburg at Stalag XIIA.

STALAG XIIA

This camp was located at Limburg, Germany. The transit camp consisted of a number of concrete block buildings with dirt floors. There was no heat, the roofs leaked, and most of the windows were broken out. A few single story barracks were located in the camp. They were divided into four sections with approximately 20 to 30 men per section. The bunks were three tier. Mattresses were filled with straw. In some cases there were no mattresses provided. Open pits were used for human waste. The camp was infested with fleas, body lice, and other vermin. The food consisted of a watery soup with potato peels on occasion, barley bread, and acorn coffee. At the end of the war the conditions were compounded by overcrowded conditions.

THE SHORT STAY AT STALAG XIIA

Alvel and the other prisoners were starved. After two weeks of marching with little food they were hoping for something more to eat, but little changed. They were given some watery soup and a small piece of bread to eat. "We were thrown into a concrete building with straw floors like cattle. There were so many of us we barely had the room to lay down. The straw was full of body lice and fleas. We had them all over us.

SGT. STRICKLIN IS MISSING

Son of Mr. and Mrs. Leo Stricklin Reported Missing In Germany.

Sgt. Orville Lee Stricklin, has been reported missing in action in Germany, his parents. Mr. and Mrs. Leo Stricklin of Stone Fort RFD 2, learned in a telegram received last Wednesday from the War Department.

Sgt. Stricklin, only son of Mr. and Mrs. Stricklin, entered the service two years ago in March and has been over seas several months. He was originally with the Tank Division but had been transferred to the Infantry. He is a nephew of Mrs. Bertha Williams of 710 North Washington Street. Marion.

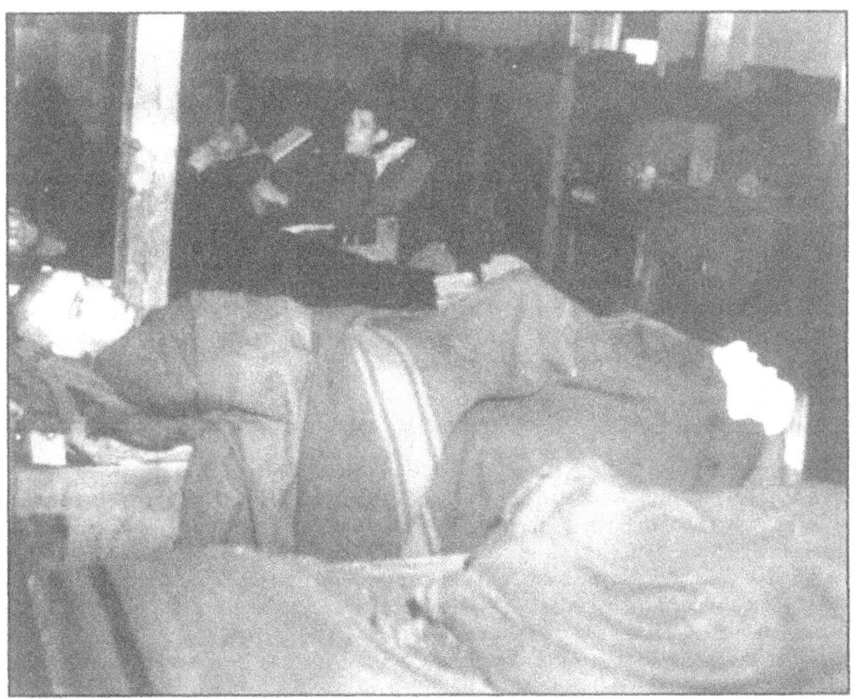

American POW in the hospital (Lazarett) of Stalag 12A at Limburg, Germany after their liberation on 26 March.

Main gate at Stalag XIIA after liberation.

A couple of days later one of my buddies died. I was on the burial detail. We took him up on a hill and wrapped him in a sheet. He was buried with four other prisoners in the same hole.

Then a couple of days later they moved me again."

THE FORTY AND EIGHTS

They took Alvel and several hundred other prisoners to the marshalling yard near Stalag XIIA. They were loaded aboard boxcars and moved out. "We were jammed in the boxcars to the point that all we could do was sit. One man between the legs of another. We never got anything to eat and only a little water. When one of us had to relieve ourselves we would do it in a helmet and pass it from one person to another until the man next to the air vent could pour it out. Those conditions along with the horse manure on the floor of the train made the smell really foul. Our planes bombed us, not knowing we were POWs and the Germans wouldn't let us out of the boxcars. We were lucky our train never got hit. We traveled for four days and finally arrived at Nienburg, Germany."

STALAG XC

The camp was located at Nienburg, Germany in Northern Germany.

The usual one-story wood and tarpaper type barracks were used. The barracks had two sections with a washroom in the middle. The facilities consisted of one cold water tap and one latrine hole emptying into an adjacent cesspool. There was a stove in each barracks, but no wood or cold to warm the barracks. The bunks were triple-deckers. Mattresses full of straw were provided for the bunks. One blanket a piece was issued to the prisoners, but it was not enough to fight against the bitter cold winter. Prisoners huddled together in three or four men to a group to stay warm. The barracks were in a state of disrepair; roofs leaked; windows were broken; and their was no lighting. Every building was infested with bedbugs, fleas, lice, and other vermin.

LIFE AT STALAG XC

"The conditions at this camp was a little better, but not much," Alvel explained. "We got soup most of the time, but we got some Red Cross parcels in this camp. They really helped because the thought on all the POWs minds foremost was food. One day I was looking out the window and I saw this dog coming down the road. Every barracks that it passed prisoners were calling the dog trying to get it to come to them. It finally went into one barracks and it never came out.

We didn't work in the camp so all we did was wait on time. The conditions didn't help. We all had body lice. I never washed, I never shaved, and I had the same clothes on that I was captured in. They had never been washed. It made the days long and the nights miserable. I don't know if I would have made it if I had been captured early in the war."

LIBERATION
April 25, 1945

Alvel and the other prisoners were liberated by the British on April 25, 1945. In the three months that he had been a prisoner he had dropped his weight from 160 pounds to a mere 89 pounds. He also developed hepatitis and was shipped to a hospital in France. After two months in the hospital he was released.

HOME
June 19, 1945-December 8, 1945

Alvel crossed the Atlantic by ship and arrived in New York Harbor on June 21, 1945. He was sent home on furlough and after reminiscing with his family returned Florida for rest and recuperation. He was Honorably Discharged on December 8, 1945.

EPILOGUE

Alvel married Florence Know in 1946. They had two children Monty Lee and Johnny. Alvel worked in the coal mines and farmed part-time until his retirement in the 1980s.

In 1984 his wife died and several years later he married his present wife Wanda. They now live on a farm in Southern Illinois and enjoy retirement. Alvel has stayed I in contact with his fellow ex-POWs. Once a month they get together and talk about the old times.

Liberated American POWs in a field near Stalag XIIA.

Sgt. Arvel Lee Stricklin, who landed in Boston, Mass., June 21, arrived home last Tuesday. Sgt. Stricklin was released from Stalag 10-C prison camp by the British 2nd army on April 28, having been a prisoner there since Jan. 21. He gives the Red Cross much praise for alleviating their suffering while in prison. He has regained the many pounds lost and looks well. He is to report back to duty at Miami Beach, Florida at the close of a 60 day furlough.

ABOUT THE AUTHOR

Harry Spiller, Author (Photo credit Bill Erwin)

Harry Spiller was born on July 3, 1945, in Marion, Illinois. He lived in Southern Illinois until he graduated from Marion High School in 1963.

On June 3, 1963, five days after graduation, at the age of 17 he reported to San Deigo, California for recruit training with the United States Marine Corps. He served ten years in the Marines which included two tours of duty in Vietnam.

From 1967 through 1970 the author served as a recruiter in Southeast Missouri. Part of his duties was to handle death messages and organize military funerals for those killed in action in the eleven county recruiting area.

After being discharged from the Marines in 1973, Spiller returned to Southern Illinois where he worked as lawman. He completed a BS in Criminal Justice, a BA in Political Science, and an MPA in Public Administration at Southern Illinois University. In 1982, he was elected Sheriff of Williamson County.

In 1989, he resigned as Sheriff to take a position as Associate Professor in Criminal Justice at John A. Logan College in Carterville, Illinois.

Spiller wrote two books on his experiences in war: the first, *Death Angel* (1992), about his experiences in Vietnam and as a recruiter delivering death messages, and a second, *Scars of Vietnam* (1994), of 17 personal accounts of these men and their families twenty years after the war. Since that time he has written numerous True Crime stories for National Magazines and a third book on POWs in Nazi Prison Camps during World War II.

Spiller and his wife Shirl have two children, Lisa, 16, and Chad, 10. He continues to teach and write. *From Wake Island to Berlin* is his fourth book.

APPENDIX A

JAPANESE PRISONER OF WAR CAMPS
WORLD WAR II, 1941-1945

CAC OR CIC-CIVILIAN PRISON CAMPS
POW-MILITARY PRISON CAMPS

PHILIPPINE ISLANDS

MANILA AREA: 31
Assumption Convent
Atenco De Manila
Bachrach Garage
Bilibid
Camp Murphy
Christ the King Seminary
Doctors Hospital
Ft. Mckinley
Ft. Santiago
Engineer Island
Holy Ghost Children's Home
Hospico de San Jose
Las Pinas (at Paranaque)
Malate Church
Mary Chiles Hospital
National Psychopathic Hospital
Nichols Field
Nielson Field
Paranaque
Philippine T.B. Hospital
Port Terminal Bldg.
Remedio's Hospital
San Lazaro Hospital
Santa Catalina Hospital
St. Joseph's Hospital
St. Luke's Hospital
Santiago Hospital
Santo Tomas University
Sternberg General Hospital
Sulphur Springs Hotel
Zablan Field

LUZON ISLAND OTHER THAN MANILA:

BAGUIO: 4
Baguio Hospital
Brent School
Camp John Hay
Camp Holmes
Bayambang
Bilibid, New, at Mutinlupa
CABANTUAN: 3
Cabanatuan No. 1
Cabanatuan No. 2
Cabanatuan No. 3

Clark Field
Limay, Bataan
Lipa, Batangas
Los Banos
Nasugu
O'Donald
Paracale
Pasay
POW Camp No. 17
San Juan Camp
Tagaytay
Tarlac
Tayabas
Tuy A.F.B.

OTHER ISLANDS IN THE PHILIPPINES:

BOHOL I.
Tagbilaran

CABALLO I.
Ft. Hughes

CEBU
Cebu City

CORREGIDOR: 3
Ft. Mills (Camp No. 7)
Malinta Tunnel Hospital
Ninety-second Gargae

COYU I.

EL FRAILE I.
Ft. Drum

LEYTE I.
Tacloban

MANAMOC I: 7
Davao Penal Colony (DAPECOL)
Davao Port Area
Lasang
Malabalay
Matina Airfield
Sasa Airfield
Zamboanga

NEGROS I.
Bacolod

PAWAWAN
Puerto Princessa

PANAY
Lloilo City

SAMAL. I.
Santa Mesa

GUAM ISLAND

Agana

WAKE ISLAND

INDONESIAN ISLANDS OF S.E. PACIFIC

AMBON: 7
Camp Benteng
Galala
Laha
Liang
Tentoey (Tantoei)
Victoria Barracks, Ambon Town
Town Gaol

BORNEO: 5
Balikpapan
Jesselton
Kuching, Sarawak
Pontinak
Sandakan

CELEBES: 6
Makassar City
Menado Gaol (Military Prison)
Menado Military Barracks
Pare Pare
Poso
Rapang

LESSER SUNDRA ISLANDS: 7
Ampenan, LOMBOK I.
Foelie
Makoronen
Maumere
Oesapa Besar

TIMOR I.
Atamboea
Dilli

MOLLUCAS: HAROEKOE I: 2
Haroekoe
Pelauw

NEW BRITAIN I.: 3
Bita Paka
Kokupo
Rabaul

NEW GUINEA: 4
Manokwari
Prafi River Camp
Windehsi
Wiringgi

NEW IRELAND

Kavieng: 2

SUMATRA: 19
Bangkal Pinang (Banka)
Djambi
Galang
Kebondoerian-Camp 4
Koetatjane
Loeboekrama
Medan: 4
  Belewan, Medan Harbor
  Medan Old City Guard Bldg.
  Medan Roman Catholic Church
  Poeloe Brajan
Padang
Palembang
Pakanbaroe
Pakoe
Rantauparpat
Sikarakara
Soengel Kariau
Talang Semoet (near Palembang)
Tandjoeng Balai

JAVA

BANDUNG (BANDOEENG):7
Artillary Barracks
Bandoeng (Tjimahi)
Exhibition Building
XV Inf. Bn. Barracks
First Depot Bn.
134th Depot Bn.
Soeka Miskin Prison

BANDOENG AREA CIVILIAN CAMPS: 9
Ambarawa
Bantjeu Gaol
Karees Camp
Mageland
Moentilan
Semarang
Sindanglaja
Soerakaboem
Tjhapit Camp
Cheribon (Tjirebon)

DJAKARTA (BATAVIA) CAMPS: 8
Adek Building
Batavia Bicycle Camp
Buitenzorg
Depok
Diaroza Hospital
Glodok Prison
Struswyk Prison
10th Bn. Barracks

DJAKARTA CIVILIAN CAMPS: 16
Boekit Doeri Prison
Galoekan
Gang Kanario
Gen Hauber
Kramat Rd.
Matramin Rd.
Meester Cornelius
East of Meester Cornelius
Ngawi
Petodjo Area
Soerakarta (Surakarta)
Struiswijk Prison
Tangerang
Tenah Abang
Tjipinang Gaol
Ziekensorg Hospital

Djokjakarta
Ft. Vredenburg
Lelos
Malang
Poerwekerto
Serang City Jail
Serang Movie Theatre
Soekaboemi (Sukabumi)

SUBURAYA POW CAMP: 4
Darmo Barracks
Grissee (Gresik)
Jaarmarket
St. Vincent's Hospital

SURUBAYA AREA CIVILIAN CAMPS: 6
Banjoewangi
Blambangan
Kesilar
Malino
Pamekssan
Tegalsanggar

TANDJONG: 3
Tandjong Priok (Kampong Kodja)
Tandjong Priork
Tandjong Police Barracks

Other camps named:
Camp C
Camp D
Camp X
Camp Y

S.E. ASIA MAINLAND

SINGAPORE: 30
Alexandra Barracks
Batutiga
Bidaderi Camp
Blakenmat
Bukit Is.
Buller Camp
Changi Barracks
Changi Prison
Changi Seletar
Chinese School, Katong Rd.
His Majesty's Central Prison
Holland Village
Krangi Hospital
McPherson Road Camp
Nee Soon
Old Race Course
Orchard Road
Palau Brani Island
Palau Damar Laut (Jeep Island)
Paulau Blakang Miti
Pasir Panjang
Revalvary
Seletar Airfield and Naval Base
Sime Road Camp
Syonon Changi
Tanglin
Tengah
Thompson Road
Tyersall Park
Woodlands Road

MALAYA: 27
Alor Star (Kedah)
Ayer Hitam (Johore)
Batu Pahat (Johore)
Beng Nha Hang
BINTON IS.
Endau (Johore)

Ipoh (Perak)
Jitra (Kadah)
Johore Bahru Hospital
Kluang (Johore)
Kluang non-I.N.A. Camp
Kota Braru
Kota Tinggi
Kualar Kangsar
Kuala Lumpur: 5
"A" Camp, Military Barracks, Ipoh Rd.
"B" Camp (Western Camp)
"C" Camp (Chinese School near flour mills)
"D" Camp (Chinese School near flour mills)
Main Camp, Chinese School, Batu R.
Malacca
Muar (Johore)
Penang, PENANG IS.
Port Swettenham (Selanger)
Seremban
Taiping Gaol (Perak Dist.)
Talok Paku
Yala

FRENCH INDOCHINA:

SAIGON:
Baria
Civil Jail
Nha Be
Polyclinque-Camp B
Saigon Docks, Jean Eudel St.
Warehouses 10 and 11
Tan Son Nhut Airfield

Baster
Battambang
Cholong
Haiphong Road Camp
Hanoi-Gialam Airport
Hanoi
Mytho
Phnom Penh
Savannaket
Tankin

INDIA

ANDAMAN I. Port Blair Jail
142nd Field Hospital, Calcutta

BURMA
Akyab Jail
Bhamo Jail
Kalewa-Mawlaik
Mandalay Jail and Fort
Maymyo Jail
Maynigo Jail
Merqui Jail

MOULMEIN:
Moulmein Jail-Camp No. 3
Wegale Camp No. 5
Mytkyina

RANGOON:
Chettiar School, kambe
Judson College
Kempelai Jail
New Law Courts Jail
Rangoon Central Prison

ROSS I.
Tavoy
Thanbyuzayat
Victoria Point
Ye

BURMA-THAILAND RAILROAD WORK CAMPS (North to South by location on R.R.): 61
4K. Camp-Khandaw
8K. Camp-(Dutch)
25K. Camp
26K. Camp-(Australian)
30K. Camp-Retphaw (Retpu)
40K. Camp
Anankwin
55K. Camp-(Hospital)
62K. Camp-Mezali
70K. Camp
75K. Camp-Milo
85K. Camp
Apalon
105K. Camp-Angenaung
Tadein
108K. Camp-(Dutch)
Payu Thonzu Tuang
(Burma-Thai Border-3 Pagodas Pass)
Ban Naung Lu
Dhamayiew No. 2
Dhamayiew No. 3
Dha Khanum (Takanum-Tauchan)
Kui Youg
Lin Thin (Rin Tin)
Gai Zai Yok (Kinsao)
Zai Yok (Konu)
Sra Si Mum (Tampli)
Tah Takua (Nong Takay-Toncha So.)
Ban Wang Yai (Tarsao)
Ban Lum Sum
Chungkai (Chonkel-Chong Kwai)
Ban Ko Krang
Tha Ma Kham
Ban Tah Maken (Tamaken-Tamarkan-

Tamarkam)
Ban Nua
Kanburi Bae Hospital
Kanchanaburi
Ban Khao Pun (Cugkai-Khao Chong Kwai)
Ban Tai (Ban Dai)
Koh Samrong
Ban Kao
Wangkanai (Tonsamrong-Talat Tah Muang-Tamuang)
Non Tha Buri (Nondhaburi)
Nakhon Pathom
WAMPO: 8K. From Kanburi-double camp on both sides of river)
Bang Pong, North Camp
Bang Pong, South Camp
Ban Pong Hospital
Ban Pong (or Thai) Camp K. 1 from Ban P
Plek Ret
Non Pla Duk (Nong Paydock-Hnohnpladuk
Ban Haui Pong
Tagloh (Ban Pong)
Ban Muang

THAILAND CAMPS NOT LOCATED:
Wat Krang
150K.-Kanty
193K. From Ban Pong
260K. From Ban Pong
Conta (or Kanyu)
Kinranjok
Kunnyok
Tanrizaya Niaru
Tamajo

THAILAND:

BANGKOK: 7
Don Muang Rd., near airfield
Klong Toj No. 1
Klong Taoi No. 2
National Stadium, Bankok
Rifle Range, near airfield
Vajiravudh College (Royal Pages College) Civilian Group
Vajiravudh College POW Camp

Bawa Sane
Chieng Mai
Hindat
Nagorm Nayok (Prachinburi)
Nike
Pechaburi (Pentenburi)
Rataburi (Rajaburi), Muang
Songkia (Singora)
Sukotai-Mesoth Road
Trang
Ubon (Ubonrajthani)
Uttaradit
Yang Yohng

NORTHEAST ASIA MAINLAND

CHINA

CANTON: 14 small work camps, including:
Anton
Cheung Ping
Cheung Pang
Honam I.
Pekkai
Pokong
SHEMEEN I.

HAINAN ISLAND: 7
Cheung Kong
Hachow (Aichow)
Hoihow
Paksha Kong (Patsho Camp or Patano)
Samal Naval Base
Shinhlushan
Tinduk Mine

HONG KONG: 12
Argyle St. Military Camp
Bowen Rd. Military Camp
Kowloon Section, Military Camp
Lai Chi Kok
Ma Tau Chaung (Matachung, Kowloon)
North Point Camp
Rosemarie Hill Convent
Samshuipo (Shamshuipo) (Camp S-Kowloon)
Sham Shui Po (Camp N)
Stanley Camp (Military Internment Camp)
STONECUTTERS ISLAND
Yaumati

KANKOW (Hancow) Internment Camp

NANKING

PEKING (Peiping): 7
British Embassy
Fengtai Camp
Likuany Kiso Monastery (Linkuangkiso-Christ the King Convent)
Pataowan Monastery
Tai-Ping-T'sang Monastery
Prison Camp No. 1407, Peking

SHANGHAI: 19
Ash Camp
Bridge House Jail
Colombia Country Club

Civil A.C. Eastern Area
Chapel C.A.C.
Franciscan House
Haiphong Road Internment Camp Shanghai
Jessfield Road Police Station
Lin Cha Lu
Lincoln Avenue Camp
Naval POW Camp
jPootung
Sacred Heart Convent
Shanghai Power Station
Shanghai Water Works
Ta Hsi Lu (No. 65)
Ward Road Jail
Yu Yuen
Zikawei

SHANGHAI AREA: 9
Chin Hua
Civic Center
Hong Chi Salt Godown, Kinhua
Kiangsu Middle School
Kiangwan
Linghwa
P'U-T'O SHAN I. (Chusan Archip.)
Chikiang
TINGHAI I. (Vhusan Archip.) Tingaad
Woosung

SHANTUNG PROVINCE:
Chefoo, Temple Hill CIC
Tsingtao CIC
Weihsein

Swatow
Tientsin
Yangchow: Civilian Assembly Center, Kiangsu:
Camp A
Camp B
Camp C

YUNNAN PROVINCE:
Chaiotoukai
Huangsikan (Wanglike)
Lungling
Mangshih
Shangkiakai (Maglien)
Teng Chung

MANCHURIA:

MUKDEN: 10
Fushun CIC
Hoten (Temporary)
Hoten-Main Camp
Hoten Branch No. 1-tannery
Hoten Branch No. 2-textile factory
Hoten Branch No. 3-steel and lumber mill
Hoten, North Camp-U.S. Consulate Bldg.
Mukden Club Internment Camp
Mukden Military Hospital
Peiling Internment Camp
Hoten Branch No. 4-Cheng Chia Tun
Kobahhashi Dairen
Sian (Changchun-Hsinking-Seihan)
Ssupingkai Internment Camp (Shihel)

KOREA (CHOSEN)
Jinsen Divisional Camp
Keijo: 3
Main Camp
Branch Camp No. 1
Dispatch Camp No. 1
Konan
Korea Divisional Camp
KOSHUYU I.
Pusan (Fusan)
Rempo
Repho
Ryuzan
Seishin

FORMOSA (TAIWAN)
Heito Prison Camp No. 3
Ingrin
Karenko
Keelung
Kingaseki
Shirakawa-Kagi, Camp No. 4
Taichu-Camp No. 2
Taihoku-Camp No. 1
Taihoku-Camp No. 5-Muksaq
Taihoku-Camp. No. 6
Takao Hospital Camp
Takao POW Camp
Toroku
Tosei

JAPAN

HOKKAIDO I.
Asahigawa
Bibai-Machi (Branch Camp No. 3)
Hakodate Main Camp
Hakodate Divisional Camp
Kamiso Sub-Camp (Sub-Camp No. 1)
Mitisuishi
Muroran Camp (Kamiso Machi Camp. No. 73)
Otaru
Sapporo Penitentiary
Temiya Park Stadium
Tomakomai
Utashinia (Hakodate Branch Camp No. 2)
Utashinai (Divisional Camp of Hakodate, No. 3)

FUKUOKA-KYUSHU ISLAND CAMPS:
AMAMI I., (Ryukyu Archipelago)
Aokuma, Camp. No. 22
Arao
Beppu
Camp No. 11
Futase, Camp No. 7 (or 10)
Lizuka
Kashi, Camp No. 1 (Pine Tree Camp; also spelled Kashi)
Koyagi Shima
Kumamoto Barracks
Kurume
Moji: 2
  Moji Camp No. 4
  Moji Hospital
Nacama Camp No. 4
Najasaki: 4
  Camp No. 2
  Camp No. 14
  Camp No. 24 Senryu
  Nagasaki Camp-former Franciscan convent
Omuta, Camp No. 17
Sasebo Naval Base
Sub-Camp No. 12
Tobata
Yawata, Camp No. 3

HONSHU (Southern) ZENTSUJI, FUKUO

KA CAMPS
Camp No. 23
Higashi-Misome, Zentsuji Sub-Camp No. 10
INNOSHIMA ISLAND, Sub-Camp No. 2
Kochi (Kochi Ken)
Kure
Mitsu, Branch Camp No. 5
Motoyama, Sub-Camp No. 8
MUKOJIMA ISLAND Sub Camp No. 1
Myoshi
Niihama, Branch Camp No. 2
Ohama, Sub-Camp No. 9
Omine, Sub-Camp No. 6 (Higp Tonoura)
Onoda, Branch Camp No. 8
Onoda, Branch Camp No. 9
Shimonoseki
Tamano, Branch Camp No. 3
Ube, Sub-Camp No. 7
Zentsuji Principal Camp
Zentsuji Sub-Camp No. 3

OSAKA-KOBE GROUP CAMPS

KOBE: 12
Futatabi, Hoyoga No. 1
Kobe (7 miles west on Kako River)
Ito Machi, CIC Sub-Camp No. 11
Kawasaki Camp-Kobe
Kobe Divisional Camp
Kobe POW Camp No. 31
Kobe POW Hospital
Koshian Hotel
Pago Camp No. 2-Eastern Lodge CIC
Pago Camp No. 3-Butterfield Swire
Seaman's Club CIC, Camp No. 4
Suzurandai POW. Camp

OSAKA: 9
Amagasaki Sub-Camp
Minato-Ku
Osaka Central Market Company
Osaka No. 1 Headquarters Camp (Chikko)
Sakai Prison
Sakurajima Camp
Sakurajima Sub-Camp. Ichioka School
Sumiyoshi-Ku
Umeda Bunsho

OSAKA-KOBE AREA:
Nagoya: 4
  Aichi CIC
  Nagoya Main Camp
  Narumi, Nagoya Sub-Camp No. 2
  Nagoya Sub-Camp No. 10
Aioshi
Akenobe, No. 6-B Divisional Camp
Funatsu
Furashi
Fuse
Gifu (Nagara Hotel)
Harima, Camp No. 29, Wakayama
Himeji
KiroHata Divisional Camp
Kamioka
Kyoto (Branches Hakata, Kaira and Choki)
Maibara
maisure (Maitsuri, Maizuru)
Notogawa
Oeyama (Oyama)
Roku Roshi
Shingu
Tanagawa
Toyooka
Tsuruge, Divisional Camp
Wakayama
Yodagawa Bunsho
Yokkaichi
Yonago
Yura

TOKYO:
Akasaka Area
Franciscan Monastery
Kagawa Christian Fellowship House

Mizonkuchi
Narashino Airport
Omori Main Camp
Sekiguchi at Koishikawaku
Shibaura
Shinagawa:
  Main Camp
  POW Hospital
Shinjuki, Camp No. 1
Sumidagawa
Sumirejo
Suziki Aio No Moto Factory
Takadanobaba Camp

KAWASAKI:
Kawasaki No. 1 Bunsho
Kawasaki Dispatch Camp No. 5
Kawasaki Sub-Camp No. 2

YOKOHAMA: 12
Achi Yamakita
Kanagawa, Tokyo 2nd Div.
Kanagawa Kenko
Negishi Race Course
Nogeyama Park
Ofuna Camp
Old City Hall
Park Central Camp
Park Central Stadium
Totsuka
Yacht Club Boathouse
Yokohama No. 5

NORTH HONSHU-TOKYO CONTROL CAMPS
Akita
Aomori
Ashikago
Atami
Chiba
Chuzenji
Fukushima
Furmaki
Futatsui City
Fuji
Hakone
Hanawa, Sendai No. 6
Hiraoka Sub-Camp No. 3
Hayashi Village, Yokosuka Dist.
Hitachi Ibaragi-Ken Camp (D-12)
Hitachi Motoyama
Kamita Kozan, Sendai Camp No. 11
Kanazawa
Kita Cotygara, Mura
Kosaka
Matushima, Camp 2-D
Mito
Morioka
Murakami
Nooetsu Prison Camp (Niigata Ken)
Niigata Sub-Camp No. 5
Odate
Ohashi
Sendai
Shimodate
Shimomago, Hitachi
Shizuoka
Toyama
Tsurumi Sub-Camp No. 5
Uraga
Urawa International Camp (Saitama)
Utsunomiya
Wakasen
Yamakita
Yamashita Camp No. 1
Yuwake Prison Camp (lwake)

APPENDIX B

NAZI PRISON CAMPS

STALAG-Main Camps
MARLAG-Camp for Sailors
OFLAG-Camp for Officers
LUFT-Camp for Airman
DULAG-Camp for Officers
LAZARETT-Hospitals

The below list is of Nazi Prison Camps, Hospitals, Work Camps and their approximate Locations. Allied prisoners of war were held in these camps throughout the duration of the war.The information of these camps and their locations came from the International Red Cross, Prisoners of War, and Allied Intelligence as the Camps were liberated at the end of the war.

PRISON CAMP PROXIMATE LOCATIONS

STALAG IIA Neubrandenburg, Machlenberg, Germany
STALAG IIB Hammerstein, Germany
STALAG IIE Mecklenburg, Germany
STALAG IIIA Brandenburg, Germany
STALAG IIIB Furstenburg, Germany
STALAG IIIC Altdrewitz, Germany
STALAG IVA Hohnstein, Germany
STALAG IVB Muhlberg, Germany
STALAG IVC Wistritz, Czechosovaki
STALAG IVD Saxony, Germany
STALAG IVD/2 Saxony, Germany
STALAG VA Ludwigsburg, Germany
STALAG VB Villingen, Germany
STALAG VC Offenburg, Bavaria
STALAG VIC Osnabruck, Bavaria
STALAG VIG Bonn, Germany
STALAG VIIA Mooseburg, Germany
STALAG VIIB Memminggen, Germany
STALAG VIIIA Gorlitz
STALAG VIIIB Teschen, Poland
STALAG VIIIC Sagan,
STALAG IXB Hessen-Nassau
STALAG IXC Thuringia
STALAG XB Hanover
STALAG XC Nienburg
STALAG XIA Saxony
STALAG XIB Fallingbostel
STALAG XIIA Limburg, Germany
STALAG XIID Waldbreitsback, Bavaria
STALAG XIIF Freinschein, Bavaria
STALAG XIIIB Weiden, Baveria
STALAG XIIIC Hammelsberg, Bavaria
STALAG XIIID Nurnberg, Bavaria
STALAG XVIIA Kaisersteinbruck, Austria

STALAG XVIIB Gneixendorf, Austria
STALAG XVIIIA Wolfsberg, Austria
STALAG XVIIIC Markt Pongau, Austria
STALAG XXA Torn, Poland
STALAG XXB Marienburg, East Prussia
STALAG XXIA Posen, Poland
STALAG 344 Lamsdorf
STALAG 357 Kopernikus, Poland
STALAG 383 Hohenfels, Bavaria
STALAG 398 Pupping, Austria
Work Camp 21 Blechhammer

MARINE CAMP AND OFLAG PROXIMATE LOCATIONS

Milag-MarlagTarmstedt, Hannover
IVC Colditz
VIIB Eichstatt, Bavaria
VIIIF Brunswick
IX Hessen-Nassau
IXA/Z Rotenburg
XB Westphalis
XIIIB Hammelburg, Baveria
XIIIC Ebelsbach, Baveria
XXI B Alburgund, Poland

LUFT CAMP PROXIMATE LOCATIONS

LUFT I Barth, Pomerania
LUFT III Sagen
LUFT VII Bankau
LUFT IV Pomerania
LUFT VI Heydekrug, East Prussia

DULAG LUFT PROXIMATE LOCATIONS

DULAG IVA Saxony
DULAG IVG Leipzig
DULAG VB Rottenmuster
DULAG VIC Hanover
DULAG VIG Gerresheim. Rhineland
DULAG VIJ Dusseldorf, Rhineland
DULAG VIIA Freising, Bavaria
DULAG IXB Hessen-Nassau

LAZARETT PROXIMATE LOCATIONS

LAZ IXC(A) Thuringia
LAZ IXC(b) Meiningen
LAZ IXC(c) Hildurghausen
LAZ XA Schleswig
LAZ XB Hanover
LAZ XIIID Nurnberg
Marine LAZ Cuxhaven, Hanover
Luftwaffen LAZ Wismar

APPENDIX C

Office Of The Commanding General Army Service Forces

The German prisoner of war regulations translated in this volume were located by a member of the Provost Marshal General's Office shortly after the termination of hostilities in Europe.

They have been translated and issued through the efforts of the Liaison and Research Branch of the American Prisoners of War Information Bureau.

B.M. Bryan
Brigadier General
The Provost Marshal General

Abbreviations of German Military Terms

Abbreviations	Translation
Abw	Counter Intelligence
Ag.E.H.	Section for Replacement Training and Army Matters
AHA	General Army Office
Arb. Ndo.	Work detail
AWA	Section for General Armed Forces Armed Forces Matters
B.d.E.	Commander of the Replacement Training Army
Bkl.	Clothing
Ch.H.Ruest	Chief of Army Equipment
Dulag	Transit camp for prisoners of war
Gen.D.Pi.	General of the engineers
Gen.Qu.	Quartermaster General
Genst.D.H.	Army General Staff
GVF	Fit for garrison duty in the field
GVH	Fit for garrison duty in the interior
H.D.St.O.	Army Disciplinary Regulations
H.Dv.	Army Service Regulations
H.P.A.	Army Personnel Office
HV	Army Administration
H.V.B1.	Army bulletin
In.Fest.	Inspectorate of fortresses
Kriegsgef.	Prisoner of War Department
Kv.	Fit for war service
Oflag	Officers' prisoner of war camp
Ob.d.L.	Commander-in-Chief of the Air Force
O.K.H.	Army Supreme Command
O.K.M.	Navy Supreme Command
O.K.W.	Supreme Command of the Wehrmacht (Armed Forces)
P.A.	Personnel Office
P.U.	Mail censorship
R.d.L.	Reich Minister of Aviation
S.D.	Security Service
S.S.	Elite Guard of the National Socialist Party
Stalag	PW camp for enlisted men
VA	Army Administration Office
VO	Decree
Wam.	Guard detail
W.A.St.	Information Bureau of the Wehrmacht
W.F.St.	Armed Forces Operations Staff
W.Pr.	Wehrmacht Propaganda
W.V.	Army administration

Supreme Command of the Wehrmacht Berlin-Schoeneber, 16 June 1941

I. Chief Group

1. Prisoners of war of alien nationalities in enemy armies.

Frequently recurring doubts in determining the nationality of alien prisoners of war are now definitely resolved in that the *uniform* is the determining outward factor in establishing the fact of the prisoner's belonging to the respective armed forces. Accordingly, Polish prisoners of war captured in French uniforms will be considered Frenchmen, while Poles captured in Polish uniforms will be considered Poles.

2. The title "camp officer" instead of "camp leader."

The title "camp leader" is not accepted in any of the regulations. It is therefore no longer to be used and is to be replaced by: "first camp officer" and "second camp officer."

3. Reward for the recapture of escaped prisoners of war.

The OKW has requested the German newspapers to publish the following: In view of the increase in the number of escape attempts by prisoners of war commonly occurring in the spring, the military and police services will welcome the cooperation of the general public. Persons offering effective aid in apprehending escaped prisoners of war may be granted financial awards, applications for which must be directed to the respective prisoner of war camp.

The reward herewith provided for are to be paid out of Reich funds... The reward of one individual shall not exceed 30 marks even when several prisoners of war are apprehended. The amount is fixed by the Commander of Prisoners of War having jurisdiction respective prisoner of war camp.

II. Group I.

4. Personal contact of prisoners of war with women.

Certain inquiries addressed to the OKW make it necessary to point out the following: The prohibition of 10 Jan 1940 applies only to association of prisoners of war with German women.

It is therefore not necessary to submit a detailed report in cases of illicit traffic of prisoners with women of foreign nationality, unless certain circumstances make it a penal offense (rape, intercourse with minors, etc.).

The question as to the prisoner's liability to disciplinary punishment is left to the discretion of the disciplinary superior officer. The inquiry of the Army District Command V of 29 April 1941, I 3330 is thereby settled.

5. Questionnaires for French officers.

The French Armistice Commission had sometime ago requested, in connection with the reconstitution of the French army, that newly arrived French prisoner of war officers in all the camps fill out questionnaires. Since the work is now finished, the questionnaires need not be filled out any longer.

6. Transfers to officers' Camp IV C Colditz.

Several officers' camps frequently transfer to officers' Camp IV C prisoner of war officers who have not yet completed disciplinary sentences pending against them.

As the few guardhouse cells in officers' Camp IV C are currently occupied by prisoners of war officers serving sentences imposed by the headquarters of the camp, the transfer of officers to officers' Camp IV C may be undertaken only after they have completed their previously imposed disciplinary sentences.

7. Jews in the French Army.

A transfer of the Jews to special camps is not intended; they must, however, be separated from the other prisoners of war and, in case of enlisted men, must be assigned to work in closed groups outside the camp.

Jews are not to be specially marked.

8. Punishment of prisoners of war by the suspension of mail service.

Several cases have been recently reported where camp commandants have suspended prisoners of war mail service as a disciplinary measure.

Attention is called to Article 36, Section 1 of the Geneva Convention of 1929 prohibiting the stoppage or confiscation of incoming or outgoing mail of prisoners of war.

Article 57, Section 2 merely provides that packages and money orders addressed to prisoners of war undergoing disciplinary punishment may be handed to them only after the completion of their sentence.

The decision as to whether mail is to be handed out to prisoners of war under a court sentence rests with the competent penal authorities.

Supreme Command of the Wehrmacht Berlin-Schoeneberg, 23 July 1941

3. English books for training in radio broadcasting to foreign lands. (Talk work).

In camps occupied by British prisoners of war, several copies of the books named below will probably be found in possession of the prisoners:

Field Service Regulations, Volumes I and II
Manual of Organization and Administration
Field Service Pocket Book
Infantry Training, Volumes I and II
Cavalry Training
Artillery Training
Infantry Section Training
Engineer Training

It is requested that one copy of these books be procured and forwarded directly to the OKW/W pr (IV h i) Berlin W 35, Bendlerstr. 10.

Should other books of similar nature not mentioned above be found, it is requested that one copy of these, too, be forwarded.

No statement as to where the books are being sent is to be made to the Prisoners of War.

14. Questionnaires on cases of death of prisoners of war.

In case of death of a prisoner of war, in addition to the report to the Information Bureau of the Wehrmacht, a special questionnaire must be immediately filled out and submitted to the German Red Cross, Berlin SW 61 Bluecherplatz 2, so that the relatives of the deceased can be notified without delay (OKW file 2 F 24. 62a. Kriegsgef. Vi No. 135/11 dated 7 Jan 1941). Direct notification of the next of kin of the deceased is not permitted. Double reports are to be avoided. Should the prisoner of war die while in a hospital, the camp is to be informed of the date on which the questionnaire has been forwarded to the German Red Cross. No questionnaires are to be filled out in cases of death of Russian prisoners of war.

Supreme Command of the Wehrmacht Berlin-Schoeneberg, 1 September 1941

4. Religious functions at prisoner of war camps.

In view of the general lack of interpreters, it will be sufficient for a specially selected, qualified guard to be present at divine services in which only the Sacrifice of the Mass is performed and communion is given, in order to see to it that the minister does not add anything in the way of a special sermon.

11. Guard personnel in officers' camps.

Complaints have been repeatedly made that guards, who are entirely unfit for their task by reason of physical disabilities (club-foot, impaired hearing, marked nearsightedness, etc.) or low intelligence are being used for the surveillance of prisoner of war officers.

For the sake of the prestige of the German Wehrmacht, officers' camps are to use only such personnel as are physically and mentally unobjectionable and who are thus not liable to produce an unfavorable impression on the prisoner of war officers. An appropriate exchange of personnel within the guard battalions is to be undertaken immediately.

Supreme Command of the Wehrmacht Berlin-Schoeneberg, 8 December 1941

14. Supplying camp canteens with rubber collars for Yugoslav prisoner of war officers.

The firm "Rheinische Gummi & Celluloid Fabrick," Mannheim, was exporting before the war considerable quantities of rubber collars to Yugoslavia, for use by officers of the Yugoslav army. The firm still has on hand about 700 dozen collars, left from an order which could no more be delivered and otherwise disposed of.

The Chamber of Industry & Commerce in Mannheim has approached the OKW with the request to be permitted to sell the collars to canteens of those camps where Yugoslav prisoner of war officers are interned.

Since the disposal of these collars, usable only by Yugoslav officers, is in the interest of our national economy, the prisoner of war camps in question are being informed of the opportunity to purchase rubber collars from the firm, Rheinische Gummi & Cellulois Fabrik Mannheim.

Supreme Command of the Wehrmacht — Berlin - Schoeneberg
Prisoner of War Department — 31 December 1941, Badenschestr 51

7. Re: Tin boxes of British fliers

British fliers brought down have been found to carry with them tin cans containing a small saw made of steel, a map of northern France and of the North-German Coast, Chocolate, and concentrated food tablets. These tin cans presumably are to help the Britishers to avoid capture or to escape from imprisonment after capture. Such special equipment has been repeatedly found on British fliers. It apparently belongs to the "iron rations" (emergency kits) of the British air force.

Special attention is to be paid to this when capturing British fliers shot down or delivering them to a prisoner of war camp.

8. Re: Informing newly arrived prisoners of war of camp regulations.

There are cases on record where prisoners of war, newly arrived in a collecting camp to be released, and unfamiliar with the regulations of the new camp, were severely wounded or killed by warning shots or by deliberate fire.

Since the same regulations governing order and discipline in camps do not apply in all camps, care must be taken that newly arrived prisoners of war be immediately made familiar with the new regulations, even if their stay at the camp is to be temporary.

Posting alone on blackboards and in the halls is not sufficient.

A reliable prisoner of war non-commissioned officer or the camp spokesman may be entrusted with this task.

Supreme Command of the Wehrmacht — Berlin-Schoeneberg
Chief of the Prisoner of War Department — 11 March 1942, Badenschestr. 51

5. Re: Marking of Jews

The Jews in Germany are specially marked with a star, as a measure of the German government to identify them in the street, stores, etc. Jewish prisoners of war are not marked with a star, yet they have to be kept apart from the other prisoners of war as far as possible.

23. Re: Cases of death of prisoners of war.

Reports to the Information Bureau of the Wehrmacht on deaths of prisoners of war and the corresponding notices to the German Red Cross through questionnaires are to be drawn up in such a way as to obviate the necessity of further time consuming inquiries.

The following is therefore to be observed:

1. The report of the death of a prisoner of war to the Information Bureau of the Wehrmacht must indicate the cause of death in exact accordance with the facts, and also give the place of death in a way to make the competent registrar's office easily identifiable. It is not enough, for instance, to state: "Shot." Rather must it be worded: "Shot while trying to escape," or "Shot in execution of sentence pronounced by... dividion on..." It is likewise not enough to give as place of death merely "Camp Erlensbusch," but rather "Camp Erlensbusch near Village X. The exact location of a work detail in a death report is essential even when such detail is located near a Stalag, as it cannot be automatically assumed that the two places belong to the same registrar district.

2. The report on the death of a prisoner of war to the Presidency of the German Red Cross constitutes the basis for the notification of the family of the deceased. The death notice is prepared by the German Red Cross and is transmitted to the next of kin through the local Red Cross office of the latter. The questionnaire proper is then forwarded by the German Red Cross to the International Red Cross in Geneva.

In preparing the "death-notice questionnaire" the following is to be observed:

a. The questionnaire must be speedily and fully filled out and promptly forwarded to the Presidency of the German Red Cross, Berlin S W 61 Bluecherplatz 2. Only this agency is competent to receive such questionnaires. Sending same to any other agency is not permitted, even though the questionnaire was made up by the International Red Cross in Geneva.

b. Careful formulation of the cause of death in case of unnatural death, as the questionnaire is to be sent abroad (International Red Cross).

c. The nationality of the deceased must be given right after the name, and the name of the country after the address of his next of kin.

d. The last question must be answered in the greatest detail, in so far as there are no objections to the answer becoming known abroad.

3. For the time being no questionnaire is to be filled out for deceased Soviet prisoners of war.

4. Deaths of prisoners of war are not to be reported to the Protecting Powers either by camp commandants, or by the spokesmen.

46. Re:Poaching by prisoners of war.

The Reich Master of Hunting reports a recent increase in cases of poaching by prisoners of war doing farm labor - particularly French.

Prisoners of war are to be told that violations of German laws are severely punished.

56. Re: Polish soldiers belonging to the French army.

The nationality of a soldier is determined by the uniform he is wearing at the time of capture.

In doubtful cases, the place of residence of the prisoner of war before the war and the present residence of his next of kin will determine his nationality.

59. Re: Engagements for work by British non-commissioned prisoner of war officers.

British non-commissioned officers who signed a pledge to work but are no longer willing to do so are to be returned to the camp. Their unwillingness is not to be considered as a refusal to work. The employment of British non-commissioned officers has resulted in so many difficulties that the latter have by far out-weighed the advantages. The danger of sabotage, too, has been considerably increased thereby.

75. Re: Contact between French and Soviet prisoners of war.

Soviet prisoners of war must be strictly kept apart from prisoners of other nationalities, particularly Frenchmen. They should also be permitted no opportunity for establishing such contacts at their place of work.

Strictest measures are to be taken against contractors who fail to comply with the above security requirements.

79. Re: Position of prisoner of war officers with respect to German personnel.

A particular incident has moved the Fuehner to emphasize anew that, when considering the relationship between prisoner of war officers and German camp personnel, the most humble German national is deemed more important than the highest ranking subject of an enemy power.

81. Re: Smoking by prisoners of war.

Complaints are voiced by the Reich Conservator of Forests that prisoners of war smoke in the forests and thereby increase the danger of forest fires.

Reference is made to Section 15 of the Compilation of Orders #5, dated 10 October 1941. Attention of the prisoners of war is to be particularly called to the fact that smoking in forests is forbidden and that any infringement will be severely punished under German law.

85. Re: Beards of prisoners of war.

Prisoners of war wearing beards for religious reasons, e.g. Indians and orthodox clergymen, may continue to do so. Individuals enjoying a non-prisoner status, such as medical officers, army chaplains, and medical corps personnel may also keep their beards if any.

109. Re: Subjecting enemy prisoners of war to the operation of the Military Penal Code.

The order of 10 January 1940 forbidding association with German women and girls is to be made known also to French medical corps personnel taking the place of, or about to take the place of the former medical personnel by way of exchange.

110. Re: Handling of medicines.

The provision contained in Section 22 of the Compilation of Orders #5 concerning the handling of medicines sent in packages to prisoners of war is hereby canceled.

The order OKW 2 f 24, 82 u Kriegsgef. Allg. (A) AbW III (Kgf.) remains in force. The latter provides that packages found to contain medicines, restoratives, etc., are to be confiscated and their contents disposed of in accordance with Section 3 of the order. Medicines, etc., are to be destroyed.

111. Re: Prisoners of war as blood donors.

"For reasons of race hygiene, prisoners of war are not acceptable as blood donors for members of the German community, since the possibility of a prisoner of war of Jewish origin being used as a donor cannot be excluded with certainty."

114. Re: Killing and severe wounding of British prisoners of war or civilian internees.

Every case of the killing and severe wounding of a British prisoner of war or civilian internee must be reported immediately.

An investigation is to be initiated by a judicial officer or an otherwise qualified officer. Where comrades of the prisoner of war or the civilian internee were witnesses to the incident, they, too, must be heard.

The result of the investigation and the minutes of the depositions are to be forwarded to the IKW/Kriegsgef. Allg. for notification of the Protecting Power.

167. Re: Poison in possession of prisoners of war.

Narcotic poisons such as "Kif," "Takrouri," and "Souffi," have frequently been found in parcels addressed to Arabian prisoners of war under the guise of tobacco packages.

These poisons are extremely harmful to health and are therefore forbidden in the French army. When searching parcels, particular attention is to be paid to these substances. They are neither to be delivered to the prisoners of war, nor to be kept by the guards. The packages are to be immediately destroyed.

171. Re: Display of flags in prisoner of war quarters.

Since the British government has forbidden the display of German flags in prisoner of war quarters, British flags are to be immediately withdrawn in all German camps. The prisoners are to be notified of the above reason during the roll call.

176. Re: Reparation for willful destruction.

Prisoners of war proved guilty of willfully destroying or damaging state or other property as, for instance, in connection with tunnel construction, are to be punished and, in addition, made liable for damages. Should the actual perpetrators not be discovered, and should the prisoners of war involved be British, the whole camp community may be collectively held responsible for damages - which is the customary practice in England and Canada (canteen funds.)

179. Re: "Warning" wire: testing of wire enclosures in prisoner of war camps.

Experience has shown that weeds growing within the stockade seriously obstruct the view of the enclosure. Several escapes in day time may be attributed to this fact.

Since the removal of the weed is in most cases not feasible, a "warning" wire is to be strung within the camp - if this has not been done already - at least two meters away. The space between the warning wire and the main stockade is to be kept free of weeds.

Several escapes have recently been made possible by the fact that the wire fences, more than three years old in most camps, were damaged and rusted through.

These wire fences must be carefully inspected for reasons of security and existing defects corrected. Reconstruction or repairs should be proceeded with only within the limits of the available supplies of barbed wire. A new supply of barbed wire over and above the fixed quota is not to be reckoned with.

189. Re: Treatment of Soviet prisoners of war refusing to work.

Cases have been observed in some places where Soviet prisoners of war did not receive their prescribed food rations or received rations of inferior quality. This was due in part to shortages of supplies in some areas (e.g. potatoes), and in part to faulty organization in delivery of food (dinner at 8 P.M.)

The resulting drop in efficiency was frequently interpreted as a deliberate refusal to work and was punished accordingly.

Commandants are again directed to pay close attention to the feeding of Soviet prisoners of war and to remove any difficulties of local characters. Should the contractor not be able to supply the prescribed food rations, the prisoners of war must be withdrawn to preserve for the Reich this valuable manpower before it had been rendered useless.

190. Re: Withdrawal of boots and trousers from prisoners of war.

The Commanders of Prisoners of War may direct within the military districts that boots and trousers of prisoners of war may be left with the latter for the night: in large work details to save time; in work details exposed to air raids; for working non-commissioned officers.

191. Re: Money rewards for recapture of escaped prisoners of war.

Supplementing the reference order:

Rewards may also be paid for successful prevention of escape. The decision as to whether the action of a person not qualified to belong to the army, the police, or the frontier guard may be considered as having foiled an escape lies with the camp commandant.

199. Re: Handling of tin cans for prisoners of war.

In a few camps it has lately become common practice, when issuing tin cans to prisoners of war, to be satisfied with the opening of the can and a superficial examination of its contents, and then to hand the open can and contents to the prisoner. When under way, even unopened cans are issued as marching rations. It is again pointed out that, for reasons of security, only the contents of the tin can may be issued to the prisoner of war. Deviation from this rule may be permitted only in exceptional cases, as when other receptacles are not available. In such cases the tin cans themselves must be examined as a security measure prior to their issuance.

202. Re: Sports events in prisoner of war camps.

Since sports contests between prisoners of war of different nationalities have resulted in brawls, such contests are prohibited in the interest of good discipline.

223. Re: Shooting and severe wounding of prisoners of war and civilian internees (except Poles, Serbs and Soviet Russians).

An inquiry by a court officer or any other qualified officer is to be initiated in each case of fatal shooting or wounding of a British, French, Belgian or American prisoner of war or civilian internee. If comrades of the prisoner of war or civilian internee were witnesses of the incident, they, too, will be heard. The result of the inquiry and a copy of the examination proceedings are to be submitted immediately to the OKW Kriegsgef. Allg. (Ia), reference being made to the file number below. This report is to be designated as "Report on the use of arms by soldier X." A detailed report against soldier X will be necessary only when there is a suspicion of the latter having committed a legally punishable act and when an immediate court decision appears desirable.

2. Re: Casualties of British, French, Belgian and American prisoners of war resulting from enemy air raids.

Deaths and injuries of British, French, Belgian and American prisoners of war resulting from enemy air raids are to be reported in writing immediately after the raid to the OKW/Kriegsgef. Allg. (V), giving the file number below. The following are to be stated in the report:

1. First name and surname
2. Rank
3. Prisoner of war number
4. Date of birth
5. Wounded or dead
6. Address of next of kin

In addition, the camp headquarters are to send carbon copies of the reports directly to: the Bureau Scapini, Berlin W 35 Standarten strasse 12 - when French prisoners of war are involved, and to the Belgian Prisoner of War Committee, Berlin W. 8, Hotel Adlon, Unter den Lindenwhen Belgian prisoners are involved.

A report is also to be submitted to the Information Bureau of the Wehrmacht.

The reports concerning special incidents to be submitted in accordance with the order OKW file 2 f 24. 83n Kriegsgef. Allg. (Ia) No. 71/42 of 17 February 1942, are not affected hereby.

228. Re: Prohibition of the so-called "Dartboard Game."

The so-called "dartboard game" is forbidden, as the darts needed for this game are to be considered as weapons and may be employed in acts of sabotage. The game is to be confiscated.

239. Re: Transport of recaptured or unreliable prisoners of war.

A certain case where a guard was murdered by four recaptured Soviet prisoners of war during transport after dark makes it appropriate to point out that recaptured prisoners of war or prisoners known to be unreliable should, as far as possible, not be transported after nightfall. Should the transport after dark be unavoidable, at least, two guards must be assigned to the detail.

240. Re: Association of prisoners of war with German women.

There are several cases on record where judicial prosecution and punishment of prisoners of war for association with German women was frustrated by the fact of their having been already punished disciplinary, the matter being apparently considered as but a slight offense.

The camp commandants must apply the most rigid criterion in deciding whether the case is a mild one, as the association of prisoners of war with German women must be prevented at all costs.

243. Re: Consumption of electricity by prisoners of war.

In order to assure the most economical consumption of electricity, all lighting installations in the prisoner of war quarters are to be examined again; all superfluous lights are to be eliminated.

Lighting installations are allowed, where necessary, within the limits of the quota of Wm. Verw. V., part II, appendix 14, same as for squad rooms in barracks.

The following are thus allowed in officers quarters:

In rooms occupied by 1-4 men—40 watts
In rooms occupied by 5-8 men—75 watts
For every additional man—additional 10 watts

Quarters of non-commissioned prisoner of war officers and men are allowed 1/2 of this quota.

For the use of electric utensils for cooking gift food etc., written permission of the camp headquarters in each individual case is necessary.

246. Re: Securing prisoner of war camps against escape attempts.

1. Fencing in of the camp. The wire entanglements between the inner and outer fences must be so constructed that an escaping prisoner of war will be able neither to climb over them, nor to crawl under them. Anchor posts should be just only slightly out of the ground.

2. The foreground of the stockade, as well as the space between the warning wire and the fence must present an open field of view and of fire. It is therefore to be kept free of brushwood and all other objects impeding vision.

3. Watch towers. There are no generally applicable detailed instructions for the construction of watchtowers. It depends on the topographic and climatic conditions of the camp and must provide the best possible field of view and of fire.

The functional shape of the watchtower is to be determined by the camp commandant.

252. Re: Repair of private apparel of prisoners of war.

Prisoners of war are permitted to repair their private apparel (including shoes) with materials from collective gift shipments. Such repairs are to be made primarily by the prisoners of war themselves. In case they are not able to do so, the repair job may be performed in the camp repair shops.

259. Re: Supervision of enemy Army chaplains and of prisoner of war chaplains.

1. Enemy Army chaplains and prisoners of war chaplains have repeatedly abused the permission to minister to the spiritual needs of the prisoners of war by creating unrest among the latter through inflammatory speeches.

All chaplains are to be advised that they must, in their contacts with prisoners of war, refrain from exercising over them any inciting influence. They must be given emphatic warning and their activity must be strictly supervised.

Chaplains engaged in inciting prisoners of war are to be denied the right to perform their pastoral functions and are to be called to strict account; the military district is to be notified of the matter simultaneously.

In critical times visits to several work details by one chaplain (traveling preacher) will be forbidden on short notice and for a limited period.

2. Attention is again called to the reference orders stipulating that sermons many not be preached by field chaplains and by prisoner of war chaplains except in the presence of an interpreter.

3. In the event the divine service for a work detail can be held neither in the quarters, nor in the open, it is the task of the Stalag to provide a suitable room. The contractor may request, but not demand, that such a room be placed at the disposal of the prisoners of war.

271. Re: Raising rabbits in prisoner of war camps.

In the future, the raising of rabbits in prisoner of war camps will be governed by the provisions of reference order 2 above. The OKW decree - file 2 f 24. 20 Kriegegef. (II) No. 1261/49 is canceled.

The cost of raising rabbits will hence forth be charged in all the camps to the Reich. Angora rabbits, warrens, tools, etc., till now maintained with canteen funds, are to be taken over by the Reich at a price fixed by an agricultural expert of the Military District Administration. The proceeds of the transaction are to be turned over to the prisoner of war canteen.

272. Re: Procuring wrapping paper for Soviet corpses.

The camp headquarters will henceforth report the amount of oil paper, tar paper, and asphalt paper needed for the burial of dead Soviet prisoners of war directly to the nearest paper wholesaler. The latter will then apply to the competent Army Raw Material Board for an Army paper ration certificate. The further procedure is familiar to the wholesalers.

In view of the scarcity of the above kinds of paper, they may be used only for wrapping corpses. Their use is to be held to the barest minimum.

278. Re: Interment of fallen or deceased members of the enemy armed forces.

To remove any doubt as to whether prisoners of war shot during flight or in acts of insubordination are entitled to burial with military honors, the following is ordered:

1. As a matter of principle, every honorable fallen enemy is to be buried with military honors.

2. Flight is not dishonorable, unless dishonorable acts were committed during such flight.

3. Cases of insubordination must be individually examined as to whether acts reflecting on the soldiers honor have been committed. Where such violations of the soldiers code of honor have been established without question, military honors during burial are to be excluded.

279. Re: Accepting bribes by guards.

A private first class on guard duty in a certain camp has on several occasions accepted bribes of cigarettes and chocolate from prisoners of war and permitted them to escape without interference, instead of reporting them to his superior at their very first suggestion. He was sentenced to death for dereliction of guard duty, for willfully releasing prisoners of war, and for accepting bribes.

All guard personnel entrusted with the custody of prisoners war is to be informed of the above with the appropriate comments. The announcement is to be repeated at least every three months.

307. Re: British prisoners of war.

The instructions contained in the OKW memorandum: "The German soldier as prisoner of war custodian" outlining the duties of German guard personnel assume a particular importance with reference to British prisoners of war, whose frequent display of arrogance toward guards and civilians is not in keeping with the discretion expected of a prisoner of war.

The guards are to be instructed to severely repress any attempt of British prisoners of war to evade their full work duty or to associate with civilians beyond the limits set by the circumstances of their employment.

Only British noncommissioned officers who exert a beneficial influence on their British subordinates may be used in supervisory capacities. British noncommissioned officers found unsuitable for this task are to be replaced. Unless they volunteer for a job, they are to be transferred to Stalag 383, Hohenfels.

313. Re: Death sentence of a prisoner of war guard member of a regional defense unit.

Private First Class Jungmichel, assigned to a guard detail at a officers' prisoner of war camp, entered into personal relations with a Polish officer interned at that camp. He supplied the officer, at the latter's request, with various tools, maps and other items intended to facilitate the escape of this and other prisoners of war. Jungmichel was sentenced to death by the Reich Court Martial for war treason. The sentence was carried out on 5 March 1943.

The above sentence is to be made known to all the members of the administration headquarters and the guard units.

324. Re: Use of identification tags by prisoners of war.

To prepare and to conceal escapes, more and more prisoners of war use the device of exchanging identification tags with other prisoners, or of getting rid of them altogether. Such practices are to be prevented by the imposition of heavy penalties, if necessary. When calling the roll, a check of the identification tags must not be neglected.

325. Re: Prevention of escapes through the gate in officers' camps.

The entrances and exits in officers' camps - where this has not yet been done - must be shaped like sluices and provided with a double control. At least one of the two consecutive gates is to be occupied by a qualified noncommissioned officer, thoroughly trained for the task, from headquarters.

397. Re: Taking winter clothing away from prisoners of war during summer months.

No objections may be raised to the practice of leaving overcoats with prisoners of war, even in summer months, in areas subject to air raids - a practice designed to enable the prisoners to take these along to the air raid shelters during an alarm for protection against colds and to lessen the danger of the coats being destroyed by fire. For all other prisoners of war doing outside work and exposed to the inclemencies of the weather, the unit leaders are to decide on their own responsibility whether the overcoats are to be taken along to the place of work or are to remain in storage. The use of overcoats for additional blankets is forbidden.

404. Re: Preventing escape by taking away trousers and boots.

When establishing new work details, an appropriate room is to be set aside for the safe storage of trousers and boots taken from the prisoners of war for the night.

409. Re: Transfer of prisoners of war.

To reduce the number of escapes, prisoners of war scheduled for transfer to another Stalag are to be notified as late as possible of such transfer, and not at all of their new place of interment.

421. Re: Sale of cellophane envelopes and China ink in prisoner of war camp canteens.

Effective immediately, the sale of cellophane envelopes and China ink to prisoners of war is forbidden, since these have been misused to prepare and carry out escapes.

422. Re: Thefts from bomb-wrecked homes.

When prisoners of war are assigned to wreckage clearing jobs after air raids, their attention is again to be called to the death penalty as provided by the reference order.

429. Re: Escape of prisoners of war in civilian clothes.

Escapes of prisoners of war in civilian clothes are on the increase. Frequently civilian clothes are kept hidden in the barracks. The latter, therefore, as well as all other premises and spots accessible to the prisoners of war (corners under staircases, basements, attics) are to be constantly searched for such hidden articles. The contractors are to be urged to proceed in like manner in places accessible to prisoners of war during working hours.

431. Re: Malingering by prisoners of war.

Recent reports indicate that French prisoners of war frequently claim to suffer from stomach ulcers, the effect of which is produced by swallowing small balls of tinfoil showing under x-rays as black spots, similar to those produced by ulcers. The possibility of malingering must be kept in mind by the chief surgeons and camp physicians when prisoners of war are suspected of suffering from stomach ulcers.

462. Re: Timely use of arms to prevent escapes of prisoners of war.

In view of the increasing number of individual and mass escapes of prisoners of war, it is hereby again emphasized that guards will be subject to the severest disciplinary punishment or, when a detailed report is at hand, to court-martial, not only for contributing to the escape of prisoners of war through negligence, but also for failure to use their arms in time. The frequently observed hesitancy to make use of firearms must be suppressed by all means.

Guard personnel must be instructed in this sense again and again. They must be imbued with the idea that it is better to fire too soon than too late.

504. Re: Use of firearms against prisoners of war.

The service regulations for prisoner of war affairs do not provide for any warning shots. Should the occasion for the use of firearms arise, they must be fired with the intent to hit.

513. Re: U.S. prisoners of war in British uniforms.

Prisoners of war of U.S. nationality captured as members of the Canadian armed forces are considered British prisoners of war regardless of whether they joined the Canadian services before or after the entry of the U.S. into the war.

The uniform is the deciding factor.

517. Re: Fuel.

To stretch the supply of fuel, experiments are to be made in the use of a mixture of coal dust (50%-75%) and clay, formed into egg-shaped bricks, for the heating of prisoner of war quarters wherever local conditions permit.

The result of the above experiments are to be reported by the Military District Administrations not later than 15 June 1944.

522. Re: Pay of American prisoner of war noncommissioned officers and enlisted personnel.

The American authorities pay to all German prisoner of war noncommissioned officers and enlisted personnel an allowance of $3 per month regardless of whether they are employed or not.

As a reciprocity measure, all American prisoner of war noncommissioned officers and enlisted personnel are to receive, effective 1 November 1943, 7.50 marks per month.

The American prisoner of war noncommissioned officers and enlisted personnel are to be notified of the above through their spokesmen.

534. Re: Transport of prisoners of war in motor busses.

In accordance with the existing regulations of the German Post Office Department, the transport of prisoners of war in motor busses is not permitted. No motor-bus vouchers may thus be issued for prisoners of war, nor may the latter be allowed to use motor busses accompanied by guards.

In view of the special operating conditions of the motor busses, it is not possible to relax or cancel these regulations.

546. Re: Enemy leaflets in possession of prisoners of war.

Prisoners of war must immediately deliver to their military superiors (camp officers, leaders of work details, etc.) all leaflets, weapons, munitions and some other prohibited articles found by them after enemy air raids, or obtained in some other way.

This, together with the punishment to be expected for disobedience in more serious cases, is to be made known to all the prisoners of war.

565. Re: Reports on British and American prisoners of war.

For reasons of reciprocity, each capture of a British or American prisoner of war must be reported by the Supreme Command of the Wehrmacht by telegram to the respective enemy powers. The camp commandants are responsible for the immediate submission of a written report to the OKW/Chef Kriegsgef. Allg. V on all new British or American prisoners of war upon their arrival in the first Stalag. Such report must contain the following data: Last and first name, rank, date and place of birth. The report to the Information Bureau of the Wehrmacht is not affected hereby.

572. Re: Mail for British and American prisoner of war airmen.

All incoming mail for British and American prisoner of war airmen is centrally examined in Stalag Luft 3 Sagan. The prisoners are to be instructed to indicate this camp only, under the heading "Sender," on all outgoing mail, so that the incoming mail is forwarded directly to Stalag Luft 3. A further examination of the mail in the individual prisoner of war camps is unnecessary.

573. Re: Prisoner of war camps.

The prisoner of war camps must do everything within their power to prevent the rifling of gift shipments for prisoners of war, and to have such thefts uncovered immediately.

Particular attention is to be paid to the shipment of gifts from camps to work details, carried out on the responsibility of the military services. Pilfering of gift shipments by the prisoners of war themselves is to be reported to the OKW, giving the name of the offender.

576. Re: British and American parachutists, airborne troops and anti-aircraft personnel.

Parachutists, airborne troops and anti-aircraft units are constituent parts of the British and American armies. Prisoners of war from these troops categories do not thus belong to the "prisoners of air force proper" in the sense of the "Provisions Concerning Prisoners of War" of 30 May 1943. They are therefore not quartered in the prisoner of war camps of the Luftwaffe (air force), but in those of the OKW.

They are put to work in accordance with the rules in force for prisoners of war of the respective nationality. However, paratroopers are to be assigned to work in closed groups and under special guard.

Since the above service branches within the German armed forces are parts of the Luftwaffe, the questioning of newly arrived prisoners of war for intelligence purposes is the task of the Luftwaffe.

Newly captured British and American parachutists, airborne troops and members of air defense units are therefore to be sent for interrogation to the "evaluation center," West Oberursel/Taunus where only small units are involved (up to 20 prisoners). Where the number of such prisoners brought in at one time is 20 or more, arrangements are to be made in each case over the telephone as to whether the prisoners shall be taken for interrogation to Oberursel/Taunus, or whether the evaluation center West should send an interrogation detail to the spot.

At the end of the interrogation the respective prisoners of war are sent to the prisoner of war camps of the OKW.

583. Re: Return of prisoners of war, recovered from illness, to their old place of work.

Complaints are heard from management quarters about the slow return of prisoners of war from hospitals to their old place of work after recovery. The prisoners of war, again able to work, are kept too long in the camps after their release from the hospital.

It is the duty of the camp commandants to see to it that prisoners of war, released from hospitals as fully able to work, be sent back in the quickest possible way to their former places of work.

584. Re: "Stepping out" by prisoners of war during work.

Since the prisoners of war misuse the unauthorized "stepping out" for the purpose of escape or loafing, it may be recommended - as has already been done in some plants - that a fixed time be set for such practice. Exceptions are to be permitted only for reasons of health.

No generally binding rule is possible in view of the varying local conditions, the strength of the work details, etc. However, the Stalags are to keep an eye on the problem, since uniformity, wherever possible, is greatly desirable as a means of avoiding the above stated difficulties. Appropriate rules might be incorporated in the plant regulations applying to prisoners of war.

The Stalags are to instruct the leaders of the larger work details to communicate with the plant managers in regard to the above matter.

589. Re: Gate control of incoming and outgoing vehicles.

Reports on escapes of prisoners of war indicate that the control of incoming and outgoing vehicles at the gates is not always carried out with the proper care. There are cases on record where prisoners of war have left the camps undisturbed, hidden under loads of sand, linen, etc. Care is to be taken that the vehicles are always closely scrutinized.

590. Re: Quartering of mentally ill prisoners of war or internees.

There is occasion to point out that prisoners of war or internees suffering from mental disorders but not requiring confinement in a closed institution must be kept in camps or hospitals in such a way as to avoid, under all circumstances, the possibility of mishaps (such as entering the area outside the warning wire without permission).

591. Re: Organization of the Bureau Chef Kriegsgef.

The Bureau Chef Kriegsgef is organized as follows:

I. Chef Kriegsgef: Colonel Westhoff

Staff Group: Major Baron V. Bothmer

Central processing of all basic matters and of those affecting in common the divisions Kriegsgef. Allg. and Kriegsgef. Org., with the:

a. Paymaster, administration, salaried employees and workmen.

b. Registry.

II. Chef Kriegsgef. Allg.: Colonel Dr. V. Reumont–General and political affairs of the prisoners of war set-up.

Group Allg. I: Lieutenant Colonel Krafft–Treatment of prisoners of war and effects of the prisoner of war problem on national policies.

Group Allg. II: Major Roemer–The prisoners of war problem in its foreign-political aspects; escorting of representatives of the protecting powers of the IRC, etc. on their visiting trips.

Group Allg. III: Major Clemens–German prisoners of war in enemy lands and members of the Wehrmacht interred in neutral countries.

Group Allg. IV: Oberstabsintendant Dr. Fuchs–Problems of administration of the prisoner of war set-up.

Group Allg. V: Captain Laaser–Welfare of prisoners of war in Germany, mail and parcel service. Co-operation with German Red Cross and IRC.

Group Allg. VI: Captain Recksiek–Exchange, furloughs and release of prisoner of war. Problems of minorities.

III. Chef Kriegsgef. Org.: Colonel Diemer-Willroda

Organization of the prisoner of war set-up.

Group Org. I: Major Dr. Hausz–The functioning of the German prisoner of war bureaus and custodial forces. Distribution of prisoners of war (planning); statistics.

Group Org. II: Lieutenant Colonel Reinacke–Officer personnel matters (commanders of prisoners of war, prisoner of war-district commandants, camp commandants and their deputies.

Group Org. III: Colonel Lossow–Labor service and transport.

Group IV: Major Eickhoff–Camp management, index-files of prisoners of war.

595. Re: Individual requests for enemy clergymen for prisoner of war camps.

Individual requests for enemy clergymen are no more to be submitted. Requests for enemy clergymen are to be collected and presented quarterly at a fixed date by the Military District Commands, as per Model I and II contained in order OKW, file 2 f 24.

596. Re: Spiritual care in Army prisons.

1. In accordance with the reference order, no religious services are to be held for prisoners of war in Army prisons. Army chaplains, civilian and prisoner of war clergymen may render spiritual aid to a prisoner of war only when the latter is gravely ill or under death sentence.

2. The reference order is relaxed in that prisoners of war in military prisons may hold religious services among themselves provided they request it specifically in each case.

619. Re: Securing of prisoner of war transports against escape.

The freight cars for the transport of prisoners of war frequently carry boards in the sliding doors, arranged so as to pass in stove pipes. These boards are to be removed before shipping the prisoners of war, since they render the barbwiring of the doors difficult and can easily be forced.

To better secure the sliding doors of these freight cars, not only the bolts, but also the door casters may be wired.

640. Re: Reward for capture of fugitive prisoners of war.

The Reichsfuehrer and the Reichsminister of Interior have authorized the Criminal Police, in the decree of 14 December 1943, S V A 1 No. 978/43, to pay a reward of up to 100 marks for assistance in apprehending fugitive prisoners of war or other wanted persons. In case more than one person participated in the capture, the reward is to be divided proportionately. Should the amount of 100 marks not suffice to properly reward all the participants for their cooperation, the matter of increasing the amount is to be submitted for approval to the Reichsfuehrer and the Reichsminister of Interior.

Rewards for capture of fugitive prisoners of war are not to be paid anymore by the prisoner of war camps.

646. Re: Confiscation of gifts from the American Red Cross bearing propaganda legends.

Gifts of tobacco supplies have recently arrived from the American Red Cross bearing propaganda legends on the wrappings. Most characteristic are packages of cigarettes with the word "Freedom" printed thereon. These articles were confiscated on several occasions because of this legend. It has been found that smokes with these legends were sent to the prisoner of war camps with no malicious intent, but that it was a form of propaganda for American consumption only commonly used in America. Such articles with propaganda legends should not be confiscated, provided the legends are not of outspoken anti-German character and provided there was no malicious intent on the part of the sending agency. The tobacco articles are to be released upon removal of the wrapping. In case of doubt the OKW is to be consulted.

The American Red Cross has been notified and has promised to make sure that further gifts to prisoners of war are free of all propaganda; it has however, requested that shipments already packed be accepted.

647. Re: Handling of prisoner of war mail for American prisoners of war and civilian internees.

Letters and parcels arriving from USA for American prisoners of war and civilian internees have in a number of cases not been released by the camps for distribution because the US post-mark stamps contained advertising matter. These stamps were placed on the prisoner of war mail for no special purpose; they are the same used in the postal service within the USA. The US government has promised henceforth to refrain from placing on prisoner of war mail any legends relating to the present war. Mail is therefore to be released for distribution provided the postmark stamp and other legends are not of an outspoken anti-German character and where no malicious intent is discernible.

677. Re: Supplying prisoners of war with beer.

The reference order is hereby modified to the effect that henceforth not more than 5 liters of beer may be released monthly for prisoner of war and military internees in prisoner of war camps (Polish and Soviet-Russian prisoners included).

679. Re: Fixing of bayonets while guarding prisoners of war.

It is in order to call attention to Section 475 of the Compilation of Orders 30 of 16 Oct 1943, whereby guards are to stand with their rifles loaded and placed at "safe," and their bayonets fixed, unless the camp commandant, for special reasons, orders a deviation from that rule. This order is extended to provide that guard details accompanying prisoners of war on transports, or on their way from and to work, have their bayonets fixed. French bayonets, which are too long, can be ground down to the standard size of German bayonets.

685. Re: Use of sidewalks by prisoners of war.

It is in order to point out that prisoners of war conducted through cities by guard details, singly or in groups, are not permitted to use the sidewalks but must use the roadway, like the smallest troop unit on the march.

Prisoners of war from broken ranks of work commandos marching alone from and to work are permitted to use the sidewalks, but must, when same are crowded, step off into the roadway.

687. Re: Private conversation between German soldiers and prisoners of war.

All conversation between German soldiers of war not justified by the needs of the service or the work assignment is forbidden.

It is the primary responsibility of the company commanders to educate their subordinates to the importance of maintaining the proper distance between themselves and the prisoners of war and to put a stop to all attempts of the prisoners to start unauthorized conversations.

692. Re: Assault on guards.

Lately, several guards have been attacked and killed while transferring prisoners of war after dark.

Prisoners of war are to be moved on foot after dark only in case of utmost necessity and only under particular vigilant surveillance.

Attention is to be directed continually to this prohibition and to the danger of attack.

713. Re: Instructing guard personnel in the guard regulations.

There is reason to point out that guard personnel engaged in guarding prisoners of war must be given continuous instruction in guard regulations. It does not suffice to hand the guard personnel a copy of the regulations and to expect them to study its contents by themselves.

714. Re: Taking away boots and trousers from prisoners of war in work details.

In order to render more difficult the escape of prisoners war assigned to and quartered in work details, their boots and trousers are generally to be taken away for the night and stored in such a manner as to make their recovery by the prisoners impossible.

715. Re: Air defense measures in the prisoner of war service.

During an air raid alarm prisoners of war may be assigned to the defense of their own quarters and workshops in exactly the same manner as the German employees.

After the all clear signal they may also be assigned to damage control work in other places, but, in this case, must be kept under safe, regular surveillance.

716. Re: Disposal of tin cans sent to prisoners of war.

The regulations contained in the above reference, in so far as they concern the handling of tin cans sent to prisoners of war, are summarized, changed as follows:

1. Tin cans of all kinds, with or without their contents (from parcels received from home, from love gifts, from rations supplied by the Army or the manager of the plant) may be left in the hands of individual prisoners of war in strictly limited quantities and under strict supervision.

Purpose of this regulation:

a. To prevent the accumulation of larger amounts of food stuffs to facilitate escape.

b. To eliminate empty tin cans as means of escape, such as in the construction of tunnels, the preparation of imitation buckles, etc.

c. To prevent the smuggling of forbidden messages and of objects useful in escape, espionage and sabotage.

2. The individual prisoner of war may be allowed a maximum of six tin cans for the storage of his food supplies (meat, spread on bread, sugar, tea, etc.) provided no other means of storage are available in sufficient quantities and provided there is no danger of the wrong use of these cans.

Before a filled tin can is issued, it must be examined before and after opening; such examination may be limited to random sampling in the case of tin cans (and tubes) sent by the British and American Red Cross in standard packages.

3. When new tin cans are issued, the old ones must be withdrawn.

Used tin cans must be emptied, cleaned and stored in a place out of reach of the prisoners of war. They must be sent every three months to the scrap metal recovery place, together with tin cans used by the German troops.

4. Compliance with regulations 1, 2 and 3 is to be enforced by orders of the camp commandants; these are to reach down to the smallest labor commandos.

718. Re: Behavior of prisoners of war during air raids.

1. Guarding of prisoner of war labor commandos.

In work shops which, according to the air defense regulations, must be vacated by their crews during air raids, provisions must be made, in agreement with the shop management, that the prisoners of war be kept at all time under surveillance by the guards and latter's assistants while leaving the premises and remaining outside of same, as well as while returning thereto. Alarm plans are to be prepared fixing the place of the air raid shelters and the ways of reaching same.

2. Marching prisoners of war seeking protection in public and private air raid shelters.

No objection may be raised against prisoners of war on march seeking protection in public air raid shelters in a sudden air attack; private shelters, too, may be used by prisoners of war in an emergency, provided the number of the prisoners is small.

It is presumed that the German civilian population will take precedence and that the prisoners of war will be kept close together in one room or one place. Dispersal among the civilian population is forbidden. In case of need, the prisoners of war may be distributed under guard in smaller groups in several parts of the air raid shelter.

Details are to be fixed in agreement with the local air raid authorities.

729. Re: Civilian clothing confiscated from individual packages sent to prisoners of war.

Civilian clothes sent to prisoners of war by their next of kin are not to be placed in safe-keeping, but must be confiscated. Relatives of prisoners of war well know that civilian clothes are not allowed to be sent to the latter. Confiscated civilian clothes are to be treated like clothes of recaptured escaped prisoners. Civilian clothes must not be sent to receiving camps for safe-keeping when prisoners of war are transferred (also when they are delivered at Army prisons).

738. Re: Air raid shelter trenches.

In a number of cases prisoners of war have declared through their spokesman their unwillingness to work on air raid shelter trenches. Such a refusal on the part of a group of prisoners of war, in view of the internationally binding provisions of the Convention of 27 July 1929, is to be ignored.

The construction of temporary air raid trenches must therefore be continued without fail.

739. Re: Use of confiscated gift packages.

When gift packages of collective shipments are confiscated on the basis of the above order, or for some other compelling reason, the confiscated items are to be disposed of as follows:

1. Confiscated articles of food from gift packages are to be used in the preparation of meals in the kitchen; in that case the food rations supplied by the Reich may be correspondingly cut.

2. Confiscated articles of consumption like coffee, cocoa, tea, etc., are likewise to be used in the community kitchen in the preparation of breakfast and supper.

3. Confiscated soap is to be used in laundries servicing prisoners of war, or to be given to prisoner of war hospitals for use in their respective laundries.

4. Confiscated tobacco supplies may be distributed as a reward for good work to prisoners of war of all nationalities, including Soviet Russians. A receipt is to be issued and entered on the records of the respective camps.

Care must be taken that members of the German armed forces and other German nationals have no share in the confiscated gift packages, and that the assignment of the confiscated items for the sole use of the prisoners of war may be conclusively proved to the representatives of the Protecting Powers or the International Red Cross.

743. Re: Working together of prisoners of war and concentration camp internees.

The working together of prisoners of war and concentration camp internees has repeatedly led to difficulties and has unfavorably affected the efficiency of the prisoners of war. Employment of prisoners of war and of concentration camp internees on the same job at the same time is therefore forbidden. They may be employed in the same shop only when complete separation is assured.

745. Re: Civilian clothes in prisoner of war barracks.

Attention is again called to the regulation which forbids prisoners of war to have in their possession civilian articles of apparel, except properly marked work clothes. Such articles of apparel arriving in packages for prisoners of war are to be confiscated. Prisoners of war are allowed only pull-overs and underwear, in so far as the latter cannot be used as civilian apparel. Sport clothes, especially shorts, are to be handed out only after they have been specially marked as prisoner of war apparel. The way of so marking is left to the discretion of the camps. The prisoner of war quarters are to be checked again and again for civilian articles of clothing.

784. Re: Ecclesiastical Services for Prisoners of War.

Ref. 1. Order OKW file 31 AWA/J (Ia) No. 2411/41 of 12 May 1941 paragraph IV.
2. Order OKW file 2 f24. 72 f Kriegsgef. Allg. (Ia) No. 10/44 of 10 Jan 1944, section 3.

In order to clear up certain doubts concerning the use of enemy clergymen is pastoral capacity at prisoner of war reserve hospitals, attention is called to the following:

1. In accordance with reference order 1, surplus prisoners of war clergymen, enlisted men or noncommissioned officers (i.e. members of enemy armed forces who were clergymen in civilian life and were captured as soldiers with arms in the hands) are to be assigned, as far as possible, to prisoner reserve hospitals as medical corps personnel. There they will perform their ecclesiastical duties in accordance with the provision in sections 7 and 8 of this order.

(The next page has been received from the archives missing a part so will pick it up it.)

...allowed to perform their pastoral duties in: Stalags for enlisted men, prisoner of war hospitals, prisoner of war construction and labor battalions, provided they assume these duties voluntarily.

b. The same applies to enemy field chaplains, provided they volunteer for service.

c. The use of these clergymen in accordance with 2a and b is contingent upon their steady residence at the place where they are employed.

810. Re: Prohibition of the use of ink and colored pencils in letter writing by prisoners of war and military and civilian internees.

Several cases are on record where prisoners of war have dyed their uniforms, blankets and underwear with ink and colored pencils for the purpose of escape.

Ink and colored pencils in possession of prisoners of war and military and civilian internees are therefore to be confiscated immediately. Ink and colored pencils are no longer to be sold in camp canteens, and the issuance of same in all private shops for prisoners of war is to be permitted.

Outgoing mail written with ink and colored pencils before this order was announced is to be forwarded. Such mail received for delivery after the announcement is to be destroyed.

Colored pencils may be acquired from time to time in the open market in limited quantities for drawing and instructional purposes; these are to be taken away every day after use and kept under lock and key. Strict control is necessary to avoid misuse.

812. Re: Forbidding prisoners of war to produce glider models.

Prisoners of war are for security reasons forbidden to produce models of gliders.

822. Re: Working time of prisoners of war: Here: On Sunday.

As a matter of principle, prisoners of war are to work the same number of hours as the German workers on the same job. This principle applies also to Sunday work; it is to be noted, however, that prisoners of war, after three weeks' continuous work must be given a continuous rest period of 24 hours which is not to fall on Sunday.

When a plant which normally works on Sunday is closed for that day, the right of the prisoners of war to a continuous period of rest is still to be respected. However, no objection can be raised to prisoners of war working beyond the usual working day and on free Sundays on emergency jobs when German workers or the German population are required to take part in such emergency projects.

However, the rest period thus lost on the emergency jobs must be made up, even on a week day, if the last continuous rest period was taken at least three weeks back.

In special emergency cases prisoners of war may be called upon to work for the relief of same even when the services of German workers or the German population are not required. The decision in the matter lies in each individual case with the respective camp commandant, in agreement with the local authorities, the competent Labor Office and the agency in need of assistance.

837. Re: Verification of personal data supplied by escaped and recaptured prisoners of war.

Recaptured prisoners of war often falsely give to the camp authorities, to whom they have been delivered, names and identification numbers of other prisoners of war of their former camp and of the same nationality, known to them as having likewise escaped. Now and then they try to hide behind the name and the identification number of prisoners of war whose approximate description and circumstances of whose escape they had learned at the very time of their own escape. Such attempts at camouflage are made particularly by escaped and recaptured prisoners of war having a court suit pending against them at their former camp.

Security officers of prisoner of war camps are to verify in each case the personal data supplied by recaptured prisoners of war from other camps.

838. Re: Death penalty for prisoners of war for illicit intercourse with German women.

The Serbian prisoner of war Private Pentalija Kabanica, identification number 104325YB, was sentenced to death by a court-martial for the military offense consisting of illicit traffic with a German woman, combined with rape. He had rendered defenseless the peasant woman, in whose farm he was engaged as laborer, then used her sexually.

The sentence was carried out on 14 Sep 1944.

The sentence is to be made known in this version to all the prisoners of war.

840. Re: Killings and serious injuries of prisoners of war and civilian internees (except Poles, Serbs and Russians).

The reference order has often not been observed, with the result that the OKW has had again and again to learn of cases of violent deaths of prisoners of war through the Ministry of Foreign Affairs or the Protecting Powers. This situation is unbearable in view of the reciprocity agreements with the enemy governments. The following additional orders are therefore announced herewith:

To 1. Every case of violent death or serious injury is to be promptly reported through channels to the OKW/Kriegsgef. Allg. (IIb) (for exception see 2). In cases involving the use of arms, written depositions of the participants and witnesses, including prisoners of war, are to be attached; action is to be taken by the camp commandant and the prisoner of war commander (kommandeur).

The name, camp, identification number, and home address of the prisoner of war involved must be given. Should a long search for these be necessary, a preliminary report is to be submitted at once, and the result of the search reported later.

Reports are also necessary, in addition to cases involving the use of arms. in cases of accidents of all kinds, of suicides, etc.; written depositions of witnesses will be mostly unnecessary here.

To 2. Losses due to enemy action are to be reported immediately to the OKW/ Kriegsgef. Allg. (V) in the form prescribed by reference order to 2.

848. Re: Rendering prisoner of war camps recognizable.

Prisoner of war camps in the home war zone are not to be made recognizable for enemy air forces.

851 Re: Transport of enemy fliers brought down or prisoner of war officers.

In view of the present state of transportation, especially in Western and Southwestern Germany, no more railway compartments may be ordered or used in the trains of the public railway system for the transport of enemy fliers brought down or prisoner of war officers to and from prisoner of war camps (also camps for interrogation and classification of prisoners of war). In agreement with the competent Transport Command Headquarters (Transport Kommandantur), freight cars are to be requisitioned instead and attached, as far as possible, to passenger or fast freight trains; in order to economize on rolling stock in small transports, the number of prisoners of war on each trip must be correspondingly increased. In particularly urgent cases troop compartments may be used in FmW, DmW and SF trains (Eilzug mit Wehrmachtabteile; Durchgangszug mit Wehrmachtabteile; Schneller Frontzug).

853. Re: Prisoners of war mustered into Waffen SS (volunteer groups).

Prisoners of war who have voluntarily reported for service in the Waffen SS have had their lives threatened by their fellow prisoners of war for their friendliness to Germany and their willingness to serve.

Representatives of the main SS office engaged in recruiting prisoners of war for the Waffen SS in the prisoner of war camps are to be reminded by the camp commandants that the security of these prisoners of war requires that steps be taken to have them speedily removed.

Should the enlisted prisoners of war not be able to take their physical examination at the SS, the representatives of the main SS Bureau must, when taking the prisoners away, report those turned back to the original camp in order that they may be assigned to another camp.

876. Re: Treatment of Jewish prisoners of war.

Ref. 1. Compilation of Orders No. 1 of 16 June 1941, Section 7.

2. Compilation of Orders No. 11 of 11 March 1942, Section 5.

The combined above reference orders provide as follows:

1. The bringing together of Jewish prisoners of war in separate camps is not intended; on the other hand, all Jewish prisoners of war are to be kept separated from the other prisoners of war in Stalags and officer camps and, in the case of enlisted personnel, to be grouped in closed units for work outside the camp. Contact with the German population is to be avoided.

Special marking of the clothing of Jewish prisoners of war is not necessary.

2. In all other respects Jewish prisoners of war are to be treated like the other prisoners of war belonging to the respective armed forces (with respect to work duty, protected personnel, etc.)

3. Jewish prisoners of war who had lost their citizenship by Regulation 11 of the Reich Citizenship Law of 25 Nov 1941 (R.G.B.I. 1941 I p. 722), are to be buried, in case they die in captivity, without the usual military honors.

894. Re: Reports on escapes of prisoners of war.

Mass escapes, escapes of small groups or single officers, from colonel upward, as well as of prominent personalities represent such a menace to security as to render the disciplinary handling of the matter in accordance with paragraph 16a K St Vo entirely inadequate, in view of the possible consequences of such escapes. Detailed reports must under all circumstances be submitted concerning the activity of the custodial agencies which made such serious flights possible, whether through dereliction of duty or through mere carelessness.

895. Re: Strict house arrest and preliminary (Investigation) arrest of prisoners of war, including prisoner of war officers.

A concrete case makes it appropriate to point out the following regulations:

1. An increase in rations through delivery of food and other articles of consumption by all outsiders, including the International Red Cross, is absolutely forbidden.

2. Additional food and other articles of consumption may be obtained by prisoner of war officers only through purchase, contingent upon good behavior, and in moderate quantities. In each individual case the approval of the camp commandant is necessary.

3. Tobacco may be obtained in quantity within the general limits provided in the smoker's card, but only when the danger of fire or disturbance of discipline is absent.

Note to 1-3: Prisoners of war under preliminary arrest, in order to obtain additional items of food and of general consumption, must also secure the consent of the investigation officer (leader) or the state attorney.

897. Re: Escapes during transport.

There is reason to point out that prisoners of war during transport sometimes try to use the toilet for escape. The guards must therefore, as a rule, accompany the prisoner of war to the toilet on transports and must keep their eyes on him with the door open. Should the prisoner of war close the toilet door with the intention to escape, the guard must fire on him through the door without warning.

Publisher's Message

Dave Turner, President

The American soldier is known throughout the world for his courage, his bravery, his resourcefulness under the gravest of pressure. This was one of the reasons for our victory in the Pacific Theater: our men, taught to think on their feet, were simply better fighters than the Japanese.

One quality of the American soldier that doesn't receive enough recognition is his capacity for sacrifice. Talk to any soldier, anywhere in the world - and you'll find the hardest sacrifice any of them could make would be to spend the duration of a conflict as a prisoner of war.

My utmost respect goes out to those Americans - and far too many of them there were - who had to serve their country in this fashion. Who among us who has not experienced it could possibly understand the frustration, the anger, the painful loss experienced by prisoners of war?

It is for these brave Americans this book is written and published; I think Professor Spiller's work speaks for itself.

Sincerely,

Dave Turner
President

100 Kilo Camp 40, 44
18 Kilo Camp 38
80 Kilo Camp 40, 44
85 Kilo Camp 40

-A-

Adaberry 209
Africa 133
Aioshi, Japan 23
Akami, Colonial 21
Alabama 173
Albania 134
Algiers 143
Alkire, Darr H. 138, 140, 141
All, Germany 212
Altdrewitz 178
Andler 210
Angert, A.A. 68
Anzio 109, 135, 144
Aparri 58
Aragon, J. 68
Ardennes 209, 210, 220, 221
Arthur, Steven 5
Artman, Ralph T. 68, 74
Arwood, W.D. 68
Asia 6, 58
Australia 30, 31, 75
Austria 6, 135
Auw, Germany 210, 211

-B-

Bad Orb, Germany 213, 214
Baguio 59
Bailey, William 19
Baits, W.V. 68
Baker, H.W. 68
Baker, R.E. 68
Baltic 161, 171, 194, 206
Baltic Sea 162, 193
Baltimore, Maryland 143
Ban Pong 36
Bangkok 36, 38
Barth, Germany 193, 194, 202, 203, 205, 206
Barton, R.S. 68
Basha 103
Baskin, J.P. 68
Bataan 58, 60, 61, 63, 64, 82, 84, 210
Batavia 31, 34
Bavaria 110
Belem, Brazil 133
Belgard 165
Belgium 210, 219, 221
Bengazi, Libia 116
Berga 213
Berlin 111, 151, 152, 153, 154, 155, 163
Bhamo 98
Bicycle Camp 33
Bilbid 58
Bilibid Prison Camp 66, 67, 82, 83
Bitterfield, Germany 171
Bizerta, North Africa 108
Black, W.J. 68
Blackman, J. 68
Blair, Major 97
Boardman, Brenda 187
Boardman, Caretta 182, 187
Boardman, Thomas Harold 182, 183, 184, 186, 187, 190
Boardman, Kevin 187
Boardman, Marcus 187
Boardman, Michael 187
Bogie, T.H. 68
Bombay, India 96
Bora Bora 96
Born, Belgium 209
Borneo 6, 34
Bowman, L. 68
Bradley, William "Bill" C. 143, 144, 146, 147, 149, 151, 152, 153, 154, 155, 156, 157, 158, 159
Bradley, Bruce 159
Bradley, Cindy 159
Bradley, Craig 159
Bradley, Flo Allen 159
Bradley, Kathleen Ketti 159
Bradley, Keith 159
Bradley, Sandy 159
Bradshaw 204
Brann 116
Branum, Charles C. 58, 68, 70
Branum, David 73, 74
Branum, Mary Etta 73, 74
Branum, P.V. 66
Braunau, Austria 120
Brereton, General 135
Brownstown 159
Brownsville, Texas 97
Buchenwald Death Camp 7, 213
Budapest, Romania 135, 137
Burma 6, 7, 34, 30, 35, 36, 37, 38, 40, 42, 46, 95, 106, 107
Burrow, Charles 143
Busell, R.M. 68
Butts, Gordon K. 132, 133, 134, 135, 136, 141, 142

-C-

Calcutta, India 96, 97
California 30, 75, 103, 159, 173, 181, 188

Calvert City, Kentucky 131
Calvin, C.E. 68
Camacho, A.R. 68
Camp Atturbury 142
Camp Buckner 173
Camp Changi 35
Camp Grant, Illinois 221
Camp Hay 59
Camp Hosi 95
Camp Kawasaki 85, 87
Camp Kilmore, New Jersey 216
Camp Lucky Strike 130, 158, 172, 185, 187, 216
Camp Meade 143, 173
Camp Mukaishima 68
Camp Nakhon Pathom 52
Camp Niigata 75, 92
Camp O'Donald 58, 64, 65
Camp Roberts 30, 44
Camp Roker 173
Camp Tamarkan 48
Camp White Pagoda 53
Cape Girardeau, Missouri 73, 92
Carabine, D. 68
Carlsen 190
Carr, William Robert 160, 161, 162, 163, 165, 166, 167, 171, 172
Carr, Michael 172
Carr, Richard 172
Carr, Veneta 172
Casablanca, North Africa 108, 143
Cassino, Italy 135
Chaffee, Missouri 92
Chambers, Slim 52
Charkow 220
Chavez, C.P. 68
Check, Lt. 116
Cheves, General 97
Chicago 25, 71, 130, 181, 208, 216, 217
China 21, 24, 37, 106
Chism, A.L. 68
Chosen, Korea 85
Chovan, E.E. 68
Christman, Wayne 99
Churchill 133
Ciborek, A.P. 68
Coats, C.A. 68
Coby, Japan 21, 68
Coffey, Robert 57
Cook 205
Cooper, J. 68
Copeland, J.D. 68
Corona, R. 68
Corregidor 25, 58, 59, 60, 84
Coxey, E.W. 68
Cummins, F.E. 68
Curtis 189, 190
Czechoslovakia 6

-D-

Dachau 7
Dai Moji Maru 36
Dai Nichi Maru 35
Dakar 133
Dalton, Georgia 131
Dann, Michael 5
Daun, W. 68
Davis, J.H. 68
de Mendana, Alvaro 9
DeBauche, A.R. 68
Del Monte 76
Denver, Colorado 115
Douglass, Beth Florence Hale 181
Douglass, Frank Lee 181
Douglass, Harold Ray 181
Douglass Jr., Edwin 173, 174, 175, 176, 178, 179, 180, 181
Douglass, Maxine 181
Dunn, Ernest B. "Benny" 30, 32, 33, 34, 35, 36, 37, 44, 49, 50, 51, 52, 53, 54, 55, 56, 57
Dunn, Joe 57
Dunn, John 6
Dunn, Thomas 49, 50, 51, 57
Durchgangs Lager 6

-E-

Earing, D.P. 68
East Prussia 6
Eastman 189, 190, 191
Eau Claire, Wisconson 74
Edwards, J.E. 68
Eggers, Sgt. 97
Eisenhower, General 205
El Toro 115
Elderge, Bob 72
Elrod, Hank 11
Elster 213
England 182, 188, 190, 204, 209
Erwin, Bill 5, 226
Escalente, A.R. 68
Eubanks, Colonel 30
Europe 116, 132
Everett, Washington 114

-F-

Fields, Corporal 97
Florida 130, 217, 224
Flossenburg Concentration Camp 7
Folksstrom 191
Formosa 84
Fort Jackson, South Carolina 208
Fort, S.E. 68
Fox, Leonard O. 26
France 130, 135, 158, 178, 181, 183, 184, 189, 190, 206, 209, 221, 224
Frankfort, Germany 117, 184, 188, 193, 213

Franklin, Indiana 142
Franklin, Theodore D. 18
Freemantle, Australia 95
Furstenburg 151

-G-

Garden Dale, Texas 181
Geissen Prison 191
Georgetown 36, 133
Geraldsden, Germany 213
Germany 6, 92, 110, 111, 137, 146, 160, 178, 179, 182, 183, 188, 189, 190, 194, 205, 213, 224
Gerola, D. 68
Gillespie, L.J. 68
Gioia Del Colle, Italy 134
Glennister 116
Golisch, Lt. 116
Gonzales, Roy J. 19
Greenland 188
Greenlee, Robin 5
Greensboro, North Carolina 143
Gregory, J.D. 68
Gross Sycrow, Pomerania 165
Guam 8, 23
Gump, Chaplain 97
Gunnip, W.J. 68
Guyana 133

-H-

Halapy 116
Halle 190
Hally, John 151
Hamilton, Hartis 131
Hammerstein 112
Hannum, Earl R. 19
Hardwick, England 116
Harlington, Texas 132
Harrill, T.T. 68
Hart, Betty Craig 106
Hart, Jerry 106
Hart, Jim 106
Hart, Joseph 106
Hart, Loren Thomas 107
Hart, Thomas J. 95, 96, 97, 98, 99, 101, 102, 106, 107
Hauptlager 110
Haure 206
Hawaii 8, 25, 27
Hawaiian Islands 75
Hays, John 107
Hazeltine, Colonel 97, 98
Heath 189, 190, 191
Herbstein, Germany 191
Hessen 213
Hicks, H.E. 68
Hilderberghausen 158
Hill, Ralph 151
Himes, G.C. 68
Himnler 194
Hiroshima 68, 70, 71
Hitler 6, 7, 111, 157, 175, 191, 210
Hobbs, H.B. 68
Holly, Germany 160, 172
Holman, G. 68
Homma, General 58
Honshu 68
Hopkins, W. 68
Horn, R.L. 68
Horton, F. 68
Houston, Texas 31, 34
Howard, R. 68
Howell, L.E. 68
Hryn, J. 68
Hulsey, Imogene 117, 120, 121, 122, 123, 124, 125, 126, 130, 131
Hulsey, Julie Alles 131
Hulsey, Russell L. 115, 116, 117, 118, 119, 120, 121, 122, 123, 124, 125, 126, 130, 131
Hungary 135
Hutso, J.H. 68

-I-

Illinois 106, 181, 225
India 38, 40, 55, 96, 97, 106
Indiana 95, 106
Indianapolis, Indiana 95, 132, 208, 209
Island of Honshu 68
Italy 109, 110, 134, 135, 136, 143

-J-

Jakarta 30, 34
Jakubowski, P. S. 68
Japan 6, 8, 15, 18, 19, 21, 23, 25, 34, 37, 68, 69, 72, 73, 74, 84, 85, 86, 90
Java 6, 31, 30, 32, 33, 34
Jefferies, Colonel 97
Johnson, H.F. 68
Joplin, R.E. 68

-K-

Kafer, O.R. 68
Kanchanaburi, Thailand 52
Kawasaki, Japan 75, 85, 88, 89
Kawasaki Prison 87
Key, Dempsey 53
Kiangwan, China 19
Kilo 105 46
Klosowski, Adam 186
Knight 98, 101
Kommandos 6
Kondo 85, 87
Krems, Austria 117
Kunming, China 106
Kuriyama 85, 87

Kuslak, J. 68
Kwai Camp 53

-L-

LaHaure 206
Lambert, John W. 18
Laon, France 206
Lape Sr., Ralph L. 75, 76, 77, 82, 85, 86, 87, 88, 89, 90, 91, 92, 93, 94
Lape, Steven 92
Larado, Texas 182
Lawrence, W. 68
Lazarett 223
Leaf, Bob 214
Leavins, I.R. 68
Lee, Bobby 214
Lee, Monty Stricklin 225
Leg, Henry 111
Lewis, Joe 151
Limburg, Germany 176, 213, 222, 223
Lingayen 58, 84
Liverpool, England 160
Lloyd, R.A. 68
Long, L.L. 68
Lowe, H.E. 68
Luckenwalde 179
Ludwigshaven, Germany 184
Luxembourg 210
Luzon 64, 75, 85

-M-

MacArthur 72, 92
Malaya 6
Malaybalay 77, 83
Malia 35
Malikowski, F.W. 68
Manchuria 84
Manila 58, 59, 66, 82, 84, 92
Mapes 116
Marrekeck, Morocco 133
Martin, L.I. 68
Martinez, G. 68
Mason, Noel 33
Mauthasen Concentration Camp 7
McGee, .W. 68
McGuiness, R. 68
McHenry, W.W. 68
McLaughlin, Alec 114
McLaughlin, Ambre 114
McLaughlin, Gage 114
McLaughlin II, John 114
McLaughlin, John 108, 109, 110, 111, 112, 114
McLaughlin, Mark 114
McLaughlin, Norma Stewart 114
McLaughlin, Scott 114
McLaughlin, Vicky 114
Meade, Maryland 173
Medell 209
Medin 134
Merseburg 193
Metropolis, Illinois 207
Meyer, F.J. 68
Midway Islands 8
Mifflin, Johanna 57
Mihalopoulos, G. W. 68
Miller, Diane Lape 92
Milsap, E.L. 68
Mindanao 75
Missouri 27
Mizuno 85
Moji, Japan 84
Montargis 174
Montgomery, Alabama 132
Montgomery, F/M 203, 204
Moore, A.B. 68
Mooseberg 141
Mortain 174
Mostar, Yugoslavia 132
Moulmein, Burma 38, 51
Mt. Carmel, Illinois 209, 217, 219
Mt. Vernon, Illinois 114
Mukaishima 58
Munich 110
Myazaki, Lt. 85, 87
Mytchinaw 97

-N-

Nadolny, S.A. 68
Nagatoma, Y. 37, 38
Nakhon Nayot 54
Nancy, France 173, 174, 175
Naples, Italy 114, 144
Nassau 213
Natal, Brazil 133
Neilson 67
Netherlands East Indies 30
Nettles, Pappy 76, 77, 89
Nevada 115
New Guinea 6
New York 153, 155, 172, 187, 209, 216, 224
New York City 143
Nicholson, Colonel 53
Nienburg, Germany 224
Nike, Thailand 49
Nippon 37, 38, 85
Nordlager 110
Norfolk, Virginia 27
North Africa 108, 116, 142
North Carolina 108, 173
Nurnberg 140

-O-

Oakland 25
Odessa, Russia 114
Okinawa 22, 72, 92

Oklahoma City 27
Omtvedt, Clifford M. 68, 74
Onomichi 72, 74
Opalocha, Florida 25
Osaka, Japan 8, 22, 23

-P-

Packer, Colonial 194
Paden, G.W. 68
Panama 132
Paris 158, 183, 206
Patton, General 130, 142
Peale, Titian 9
Pearl Harbor 8, 10, 25, 27, 30, 58, 208
Peleiu Rock Islands 25, 28
Philippine Islands 6, 30, 58, 75, 77
Philippines 25, 30, 58, 66, 75, 76, 77, 85, 102
Pickett, L.V. 68
Piercey, I.B. 68
Ploesti 135, 136
Plymale, C.A. 68
Poland 6, 113, 114, 156, 165
Pope, E.L. 68
Potris, J.F. 68
Preston, Al 186
Prestwick, Scotland 182
Prussia 213
Puerto Rico 133

-R-

Rangoon 36, 38
Rapid City, South Dakota 160
Ratburi 53
Rayborn, B.R. 68
Reed, Walter 56
Regensburg, Germany 135
Reims, France 142, 206
Remy, Betty Taylor 190, 207
Remy, Carl W. 188, 193, 194, 207
Remy, Stephen T. 207
Remy, Suzanne Ware 207
Rentfro, Terri 5
Reveglia, A.J. 68
Rhoads, Lt. 97, 98
Rio Hata, Panama 132
Roberts, N.W. 68
Roosevelt, Franklin D. 11, 91, 133, 203
Rostock 194, 203
Rote, R.W. 68
Rumania 135, 136
Russia 113, 114
Russland 220
Ryan, M. 68

-S-

Sagan 111, 137, 139
Saigon 34
Saint Ive, England 174
Saint Lo, France 174
Saint Marcas, Texas 188
Saipan 23
Saito 85
Salt Lake City, Utah 94
San Antonio, Texas 158
San Diego, California 8
San Fernando 64
San Francisco, California 25, 34, 75, 92, 95, 159, 217
Sanborn, S/Sgt 137
Sarajevo 137
Schemeling, Max 155
Schonberg, Germany 210
Scotland 182, 209
Scott, G.B. 68
Seamancheck, J. 68
Seattle, Washington 95
Senegal 133
Shanghai, China 19, 20
Shannon, H.O. 68
Shiozawa 85, 87
Shuford, J.H. 68
Sicily 108, 109
Sikeston, Missouri 73, 187
Simpson 68,203
Singapore 6, 30, 34, 35, 36, 46, 53
Sioux Falls, South Dakota 182
Skagway, Alaska 95
Slovakia 7
Smith, Kenneth M. 208, 209, 210, 211, 213, 216, 217, 218, 219
Smith, Mary 217, 218
Smith, Pam 218
Soerabaja, Java 30
Sohonberg 210
Solingen, Germany 115
Soliski, Lt. 116
Sourbergenon, Germany 160
South Bend, Indiana 132
South Carolina 143, 151
South Viet Nam 106
Southeast Asia 6
Spiller, Harry 226
St. Louis, Missouri 72
St. Valery, France 206
Stalag 12A 223
Stalag 17B 117, 118, 121, 122, 123, 124, 125, 126, 131
Stalag I 188, 193, 205
Stalag IIB 108, 112, 113
Stalag III 7, 18, 108, 111, 132, 137, 139
Stalag IIIA 143, 154, 155, 156, 173, 178, 179, 180, 181
Stalag IIIB 143, 151
Stalag IIIC 173, 178, 181
Stalag IV 160, 165, 182, 193

Stalag IXA 213
Stalag IXB 7, 208, 213, 214, 215, 219
Stalag IXC 213
Stalag Stamm Lager 6
Stalag VI 186
Stalag VII 7
Stalag VIIA 108, 110, 132, 141, 142
Stalag XC 221, 224
Stalag XII 178
Stalag XIIA 173, 176, 177, 221, 222, 223, 224, 225
Stalag XIIID 132, 140
Stambaugh, M.J. 68
Stanley, A.J. 68
Steinbuchel, Jupp 220
Stettin 203
Stone, England 182
Stricklin, Alvel L. 221, 224, 225
Stricklin, Florence Know 225
Stricklin, Johnny 225
Stricklin, Wanda 225
Strunc, Hank 205, 206, 207
Sturgeon, David 27
Sturgeon, Edward 8, 9, 10, 11, 12, 13, 15, 21, 22, 26, 27, 28
Sturgeon, Joyce 27
Sturgeon, Linda 27
Sturgeon, Theresa 27
Suedlager 110
Sugamo 87
Sunda Strait 31
Swann 190, 191
Sweden 190, 206
Switzerland 138, 141, 189, 190, 205

-T-

Tacoma, Washington 75
Takao, Formosa 84
Tanjong Priok 32
Tanjong Priok Harbor 31
Tennessee 143, 173, 208, 211
Texas 30, 31, 73, 97, 131, 160, 181, 217, 221
Thailand 6, 30, 34, 36, 38, 46, 48, 50, 52, 54, 57
Thanbyuzayat 36, 37, 38
Thomas, Loren 107, 116, 212
Thompson, Dick 97, 98
Thye, Norm 186
Tittle, S/Sgt 137
Tjilatatjap 32
Tokyo, Japan 19, 23, 24, 85, 86, 90, 91, 92
Totington, England 209
Troyes 174
Tuscon, Arizona 115
Twigg, W.E. 68
Tyrrell, E.W. 68

-U-

United States 10, 19, 58, 107, 116, 130, 172, 173, 182, 206, 216
Utah 75

-V-

Venable, Ted 86, 87, 93
Vienna, Austria 117
Virgan 58
Virginia 74, 173
Vistula, L. 68

-W-

Wackler 101
Wagner, Donald 186
Wagner, L.M. 68
Wainwright, General 77
Wake Island 7, 8, 9, 10, 11, 12, 13, 14, 15, 17, 18, 19, 25, 26, 27, 30
Wake, Samuel 9
Washington, D.C. 7, 56, 74
Watanabe 85, 87
Weatherall, Phil 153
Webb, Sergeant 208, 211
West Africa 133
West Palm Beach, Florida 133
West Plains, Missouri 82
Wheatley, V.A. 68
Whitecotton, N. 68
Wichita Falls, Texas 188
Wiemar 204
Wilkenson, Lt. 116
Wilkes, Charles 9
Wilkes Island 9
Williams, G.L. 68
Wisecup, John 41, 42, 45, 57
Woo Sung 8, 19, 20, 21
Wyoming 217

-Y-

Yamaguchi, Ei 26, 28, 29
Yokohama 20, 24, 92
Younts 189
Yugoslavia 136
Yuma, Arizona 160

-Z-

Zamboanga, Mindanao 84
Zempke, Colonel 194, 202, 203, 205
Zielinski, E.S. 68
Zigenheim 213
Zimmerman 116

POWs at Stalag IXB.

At O'Donald the healthiest POWs were seated at the noon meal. After the photos were taken by the Japs, the rice was thrown out.

American POWs captured during the Battle of the Bulge. Photo taken by the Germans.

One month after Camp O'Donald opened the Japs took this photo of the men who were the healthier to show that their treatment was good. Little did the world know that men were dying rapidly from starvation.